Shanghai Tai Chi

Shanghai Tai Chi offers a masterful portrait of daily life under socialism in a rich social and political history of one of the world's most complex cities. Hanchao Lu explores the lives of people from all areas of society – from capitalists and bourgeois intellectuals to women and youth. Wielding the metaphor of Tai Chi, he reveals how people in Shanghai experienced, adapted to, and manipulated the new Maoist political culture launched in 1949. Exploring the multifaceted complexity of everyday life and material culture in Mao's China, Lu addresses the survival of old bourgeois lifestyles under the new proletarian dictatorship, the achievements of intellectuals in an age of anti-intellectualism, the pleasure that urban youth derived from reading taboo literature, the emergence of women's liberation and the politics of greening and horticulture. Lu argues that an undercurrent of non-confrontational but nevertheless powerful and effective defiance characterized Mao's China, paved the way for the post-Mao reform, and illustrated how the public might, through accommodation and manipulation, resist even the most repressive of regimes.

Hanchao Lu is Professor of History at the Georgia Institute of Technology and Director of the China Research Center in Atlanta. He is the author of three award-winning books: *Beyond the Neon Lights* (1999), *Street Criers* (2005), and *The Birth of a Republic* (2010).

Cambridge Studies in the History of the People's Republic of China

Series Editors

Jacob Eyferth, Daniel Leese, Michael Schoenhals

Cambridge Studies in the History of the People's Republic of China is a major series of ambitious works in the social, political, and cultural history of socialist China. Aided by a wealth of new sources, recent research pays close attention to regional differences, to perspectives from the social and geographical margins, and to the unintended consequences of Communist Party rule. Books in the series contribute to this historical re-evaluation by presenting the most stimulating and rigorously researched works in the field to a broad audience. The series invites submissions from a variety of disciplines and approaches, based on written, material, or oral sources. Particularly welcome are those works that bridge the 1949 and 1978 divides, and those that seek to understand China in an international or global context.

Map 1. Shanghai Municipality

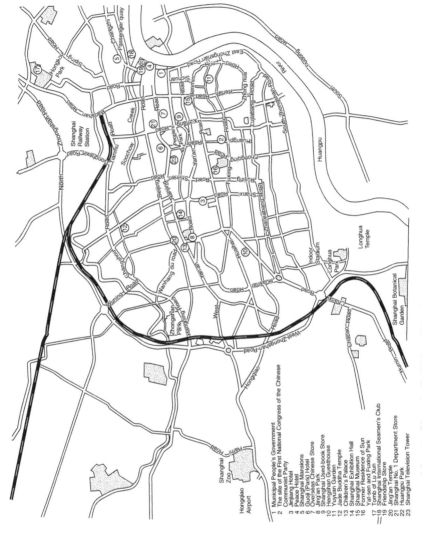

Map 2. Shanghai's Urban Districts

Shanghai Tai Chi

The Art of Being Ruled in Mao's China

Hanchao Lu

Georgia Institute of Technology

Shaftesbury Road, Cambridge CB2 8EA, United Kingdom

One Liberty Plaza, 20th Floor, New York, NY 10006, USA

477 Williamstown Road, Port Melbourne, VIC 3207, Australia

314–321, 3rd Floor, Plot 3, Splendor Forum, Jasola District Centre, New Delhi – 110025, India

103 Penang Road, #05–06/07, Visioncrest Commercial, Singapore 238467

Cambridge University Press is part of Cambridge University Press & Assessment, a department of the University of Cambridge.

We share the University's mission to contribute to society through the pursuit of education, learning and research at the highest international levels of excellence.

www.cambridge.org
Information on this title: www.cambridge.org/9781009180986

DOI: 10.1017/9781009180979

© Hanchao Lu 2023

This publication is in copyright. Subject to statutory exception and to the provisions of relevant collective licensing agreements, no reproduction of any part may take place without the written permission of Cambridge University Press & Assessment.

First published 2023

Printed in the United Kingdom by TJ Books Limited, Padstow Cornwall

A catalogue record for this publication is available from the British Library.

Library of Congress Cataloging-in-Publication Data
Names: Lu, Hanchao, author.
Title: Shanghai tai chi : the art of being ruled in Mao's China / Hanchao Lu, Georgia Institute of Technology.
Other titles: Art of being ruled in Mao's China
Description: Cambridge, United Kingdom ; New York, NY : Cambridge University Press, 2023. | Includes bibliographical references and index.
Identifiers: LCCN 2022029325 | ISBN 9781009180986 (hardback) | ISBN 9781009180979 (ebook)
Subjects: LCSH: Shanghai (China) – History – 20th century. | City and town life – China – Shanghai – 20th century. | Mao, Zedong, 1893–1976 – Influence. | Shanghai (China) – Politics and government – 20th century.
Classification: LCC DS796.S25 L8127 2023 | DDC 951.132–dc23/eng/20220706
LC record available at https://lccn.loc.gov/2022029325

ISBN 978-1-009-18098-6 Hardback

Cambridge University Press & Assessment has no responsibility for the persistence or accuracy of URLs for external or third-party internet websites referred to in this publication and does not guarantee that any content on such websites is, or will remain, accurate or appropriate.

To my family on both sides of the Pacific

Contents

List of Figures	*page* x
List of Maps	xii
List of Tables	xiii
Acknowledgments	xiv
Notes on the Text	xvii
Introduction	1

Part I The Condemned

1	The Upper Crust	21
2	The Stinking Number Nine	55

Part II The Liberated

3	The Power of Balzac	99
4	Alleyway Women's Detachments	139

Part III Under the French Parasol Trees

5	Everyday Flora	169
6	In the Eyes of Foreign Onlookers	201
7	The Essential Does Not Change	216

Conclusion	249
Appendix	257
Notes	265
References	311
Index	345

Figures

I.1	Communist soldiers resting on the sidewalks of Shanghai, May 1949	*page* 4
I.2	Spectators at a government-organized Liberation parade in 1949	5
I.3	Gangster Huang Jinrong, 1868–1953	6
I.4	Mao's regime excelled in mass mobilization and propaganda	8
I.5	Mao meeting with intellectuals and cultural figures, Shanghai, 1957	14
I.6	Xinghuo Convenience Store	16
1.1	A Socialist Nationalization Campaign rally, Tiananmen Square, 1956	22
1.2	Celebrating "Joint state–private enterprise" events on Nanjing Road, 1956	23
1.3	A meeting in Shanghai for capitalists' spouses, 1956	25
1.4	A socialist nationalization rally at the Sino-Soviet Friendship Hall, 1956	29
1.5	Mao receives "red capitalists," January 30, 1956	32
2.1	Fu Lei's secluded comfort	61
2.2	Li Jinhui adapted to the new era	77
2.3	Shao Xunmei and Emily Hahn	79
2.4	Lu Xiaoman and Weng Tonghe	85
2.5	Jing'an shopping area, ca. 1960	88
2.6	Autographed photos of Lu Xiaoman for her "teacher" Hu Shih	94
3.1	The largest used-book store on Fuzhou Road	107
3.2	A hand-copied underground manuscript, *A Maiden's Heart*	110
3.3	An open-air urinal in a residential alley, ca. early 1980s	112
3.4	Pavel and Tonya	128
3.5	The center of Shanghai, 1973	134
4.1	Downtown Shanghai before 1949	142
4.2	A neighborhood sewing workshop in Zhangjiazhai, 1958	143
4.3	Manned public telephone booths run by APTs	148

4.4	Moved by pedal power	156
5.1	People's Park, Shanghai, ca. 1965	176
5.2	The marble pavilion inside the Bubbling Well Cemetery	177
5.3	Paintings of parks in Shanghai during the Cultural Revolution	180
5.4	Taking up gardening	183
5.5	Shanghai's "foreign garden homes," ca. 1964	194
6.1	The annual Buddha Bathing Festival in 1958	205
6.2	Tai chi on the Bund, 1979	210
6.3	Shanghai Overseas Chinese Store, ca. 1975	212
6.4	The Shanghai Friendship Store, ca. 1960	214
7.1	*Fu-Zhuang*, 1958	220
7.2	An alleyway tailor shop, Shanghai	228
7.3	Mao receiving Imelda Marcos, 1974	234
7.4	Queuing up for food, 1956	244
C.1	Shanghai shortly after the Mao era, 1980	253

Maps

Map 1. Shanghai Municipality *page* iii
Map 2. Shanghai's Urban Districts iv

Tables

2.1	Shanghai's private telephone lines in various years during the Mao era	*page* 62
2.2	Fu Lei's published translations of French literature, 1949–1963	63
4.1	Neighborhood organization-sponsored work units in Shanghai, December 1959	144
4.2	Types and sizes of APTs in Shanghai, 1965	146
4.3	Waste reclamation depot rates, 1965–1979	147
4.4	A typical alleyway communal canteen menu, 1960s–1970s	150
4.5	Level of education of 115,324 new women factory workers in Shanghai, 1958	158
5.1	Public green space per capita in Shanghai, selected years of significance during the Mao era	172
5.2	Major chrysanthemum exhibitions in Shanghai's parks, 1954–1977	181
6.1	Overseas remittances to Shanghai residents, 1953–1982	213
7.1	Prices of non-staple foods in Shanghai, 1963–1977	242

Acknowledgments

This study is the culmination of a project launched in 2013–2014 when I was the William Bentinck-Smith Fellow of the Radcliffe Institute at Harvard University. I would like to thank the institute for providing an excellent research environment. The dean of the Radcliffe Institute, Lizabeth Cohen, and the associate dean of the Fellowship Program, the late Judith Vichniac, were constant sources of support. I was inspired by numerous presentations at the institute as well as by stimulating conversations over lunch and coffee with scholars at Harvard. Although not all of the presentations were directly related to my research interests, a substantial number of them were. I would like to thank Paul Cohen, Mark C. Elliott, Bill Kirby, Daniel Koss, Jie Li, Elizabeth J. Perry, Eugene Y. Wang, James L. (Woody) Watson, and Martin King Whyte for their graciousness and inspiration during my sojourn. Ann Karnovsky, a Radcliffe College alumna and a benefactor of the institute, kindly shared her photos, slides, and notes of her visits to China during the late Mao years. I enjoyed being a guest at her home in Cambridge. Her hospitality was particularly meaningful to me as my visits turned out to be part of a few small gatherings in the final months of her life.

At the Harvard-Yenching Library, I benefitted from James Cheng's and Xiaohe Ma's extensive knowledge of source materials. I thank them for their generous help. My student assistants, Brooke K. Nowakowski, Ezra Stoller, and Rose-Ann Thomas, were diligent and resourceful. Despite the demands of their own coursework at Harvard, each spent several hours a week in spring 2014 helping locate source materials for this study. Some of the journalist accounts used in Chapter 6 are a result of their research.

I also had the honor of being a Visiting Research Fellow and Guest of the Director of the IGK Work (re:work) and Human Life Cycle in Global History of the International Research Center, Humboldt University of Berlin in 2017 when I was working on Part II of the book. I thank the re:work Program Manager Felicitas Hentschke and Director Andreas Eckert for their support and hospitality during my visit and for

Acknowledgments xv

keeping me informed of the program thereafter. My fellow visiting fellow Susan Zimmermann, University Professor at the Central European University, Budapest, generously shared her research on women workers in East European countries under socialism, which helped shape Chapter 4 of the book. Thanks to Barbara Mittler, I was able to present part of my research at the Heidelberg University in Heidelberg, Germany.

I have the fortune of enjoying a longtime association with the Shanghai Academy of Social Sciences (SASS) and the Shanghai Research Center at Fudan University. Both institutions provided much-needed assistance for my fieldwork. In particular, I thank Xiong Yuezhi and Song Zuanyou for their friendship and support. Many thanks are due to all my informants, who generously shared their life experiences in Mao's China with me. Their support has made the book much better than it otherwise would be. I also thank Denise Ho, Jin Dalu, Jin Guangyue, Ma Jun, and Sun Peidong for inviting me to conferences and presentations and for stimulating conversations about our shared interest in social history.

Parts of the research have been presented in conferences and workshops over the years in various locations. I would like to thank the organizers and the participants who offered their comments on the research at the following events: History, Images, and Politics in the PRC: An International Workshop, Stanford University, January 24–25, 2019; the 12th Annual China Goes Global Conference, Shanghai, June 18–20, 2018; the International Conference on Urban Cultural Heritage: Research and Protection in an Interdisciplinary Perspective, Shanghai Academy of Social Sciences, July 18–19, 2017; and Work and Life Cycle in Global History, Humboldt University of Berlin, June 13 and July 7, 2017. I would also like to thank the following journals for allowing me to use some of the materials from my previously published articles: *Journal of Social History* (vol. 52.1: 74–100), *Urban History* (vol. 45.4: 660–681), and *The China Quarterly* (no. 243: 757–779). Zhang Nianchi, a historian and counselor of the Shanghai municipal government, kindly sent me an album of his paintings and gave me permission to use in this book four pictures that he painted during the Cultural Revolution.

At my home institution, Georgia Institute of Technology, humanities and social science research are important pursuits and are strongly supported, much more than what one might assume for a major technological university. I would like to thank my colleagues Jacqueline J. Royster, Kaye Husbands Fealing, Willie Pearson, Jr., Steven Usselman, and Eric Schatzberg for their leadership and support of my research and scholarship. I thank Robert Hampson for his administrative skills, which greatly eased the tension between my research and administrative responsibilities. The study-abroad programs of Georgia Tech's School of Industrial and Systems Engineering (ISyE) and School of Electrical and Computer Engineering (ECE), two schools that might seem entirely unrelated to my field, provided me with numerous opportunities to go Shanghai for research. I would like thank my colleagues who led these programs, Chen Zhou and G. Tong Zhou, for their support. I would also like to thank the Georgia Tech Foundation for years of travel grants which made possible trips to Asia to attend conferences and conduct research related to this study.

Richard Gunde once again most generously lent me his expertise in every possible way and shared with me countless thoughts about this book project. His help saved me from numerous embarrassing errors and greatly improved the manuscript, for which I am truly grateful. A special thanks is due to Jeremy Brown, a fellow historian of modern China at Simon Fraser University, who introduced this book project to Cambridge University Press. At the press, Rachel Blaifeder, Political Science and Sociology Editor, appreciated the value of the manuscript and initiated the process leading to publication. Senior Commissioning Editor Lucy Rhymer, Editorial Assistant (History) Emily Plater, Content Manager Stephanie Taylor, and Narmadha Nedounsejiane (Senior Project Executive at Lumina Datamatics, Ltd), and Carol Thomas were very helpful in every step toward production. I thank them for their expertise, efficiency, and professionalism. Janet Beckley, Evelyn E. Pike, Erik Rostad, and Patrick Sonnett helped with the illustrations, which serve as important allies of the text.

Last but not least, I would like to thank my family on both sides of the Pacific for their support in the making of this book. My brother Hanlong, one of the key sociologists responsible for the revival of sociology in post-Mao China, has always happily shared his thoughts on myriad topics. My sister Xiuyu arranged several of my interviews with Shanghai residents who provided valuable details for this project. I would also like to thank Hanyi and Handing for being caring elder brothers. Back home in Atlanta, Linlin has been a constant source of love and support since we first met at the Institute of History of SASS in 1982, when she had just graduated as a history major from Fudan University. I am immensely grateful to her for the warmth of our home and for sharing my love of history. Finally, our sons Frederic and Jeffrey, despite following career paths far from history, have become history buffs to whom I can always turn to for stimulating tête-à-têtes. It is to my family that I dedicate this book.

Notes on the Text

yuan　　Chinese currency. During most of the Mao era, the official exchange rate was stable, at about US$1 = 2.46 yuan.
fen　　1/100 of a yuan, referred in the text as "cent."
catty　　*jin*, 500 grams
tael　　*liang*, 50 grams (effective June 1959)
chi　　one third of a meter = 1.09 feet
cun　　1.3 inches
mu　　0.165 acre

Chinese terms and personal names are rendered in pinyin transliteration, with a few exceptions for those that are conventionally spelled other ways, such as Chiang Kai-shek (instead of Jiang Jieshi), Hu Shih (instead Hu Shi), and tai chi (instead of taiji).

Introduction

The People's Republic of China (PRC), founded in 1949, has been the longest lasting Communist state in the world.[1] In its formative stage – the Mao era (1949–1976) – the country experienced decades of international isolation as well as political chaos, economic disasters, and cultural and social decay, causing tens of millions of premature deaths in peacetime and leading the economy to the edge of collapse. Yet not only did the regime survive, but, in the post-Mao era, the country became a global power so strong as to convince many observers that China and the United States are caught in what the political scientist Graham Allison called a Thucydides Trap, "a deadly pattern of structural stress that results when a rising power challenges a ruling one."[2] Despite the never-ending predications of the "coming collapse of China" and of China's "peaceful evolution," there is little sign that either will come to pass in the foreseeable future.

What has given the Chinese and their system the strength to endure decades of turmoil and catastrophe yet not merely survive but thrive? Answering this question requires a multidisciplinary examination of every layer and aspect of the Communist system and Chinese society. This study, unlike most other works that try to account for the strength and endurance of China's Communist system, does not examine politics at the top level nor on a national scale, but instead explores the quotidian aspects of people's lives during the Mao era in China's largest and arguably most cosmopolitan city, Shanghai. A micro social history can be a powerful lens for perusing the real lives of people, and thus provide a human face for politics and society. And, as a Chinese metaphor puts it, by looking at one spot, the whole leopard may be inferred.

Few cities in the world have generated so many strikingly different images as Shanghai. Since the late nineteenth century, Shanghai, literally meaning "upper sea" for its location at the outlet of the Yangzi River to the Pacific, has been known as a preeminently Westernized city, a city "in China but not of it," a city that was "another China." Shanghai has been considered a key to understanding modern China and, in the eyes of most Chinese, a portal through which virtually everything foreign – which is to say, all things advanced, exciting, dangerous, and Western – flowed into the nation. In popular writings, Shanghai has been depicted as a city of foreigners, compradors, bankers, gangsters, coolies, and prostitutes. It was declared a sin city, an adventurer's paradise, and a gigantic dye vat in which everyone was tinted the same color.[3] A standard guidebook published during the heyday of the city in the 1930s describes Shanghai as a "city of amazing paradoxes and fantastic contrasts," calling it "the beautiful, bawdy, and gaudy; [a] contradiction of manners and morals; a vast brilliantly-hued cycloramic panoramic mural of the best and the worst of Orient and Occident."[4] US journalist Edgar Snow (1905–1972) called it "the wickedest and most colorful city of the old Orient."[5] Such contradictory images also exist in the Communists' descriptions of the city. For the Communists, Shanghai, the birthplace of the Chinese Communist Party (CCP), was a city with a glorious revolutionary tradition and stood at the forefront of the party's anti-imperialism and anti-feudalism mission. At the same time, it was a "parasitic" city, the bridgehead of imperialist aggression again China, and the headquarters of China's domestic reactionaries.[6]

Shanghai's Fall ... or Liberation

In the middle of the night on May 24, 1949, a detachment of the People's Liberation Army (PLA) crept into Shanghai. Since there was a 9:00 p.m. curfew that day, which silenced "the city that never sleeps," their arrival was unknown to most of the slumbering population. At dawn the next day, the troops occupied the city proper and two days later, the Communists officially declared the city "liberated."

This was not the first time the city had experienced war and occupation. A century before, during the Opium War of 1840, Shanghai, then a prosperous port specializing in the cotton trade, was attacked and occupied by British troops, leaving the town, as an eyewitness described it, with "no pedestrians on the streets and no dogs barking."[7] Since then the city has been caught up in numerous wars, both domestic and international. In the early 1860s, the Taiping rebels attacked Shanghai three times and occupied the suburb of Xujiahui, just five miles west of the walled town at the center of the city. In the Republican Revolution of 1911, troops occupied the city's Chinese districts and declared them independent of the imperial Qing dynasty. Shanghai was a battlefield in the 1924 war between the warlords of Jiangsu and Zhejiang. Eight years later, Japan attacked and bombed Shanghai. During the Sino-Japanese War of 1937–1945, Japan occupied the Chinese portions of the city for four years before it moved to take the core of the city – the International Settlement and the French Concession – after the outbreak of the Pacific War. The Japanese occupation continued till the end of the war in 1945.[8]

This time, things were different. The occupation was part of a great regime change and marked the beginning of what was essentially a rural-based revolution that seized and reshaped China's most industrialized and Westernized city. As the sociologist Martin King Whyte has pointed out, "China's new leaders were not, of course, country bumpkins: Most had had considerable urban experience before they took to the hills in 1927. Still, the task of bending the cities to suit the programs of the new government appeared formidable."[9] The Communists were well aware of the challenges facing them, especially in Shanghai. The Communist leader Mao Zedong (1893–1976) worried that a military occupation of Shanghai would paralyze the city. Just two months before the battle for Shanghai, Mao expressed his hesitation to Ivan Kovalev (1901–1993), the CCP's top Soviet advisor, saying it would be more difficult to govern Shanghai than to occupy it. In particular, Mao asked the Soviet Union to send experts to help with governing the city.[10]

The takeover of Shanghai turned out to be surprisingly uneventful. For two months before the Communist military attack, the PLA had troops stationed in Danyang, a town in Jiangsu about 130 miles north of Shanghai. The battle of Shanghai was fiercely fought, but mainly in the rural areas surrounding the city. To avoid "being caught like rats in a china shop," as war in the city proper was described, the Communists adopted a strategy of luring the Nationalist army in Shanghai to fight on the outskirts of the city, and it worked. Meanwhile, the CCP's subversive cells, which had actively operated underground for decades in the city, also played a crucial role. They managed to incite a number of defections of Nationalist military leaders, including an army corps commander who ordered his more than 10,000 troops stationed in the city to put down their weapons. The CCP's strong underground network within various trade unions played a key role in preventing the Nationalists from implementing an intended scorched earth plan, leaving the city to fall into the Communists' hands largely intact.

By the time the PLA reached the city proper after midnight of Tuesday, May 24, it was remarkably quiet. George Wang (1927–), a local resident who was at the time employed by the *China Weekly Review*, an American edited English-language newspaper published in Shanghai, recalled that while he was on his way to the office in the morning of May 25, "apart from the fighting along [Suzhou] creek, everything else downtown seemed perfectly normal. There were cars and trams on the streets; people were walking to work or back from the market as usual.... Everything looked the same as ever, even the policemen on the street."[11] Just two days earlier, the Nationalist government had organized a parade on Shanghai's streets to celebrate its "victory" in defending the city. Although people were skeptical of the claim of victory, no one realized that it was completely ridiculous, nor that the fall of the city to the Communists was imminent, not to mention that it would be uneventful.

"Shanghai was the greatest colonial city the world has ever known," historian Ian McLachlan melodramatically wrote, "but when it fell, nothing happened."[12] Mak Lai-heung, then a journalist in Shanghai, recalled that the radio was still broadcasting music after midnight on Tuesday, only it went on and on – apparently no one was at work in the studio. The music was Beethoven's Ninth, and Mak literally hailed the day – and the historical event – amid that music:

> By two there was nothing happening, so we switched it off and went to bed. The next morning I ventured out into the street and I saw the Liberation army men sleeping right there at the entrance to our lane. I went over and talked to one of them who was awake. I said "When did you get here?" He said "one o'clock in the morning." We were still listening to the radio at that time and they were already outside. They made no noise at all (see Figure I.1).[13]

Figure I.1 Communist soldiers resting on the sidewalks of Shanghai after taking over the city during the night of May 25, 1949. The soldiers' pillows are their bags of millet and each solider carries an enamel bowl for food and water. The PLA issued a "do not disturb the residents" order upon entering Shanghai, contributing to the military's reputation as a genuine "people's army." *Source:* Shanghai Municipal Library.

Introduction

It was all over by Wednesday morning. Residents noted that by 9:00 a.m., "shopkeepers in the side streets were even taking down their shutters and opening up for business."[14] Robert Guillain (1908–1998), a French journalist who was in Shanghai at the time, sent a cable to *Le Monde* reporting what he saw:

Shanghai, 25 May.—This morning, I saw the Communist spearhead arrive at the heart of Shanghai along the Nanking Road and the Bund. At the foot of the giant buildings, small, khaki-clad, mud-spattered young men advanced methodically. They were moving in small groups, hugging the walls in the empty streets and jumping from one crossing to the next.... During their short periods of rest, these peasant-soldiers craned their necks to stare at the tops of the 15- or 20-storey buildings, an obviously unfamiliar sight to them.[15]

Soon thousands of Communist soldiers and cadres, mostly from rural Shandong and northern Jiangsu, were handed responsibility for running the city. Parades were organized on the major boulevards of the city, ceremonially announcing the birth of a new regime (Figure I.2). By the

Figure I.2 Spectators at a government-organized Liberation parade on October 8, 1949, at Bubbling Well Road (West Nanjing Road) near the corner of Gordon Road (Jiangning Road). Unlike Communist propaganda that portrayed the audience as enthusiastic citizens welcoming liberators, most people in the city had little idea of what to expect in the new era. Anxiety, apprehension, and curiosity were the main chord of the day. Photo by Jin Shisheng (1910–2000). *Source:* Shanghai Photographers Association.

Figure I.3 (a) *Left*, Huang Jinrong (1868–1953), Shanghai's most senior gangster boss, chose to stay in Shanghai after Liberation and submitted a confession to the authorities. Nicknamed "Pockmarked Jinrong," Huang had been the chief detective in the French Concession and, as one of the leaders of the so-called Green Gang – the biggest in Shanghai – allegedly was in cahoots with Chiang Kai-shek. Huang's confession, which was published in Shanghai's *Daily News* and *Wenhui Daily*, on May 20, 1951, read in part, "to return the great kindness of the People's Government, I will help the government in suppressing counterrevolutionaries." (b) *Right*, To show the public that Huang had totally capitulated to the new regime, he was handed a broom and, at the age of 83, he swept the street in front of the Great World amusement arcade and entertainment complex. *Source*: Xinhua News Agency.

summer of 1949, not much seemed to have changed. Shanghai was still ablaze with neon lights and its major boulevards were still lined with luxury shops and nightclubs. Soldiers patrolling the streets downtown exclaimed, "Even the wind on Nanjing Road smells fragrant."[16] But thereafter changes came quickly. Just eight months after the takeover, an American who flew on a Nationalist air raid over the city proclaimed, "From a Chinese air force B-25 over this Communist held metropolis, it is plain that Shanghai is a dying city."[17] On the ground, the city crawled with rich conspirators who believed in the power of corruption and whispered to each other: "The Reds are arriving in Shanghai, but they will soon become black here."[18] According to private reports from the city, many Shanghainese were "still denouncing the existing Government in private while cooperating with it in public and hoping for deliverance by somebody else."[19]

But all those who thought Shanghai was dying, or that it would seduce the Communists, or that "deliverance" was just around the corner were soon to be disappointed. In fact, after Liberation (as the Communist takeover is commonly called in China), as one author put it, "Shanghai made the transition to life without John Bull and Uncle Sam quite smoothly."[20] Within just a few months, the Communists had established a well-run government and successfully crushed currency speculation and contained inflation, two huge problems that to a great extent led to the downfall of the previous regime. In less than three years, the new government had decisively eliminated the major social vices of prostitution, drug trafficking, and gambling. The city's notoriously powerful gangs were pulverized (Figures I.3a and I.3b). Shanghai, the city where the CCP was secretly founded with just twelve delegates twenty-eight years earlier, was now firmly in the grip of the Communists.

In the next three decades, the city, like the nation, was largely cut off from the rest of the world and became a major locus of Maoist politics and programs (Figures I.4a and I.4b). It bore the brunt of numerous political campaigns and finally became the breeding ground of the Gang of Four, the Maoist radical clique that was a mainstay of the disastrous Cultural Revolution (1966–1976). Economically, the Communists vowed to transform Shanghai from a city of consumption to a city of production. Building on the city's manufacturing foundation inherited from its colonial past, new industries, especially light industry, were developed. For decades after 1949, "made in Shanghai" meant quality and style, and consumer products from Shanghai were coveted by customers throughout the country.

8 Introduction

Figure I.4 Mao's regime excelled in mass mobilization and propaganda. (a) *Left*, Residents of two alleyways on Pingliang Road in northeastern Shanghai listen to a radio broadcast about China's new Marriage Law, implemented on May 1, 1950. The law stipulated that men and women have equal rights, prohibited concubinage, and contained a host of other provisions to end the patriarchal practices of China's "feudal" society. (b) *Right*, Teaching revolutionary songs in a Shanghai alley, ca. 1952. *Source:* Shanghai Municipal Library.

However, under the socialist planned economy, the central government treated Shanghai as a cash cow. For more than three decades, the city contributed an astonishing one-sixth of the central government's annual revenue, leaving little for the city's own needs. By the end of the Mao era in 1976, Shanghai was a jam-packed metropolis of over ten million people. It has remained China's largest and most industrialized city, but its urban infrastructure very much lagged behind: By the end of the 1970s, average residential housing space per capita was 4.5 square meters and average paved street space per capita was only 0.8 square meters.[21]

The State–Society Paradigm

China's most capitalistic and cosmopolitan city was thus engulfed in the Maoist rural-based revolution and run by a zealous Communist administration. Two decades after the takeover, in the words of historian

Introduction 9

Anthony Kubek (1920–2003), the thriving metropolis known as "the New York of the Far East" was reduced "from the fourth largest port in the world and great international clearinghouse for trade and ideas, to a sullen Chinese provincial town under the iron heel of a Communist agrarian bureaucracy with little sympathy for urban peoples in general and none for those in Shanghai in particular."[22] Despite its Cold War tone, this assessment was largely correct. But a key question, even after another half a century has passed, remains: How did ordinary people cope with the extraordinary changes brought by the regime change and Mao's continuous revolution thereafter? To what extent did the city's old cosmopolitanism survive? Does Shanghai's stunning resurgence as a global megacity today represent a complete break with the Maoist "dark ages" half a century ago or might it have its roots there? What does Shanghai's experience tell us about the nature of Communist rule in China, and, despite its twists and turns, does any of that experience remain relevant today?

For decades, writings about the Mao era have mostly looked at the politics within the Communist Party, political campaigns, and their ramifications in society. Given the Communists' one-party rule and limited information on a society that was largely closed at the time, this approach was appropriate and sensible. In recent years more scholars have started, with good reason, to treat the period as a historical subject and to view the Mao era from a bottom-up perspective. Chronologically speaking, inasmuch as the era ended with Mao's death nearly half a century ago and epic changes have occurred since then, it is now truly a part of history. Practically speaking, the opening of various archives in China (though in many cases the opening is still partial), the possibility of conducting fieldwork at the local level, and the availability of unofficial materials (*minjian ziliao*) via unconventional channels, such as flea markets and private collections, have greatly diversified scholarly approaches to the era and contributed to a new trend of exploring Mao's China from below.[23] A more profound reason, however, has to do with philosophy: In attempting to know the history of a nation, the lives of the common people and the everyday rhythm of grassroots society are now seen as important as – if not more important than – elite politics.

The result is that research in the field has revealed a more complex and multidimensional picture of Mao's China, exceeding what we knew just a decade or so ago. One area of particular concern has been the limits of the state versus society paradigm, an issue raised by Elizabeth Perry some twenty-five years ago.[24] As has now been well documented, for most of the Mao era, a radical ideology based on the notion of class struggle reigned supreme in the party and dictated the course of the party's policies.[25] In the CCP's post-Mao political language, there had been a persistent "left" deviation in the Mao era, which obstructed the party's "correct line."[26] We now also know that the factionalism within the party was not limited to a struggle among the party's top leaders, but involved all levels of the party-state apparatus.[27] Sporadically, moderate party leaders were able to implement some relatively mild or pragmatic policies on the ground while legitimizing them with Mao's own words. Simply put, the state itself had a split personality.

Society was also divided, and in fact in its dealings with the party's politics it was more variegated than the party itself. First of all, the majority of the people were all too ready to take advantage of the divisions at the top and find nooks and crannies where they could, to one extent or another, think and act as they wished. Then, there was a considerable portion of the population who were eager to swim in the mainstream of Maoism in order to advance their own interests. Furthermore, there were people who wangled and finagled in order to get on in the system no matter what direction the wind blew. All these various responses were frequently entangled with the party's own fractures and inconsistent policies that, like a pendulum, swung from one extreme to the other. Any view of Mao's China that sees no more than simple dichotomies cannot help but be blind to the heterogeneity in society and to some of the most intriguing, revealing, and significant aspects of society in those years.

Building on this understanding, this book aims to provide a multidimensional portrait of daily life in Shanghai during the Mao era, with a "thick description" (to use anthropologist Clifford Geertz's term) of how a wide array of people, including industrialists, intellectuals, students, factory workers, and what were generally called "petty urbanites" (*xiao shimin*, or "little urbanites"), denizens of the city's crowded alleyway house (*lilong*) neighborhoods, actively coped with "high socialism" in the search of material well-being, social status, intellectual satisfaction, and aesthetic pleasure.[28] This search was not always in compliance with the party's dictates; quite the opposite, it often defied political orthodoxy, even if the defiance was mostly unintentional.

There were a number of the party's proclaimed principles and their associated policies that facilitated the above-mentioned activism at a time of Maoist political oppression and material scarcity. Before perusing snapshots of how these policies were implemented on the ground and the contextual details of how people exploited the party's policies for their own benefit, it is necessary to put into perspective the party's principles and policies that helped make grassroots-level activism possible.

Introduction

The United Front

One of the CCP's long-standing strategies was the united front, based on the notion of uniting with one's lesser adversaries to fight against the primary adversary. During the revolution, the Communists vigorously pursued the united-front strategy and Mao explicitly claimed that it, together with armed struggle and party building, was one of the "three principal magic weapons for defeating the enemy in the Chinese revolution."[29] Two major united fronts were formed in the Republican era (1911–1949): First, the coalition between the Nationalists and Communists during the Northern Expedition of 1926–1927 against the warlords, and second, the alliance of the two during the Sino-Japanese War of 1937–1945. After the Communist victory, and especially after the "New Democracy" promised by the party was quickly replaced by a radical "socialist transformation" in the mid-1950s, the united front seemed to fade away, remaining relevant mostly in issues related to national unity such as those involving Taiwan, Tibet, religious groups, and ethnic minorities.[30]

By the time the Cultural Revolution exploded on the scene in 1966, it looked like, as the historian Lyman Van Slyke noted, "the united front may have become largely irrelevant to concrete problems within China. It may have become somewhat formalized and dogmatic at the theoretical level."[31] However, as we will see later in this book, the united front was very much still alive in the Mao era despite the Maoist "class and class struggle" rhetoric and fanaticism. It was not only formalized and dogmatized at the theoretical level – the most obvious emblem here was the Chinese People's Political Consultative Conference (CPPCC), established as a state apparatus at the central and local levels, with members from both the Communist Party and the eight other legally permitted but powerless political parties, to serve as an indispensable symbol of "people's democracy" – but also functioned in such a way as to have real consequences for people's lives.

The united front served to validate giving some Nationalist Party figures and capitalists, both avowed targets of the revolution, political status as "united front personages" (*tongzhan duixiang*). As such, they enjoyed high salaries, kept their garden homes, still employed servants, and indulged in luxuries. Their privileged lives were also used to impress foreign visitors and helped with the party's broad united-front strategy overseas. Except for the most radical years between late 1966 and early 1972, when these policies were mostly suspended, the privileges and bourgeois comforts protected by the united front indicated that Mao's "magic weapon" was alive and well.[32]

Thus, although condemned and politically disadvantaged, in day-to-day life the old rich in the city, former capitalists, Nationalist officials, and so-called higher intellectuals still lived life at a level significantly above that of the common people and, indeed, became the envy of party cadres themselves. At the time of the Communist victory, there was a proposal in the PLA, initiated by a general and supported by many cadres, that soldiers' pay should be raised. It was argued that a capitalist's meal consisted of five courses whereas a PLA soldier had only salt water plus some pickled cabbage, and that wouldn't do. Mao firmly opposed the proposal, saying, "I have always been of the opinion that the army should live plainly and work hard and be a model." The tough lifestyle of Communists, in Mao's mind, was exemplary of the revolution: "They had five courses while we ate pickles. There was politics in these pickles, out of which models would emerge. The PLA won people's hearts and minds precisely because of these pickles."[33] Mao reiterated the point numerous times after Liberation. And among the public there was an enduring apprehension that party cadres faced the danger of being felled by bourgeois "sugar-coated bullets," that is, they would be corrupted by material comfort and lose the will to fight.[34] With a certain irony, the united-front policy allowed its subjects precisely the comfortable lifestyle that was denied the party's cadres and the general public.

The Intellectuals

In a broad sense, the united front extended to the nation's educated elite, generally categorized as "intellectuals" (*zhishifenzi*).[35] In a nation where the vast majority of the people were illiterate, a school education was a privilege, mostly limited to individuals from the urban middle class or above in the pre-1949 era. Those who were educated before Liberation were to varying degrees estranged by the self-proclaimed regime of workers and peasants. Although many intellectuals joined the Communist revolution during the years of foreign aggression and civil war out of patriotism and a sense that social injustice had to be righted, they were seen to bear the original sin of being "bourgeois intellectuals" and thus not entirely trustworthy. In Mao's words, intellectuals, like "petty bourgeois," are "fellow travelers" of the party and, as the revolution continues, at various points many of them will desert.[36]

On the other side, China had a long tradition of literati serving as bureaucrats and community leaders. In modern times, Chinese intellectuals played a similar role. They had a strong sense of public responsibility and civic obligation, especially in times of national crisis. Many intellectuals were unhappy with the Nationalist government and sympathetic to

Introduction   13

the Communist revolution. In the early 1950s, while they applauded the revolution that allowed the "Chinese people to stand up," many hoped they could act as a loyal opposition under the socialist regime. This hope, or rather illusion, was soon crushed. After the Anti-Rightist Campaign of 1957, it was abundantly clear that intellectuals not only were not to be allowed to act as critics, but also that the cost of their quest for intellectual autonomy was condemnation and persecution.[37]

Much has been said about the suppression of freedom of speech in Mao's China, but perhaps no incident is more revealing than Mao's remark on the writer Lu Xun on July 7, 1957, at an officially planned social gathering in Shanghai during the so-called Hundred Flowers Campaign.[38] Thirty-six writers, composers, other cultural celebrities, and businesspeople as well as Shanghai's top party bosses attended. In a seemingly relaxed and amicable atmosphere, Mao was asked a hypothetical question about what the fate of the writer Lu Xun (1881–1936) would have been if he was still alive. While everyone in the room shuddered at the question, Mao's reply was brutally candid: If Lu Xun were still alive, he would "either be put in prison but still write his stuff or he would know that the general situation required him not to say a single word."[39] Huang Zongying (1925–), a movie actress who sat close to Mao, recalled that Mao uttered those words in a clear and forthright manner, but the statement was like "a big clap of thunder right in front of me." As she was pregnant at the time, "I felt like the baby in my womb was going to jump out" (Figure I.5).[40] Huang's reaction was nothing unusual. In public, it was Mao who revered Lu Xun as a hero of extraordinary wisdom and courage, and raised Lu Xun to the status of a revolutionary saint, perhaps next only to Mao himself. Yet in this candid conversation, Mao revealed that he would have sent Lu Xun to prison if he had dared to speak out – the mendacity was too frightening, and Mao's comment was never publicized.[41]

The Communist Party nevertheless needed the expertise and skills of professionals to carry out its project of socialist nation-building, especially in the fields of science and technology. Hence it developed what was referred as an intellectual policy, a set of vague dogmas that swung between labeling educated people "bourgeois intellectuals" who must undergo "thought reform" in order to be productive members of socialist society, and acknowledging them as among the working people who, by dint of their skill and knowledge, contributed to the cause of socialism. The pendulum, however, rested most of the time on the unfavorable side, as Mao insisted that the label "bourgeois intellectuals" remained valid even after years of thought reform.[42] However, regardless of the tag, when it came to the actual implementation of policy,

Figure I.5 Mao meeting with intellectuals and cultural figures, Shanghai, July 7, 1957. The photo was published on the front page of *People's Daily* (July 9, 1957), with a caption reading, "Chairman Mao holds a meeting with representatives of Shanghai's scientific, educational, literary, artistic and industrial and commercial circles on July 7 at Shanghai's Sino-Soviet Friendship Building. The photograph shows Chairman Mao having intimate exchanges with them." At the table behind that at which Mao sits are (*extreme left, and partly obscured by Mao's head*) Huang Zongying and her husband, Zhao Dan (1915–1980), a famous movie actor. The man to Huang's left wearing glasses is Zhang Chunqiao (1917–2005), then editor-in-chief of *Liberation Daily*, Shanghai's CCP mouthpiece. Luo Ji'nan (1898–1971), who asked the sensitive question about Lu Xun, is facing Mao (*front, back to the camera, second from the right*, wearing glasses and with unkempt hair). According to Huang, the meeting was planned as a casual social event and the seating was random. *Source:* Photo by Huo Bo, Xinhua News Agency.

"to carry out the intellectual policy" (*luoshi zhishifenzi zhengce*) meant making sensible and often favorable concessions to the people so categorized in job assignments, promotions, salaries, housing allocations, and so on.[43] In Mao's words, "bourgeois intellectuals may be bought when necessary."[44]

While intellectual life in general was straightjacketed by Maoist ideology and the party line, various fields in the humanities and social sciences were particularly hard hit. Political science, for instance, was seen as equivalent to the study of Marxism. The same applied to philosophy, and sociology as a discipline was totally eliminated.[45] One odd exception was translated literature, which thrived. Under tight political control, translation, rather than original creative writing, seemed to be ideologically safer and politically less vulnerable. The translation of literature, especially European literature, experienced a boom.

Many Communist leaders in charge of cultural affairs were familiar with and fond of the European literature that had been introduced to China in their youth in the Republican era, and they tended to be supportive of translating foreign literature. Ideological kinship gave Russian and Soviet literature a birthright in socialist China. Marx and Engels's favorable remarks on nineteenth-century European classics served as a license to publish a great variety of these works in China. As a result, translators of foreign literature enjoyed great popularity and prestige in the Mao era. Even during the Cultural Revolution, when books were burned and banned, reading among the youth was a "deep and silent undercurrent."[46] With the great increase of the literacy rate (especially in cities) and a huge amount of translated works published and available via numerous channels, Mao's youth were among the best-read generation in foreign literature in recent Chinese history.

The Economy

Frequent political campaigns and purges in the Mao era placed economic development on the back burner. After the Great Leap Forward of 1958–1962,[47] even the Soviet-style five-year economic plans were not necessarily put into effect.[48] But there was always a degree of pragmatism within the party and a group of level-headed leaders remained devoted to economic matters and day-to-day governance. Mao overall "had a very poor grasp of economics," as he himself would admit in a moment of frankness in early 1961 when famine was widespread.[49] Still, his words on the economy were taken as supreme instructions. On several occasions in the war years, Mao pointed out the importance of finance and production for ensuring the victory of the revolution. This idea was summarized in the slogan "develop the economy and ensure supplies." This became an essential strategy for safeguarding at least a modicum of rationality amid the fanatic "politics in command" (*zhengzhi guashuai*) of the Mao era.[50] Even during the most radical years of the Cultural Revolution when the entire nation seemed to have

Figure I.6 (a) *Top*, Beginning on September 26, 1968, the Xinghuo Food Store on the corner of Tibet Road and Xinzha Road in downtown Shanghai was open twenty-four hours a day, making it Shanghai's – and indeed China's – first twenty-four-hour convenience store. In addition to food, the store also stocked such common items as fuses, candles, matches, toothbrushes, toothpaste, and postage stamps, and provided services such as emergency phone calls and inflating bicycle tires. This made the Xinghuo a model of "serving the people." (b) *Bottom*, A poster titled *Spring Winds on a Snowy Night* (published in 1976), depicting fifty shoppers and shop assistants in a busy food store in the middle of a city, was said to be inspired by Xinghuo. The slogans on the wall read "Develop the Economy and Ensure Supplies" (*top left*) and "Criticize Bourgeois Rights Thinking and Serve the People Wholeheartedly!" (*top center*). *Source:* Huangpu District Archives.

succumbed to mass insanity, Mao gave his support – albeit lukewarm – to the economy in order to prevent it from collapsing and to maintain a level of basic social order. To that extent, pragmatism within the party never completely disappeared.

On September 7, 1966, just three months after Mao launched the Cultural Revolution, *People's Daily*, with Mao's approval, published an editorial titled "Grasp Revolution and Promote Production," calling for linking revolution and production. A month later, the newspaper carried another editorial with virtually the same title, reemphasizing the theme.[51] To put that theme into effect, an expanded CCP Political Bureau meeting in December adopted a resolution consisting of ten guidelines for economic production, including working hours, workplace discipline, and quality control.[52] In the next decade, as everything had to be validated under the banner of "revolution," the expression "Grasping Revolution and Promoting Production" in actuality meant the second half only, that is, putting the spurs to production. The slogan, together with "Develop the Economy and Ensure Supplies," was printed on ration coupons and inscribed with Mao's own calligraphy in wall decorations and window displays everywhere in the country (Figure I.6b). They were used to balance or, to some extent, counteract the radical theme of "politics in command" in those turbulent years, now officially pronounced to have been "a decade of great calamity."

The emphasis on production and the economy meant job opportunities and material benefits for the people. Regardless of the proclaimed ideological purposes of Mao's endless campaigns, everyday people were concerned about avoiding becoming a political target and, moreover, seeking what they called *shihui*, or "real benefits," whenever possible. Karl Gerth has demonstrated how consumerism undermined Communism in the Mao era and prepared for the varieties of capitalism in post-Mao China, arguing that "regardless of the specific institutional arrangements, the CCP was always developing one or another variation of industrial capitalism."[53] Government programs that included real benefits for the people usually worked well. One of them was women's liberation, a sociopolitical theme that the CCP had advocated since its nascent years in Yan'an (1935–1948). In the public mind, and to some extent in the party as well, women's liberation consisted most of all in women's participation in the workforce outside the home. Women's employment increased remarkably in the Mao years. As we shall see, the Great Leap Forward, despite its failures, marked the beginning of women joining the workforce on a large scale and ultimately led to near universal employment of working-age women in urban China.

The party's moderate policies such as the united front and developing the economy were frequently submerged by a flood of radical rhetoric of "class and class struggle" and "politics in command." Nevertheless, such policies endured throughout the Mao era. The pragmatism amid fanaticism served as a justification for allocating resources to improving people's lives and allowing a certain level of freedom in the pursuit of material and emotional comfort.

Researchers of Communism have noted the existence of a noncompliant "second society" in which "people offered no more than outward compliance, keeping their innermost thoughts and personal feeling to themselves" while managing "to keep a diversity of cultural traditions alive."[54] Maintaining one's own way of life in terms of material comfort and intellectual pursuits was a way of defending the type of character and individuality that Maoist radicals deemed to be deviant and dissident. Tenaciously and ingenuously pursuing "bourgeois pleasure" in daily life – a subject of the following chapters – no matter how subconsciously it might have been exercised, was, to borrow James Scott's term, a powerful "weapon of the weak."[55] Unlike Scott's peasant troops, however, here the group that wielded the weapon consisted of urbanites who, in their battle against intrusion into their private lives, had quietly become what Michel de Certeau called "a dark rock that resists all assimilation."[56]

The interaction between the party-state and society in the Mao era in a way resembled Chinese shadowboxing, tai chi, with its circuitousness, indirection, ingenuity, and accommodation of all parties involved. Part of such a haecceity is often thought to be stereotypically "Asian." Malaysian prime minister Mahathir Mohammad once suggested so, and academics such as Samuel P. Huntington apparently agreed: "Asians generally pursue their goals with others in ways which are subtle, indirect, modulated, devious, nonjudgmental, nonmoralistic, and non-confrontational."[57] This is, of course, a broad generalization, but the deep cultural roots that led to such a character have to do with living under a variety of long-lasting hierarchical institutions with total power, of which China was no doubt a prominent case. Political tai chi, so to speak, represented an often invisible and instinctively roundabout resistance against a tyranny that, paradoxically, had its own pliability and elasticity. Under the circumstances, such interaction led to a degree of balance and composure in everyday life that sustained the regime as well as the operation of society. Ultimately, such a delicate balance paved the way for Shanghai's resurgence as a cosmopolitan city in the post-Mao era. More importantly, on a much larger scale it led to the great resilience of Chinese society that has bought China to where it is today.

Part I

The Condemned

In China's cities, two groups of people were the primary targets of the Maoist revolution: The bourgeoisie and the intellectuals. The essence of Communist revolution was the belief that Communism is a "universal truth" and that it will inevitably replace capitalism. The bourgeoisie, as the *Communist Manifesto* declared, produces its own gravediggers, the proletariat. Hence the personification of capitalism, the bourgeoisie (*zichan jieji*), was the natural enemy of the revolution – the subject of the "dictatorship of the proletariat." People so labeled and their families were effectively outcasts. In Marxist doctrine, intellectuals were not a social class per se but were defined by their capacity to act as a class. Since the education Chinese intellectuals received before 1949 was condemned as "bourgeois," intellectuals bore the original sin of being associated with the bourgeoisie and were subjected to constant political scrutiny, "thought reform," and, periodically, labor reform.

Such were stories of the bourgeoisie and "bourgeois intellectuals" told by countless reports and endless research on Mao's China. Although the picture of these condemned and oppressed people was generally accurate, it was broad-brushed and incomplete. The regime was ruthless in suppressing the bourgeoisie, justified by the Marxist theory of class warfare and the Maoist notion of continuous revolution, but if one looks closely, one can discern fine and not-so-obvious brushstrokes. For instance, the CCP created an arbitrary category of "national capitalists," who were subject to the party's united front policy, and as such were treated leniently. The united front policy was also selectively applied to what the party called "patriotic personages," who were useful allies of the revolution. And intellectuals, at least in theory, could be "educated" to reform their "world outlook" and could dedicate themselves to the cause of socialism. Such moderate principles and related policies, although not always carried out in the Mao years, were an important means by which the party broadened the regime's foundation. Beneficiaries of the united front policy were well aware of the ambiguity of their status and were always ready to exploit it; some were keen to prove their trustworthiness to the party. The result was that, paradoxically, bourgeois comforts were in some instances preserved under proletarian dictatorship and the politically condemned might well at the same time be among the socially privileged.

1   The Upper Crust

China under Mao Zedong is known for its frequent political campaigns in the name of consolidating the "dictatorship of the proletariat." While virtually all the campaigns attacked what was often arbitrarily branded "the bourgeoisie and bourgeois ideology," two campaigns specifically targeted the capitalist class: The Five-Anti Campaign of 1952 and the Socialist Nationalization Campaign of 1955–1956 (officially known as the Campaign for the Socialist Transformation of Capitalist Industry and Commerce).

The so-called Five-Antis referred to five vices to be expunged from business circles: Bribery, tax evasion, theft of state property, cheating on government contracts, and stealing state economic secrets. With tens of thousands of cadres specially trained to wage the campaign, in a matter of four months the Chinese Communist Party (CCP) in effect brought China's capitalists to their knees.[1] According to the CCP's official data, the campaign scrutinized the business conduct of 999,707 firms nationwide. Businesses were investigated and then categorized into five groups. In October 1952 the results were announced: "Law-abiding" business owners made up 10–15 percent of the total; "basically law-abiding," 50–60 percent; "semi-law-abiding," 25–30 percent; "serious lawbreakers," 4 percent; and "total lawbreakers," 1 percent.[2] Although only 1,509 business owners, or 1.5 per thousand under scrutiny, were actually charged with crimes, the campaign generated over thirty trillion yuan in taxes that had been evaded and in fines, an amount equivalent to more than half of China's military expenditures for the Korean War (1950–1953).[3] However, the impact of the campaign was more political than financial. It put immense psychological pressure on businesspeople for the purpose of, in Mao's words, "making the entire capitalist class obey state ordinances."[4]

The Five-Anti Campaign cleared the way for a more substantial movement to bring capitalists to heel.[5] In June 1952 when the campaign was nearing its end, Mao indicated that from then on "China's main internal contradiction is the one between the working class and the national

Figure 1.1 A rally to celebrate the Socialist Nationalization Campaign, Tiananmen Square, Beijing, January 15, 1956. On the rostrum, Le Songsheng (1908–1968; *far left*), whose family had owned the pharmacy Tongren Tang (lit., Hall of Shared Benevolence) for thirteen generations, is handing Chairman Mao a huge envelope containing a letter symbolizing the notion that all the capitalists in Beijing supported "joint state–private ownership." On Mao's right is Premier Zhou Enlai (1898–1976), and on Mao's left, the mayor of Beijing, Peng Zhen (1902–1997). *Source:* Xinhua News Agency.

bourgeoisie."[6] Three years later, the Socialist Nationalization Campaign was launched in the name of reorganizing private businesses into firms under "joint state–private ownership" (*gongsi heying*), which was essentially, as Andrew Walder has put it, "a halfway house toward full state ownership." The "joint" category soon disappeared from government statistics (Figure 1.1).[7] However, unlike in the Soviet Union, where the state simply confiscated private businesses altogether, in China the government adopted what was known as a "policy of redemption," that is, in effect it bought out private businesses by paying the owners 5 percent in "fixed interest" (*dingxi*), based on the estimated market value of the business, for seven years (later extended to ten years).[8] Although the math was not favorable to capitalist "sellers," under tremendous political and financial pressure, virtually all owners of private businesses, save for some mom-and-pop shops that the government did not want to take on, complied with the plan. By early 1956, Chinese capitalists had become

Figure 1.2 Much publicized events on Nanjing Road celebrating "joint state–private enterprises," 1956. (a) *Top*, Dragon dance in front of the Wing On department store (founded in 1907; dubbed the Macy's of China). (b) *Bottom*, Putting up a new store sign on the Xindaxiang Silk and Fabric Store (founded in 1928) announcing that it has been nationalized. *Source:* Xinhua News Agency.

employees of what used to be their own businesses, now nominally under the institution known as the "joint state–private enterprise" (Figures 1.2a and 1.2b).[9] Nationwide there were 810,000 business owners and their agents who received quarterly "fixed interest" payments. But by then being a capitalist under the Communist class system had become such a political liability that many small business owners, if they had the choice, would probably have relinquished their "fixed interest" in exchange for the removal of the "capitalist" label and being recognized as working people.[10]

In the next two decades, China's former capitalists, constantly facing purges and political condemnation, were doomed as a class. Although up to the death of Mao in 1976, the CCP launched numerous political campaigns that were broadly anti-capitalist, none of them, unlike the Five-Anti and the Socialist Nationalization campaigns, was directed explicitly against capitalists. Nonetheless, all the campaigns were by and large driven by the notion of class warfare against the bourgeoisie and its alleged influence.

Yet in Shanghai, China's largest and most industrialized city, the representative par excellence of what Steve A. Smith has called China's "capitalist modernity,"[11] much of the lifestyle of the old capitalist class survived the harsh "dictatorship of the proletariat" and persevered beneath the surface of Communist egalitarianism and asceticism. But with the Cultural Revolution in 1966 the privileges that the formerly wealthy still enjoyed after the 1949 revolution came to a crashing end. Official records indicate that from August 1966 to the end of that year the homes of more than 48,000 Shanghai capitalists were ransacked and the households' valuables confiscated. The total value of the items seized – including bank savings accounts (certified deposits only), bonds, gold and silver, but not real estate – was 480 million yuan.[12] This means that after seventeen years of Communist rule and endless campaigns attacking capitalism, on average a Shanghai capitalist still had cash assets under the mattress, so to speak, worth more than two decades of the income of an average worker in the city.[13]

In this chapter, we examine what life at home was like for the people whom the CCP classified as "national capitalists," a bewildering and often arbitrary category that positioned business owners as an ally of the Communist revolution, a revolution aimed precisely at ending capitalism. As we will see, in the intimate aspects of their lives, the so-called national capitalists and their families were in fact comfortable and privileged – quite the contrary of the broadly accepted notion that capitalists lived in misery after the revolution (see Figure 1.3).[14] There is anecdotal evidence that even during the Cultural Revolution, the old

The Upper Crust

Figure 1.3 In his celebrated salty style, Shanghai's Mayor Chen Yi (1901–1972) instructed his party cadres that pillow talk was often more effective than official mobilization meetings in the Socialist Nationalization Campaign. Therefore, business owners' spouses were an important subject of the united front. Pictured is a meeting in Shanghai in January 1956 specifically for capitalist family members, who were briefed on the party's polices on nationalizing private businesses. Nearly all attendants were wives of well-off capitalists. The anxiety and uneasiness of some of these well-dressed women, who were still living a privileged life at home, were reflected on their faces. *Source:* Xinhua News Agency.

rich continued to enjoy a certain level of material comfort. Many of the sources used in this chapter refer to relatively big capitalists rather than small business owners. According to orthodox Communist ideology, their wealth should have put them in a truly disadvantaged position after the revolution. Yet even after their businesses were taken away, they were, during China's long period of high socialism, categorized as "objects of the united front" (*tongzhan duixiang*), a term referring to the nonparty personages whom the CCP deemed to be of value to the revolution. This status made it possible for them to continue to live what the Chinese called a "bourgeois life," a phrase connoting a wealthy and privileged (rather than "middle-class") lifestyle but one that, of course, was a political anathema.[15]

The revelation of such a hitherto largely hidden phenomenon, a product of the complexity and paradox in the Chinese Communist system, helps correct the lingering oversimplification since the Cold War era that dismisses the Chinese revolution as nothing more than tragedy.[16] As the following discussion reveals, in its social dimensions, the old and sometimes extravagant lifestyle of the capitalist class persisted in what has often been thought to have been the uniformly drab and monotonous everyday life in the Maoist period.

This complicating of the picture by no means is intended to downplay the cruelty of the regime, nor to overlook the suffering it caused, but it is to recognize that there were nuances and variations in the Communist system that were not always readily apparent, nor always consistent with the regime's political rhetoric. If we navigate through party politics and the ideological superstructure down through society in search of the quotidian aspects of life and make "home a site of inquiry,"[17] we may have a better appreciation of the resilience and elasticity of Chinese society under Communism.

The "National Capitalists"

Based on Mao's analysis of social classes, the CCP divided businesspeople – exclusive of small tradespeople, or the so-called petty bourgeoisie – into two broad categories: Comprador bureaucratic capitalists and national capitalists. The former category was designated an enemy of the people, and therefore a target of the revolution, while the latter was described as "a class with a dual character," and under certain circumstances could be an ally of the revolution.[18] This distinction was the rationale for placing national capitalists under a sort of discretionary protection via the united front, as will be discussed in this chapter. Well-established national capitalists were often dubbed "patriotic capitalists" or informally, "red capitalists," to be distinguished from comprador bureaucratic capitalists who worked for "Chiang Kai-shek's old regime of quislings" or served as compradors for foreign (therefore, imperialist) firms.[19]

As China's most industrialized city, Shanghai had the highest concentration of capitalists in the nation. In 1949, private businesses in Shanghai churned out more than a third (36 percent) of China's gross industrial output.[20] In July 1952, Shanghai had 167,716 registered private businesses.[21] By early 1956, when the Socialist Nationalization Campaign was at its height, the city had nearly a quarter million private businesspeople (including small tradespeople) out of a total population of about 5.5 million.[22] According to an official assessment by the CCP United Front Department, the market value of China's urban-based private businesses in 1956 amounted to 2.42 billion yuan; private enterprises in Shanghai accounted for over half of that (1.25 billion).[23]

The term "national capitalists" could be applied to any business owner who was neither an "enemy of the people" (i.e., a comprador bureaucratic capitalist) nor "petty bourgeois" (i.e., a small merchant). But the real beneficiaries of the title were those who received a good amount of fixed interest. Shanghai had about 10 percent of the national total of fixed-interest recipients and an extraordinary concentration of high-paid ones. By 1964, Shanghai still had 84,126 capitalists and their "agents" (high-paid business executives) who were recipients of government compensation in the form of fixed interest and high salaries known as "retention pay" (*baoliu gongzi*), both provided as part of the policy of expropriation implemented during the Socialist Nationalization Campaign in the mid-1950s.[24] Nationwide in 1964, 1,004 capitalists had a monthly salary greater than 300 yuan; fully 937 of them lived in Shanghai.[25]

The Shanghai municipal government's payroll records provide a complete list of 386 capitalists who, up to July 1966, were paid over 350 yuan a month, not including fixed interest. Twenty-six of these capitalists were also politically privileged, serving as either members of the People's Congress or of the Chinese People's Political Consultative Committee at both the municipal and national levels. The following is a breakdown of monthly salaries of these capitalists, with the number of payees in each subgroup in parentheses: 351–400 yuan (191), 401–500 yuan (132), 501–600 yuan (37), 601–1,000 yuan (23), and 1,000+ yuan (3).[26]

In comparison, the average pay for all employees in Shanghai in 1962 was 68.41 yuan (821 annually).[27] Skilled factory workers after three years of apprenticeship received about 40 yuan a month; after 1968, the rate was made uniform at 36 yuan.[28] Wang Hongwen (1935–1992), a Shanghai cotton mill worker-cadre who was handpicked by Mao as the preeminent representative of the Chinese working class and, in 1973, was made his heir apparent, had a salary of 64 yuan. Wang's wife, who worked in the same factory with Wang, was paid 24 yuan.[29] The salary of college-degree holders – the highest paid employees among the generation that grew up in the Mao era – was 46 yuan during the first year of employment and 56 yuan thereafter.[30] Even the highest salaries of China's top leaders were dwarfed by capitalists' income. Starting from July 1955, the CCP adopted a salary system to replace the wartime supply system: Chairman Mao's salary was set at 404.80 yuan and Premier Zhou Enlai's at 400.80 yuan.[31]

Bourgeois Comforts

The high income guaranteed former capitalists a comfortable life. As far as home life and material comforts are concerned, little changed for the families of wealthy entrepreneurs after Liberation. In fact, without frequent warfare, pervasive underworld gang activity, ruthless business competition, and terrible inflation – all of which were characteristic of old Shanghai – some former business owners felt their lives had become simpler and more peaceful under the new regime. Historian Marie-Claire Bergère has noted that after Liberation compensation paid to the most important heads of private businesses "certainly assured them of a living standard incomparably superior to that of the Shanghai masses."[32]

Daisy Kwok (1910–1998), whose family owned the Wing On Company – one of the "big four" department stores of Shanghai and, indeed, of China – remembered that there was actually very little difference in the daily life of her family before and after 1949. In her words, "The Kuomintang [i.e., Nationalist] flag with its blue sky and white sun had been replaced by the Communist five-starred red flag. We hardly paid any attention to the difference between the two."[33] In an interview in 2009, eighty-eight-year-old Xu Lingxian, a daughter of cement mogul Xu Meifeng (1902–1996), recalled that "when the Communists came, it was impossible not to panic unless you were a pauper. [But] it turned out that the lives of capitalists were not affected.… The capitalists who chose to stay in Shanghai after Liberation felt very contented."[34]

After his family business was nationalized in 1956, the flour and cotton milling tycoon Rong Yiren (1916–2005), who was arguably the best-known "red capitalist," told a reporter that "as for material life, indeed I lost nothing; I still live very well"[35] (see Figures 1.4 and 1.5a). Another Chinese business magnate, Liu Hongsheng (1888–1956), dubbed the "King of Matches and Wool," gave the new government a "blanket endorsement," writing to his son soon after the Communist takeover that Shanghai was "the place where all the Lius should be." He told his son that "it is generally believed that great hope lies ahead. I share this view. At home everything is fine."[36]

The feeling was not limited to business moguls but was common among less prominent capitalists as well. Despite the Five-Anti Campaign, which targeted "law-breaking capitalists," the early 1950s have been considered by some former capitalists as a golden age. As a Shanghai writer put it, the "chaos of the civil war and the uncertainty of where to go before 1949 [were] at last ended. Shanghai capitalists breathed a sigh of relief under the newly raised red flag and began to live a peaceful life. The dust had settled. There was no more war, no more rowing soldiers, no more racketeering. So long as they exerted themselves, there

Figure 1.4 A rally in support of the socialist nationalization of private businesses, Shanghai, January 20, 1956. In front on the far left is Rong Yiren (1916–2005), a key business magnate and famous "red capitalist" who cooperated with the party in the campaign and later served as the vice president of the People's Republic of China (1993–1998). The Russian- and Empire-style neoclassical building in the background is the Sino-Soviet Friendship Hall (now the Shanghai Exhibition Center), which was built just a few months earlier, in 1955, on the ruins of Silas Aaron Hardoon's residence (the Hardoon Garden), once the most extravagant private home in old Shanghai. *Source:* Shanghai Municipal Archives.

was every promise of great progress to come."[37] Even after their businesses were taken away by the Socialist Nationalization Campaign, the owners, who were battered by the revolution, realized that under Communism they still had some substantial privileges. The banker Cheng

Muhao (1898–1991) expressed such awareness when he sighed with emotion to his family, "We should be grateful to the government. If we had been living in tsarist Russia, we would have long since been executed by the Soviet regime or exiled, or live like those penniless and frustrated White Russians in [old] Shanghai."[38] This sentiment could be often found among Shanghai's old rich.

For instance, Wang Jingzhi (1933–), a scholar of Chinese classical literature, recalled how his family was politically divided, with him being labeled a rightist in 1957 and therefore resentful of the regime, and his capitalist parents, particularly his mother, being supporters. In the summer of 1989 when Wang was writing a book titled *Being Frozen for Thirty Years* about his three decades of depressive life in China, his mother said she would write a book expressing the opposite. She would title her book *The Forty Golden Years* to compare her life under Communism to her early years in the "old society," namely, China before 1949. Wang's father, who had a PhD from the Wharton School of the University of Pennsylvania, declined job offers in the United States and returned to China on the eve of the Communist takeover. Despite all the hardships this capitalist family endured in Mao's China, the mother firmly believed that the time after 1949 was the golden age of her life. Wang admitted that his mother's view "was not uncommon among people of her generation."[39]

Gu Zhimin (1903–1956) offered perhaps the most sober expression of Chinese businesspeople's feelings about the CCP. Founder of China's most popular brand of skincare cream, Pechoin (*Pehchaolin*, or "A Hundred Sparrows"), Gu was a bit down when he saw two decades of his hard work nationalized, but he soon got over it and told his family:

To compare the CCP with the Soviet Communist Party, Stalin was not at all as gentle and kind. All [businesses] were nationalized regardless of one's attitude. All capitalists became common people overnight; in fact, they were not up to the status of the common people as the Soviets killed Russian capitalists at will. The CCP pursues a buyout policy that allows capitalists to retain their salaries and keep their status in the factory, in addition to receiving fixed interest. This is indeed [as a Chinese saying puts it] "to fall short of the best but to be better than the worst!"[40]

There is little reason to doubt the sincerity of remarks such as these that entrepreneurs made privately to their families. In a way, this type of gratitude among China's former business community broadened the CCP's power base and reflected its united front policy at work.

The material life of former businesspeople was noted by foreign visitors. Barry Richman, an industrial management specialist with experience in Communist countries, visited eleven cities in China seventeen years after the Communist takeover. In his report, Richman described the life of his British-educated "Chinese capitalist acquaintance": "It was indeed disconcerting for me in Shanghai in May 1966 to be picked up by a native Chinese capitalist in a new Jaguar, taken to his large factory for a day of discussion, and later to his sumptuous home where he still lives as a wealthy industrialist does in a capitalist nation."[41]

Robert Guillain (1908–1998), a French journalist who specialized in East Asia, also experienced this type of visit firsthand. On a trip to China in 1964 he visited the home of Liu Tsing-kew (1902–1997), a Shanghai textile-business owner, and was impressed by the luxuries he saw in the Liu residence: "There was a big drawing room, hung with paintings by Chinese masters, armchairs with silk cushions, waxed floors and flowers in the vases. A maid served tea; the chauffeurs waiting with the car."[42] Liu had reason to live in luxury in socialism (Figure 1.5b). He was among the few big entrepreneurs who not only chose to stay in the mainland when the Communist victory was certain but also transferred capital from overseas to Shanghai.[43] Liu was also among the first group of industrialists who actively responded to the CCP's call for nationalization.[44] His home, an elegant European-style villa rustica located at ninety-nine Wukang Road (formerly, Route Ferguson), was originally the residence of a taipan of the well-known Shanghai-based British soft-drink company Aquarius. It was allocated to Liu in 1955 by the Shanghai mayor as the government's gesture to "industrialists and businessmen who made a special contribution to the country."[45] Financially, after his Anda Cotton Mill was nationalized in June 1955, he became even more comfortable: His annual compensation was 26,213.70 yuan.[46]

A comfortable lifestyle was not limited to a few industrial magnates that foreigners could meet but in various degrees it reflected the general situation of Shanghai's capitalist families. Liu's associate Hua Du'an (1900–1970), for instance, received an annual compensation of 6,256.50 yuan.[47] In 1946, Cheng Muhao invested in the Garden Villas, a British-style apartment complex on Bubbling Well Road (today West Nanjing Road); ten years later, in 1956, the property was put under joint state–private ownership. As compensation for his share of the property, Cheng received 32,000 yuan annually in fixed interest, which was paid until September 1966. Cheng's granddaughter, Cheng Naishan (1946–2013), called it an "astronomical figure" and reminisced that the Garden Villas "resembled the Garden of Eden." At twilight, residents in the neighborhood would play the piano. Her father, a Western music buff who had collected about a hundred recordings of classic Western music, would put on a record. The air was thus often filled with melodies such as "As Time Goes By" (from *Casablanca*) or

Figure 1.5 Mao receives "red capitalists" on January 30, 1956. (a) *Top*, Shaking hands with Rong Yiren (1916–2005), whose family owned a major flour and cotton milling business. Rong was appointed vice mayor of Shanghai the following year. (b) *Bottom*, Shaking hands with Liu Tsing-kew (1902–1997), then a member of the Chinese People's Political Consultative Conference (CPPCC). *Source:* China National Democratic Construction Association and Xinhua News Agency.

"One Day When We Were Young" (from *The Great Waltz*).[48] Even children's play remained quite British in these neighborhoods. Among the most popular children's pastimes were the singing game "My Fair Lady" (aka "London Bridge Is Falling Down") and a catch-and-run game called "Stop."[49]

The melodic atmosphere in the Garden Villas was widely shared by Shanghai's moderately comfortable neighborhoods. Zhang Zugan (1947–), who lived in a Hongkou neighborhood northeast of the city, far away from the elegant residential district of west Shanghai where the Garden Villas were located, recalled:

I remember our family life in the 1950s and 1960s before the Cultural Revolution as very happy and loving.... My parents loved classical music, so we had quite a lot of Bakelite records and a hand-operated gramophone made in the US by the Columbia Phonograph Company. The music we played consisted of pieces composed by world-class musicians such as Beethoven, Mozart, and Schubert, and famous light music. Our home thus often reverberated with the moving melodies of the *Pastoral Symphony* and the *Fate Symphony*, or the melodious sound of *Serenade for Strings*, *Light Cavalry Overture*, *William Tell Overture*, *The Barber of Seville*, "The Cuckoo Waltz" and other world-famous classics. We were all intoxicated by the music and never got tired of it. In addition to elegant classical music, at the time there was a book called *Two Hundred Foreign Folk Songs*. We often learned to sing songs from that book—although most of the folk songs we learned were from Russia, they were truly pleasant to the ears.[50]

During his visit to Shanghai in 1971, Yang Zhenning (Yang Chen-Ning, 1922–), a Nobel laureate (physics, 1957) who was among the first group of US citizens to visit the PRC, often heard the sound of piano and violin practicing in the neighborhood of his parents' home, an alleyway-house compound on Huashan Road (formerly, Avenue Haig). He thought it might be because the Shanghai Conservatory was not too far away, but he also saw young people, both men and women, riding bicycles carrying a violin on their shoulders, evidence of the popularity of the instrument.[51]

In China, perhaps no musical instrument is considered as classy or Western as the piano. Although many of the occupants of the city's upscale houses had changed, some affluent residential neighborhoods in the former International Settlement and French Concession remained. These neighborhoods retained their tranquil and elegant atmosphere, with lovely homes and tree-lined streets with few pedestrians – in the local slang these were called "upper corners" (*shang zhi jiao*). There the piano was a symbol of the good life. Chen Danqing (1953–), a local painter and writer, wrote that "on a spring day after a rain, a 'bourgeois' or their children might play the piano in their Western-style home, and the music was heard beyond the fences of their gardens. This was another

Shanghai. As a 'class,' the bourgeoisie had been subdued, but physically they were still there, together with their piano. At that time, the word 'piano' conveyed a good family background and social status."[52] In the first few months of house ransackings during the Cultural Revolution, in the alleyway neighborhoods around Huaihai Road (formerly, Avenue Joffre) alone, thousands of pianos were confiscated. Working people chuckled over the upper crust's loss of their pianos, enjoying the idea that the rich now had no toy to play with. At the same time, a secondhand store near the corner of Huaihai Road and Maoming Road (formerly, Route Cardinal Mercier) had many of the confiscated pianos for sale. The store did not have enough room for the sudden influx of the huge instruments, so pianos were set vertically on the shop floor. Eventually they were all sold – clearly there was still a market for such "bourgeois toys" even at the height of the Cultural Revolution.[53] Like many other luxury goods at the time, prices were cheap: The lowest price for a used piano at the time was 50 yuan, equivalent to about a month's salary of a typical schoolteacher.[54]

Zhang Weiqun (1949–2015), a research fellow at the Shanghai Administration Institute, made an anthropological study of Siming Villa, an alleyway-house neighborhood where his family moved when he was seven months old. His next-door neighbor Yang Diaofang (1901–1987) was a piano teacher at St. Mary's Hall (a Christian school in Shanghai established by the Episcopal Church of the United States in 1881) and played the piano at home every day and tutored private students. Although the music she played consisted of Western classics, which were labeled bourgeois, and earning money outside one's regular job was regarded as a "capitalist tail," Yang did not run afoul of the authorities. Her husband, Diao Deren (b. 1888), was a professor of political science at St. John's University (an Anglican school in Shanghai founded in 1879) and once worked for T.V. Soong (Chiang Kai-shek's brother-in-law) in the Nationalist government. Apparently, he was an "alien class element" in the eyes of the Communists, but after Liberation the party's secret dossier described him as a "decrepit element" (*laoxiu*) and he was largely left alone. Unlike in the city's more jam-packed neighborhoods where there was a great deal of interaction between people, in this moderately comfortable alleyway-house complex, neighbors only occasionally saw each other on their half-moon shaped second-floor balconies, and exchanged no more than polite greetings. But, imperceptibly, the peaceful melodies flowing from the piano in Yang's house became a part of life in the neighborhood and were missed when Yang passed away in 1987.[55]

Zhou Yi (1931–), daughter of the renowned Peking opera actor Zhou Xinfang (1895–1975), described her life after she married into an affluent capitalist family in 1952: Living in a single-family European-style house on Huashan Road (Avenue Haig) in the former French Concession, the family had maids and servants to attend them and would sleep-in most mornings. Much of the afternoon was spent reading translated Western literature available at the Xinhua Bookstore.[56] In the evening, Zhou Yi and her husband often dined out or went to the movies or had get-togethers with friends.[57] The topics of conversation at social gatherings among family friends were fashion, cars, motorcycles, cameras, and hunting rifles.[58] Another privileged "princeling," Liu Hexiang (1942–), lived in the French Concession on his family's fixed interest and overseas remittances and kept himself busy with nothing but dating and pleasure-seeking. As he remembers it, his daily routine involved sleeping until 10:00 or 11:00 a.m. and after lunch going out for coffee and cakes with the other princelings or friends on Huaihai Road (formerly, Avenue Joffre). "Then he might play a couple of sets of tennis, and in the evening, he holds parties and dances."[59] This sort of playboy life in the former French Concession was in line with that in the former International Settlement where, up to the Cultural Revolution, young men from affluent families still fancied themselves as "Mr. Three Rs," that is, having US Ray-Ban sunglasses, British Raleigh bicycles, and German Rolleiflex cameras.[60] The Three Rs were far beyond the reach of ordinary youth: Ray-Bans cost 45 yuan, and a Raleigh bike and Rolleiflex camera were several hundred yuan.[61] In the local slang children of the rich were called *xiaokai* ("little open") and showoffs or loose characters were labeled *afei*, a term derived from the English "a figure."[62]

Shanghai resident Zhang Da-Peng (1941–) recalled that a family friend, a former capitalist whom he called Uncle Hua, lived with his wife in a three-story building with over ten rooms. Hua apparently was contented with his life, as the sixty-one-year-old man told Zhang in the summer of 1963: "Even though I went through the Five-Antis and the state-private joint operation after Liberation, I still have this big house.... Now I am no longer doing business, I have savings, and every year I get fixed interest. If I spend this money for the rest of my life, I still won't have used it up."[63] In May 1966, sensing the looming political upheaval and that something bad would happen to him, Hua deposited 50,000 yuan in a number of bank accounts in Zhang's name, asking him to keep the money for use in a time of emergency. That amount of money equaled nearly a hundred years of a university graduate's salary at the time. Zhang hid the deposit receipts in an unlikely place: underneath his old bicycle seat cushion. Just a few months later, when searching and ransacking homes became widespread in Shanghai, such a hiding place proved to be ingenious.[64]

Yan Qingxiang (1899–1988), owner of the Dalong Machine Plant, had a much larger house than Hua's and was known for throwing parties at home after he retired in 1957. His imposing house in west Shanghai, a 5,416 square-meter (58,297 sq ft) northern European-style mansion with a 4,900 square-meter (52,743 sq ft) garden, remained the family's private property throughout Mao's time.[65] Often before throwing a party, Yan would call the local police station to give the neighborhood police officers a heads-up in a condescending tone: "I'll have a dance party at home and play mahjong – just to let you know."[66] The Communists had banned mahjong since August 1949, but apparently the prohibition was not strictly applied and a "national capitalist" like Yan felt no need to hide what he was doing.[67]

Yan was also known among his friends for making "happy complaints": "I have so much money in Shanghai that I really have no way to use it up." In 1961, he wired US$10,000 to his son in the United States as pocket money. On National Day in 1962, Yan reserved seventeen tables, each costing more than 100 yuan, at the Park Hotel to entertain his friends only because one of them teasingly ask him to *qingke* (host a dinner party).[68] This was a time when millions of Chinese were starving to death. When Yan was criticized for his "wastefulness," he retorted: "This is my money. Fixed interest is paid by the state, so why shouldn't I use it however I like? These chic restaurants are there and open – what are they open for?"[69]

Yan had a point. Despite the ideologically based condemnation of wining and dining as bourgeois decadence, the Shanghai municipal government in fact paid a great deal of attention to running high-end restaurants. At least eighty-two "famous restaurants of old Shanghai" survived after 1949, and many prospered.[70] The official Shanghai Municipal Public Food and Drink Company, founded in January 1956, centralized the management of all restaurants and eateries in the city. Top chefs were hired, ranked, and retained. About fifty of them were honored as "famous masters."[71] Numerous training programs and cooking competitions eventually led to the establishment of the Shanghai Culinary School in 1963.[72] Gastronomists were hired to taste food and advise chefs in high-end restaurants. They also served as judges of chefs' qualifications and graded examinations. For instance, Shen Jingshi (1898–1992), a self-made expert in gastronomy, was invited to serve as an advisor for Shanghai's six top hotels and their affiliated restaurants for a monthly payment (in the form of an honorarium) of 240 yuan. Shen's father had been a wealthy salt commissioner, which allowed the son to do virtually nothing in life but revere fine food. According to the dictates of the Communists' ideology, he could well have been categorized as a "bourgeois parasite" and banished from the city, yet he was much appreciated for his culinary judgment. In fact, his appointment was recommended by the very powerful Marshal Chen Yi (1901–1972), who served as the first mayor of socialist Shanghai from 1949 to 1958.[73]

Historian Mark Swislocki, who carried out substantial archival research on Shanghai's restaurants in the Mao era, noted that it is hard to know exactly what the party's motivations were in maintaining the city's high-end restaurant industry, since few Shanghai residents could afford to eat in these places, yet it was also clear that "there was some demand, and even expectation, that the party maintain at least some of these establishments."[74] Upscale restaurants were kept for entertaining foreign visitors, holding government banquets, and, at least in theory, feeding the public. Shanghai apparently had enough wealthy people to constitute "the public." To cope with the crisis caused by the Great Leap Famine, the state set exceptionally high prices, at least more than five times the regular prices, for certain dishes in order to "recoup funds and revitalize markets." In Shanghai, from February 1961 to July 1963, ninety-four restaurants were designated as sites for serving "high-priced dishes." While the profits on most dishes in an average restaurant in the city were set at 32–36 percent, the profits on high-priced dishes stretched up to 75–83.4 percent.[75] It was common knowledge among Shanghai's residents that those who could afford to eat in these restaurants were people who "ate" on either fixed interest (*chi dingxi*) or overseas remittances (*chi qiaohui*), which dovetailed with the government's goal of gathering funds from those who had cash.[76] When Communist cadres grumbled that the high-priced restaurants served practically only the old rich and therefore were politically incorrect, the CCP's chief economic leader, Chen Yun (1905–1995), explained that this was a way for the government to get money back from the recipients of fixed interest, and therefore it was politically shrewd.[77]

In short, Shanghai's old rich had no problem maintaining their lavish lifestyle even during the Great Famine of the early 1960s. Yan Qingxiang certainly was not alone in frequently patronizing the luxury restaurants in upscale hotels. Before the Cultural Revolution, it was common for Shanghai's still-wealthy capitalist families to spend thousands of yuan on their children's wedding banquets in the most luxurious hotel restaurants in the city, such as those at the Jinjiang Hotel, Peace (Cathay) Hotel, and Park Hotel.[78] At a time when there were virtually no taxis in the city, pedicabs were hired for such events. Hundreds of pedicabs carrying well-dressed guests to and from the hotels made an impressive scene and drew a crowd of spectators.[79] One Shanghai resident recalls seeing such a pedicab parade in 1963 when he was eleven and heard onlookers' commenting, "The rich are still rich!" and "Those who had money still have it!"[80] This kind of envy would later turn ugly when the Red Guards ransacked the homes of the old rich and some onlookers rejoiced in the suffering of others: "Those rich people deserve to be fed a little misery!"[81]

For people who felt more comfortable entertaining at home, catering from upscale restaurants was also available. Although a table for eight to ten persons cost 100 yuan, equivalent to the cost of living for about six months for an average Shanghai resident, often a dozen or more tables were ordered by one family to celebrate holidays such as the Chinese New Year.[82] Chefs could even be hired out for special occasions. In late spring of 1961, at the peak of the national famine, a Shanghai capitalist, Ye Xingshan, held a banquet with dozens of tables laden with food prepared by upscale-restaurant chefs to celebrate his birthday. The banquet was held in Wuxi, a scenic city on the shores of Lake Tai, about eighty miles northwest of Shanghai. To entertain his guests, after the dinner Ye hired two boats to tour the lake and make a stop at Mount East (Dongshan) to enjoy fresh loquats, a local delicacy that was just in season. Ye spent 6,500 yuan on that occasion.[83] No wonder one capitalist, after whining a little about losing some individual freedom under Communism, such as needing a doctor's note in order to account for an absence, said to his friends, "To be honest, life is better under the socialist system; there are no gangsters, no blackmail, and no extortion."[84]

Most capitalists did not blaze their comfort around; instead, they quietly enjoyed it, while making every effort to dodge attention. One capitalist named Lu, who worked as an engineer in the factory he used to own, always openly showed his allegiance to the party. Privately, he managed to live as comfortably as he could, wearing expensive silk gowns, drinking coffee imported from Brazil, and listening to classical music from a gramophone (one of his favorites was Schumann's "Träumerei"), all of which were considered Western and bourgeois. His home was an ivy-covered garden house on Fenyang Road (formerly, Route Pichon), in one of the city's best residential neighborhoods. Lu coveted his old lifestyle, but out of fear of political trouble he carefully concealed it from people outside the family, including his neighbor, the writer Bai Hua (1930–2019), who had lived on the first floor of Lu's house since 1957. He would always keep the volume down while playing records on his gramophone or simply turn the music off if he found a neighbor was nearby. He brewed coffee early in the morning so as to avoid any attention to this "bourgeois habit." On one occasion, Bai Hua needed to take a trip out of town early in the morning and hence encountered Lu who, dressed in white embroidered silk pajamas and a red camauro, was making coffee in their shared kitchen. Lu, apparently did not expect to see Bai in this early hour, and was a bit uneasy and self-deprecating: "Do I look like a circus clown?" He then explained to Bai Hua that the pajamas he wore were from his old stock as were the coffee beans. "Isn't it bad to waste things?" Lu stretched his reasoning: "And, coffee beans are the fruit of labor of the working people." Bai Hua found the explanation totally absurd and his neighbor pathetic. One day years later, after the Mao era, Lu walked into Bai Hua's room and offered the following heartfelt comment on his life during the Mao years:

For decades, every night I sipped a glass, just one glass, of the best French brandy, XO, and never stopped for a single day. As you probably have figured out, even during the Great Famine of the early 1960s, I still lived a bourgeois life despite cowering inside a spiral shell, so to speak. At the time, even in the vicinity of Shanghai, there were people who ate bark and grass roots for survival. Who would have thought that at the same time someone could be leisurely sipping XO? If the famine victims had known it and found out where the alcohol came from and how much it cost, for sure I would have been beaten to death.... In that bloody winter of Shanghai in 1966, every night I had old friends who committed suicide; among them, there were so-called bourgeois and also leading reactionary intellectuals. And I drank my brandy all the same![85]

The story of Lu's indulgence might be considered no more than an anecdote but it cannot be dismissed as unusual. There are indications that even the Cultural Revolution failed to uproot the bourgeois lifestyle in Shanghai. In 1972, Wang Anyi (1954–), then a Shanghai youth sent down to rural Anhui, went back to the city hoping to study music in order to join an art troupe, a route out of the countryside that many so-called sent-down youths (that is, urban youth relocated to rural areas supposedly on a permanent basis) hoped to take. Wang and her like-minded friends often got together at home for music lessons, taught by teachers who were not allowed to practice their profession during the Cultural Revolution.

One day, the gathering was for a lecture on melody in vocal music at the home of a teenage girl who had studied the cello. Like millions of other teenagers, the girl had been sent down to the countryside (in her case, in Jiangxi), but was allowed to return temporarily to the city for a visit. Her home was in a back alley near the busy Jing'an Temple shopping area in west Shanghai. Walking into the house steps away from a noisy open-air food market, Wang was astonished by the luxury within. The waxed light brown hardwood floor shone; leather armchairs and sofas formed a half circle in a corner of the living room, and there, under a floor lamp, a gentleman wearing gold-rimmed spectacles – the girl's father – was reading a newspaper. An almond-color piano occupied another corner of the room. Behind the sofa was a dining table, and further down through a half-open door, a woman in her pajamas – the girl's mother – was doing her chores. Since the living room was big and adjacent to the dining area, looking at her from a distance, with the lights illuminating only her back as she took small paces, enhanced the relaxed and comfortable atmosphere, much like a scene of middle-class life in old Shanghai depicted in Eileen Chang's novel *Red Rose and White Rose* (1944). Wang exclaimed:

Such a bourgeois life was kept so perfectly that not even its skin had been wounded. It seemed like time and misfortune had not affected it at all. In a time of stormy and violent revolution, such a lifestyle appeared extravagant. It was certainly something one could not have imagined. Such a living room could be from any time: the thirties, the forties, or it even might fit in the fifties or sixties; but it was the seventies, at the conjunction of surging upheavals. It was said that they [the bourgeoisie and their lifestyle] had no hope, but they still kept their same old selves, silently plodding through an era.[86]

This was a time when having a sofa was considered decadent. What Wang observed was a slice of the bourgeois comfort that the city's old rich strove to maintain and the city's common folk craved to have. The painter Chen Danqing (1953–) recalled what he observed in his Shanghai home:

Across from my house lived a family of capitalists who used to own the whole house. By the time of the Cultural Revolution, they lived on one floor. We children often liked to look through the window when the family ate, sitting around a huge "eight-immortal table" made of padauk [expensive Chinese redwood]. The silverware was exquisite and the food, always carefully prepared and appetizing, was served by a maid.[87]

It remained common for Shanghai's ex-capitalists to continue to have domestic servants during the Cultural Revolution, at a time these families of "black" classes lived in the garage of the houses they used to own.[88]

Elegant Homes and Extravagant Parties

As mentioned earlier, Shanghai was known for having a great variety of fine buildings and luxurious homes built in the first half of the twentieth century, earning it a reputation as a "museum of global architecture."[89] The building frenzy since the 1990s has destroyed much of the old city; still, up to 2005, the Shanghai municipal government was able to identify 742 "outstanding historical structures" in the city and order that they be protected as cultural heritage sites.[90] Most of these were European-style houses, originally the homes of affluent families. When the Communists took over the city, real estate of the "comprador bourgeoisie" and "bureaucratic capitalists" (that is, those who were associated with foreign capital or the capital of the old regime) was subject to confiscation. Private real estate owned by all other capitalists was largely untouched. During the Socialist Nationalization Campaign, privately owned homes, as long as they had not been designated as business properties, were left alone. That was why when the Cultural Revolution started, the Red Guards and the so-called revolutionary rebels were able to occupy at least 26,104 privately owned houses – more than twenty-million square feet (1,872,100 square meters). Almost all were the best houses in the city.[91]

The great majority of Shanghai capitalists who owned a home therefore were able to continue to live in their property up to late 1966. From 1950 to 1966, the average living space for Shanghai residents never exceeded 4 square meters (43 square feet) per person, and it was common for multigeneration families to live in "pigeon lofts," a single room of less than 10 square meters (108 square feet).[92] In contrast, luxury homes occupied by former capitalists with thousands of square feet of living space and large yards were not unusual.

An example is the house at 333 Tongren Road, an art moderne structure constructed in 1937. The four-story building and the wall that surrounded it were covered with green tiles and built in the shape of a luxury passenger liner. The house was graced with a 14,722-square-foot lawn. Among its dozens of rooms was a glass booth, a sunroom facing the garden, and a ballroom with a sprung floor.[93] The house was designed by the Hungarian-Slovakian architect Ladislav Hudec (or, László Hudec, 1893–1958) and was known among Shanghai's foreign community as Dr. Woo's villa or, much more commonly among Shanghai's locals, as the Green House.[94]

The premises were the home of Wu Tongwen (1908–1966), a businessman who inherited his father's fortune and invested it in the pigment business in the mid-1930s when the nationalist government was expanding the army, hence green dyestuff for uniforms was in demand.[95] For much of his life, however, Wu was not much of a businessman but an extravagant playboy "young master." The success of Wu's pigment investment was perhaps due to the guidance provided by his father-in-law, Bei Runsheng (1872–1947), one of China's pigment tycoons.[96] Or maybe it was just a matter of luck: Wu regarded green as auspicious and used it extensively. In any case, the building was an architectural gem. Hudec, who was responsible for some of the most notable structures in Shanghai, such as the Park Hotel and the Grand Theater, proudly promised his patron that the residence would stay in fashion for another fifty years, or even a century.[97]

Wu Tongwen lived in this home during one of China's most chaotic times. The year 1937 marked the beginning of China's eight-year War of Resistance against Japan. The defeat of Japan in 1945 only gave way to the civil war between the Nationalists and the Communists. But Wu was unaffected by the chaos outside his home. During that twelve-year period, he brought a mistress home, enjoyed luxury cars (his BMWs were always painted green), and frequently held glamorous parties. When the Communists approached Shanghai in 1949, Wu, then forty-one, decided to stay. His emotional attachment to the home seemed to have been the deciding factor. On Christmas Eve 1948, Wu received a handsome offer, including a passenger liner and half-a-million US dollars in cash, for his home. At the time, the Communist victory was on the horizon, and his eldest son was already in Hong Kong. Wu's second son, a graduate of Shanghai's prestigious St. John's University, urged his father to take the offer and move to Hong Kong. Outraged by his son's idea, Wu claimed his conscience was clear and so he had no reason to fear the Communists: "If I have to die, I prefer to die in the Green House!"

Wu's confidence served him well for seventeen years after the Communist takeover. He was a member of the All-China Federation of Industry and Commerce (ACFIC). Established in 1953 as China's de facto national chamber of commerce, the ACFIC was (and still is) a unit of the National Committee of the CPPCC. This meant Wu had a place in new China through the CCP's united front policy. He never had to work. Wu continued to reside with his wife and concubine in the Green House, alternating his nights between them. His children, including a daughter and a son by the concubine, all attended college and adapted well to socialist society.

Cheng Naishan, who lived only a block from the Green House, recalled that as a teenager she walked past the house almost daily on her way to school: "Often, I saw a few men and women, stylishly dressed in fashionable Western clothes, leaning against the railings and looking into the distance from the patio, where there were layers upon layers of fresh flowers and plants and elegant canvas beach chairs." Cheng commented that although this was in the 1960s, the scene had an aura of what she conceived of as "pre-Liberation life."[98]

Wu's life took a tragic turn in the summer of 1966. Soon after Red Guards trashed his home and held a "struggle meeting" against him in August, the fifty-eight-year-old and his concubine committed suicide in their third-floor bedroom. The couple took a whole bottle of sleeping pills with coffee and died side by side in an armchair, holding hands. Wu, who preferred to wear Western attire all his life, dressed in a Mao suit in compliance with the politically correct style at the time. On his lap lay an open copy of *Red Flag*, the CCP's monthly journal, turned to the page with the May 16 Circular, the CCP document officially declaring the launch of the Great Proletarian Cultural Revolution; on the document were lines upon lines of Wu's handwritten notes in red.[99] Even in death, this big capitalist still tried to reconcile with the system that aimed at destroying people of his type.

The Green House was not the only bastion of bourgeois elitism. In the former French Concession, a similar lifestyle continued at Number Three Baoqing Road, home of businessman Zhou Zongliang (1875–1957). Zhou was born into a Christian preacher's family in the city of Ningbo, about a hundred miles across the Hangzhou Bay from Shanghai. He worked as a comprador for German companies in Shanghai for thirty-five years and, like Wu, made his fortune in the pigment business. Although he left Shanghai for Hong Kong in June 1948 and stayed there until his death in 1957, his family continued to live in Shanghai. His Western-style villa on Baoqing Road featured 4,000 square meters of lavish lawn right off the city's most expensive residential area on Avenue Joffre.[100] Xu Yuanzhang (1946–2015), Zhou Zongliang's grandson who lived in the Zhou house from 1951 to 2007, described the villa home where he grew up: Five buildings sitting on a sprawling lawn. Four served as houses for the family; guests and servants lived separately. The furniture and light fixtures were imported from France, modeled after those in the homes of the European aristocrats from the Middle Ages. Two Russian guards stood at the gate.[101] After 1949, the Russian door guards were gone, but the lifestyle of the occupants continued. For instance, Zhou's third son, Xiaocun, who was in charge of the mainland part of his father's enterprises, in 1954 bought six cars at once for his personal use. On another occasion, he spent US$40,000 for a holiday in Europe. The family maintained a stable in the residence to cater to his hobby of playing polo in the garden.[102]

Dance parties were regular occurrences in the homes of Shanghai's former capitalist families up to 1966. Xu Yuanzhang recalled that in his childhood lavish all-night parties, with music supplied by record players, were held in the family home. After dancing, guests would sit on the patio chatting until the first rays of dawn appeared.[103] Although only the richest capitalists had houses as extravagant as the Baoqing Road villa and the Green House, the city had enough elegant residences still occupied by bourgeois families for such social gatherings. Typically, these parties started at eight in the evening and lasted until one in the morning. Often, dozens of pedicabs lined up outside these premises while drivers waited for their customers, not unlike the street scene of rickshaws awaiting fares in old Shanghai. A practical reason for hiring a pedicab was that the vehicle provided a certain level of privacy for the "outlandishly dressed" dancers who, as a CCP internal report disapprovingly commented, "wanted to get a bang out of every bourgeois addiction."[104]

Zhang Da-Peng recalled he was once invited to a party at a friend's house in the winter of 1963–1964. When he walked through the crowd of pedicabs into the openwork-iron-gated house, he felt "a wave of heat hit him" as inside was as warm as springtime, and the dimly lit dance hall was even warmer: "The fire [was] blazing away in the fireplace. On opposite sides of the fireplace, in each of the other corners of the room, were stoves in which fires hissed and whistled." At a time when most Shanghai families survived on coal rations that were barely enough for cooking, this was truly extravagant. Electricity was expensive – one watt could cost as much an average's person's food for a whole day – but that was not a concern here: "A crystal chandelier hanging from the ceiling was all alight, as were wall lamps that illuminated each of the beautiful paintings mounted on the walls." In such a warm and pleasant home, female guests "wore evening gowns, and some of these were even in the low-cut and bare-shoulder style. They were heavily made up and wore the latest fashion in pointed-toed high-heeled shoes." When Zhang walked into the dance room, "a melody with a graceful rhythm was being played and already there were three or four couples dancing smartly and elegantly."[105] Zhang as a first-time visitor exclaimed that he "almost couldn't believe his own eyes or ears" and that "this was a surreal world, not socialist Shanghai."[106]

The authorities attacked home parties as "black-light dance parties" (*heideng wuhui*). The term "black light" conveyed the perceived visual image of the gatherings (they were dimly lit) while also delivering a political message, since anything "bourgeois" or disapproved of by the Communists was labeled "black." A Communist Youth League report dated May 27, 1964, revealed that these parties were common at the time. In one case two whistleblowers, students at the Shanghai Number Two Medical College, told the Youth League about their fellow student who held "black-light dance parties," and the authorities investigated. The league's official report claimed that the perpetrators were mainly "college students and social youth of bourgeois families." Among the regular partygoers in this case, more than fifty were individually identified as coming from Shanghai's seven universities and colleges. According to the report:

For several years, they have get-togethers both in daytime and at night (sometimes overnight). Males and females stay together in the same room. In addition to listening to yellow music [i.e., popular music associated with eroticism and sex] holding black-light dance parties, they also hold a drawing to decide who will play the obscene game of "kissing a friend for a few minutes," "lying on a friend's chest for a few minutes," "touching each other's tongue top for a few seconds," and "showing a commonly acknowledged intimate movement." The game also includes fondling one another's breasts, touching private parts, or even having sexual intercourse in front of the others.[107]

Apparently, these parties were no less wild than their counterparts in the West (which was caught up in the sexual revolution of the 1960s), yet they occurred in a totally different world: In an isolated, anti-Western, and ascetic China. The similarity was therefore both startling and significant, revealing not only that a totalitarianism as tight and seemingly perfect as Mao's had cracks, but also, more importantly, that resistance often sprang not from conscious political dissent but sheer human desire. The report did not mention the specific sites of the parties, but the location of the Shanghai Number Two Medical College gives a hint. On its north side, the college was adjacent to the former French Concession where most of the city's elegant homes were located. Even in the years of scarcity in the 1960s, the youth of old rich families could still frequent upscale restaurants and get together at one another's homes, although not necessarily, as the report describes, for "excessive drinking and salacious behavior."[108]

Such deviations were often attributed to the residual Western influences in Shanghai, which had more of them than elsewhere in the country. But the Western bourgeois lifestyle was not restricted to Shanghai alone, nor was it limited to the younger generation whose fascination with things Western and bourgeois could have been simply because such things had been denied them. A private birthday party in 1968 for Kang Tongbi (1887–1969), daughter of the prominent late Qing reformist Kang Youwei (1858–1927), reveals that even at the height of the Cultural Revolution, right under Chairman Mao's nose at the center of Beijing, anti-Maoist social norms still flourished. Zhang Yihe (1942–, daughter of "China's number one rightist" Zhang Bojun [1895–1969]), who was living with Kang at the time, recalled how women at the party all dressed in Republican-era elitist fashions. To avoid attention, the birthday party was a secret. According to one of the guests known as "Ms. Shanghai" (a ballerina and a granddaughter of the owner of Shanghai's Wing On department store), each of the guests carried a big bag containing a qipao (aka cheongsam), high-heeled shoes, a mirror, a comb, powder, lipstick, rouge, an eyebrow pencil, etc. Kang's residence was inside a hutong alley; in front of the gate, the guests quickly changed and put on the makeup while their husbands stood sentinel. Luckily, the hutong was usually quiet and had few pedestrians. In a few minutes, they walked into Kang's home, resplendent in their party attire. Zhang Yihe was amazed by what she saw at the gathering: The living room was full of poised, well-dressed women engaged in lively conversation. It was as if she had walked into another world. "In the warm air," Zhang wrote, "the souls that had been politically repressed were released and revitalized." Zhang, dressed in Maoist khaki suit, felt she was a total outsider. For the guests, however, "the bygone attire and etiquette provided a moment of a return of the old spirit and a confirmation of their identity." Zhang could not help but sense a sharp contrast with political implications:

> In that crazy and frightening environment [of the Cultural Revolution], despite everybody living in degradation, lacking any dignity, these people struggled to keep connected with feelings and emotions of the past. The object of dressing up in old-style clothing for Kang's [party] was not to show off the material wealth they once possessed; rather, it was a way of showing their respect for the old lady and their regard for her. This lingering attachment to old-time attire and ritual was a cultural expression of a historical emotion. These people had to follow what the Communist Party said, insist on "politics in command," read the *Selected Works of Mao Zedong*, recite the *Quotations of Chairman Mao*, and live a revolutionary style of life. But deep down in their hearts, what they appreciated and cherished was a highly embellished and refined private life.[109]

That a party like this would have been seen as subversive by the government and had to be held underground reveals much about the nature of Mao's rule. But it also tells us about popular resistance. The very existence of such events despite the government's constant monitoring is evidence of everyday defiance of the Communists' policy of scrutinizing people's lives. This defiance may also explain why home dance parties quickly revived after the death of Mao and flourished into the late 1990s.[110]

Xu Yuanzhang's childhood memories about home parties were so much embedded in his mind that in the 1990s, when nostalgia for old Shanghai swept the city and was by and large politically acceptable, Xu started holding weekly parties at his home. As he described it, "We drink black coffee and dance to classic music. All of these things take us back to the good times of the past."[111] Nearly half a century after the Communist takeover, the city still had many old-timers who admired Hollywood movie stars of the era such as Robert Taylor (1911–1969), Vivien Leigh (1913–1967), and Bob Hope (1903–2003). The music to which they danced consisted of waltzes and soundtracks of old Hollywood classics. Such parties made the long suspension of entertainment under Communism seem like an easily forgettable interlude, as a journalist who visited one of the parties in Xu's house in 2002 commented: "It sounds like this dance party has been going on for half a century, as if it had never been stopped."[112] Indeed Xu accidently found that there were neon lights from the old days installed underneath the ceiling and eaves of his family's house and, as a pleasant surprise, after all those years with virtually no maintenance, the colored lights still blinked without fail.[113]

The lingering bourgeois lifestyle in the Mao era gave rise to a slang term, *laokele*, referring to those who retained a pared-down version of the aristocratic lifestyle of old Shanghai.[114] The term is a kind of pidgin English: *lao* is the Chinese word for "old" and *kele* is a transliteration of the English word "class" or "color," hence *laokele* could mean either "old class" or "old color." Few people bothered to inquire about the etymology of *laokele*; nevertheless, it was a popular expression referring to people with the mentality of an older generation. Xu Yuanzhang, born in 1945, had little experience in old Shanghai to warrant the epithet *laokele*, but he certainly derived from that social stratum and identified with it. In a 2010 interview, he mentioned that most of his friends came from rich families. They dressed formally, preferred black tea and Western food, listen to jazz from the 1920s and the 1930s, and were gentle. As for the question of whether it should be "old color" or "old class," Xu preferred the latter: "'Color' means our life was colorful and interesting because of our wealth, but I prefer the word 'class,' which indicates a hierarchy." This self-indulgenced sense of class superiority was based on what people considered to be Westernization: "We were deeply influenced by Western culture due to the foreign concessions. We were well-educated and well-mannered, had a sense of humor, and were aristocratic in both spirit and substance."[115] There were many people of his age or younger who admired and imitated that "old class." This was completely at odds with the party's ideology that "the working class is glorious" and "the working class must lead everything."

Capitalist Agent Nien Cheng

A comfortable (and sometimes extravagant) lifestyle was also enjoyed by a group of people known as "capitalist agents" (*zifang dailiren*). This CCP-designated category refers to those who did not own a business but served in high-paid positions, such as CEOs or general managers, for private businesses – more often in industry and finance than in commerce.[116] These people were grouped together with the bourgeois class in the category "capitalists and their agents" (*zibenjia jiqi dailiren*).

Perhaps no single Chinese "capitalist agent" is better known in the West than Nien Cheng (1915–2009), author of the best seller *Life and Death in Shanghai*. The book, first published in the United Kingdom in 1986, was praised as an "extraordinary story of an extraordinary woman who, despite six-and-a-half long years of imprisonment and torment in

Communist China, not only survived but endured and even prevailed."[117] Readers were struck by the tragedy of her family during the Cultural Revolution, when Cheng endured imprisonment and torment after being falsely accused of being a British spy. Cheng came out of prison with no apologies from the authorities, only to learn that her daughter, at the age of twenty-four, had been beaten to death by the Red Guards. The story is an account of life in Communist China and a powerful testimony of the cruelty of a totalitarian regime. Cheng's refusal to bend under attack has been seen as "the triumph of the human spirit over inhumanity."[118]

Cheng's testament about the brutalities of the Cultural Revolution was so devastating that it overshadowed the fact that she and her family led an extraordinarily privileged life for seventeen years under Communism. When the Red Guards accused Cheng of being a counterrevolutionary, she retorted: "I'm not a counterrevolutionary, that I know. I'm a supporter of the People's Government and the Communist Party. I have the greatest respect for our Great Leader Chairman Mao."[119] Cheng was not pretending but stating a fact. She and her daughter, Meiping, were members of one of those "capitalist agent" families who lived in comfortable and frequently luxurious three-story homes in the best residential areas in Shanghai's former French Concession and International Settlement.[120] These houses were typically filled with antique furniture, works of art, rare books, and a piano; and there were servants (Cheng had three). Cheng recalled that "an English friend, a frequent visitor to my home in Shanghai, once called it 'an oasis of comfort and elegance in the midst of the city's drabness.'"[121] To reiterate, under the united front policy, which took into consideration each family's background in determining its status, the revolution essentially did not touch these families' lifestyles. In Cheng's case, this had to do with her education.

Cheng and her husband, Dr. Cheng Kang Chi, met and married in England, where both had attended the London School of Economics. Meiping, their only child, was born in 1942 in Australia, where Kang Chi was a diplomat of the Republic of China. After living in Australia for seven years, the family returned to Shanghai on October 1, 1948, eight months before the Communist takeover. Apparently, the Western background of the couple did not prevent them from "believing the Communist revolution [was] a historical inevitability for China" and being "prepared to go along with it."[122] Kang Chi served as a foreign affairs advisor for the newly founded Shanghai municipal government. Soon, with the approval of the government, he began working as the general manager of the British-owned Shell Oil company in Shanghai, the only foreign oil company remaining in China.[123] He was the first local

PRC citizen to hold that position. After his death in 1957, his wife, Nien Cheng, was hired as an adviser to three successive British general managers for nine years. The company continued to sell various chemical products, such as fertilizers and pesticides, until May 1966.[124]

Before the Cultural Revolution, the Cheng family was not only materially privileged but also politically trusted. Shell Oil's stay in China was approved by Premier Zhou Enlai (1898–1976) and reportedly was personally arranged by him.[125] Although the Chengs were hired by a British company, in the PRC system only a politically trusted individual would be allowed to serve in such a position. Moreover, the Cheng family could travel abroad freely, a privilege denied to most Chinese at the time.

The Chengs' close ties with the regime were also reflected in Meiping's life. She was a member of the Communist Youth League, the head of the Shanghai municipal rowing team, and a promising actor with the Shanghai Film Studio. In this elitist institution, she enthusiastically participated in the political activities called for by the party, including trips to villages in rural Shandong to perform for "poor and lower middle peasants." She was favored by the studio's CCP branch and was on its list to be recruited into the party. This "Western-returned" family with a Nationalist background had lived in such harmony with the Communist regime that, in Nien Cheng's words, it "never occurred to us that our kind of people would get into trouble [with the Communist government]."[126]

But trouble indeed came in 1966. On July 3, when Nien Cheng was asked to participate in a meeting regarding the Great Proletarian Cultural Revolution, she responded, "What has a cultural revolution got to do with us? We worked for a commercial firm, not a cultural establishment."[127] Her ignorance reflected her comfort with her and her family's place within the Communist system, unaware that it would come to a abrupt end. On August 30, her home, like millions of others in China at the time, was raided by the Red Guards and all her household valuables were confiscated. The Red Guards were astonished to see the Western style of her home life. In their words, "We have been to many homes of the capitalist class. Your house is the worst of all, the most reactionary of all. Are you a Chinese, or are you a foreigner?"[128] They froze tens of thousands of yuan in her bank accounts; still, some of her property was beyond their reach – the Red Guards were unable to touch her savings in Hong Kong.[129]

After she was released from prison in 1973, Cheng was assigned an apartment with a balcony overlooking one of the most elegant residential areas in the city. The apartment was in a residential compound known as the "foreign alley," which consisted of four rows of two-story

Spanish-style houses that in the past were the homes of affluent foreigners in the French Concession. Cheng's neighbors were notable families, old fogies, and distinguished professionals.[130] Much smaller and less comfortable than her old home, her new residence could nonetheless be described as "an oasis of comfort and elegance in the midst of the city's drabness." Apparently even in the chaotic years of the Cultural Revolution, the authorities in charge of her case still had her united front status in mind when they allocated the apartment to her. Cheng had a maid at home and kept her dignity and bearing after years of imprisonment. One of her neighbors in the "foreign lane" described her as "rich and tastefully clad, going in and out of the alley looking charming and graceful." Even in this elitist neighborhood, Cheng appeared to be aloof from her neighbors and "had an expression on her face as if she would keep everybody a thousand miles away."[131] This was not only a precaution in an environment of ubiquitous political surveillance, but also evidence of her determination to protect her privacy and individuality in a revolution that aimed to destroy both.

Marxist Theory and Maoist Politics

Why did the Communist government pursue a relatively moderate policy toward the capitalists and the old rich in general except for a few radical years during the Cultural Revolution? How did it justify this from a Marxist perspective? One reason surely was the weight it placed on the policy of the united front. In analyzing the formation of the first united front promoted by the Comintern in the 1920s, Tony Saich pointed out that the Communist Party believed all "outside" factors had to be mixed with Chinese reality: "It was in China that a 'bourgeoisie,' a national revolutionary government and a Communist party had to be found and all brought together into one 'happy family.'"[132] By the 1950s and early 1960s, the political landscape of China had fundamentally changed, but the principle of bringing the great majority of the people, including the "national bourgeoisie," into the "socialist big family" remained.

The united front made sense given the country's practical need for the knowledge and resources of the relatively small number of industrialists. Liu Shaoqi (1898–1969), second only to Mao in the CCP hierarchy before 1966, repeatedly made the point in public that socialist China should allow some sort of capitalist development. "In China today," Liu declared at a workers' rally in Tianjin in May 1949, "it is not that there are too many capitalists and they are overutilized; it is that there are too few of them and they are being underutilized. Because of the underdevelopment of capitalism, workers are suffering."[133] In a series of speeches delivered in Tianjin after that industrial city and former treaty port was taken by the Communists in January 1949, Liu claimed that "today in our country, not only is capitalist exploitation not evil, but it is meritorious."[134] In November 1955, Liu instructed all provincial party leaders: "We must train a group of progressive elements among the capitalists as a core. Every city should have a few dozen or a few hundred of them. These capitalists should not be afraid of 'sharing property' [the literal meaning of the Chinese translation of "Communism"] but should be determined to support 'sharing property.'"[135]

Liu's speeches on policies toward China's capitalists were taken as evidence against him during the Cultural Revolution as being the "number one capitalist roader within the party." However, Liu's words reflected not just his own opinions but the general policy of the CCP in the early 1950s. Mao openly endorsed Liu's Tianjin speech, praising his comments as "well said," albeit with some wording needing a little modification.[136] In fact, Liu's above-quoted speech in November 1955 was a rehash of what Mao had said in a CCP meeting on socialist reform a month earlier.[137] Mao also proposed "taking into account both public and private interests, benefiting both labor and capital" as the basis for handling private businesses. This language was used in the Common Program of the Chinese People's Political Consultative Conference, which served as China's provisional constitution until 1954.[138]

Although the CCP soon greatly accelerated the pace of socialization and by the end of 1956 virtually all private businesses had been put under state or collective ownership, the policy of allowing capitalists to live in material comfort remained undisturbed. Mao personally endorsed the policy and knew the details. In a speech at a meeting of the All-China Federation of Industry and Commerce in December 1956, Mao emphasized the importance of being generous in financial dealings with China's capitalists, especially "big capitalists." As a case in point, he mentioned that "foreigners who come to China like to go to Shanghai to visit the home of Rong Yiren, to see how many cars he has, one car or two; if there is a piano in his room" and so on (see Figures 1.4 and 1.5a).[139]

Mao reiterated the importance of "not infringing on the interests of big capitalists" because "for middle and small capitalists, their interest is to remove their capitalist cap as soon as possible; for big capitalists, their interest is to have fixed interest paid as long as possible." According to Mao, all together China's "national capitalists" had only 1.7 billion yuan invested in industry, just shy of US$700 million. "Our national capitalists only had that much; no wonder the imperialists bullied our country." In Mao's words, "the redemption should be real, not deceptive …

and [paid] in full." Mao even used a class-blind (and therefore, politically incorrect) expression to legitimize a longer payment period, saying that the redemption "has to be above the bottom line of heaven's justice and human feelings" (*zongyao tianli renqing jiangde guoqu*). Clearly, in Mao's mind the political effect of the redemption policy far outweighed its economic cost, which he said "won't be much."[140] When it came to the details of nationalization, Mao's instructions usually leaned toward being generous with capitalists so long as they did not resist joint state–private ownership.

A practical issue in the nationalization was assessing the worth of each private business, as the boundaries between the "means of production" and the "means of livelihood" were not always clear. For instance, it was common for businesses to be conducted in the same premises where the owner's family resided. During the nationalization campaign, owners asked that their wives be hired as fulltime employees by the collective firm, arguing that the family lived on the premises. Mao's instruction was clear: "Let the owners' wives come into the joint enterprises. As for distinguishing means of production from means of livelihood, be generous with the latter, so that the capitalists' livelihood is not affected."[141]

No doubt Mao would have liked the outside world, particularly the West, to believe his revolution was, at the very least, benign. But it would be a mistake to think that all of this was just an orchestrated propaganda show. Mao would not have cared merely to cultivate an image had he not believed in the effectiveness of the policy. This has been proved by many of his political campaigns that were disastrous for China's international image.

The united front policy, as pointed out earlier, justified giving the capitalists certain protections and privileges (such as being paid for their businesses and receiving high salaries) and thus made possible the continuation of bourgeois lifestyles. As Lyman Van Slyke has pointed out, "the united front is not limited to any particular area, but can be applied with great flexibility to a wide variety of specific situations."[142] The CCP legitimized the policy by tracing its origins to Marx, Engels and, in particular, Lenin.[143] In Marxist theory, providing former industrialists with compensation was a recognition of the bourgeoisie's rights (generally referred to as "bourgeois right").[144] The term was first used by Marx in his *Critique of the Gotha Program* written in 1875 and reiterated by Lenin in his *State and Revolution* of 1917.[145] Despite some confusion regarding the choice of wording in translating the German word *Recht* or the Russian word *право* into Chinese, the CCP's theorists certainly understood the specific meaning of the term and used it in the context of discussing "distribution according to labor."[146]

By 1958 some in the CCP argued that it was time to set aside the principle of bourgeois right. That year Zhang Chunqiao (1917–2005), a propaganda official in Shanghai, published an article that caught Mao's attention. The article, "Eradicate the Concept of Bourgeois Right," first appeared in the Shanghai local CCP monthly, *Liberation*. Mao ordered that it be reprinted in *People's Daily*, and anonymously wrote an editorial note endorsing it.[147] Zhang's view on eliminating "bourgeois right" reflected Mao's own ideas.[148] However, after Mao endorsed Zhang's article in 1958 and through the rest of the Mao era, the original meaning of the term became less relevant; instead, the concept of bourgeois right was used to refer to anything that would either drag China back into the "old society" (i.e., capitalism) or prevent China from marching toward a truly egalitarian society (i.e., "complete Communism").[149] As Luigi Tomba has pointed out, by the time of the Cultural Revolution, the phrase "bourgeois right" (*zichan jieji faquan*) had been used as the basis for an "all-embracing theory of bourgeois legal rights," including all things old from bourgeois society, the risk of a growth in income inequality, and the inevitable emergence of a new bourgeois class.[150]

Changes in China under Mao's rule have been described as "turning heaven and earth upside down" (*tianfan difu*).[151] The scope and intensity of the revolution were indeed unprecedented in the history of China – if not the world. However, Mao was keenly aware of the tenacity of the forces that he fought against. His apprehension about "capitalist restoration" primarily had to do with forces within the CCP leadership itself – those who took a moderate line and were labeled by him "capitalist roaders." The very existence of such elements in the party, in his mind, reflected the power of bourgeois influence in society in general. In 1962, Mao warned the party and the entire nation that "bourgeois influence and the force of habit from old society still exist" in China and that "class struggle in society will be inevitably reflected inside the Communist Party."[152] On August 3, 1965, he remarked to French minister of culture André Malraux (1901–1976) that the "forces tending toward the creation of new classes are powerful."[153] The next year, at age seventy-two, he started his last and most devastating campaign against the forces that, in his mind, were ranged against revolution – specifically, "capitalist roaders" within the party. But the decade-long struggle that ensued largely failed. On October 20, 1974, in the twilight of his life, Mao told the visiting Danish prime minister Poul Hartling (1914–2000), apparently in a moment of dismay, that except for the system of ownership, China after his revolution "differs very little from the old society."[154]

Ideologically, the CCP made no secret that capitalism was the ultimate target of the revolution and in a few years after it took power it had instilled sufficient fear to keep capitalists at bay. But on the ground, it also skillfully made businesspeople the object of both favor and disfavor simultaneously, all under the broad strategy of the united front. In May 1966, Mao launched the Cultural Revolution, aiming to "boldly sweep away evil people of all kinds."[155] The essential justification for this destructive national campaign was that for seventeen years since Liberation, a "capitalist black line" had dominated many sectors of Chinese life; hence it was imperative and urgent to launch a comprehensive "cultural revolution" to clean house – that is, to "get rid of bourgeois right" and to enact "complete dictatorship over the capitalist class." We now know that aside from his ideological zeal, Mao's immediate purpose for launching the Cultural Revolution was to purge his supposed enemies in the party – the "number one capitalist roader" Liu Shaoqi and Liu's supporters in the CCP bureaucracy.

Mao's apprehensions about the danger of "capitalist restoration" in China at times may have appeared paranoid. However, as we have seen, there were grounds for his concern about the lingering of "bourgeois right" in China, thus his "continuous revolution" did make sense as far as his utopian world of revolution is concerned. As we have noted, even the Cultural Revolution did not totally uproot Shanghai's bourgeois lifestyles and was less restrictive than is often argued.[156] No doubt in the turmoil and destruction of the Cultural Revolution much was destroyed and lost. And no doubt some anecdotal observations on capitalists' well-being applied only to a tiny minority. But bourgeois comfort had always belonged to a small privileged group of people in China, both before and after the Communist revolution. Even in Shanghai, the most modernized city of the nation, bourgeois life had never been a reality for the populace, but merely an object for them to envy, admire, imitate, and long for. Therefore, the existence of bourgeois lifestyles under the "dictatorship of the proletariat" should not be seen as merely a materialistic matter, but as evidence that the Chinese state could be more flexible and elastic than has usually been thought.

There was yet another group of people who were not capitalists per se but were able to live in the material comfort that was typically associated with affluent businesspeople. In Communist terminology, these people by virtue of their education and professions were lumped into a broad – and, again, arbitrarily defined – category as "bourgeois intellectuals." Like their counterparts in business circles, bourgeois intellectuals could be privileged or comfortable under the proletarian dictatorship so long as the regime regarded them as benign and useful, as we shall see in Chapter 2.

2 The Stinking Number Nine

In a Supreme State Conference held in October 1957, Mao Zedong estimated the number of Chinese intellectuals – by which he meant college faculty, schoolteachers, scientists, engineers, technicians, journalists, actors and actresses – at about five million.[1] This was less than 1 percent of the population. Moreover, nearly all of them were urban-based and received their education during the Republican era.[2] Since the late 1930s, an increasing number of intellectuals grew sympathetic to Communism and many urban-based educated Chinese joined the revolution prior to the final victory of the Communists. Nevertheless, as Eddy U has pointed out, "Once *zhishifenzi* [intellectual] entered the CCP lexicon, possession of formal learning, a self-centered personality, and resistance to revolutionary change became core meanings of the term."[3] After Liberation the party had an uneasy relationship with China's educated elite – especially those who were not in the fields of science and technology – and lumped intellectuals together with the bourgeoisie.

The expression "bourgeois intellectual" became a standard phrase in Mao's time. It referred to educated people, especially those who had at least some college education before 1952, when the PRC government reorganized the higher education system.[4] On March 12, 1956, Mao made the definition clear at the CCP's National Conference on Propaganda Work: "The majority of our intellectuals are from the old society and their family backgrounds are non-working people. Even though some of these people come from a worker or peasant family, the education they received before Liberation was a bourgeois education, their worldviews are essentially bourgeois, and they belong to [the category of] bourgeois intellectuals."[5] After the conference, Mao made a series of inspection tours of the cities of Tianjin, Ji'nan, Shanghai, and Hangzhou, reiterating this judgment that was, obviously, taken as the party's policy.[6] On September 23, 1957, Deng Xiaoping, then the CCP's general secretary, announced on behalf of the party that, "Judging from the current situation, most intellectuals come from a bourgeois or petty-bourgeois family background; the education they received is of the bourgeois type. Therefore, for the sake of convenience, we discuss them together with capitalists."[7]

It was of course not a matter of convenience but the party's principal assessment of China's urban-based intellectuals. It reflected the party's fundamental mistrust of this group. In the nearly three decades of Mao's rule, only on two occasions, one in 1956 and the other in 1962, did the CCP acknowledge that intellectuals were part of the working people. In Marshal Chen Yi's words, the party needed to remove the cap of "bourgeois intellectuals" from intellectuals and crown them members of the "working class," a step known as "replacing the cap with a crown" (*tuomao jiamian*). These brief periods (each less than a year) of moderate policies toward intellectuals were dubbed the "intellectuals' spring." They were primarily associated with the party's off-and-on agenda of "marching toward science," which called for the use of the nation's limited intellectual resources for economic development.[8]

For the party, which intended to keep the people constantly in line with its goals and agenda, intellectuals from the "old society," as the pre-1949 era was called, had a nebulous role.[9] Their expertise in various fields was an asset to the newly established regime, but they could also be an obstacle to Communist nation-building – they were, after all, lukewarm supporters at best and recalcitrant or even rebellious critics at worst. As Richard Curt Kraus has pointed out, "It is important to bear in mind the multifaceted heritage of intellectuals in the People's Republic, with their shifting and often intangible mixture of capitalism, foreign culture, Confucian education, patriotism, and desire for social reform. With most intellectuals these values and orientations coexisted uneasily and in varying proportions."[10] Certainly, the party was well aware of the difficulty of winning the undivided loyalty of this small but important part of the population.

While it labeled these people "bourgeois intellectuals" as part of its struggle for political control, the party also exhibited a soft side when it came to the nation's educated elite. Like the entrepreneurs discussed in Chapter 1, intellectuals were frequently made subjects of the party's united front policy. In particular, well-established professionals were categorized as "high-level intellectuals" (*gaoji zhishifenzi*) and given a somewhat positive political status, such as being made members of one of the eight officially registered democratic parties or being acknowledged as "democratic personages without party affiliation" (the latter were also called "nonparty democratic patriots").[11] Financial benefits associated with that status included a high income, free VIP medical care, and housing in upscale neighborhoods.

This chapter looks at the lives of a group of Shanghai-based "bourgeois intellectuals" in the Mao era. These people belonged to an elitist cohort in the Republican era. After 1949, their previous social status was perceived variably by the party, depending on the needs of the state, the vicissitudes of top-level politics and, more often than not, the individual's personal connections in the party. In the capricious political climate of the Mao years, an individual's fortunes could change drastically and virtually overnight. In good times, they were categorized as "high-level intellectuals," placed in respected positions, and entitled to political and material benefits. In bad times, they were reduced to the ranks of the so-called stinking number nine (*choulaojiu*) – a term referring to intellectuals in general during the Cultural Revolution – and subjected to condemnation, purge, and even imprisonment.[12]

Fu Lei's Rose Garden

Fu Lei (Fou Lei, 1908–1966), a typical "bourgeois intellectual," was famous on two accounts. First, he was a renowned translator of classic French literature. His published translations amount to over five million Chinese words.[13] His translations of works by Prosper Mérimée, Romain Rolland, Voltaire, and, most of all, Balzac, influenced generations of Chinese and, in particular, those who grew up under Mao.[14] Second, he was one of the best-known victims of the Maoist dictatorship. He was labeled a rightist in 1958, an event that led his son, a Mazurka Prize winning pianist, Fu Cong (Fou Ts'ong, 1934–2020), to flee from Poland, where he was a Chinese government-sponsored music student, into exile in England – a traitorous act by Chinese standards at the time. On the night of September 2, 1966, after Red Guards had rampaged through Fu Lei's home for four days, Fu and his wife hanged themselves with a bed sheet on the French doors in their bedroom, becoming the first well-known victims of the Cultural Revolution.

Fu's beautiful translations of Western literature are admired by millions of Chinese. His tragic death, together with his wrongful label as a rightist, have made him one of the most frequently cited cases to demonstrate the Communists' oppression of intellectuals and, in larger terms, the injustice of Maoist totalitarianism. Yet Fu's fate cannot be simply depicted as a witch-hunting political persecution. The seventeen years he lived under Communism involved a complex tale of personality conflicts, misplaced loyalty, and betrayed trust in a system that intended to make human society totally uniform.

Fu Lei was born into an affluent farmer's family in Nanhui county southeast of Shanghai and studied art history and art criticism at the University of Paris from 1928 to 1931. After he returned from abroad, Fu taught Western art and literature at the Shanghai School of Fine Arts.

Although he had a vast knowledge of aesthetics, arts, and music, he chose to be a freelance translator of French literature. This meant he could pursue his calling alone in his study and avoid much of the complexity of human relations, which he often found difficult to deal with. Indeed, a courtesy or style name he gave to himself, "Angry Peace" (*Nu'an*) or a homophone, "Angry Hut" (*Nu'an*), reflects his feisty temperament.[15]

Like many other intellectuals in the late 1940s, Fu was frustrated by the corruption and incompetence of the Nationalist government and was sympathetic to the Communists, who promised a rosy future: A just society, clean government, and a strong nation. Not only did Fu stay in Shanghai after the Communist takeover, but he also became active under the new regime. In 1954, he was awarded membership in the Chinese Writers' Association (Shanghai branch), the exclusive official organization for accomplished writers in the PRC and, just before the Anti-Rightist Campaign, he was appointed a member of the secretariat of the association. From 1955 to 1957, Fu was also a nonpartisan member of the Shanghai branch of the CPPCC, and served as an associate director in charge of literature, press, and publishing affairs. All these were unpaid posts but important marks of his political status and his esteem. Fu took these responsibilities seriously, enthusiastically going to meetings, conducting fieldwork, and writing numerous reports and articles for the government. His longtime friend Luo Shiyi (1905–2001), a Communist cadre who served as the chief editor of China's prestigious People's Literature Press, was surprised to find that his usually unsociable friend had become "a busy man in political activities, having meetings all day long, sometimes coming home late at night in heavy rain."[16]

Fu's family was also privileged under the new regime. Fu's two sons were favored products of the socialist educational programs. His older son, Fu Cong, studied piano from childhood with Mario Paci (1878–1946), the Italian founder of the prestigious Shanghai Symphony Orchestra. In summer 1953, Fu Cong was selected to go to Romania with the Chinese youth delegation led by Hu Yaobang (1915–1989), the then head of the Communist Youth League. In August 1954, he was sent by the government to Poland to study at the Warsaw Conservatory with Poland's Chopin authority, Zbigniew Drzewiecki (1890–1971). Fu Cong won the special Mazurka Prize at the 1955 International Chopin Piano Competition, the first Chinese ever to win an international music competition, and afterward stayed in Poland as a government-sponsored student.

Unlike his fellow Chinese students whose passports were invalid outside Poland, Fu Cong's passport allowed him to travel in Europe, as his fame had made him a frequent invitee to perform at concerts. At a time when the vast majority of Chinese were denied a passport, this was an extraordinary privilege. Also, unlike other students, Fu Cong had a salary, his own apartment in Warsaw, and when he went out, he took a taxi. It is no surprise that his fellow students were uneasy about his "bourgeois lifestyle."[17] Fu Lei's younger son, Fu Min (1937–), also had a promising future. In 1956, he was sent to the Foreign Affairs College, the newly founded institution in Beijing created solely to train future diplomats. The college was affiliated with the Ministry of Foreign Affairs and admission was limited exclusive to the most trustworthy children of the CCP's political confidants.[18]

For Fu Cong's achievements, Fu Lei was lauded as a model father who raised a bright son who brought honor to China. Fu was asked to write about how he educated Fu Cong. For instance, his article "The Upbringing of Fu Cong" was published in *New Observations* in Beijing in April 1957; another of his articles, "Conversations with Fu Cong on Music," was published in installments in Shanghai's *Wenhui Daily* from October 18 to 21 of the same year.[19]

At the time Fu Lei was an ardent supporter of the Communists. In March 1957, he was invited as a non-Communist Party member to attend a national conference on propaganda work in which Mao gave a speech on "Let a hundred flowers bloom; let a hundred schools contend."[20] During the meeting, on March 18, Fu Lei wrote from Beijing to his son commenting on Mao's speech. His tone was nothing short of worshipful:

The speech of Chairman Mao was delivered in an extremely amiable and easy-going way, full of humor, and did not smack of lecturing people. His tone and voice were pitched at the right level, and he spoke at the right speed and paused at the right places—none of these can be conveyed in our notes of the speech. His mastery of Marxism is sublime. It comes to him all so naturally and effortlessly. His speech deeply touched the hearts and minds of the audience. The logic of his speech was inherent and invisible; [he is] a true master of [speech] arts.... He has a great vision and a liberal way of thinking; no doubt he can master statecraft. Chairman Mao is a man who has truly integrated the philosophies of past and present, East and West.[21]

Fu even used the language of the cult of Mao that was not common in the 1950s but would become emblematic of the Cultural Revolution a decade later: "Far away [from Poland] the great [leader] Chairman Mao shines with boundless radiance illuminating your way; you should not fail to live up to his majestic leadership."[22] Fu was known as an uncompromisingly honest and straightforward person who was not given to bending to what he did not believe in. These words, in a private letter to his son, must have reflected his true thoughts and feelings at the time.

But the honeymoon with the party would soon be over. In the Anti-Rightist Campaign of late 1957, Fu was criticized for expressing "anti-Soviet and pro-United States" viewpoints. His connections in the party tried to protect him, categorizing him as "in the middle ground with a tendency toward the right." However, in April 1958, at the end of the campaign, Fu Lei was labeled a "rightist" by the Writers' Association, which was not Fu's "work unit" but the organization with which he was affiliated. The decision was made at a higher level in a large part because of a personal grudge that Ke Qingshi (1902–1965), then Shanghai's first party secretary, held against Zhou Yang (1908–1989), Beijing's top official in charge of cultural affairs. Zhou intended to let Fu off the hook while Ke saw it as an infringement on his domain since Fu was a Shanghai-based writer.[23] In spring 1958 when the Anti-Rightist Campaign was drawing to its dusty end, the party decided that, based on Mao's estimation, a quota of 5 percent of the people in a unit should be designated as rightists.[24] Fu was a victim of what is known as the "makeup class" (*buke*) of the campaign, that is, a second round of purges to catch those who were missed in the first one.

Fu Lei was angry and felt betrayed. The day the announcement was made in a meeting of the Writers' Association, he went home unusually late and told his wife, Zhu Meifu (1913–1966), who was extremely worried, that if his younger son Fu Min were financially independent, he would end his life that night. Eight months later, in December 1958, Fu Cong fled from Poland to England. Fu Lei thus became a rightist with a son who was a traitor who defected to the West, one of the worst political combinations in the Communist system of class differentiation.

However, unlike numerous other rightists whose lives were turned totally upside down by this political label, Fu's daily life was little affected. His residence was in a Western-style three-story house located inside an alleyway neighborhood called Anding Fang (Alley of Peace and Stability), in one of the best residential areas in west Shanghai. The light milky yellow walls of the house were coated with pebble stones. The family had a fenced-in spacious front yard, where Fu Lei often indulged in gardening. There were pine trees, cypresses, sweet-scented osmanthus, chrysanthemums, and, most of all, roses. Fu planted over fifty types of roses in his garden, including special varieties that he ordered from Paris and London (Figures 2.1a and 2.1b).[25] The monthly rent of the house was 55.25 yuan, which equaled the monthly salary of a college-educated professional and was about enough to support an average family of four at the time.[26]

In some seemingly trivial aspects of daily life, Fu Lei's habits were regarded as Western, therefore, bourgeois. His son once summarized his way of dressing at home as "silk shirt in the summer, smoking jacket in the winter."[27] He kept smoking a pipe – and filled it with Dunhill's Royal

Figure 2.1 Fu Lei's secluded comfort. (a) *Top*, Fu and his son Fu Cong share readings while his wife knits (ca. 1956); (b) *Bottom*, the Fu and Zhu in the rose garden in front of their home (ca. 1965). *Source:* Shanghai Writers' Association.

Table 2.1 *Shanghai's private telephone lines in various years during the Mao era*

Year	1950	1958	1961	1965	1966	1970
Phone lines	25,196	16,947	15,432	14,377	7,341	960
Population (millions)	4.1784	5.8728	6.4121	6.4307	6.3621	5.8023

Source: Compiled from Shanghai tongzhi bianzuan weiyuanhui, *Shanghai tongzhi*, 6:4337–8.

Yacht pipe tobacco. He kept a habit of having butter on his bread, something considered Western and luxurious. When there were not enough supplies, Fu Cong and family friends sent them from overseas. During the Great Leap famine, Fu Lei frequently received food packages from Europe, Hong Kong, Singapore, and Australia, and sometimes directly from the Nestlé company. A barber regularly came to his home to cut his hair. He also had a telephone at home, another luxury in Shanghai at the time. After the mid-1950s, 94 percent of the phones in private homes were eliminated. In a city of over ten million, only around 15,000 private homes had a telephone line (Table 2.1).[28]

Fu Lei was among a few freelance writers who were able to maintain a comfortable lifestyle similar to the life they enjoyed before Liberation and one that continued even after they were labeled rightists. His royalty payments were higher than the usual. While the standard rate for translated literature in the 1950s was 9 yuan per 1,000 Chinese characters, his was 11 yuan.[29] Before 1964, on average his annual translations amounted to about 200,000 characters, which earned him close to 200 yuan a month, not counting royalties from sales of previous books. In fact, most of his works were published during the seventeen years between 1949 and his death in 1966 (see Table 2.2), and they were financially rewarding. According to Red Guard accounts, Fu Lei earned 33,880 yuan (approximately US$17,000) in royalties from *Jean-Christophe* alone, ranking him as the sixteenth most highly paid on an apparently incomplete list of Chinese authors.[30] Basically, his main income before 1949 was from selling farm land in Pudong that he had inherited from his parents; after 1949, his income was mainly from publishing his books of translations.[31]

From April 1958, when he was labeled a rightist, to September 1961, when the "cap" was removed, Fu could not publish his new translations because of the policy that prohibited the publication of works by rightists. However, as a way of letting him continue to have an income, People's Literature Press, which had published most of his books, proposed to publish his new translations under a pen name. Inflexibly, Fu refused the offer, insisting he would only publish under his real name. His stubbornness was tolerated and indeed accommodated. The

Table 2.2 *Fu Lei's published translations of French literature, 1949–1963*

Original title	Year	Chinese title	Place	Press	Year
Honoré de Balzac (1799–1850)					
Eugénie Grandet	1833	《歐也妮・葛朗台》	Shanghai Beijing	Sanlian Pingming Renmin wenxue	1949 1951, 1952, 1953 1954, 1963
Le Père Goriot	1835	《高老頭》	Shanghai Beijing	Sanlian Renmin wenxue	1950 1963 (2 printings)
La Cousine Bette	1846	《貝姨》	Shanghai	Pingming Renmin wenxue	1951–1954 (5 printings) 1954 (2 printings), 1963
Le Cousin Pons	1847	《邦斯舅舅》	Shanghai	Pingming Renmin wenxue	1952–1953 (4 printings), 1954, 1963
Le Colonel Chabert	1832	《夏倍上校》	Shanghai	Pingming Renmin wenxue	1954 1954
Ursule Mirouët	1841	《于絮爾・彌羅埃》	Beijing	Renmin wenxue	1956, 1958
La Rabouilleuse	1842	《攪水女人》	Beijing	Renmin wenxue	1962
Le Curé de Tours	1832	《都爾的本堂神甫》	Beijing	Renmin wenxue	1963
Pierrette	1840	《比哀蘭德》	Beijing	Renmin wenxue	1963
Prosper Mérimée (1803–1870)					
Carmen	1845	《嘉爾曼》	Shanghai	Pingming	1953, 1954
Colomba	1840	《高龍巴》	Shanghai	Pingming	1953, 1954
Romain Rolland (1866–1944)					
Jean-Christophe	1904–12	《約翰・克里斯朵夫》	Shanghai Shanghai Beijing	Shangwu Pingming Renmin wenxue	1951 1953 1957
François Marie Arouet de Voltaire (1694–1778)					
L'Ingénu	1767	《老實人》	Beijing	Renmin wenxue	1955
Zadig	1747	《查第格》	Beijing	Renmin wenxue	1956
Hippolyte Adolphe Taine (1828–1893)					
Philosophie de l'art	1865–82	《藝術哲學》	Beijing	Renmin wenxue	1963

Sources: Zhongguo fanyijia cidian bianxiezu, comp., *Zhangguo fanyijia cidian*, 222; Zhongguo banben tushuguan, comp., *1940–1979 fanyi chuban waiguo wenxue zhuzuo mulu he tiyao*, 1155–60.

press continued to pay him for his new manuscripts in the form of an advance. For instance, the press paid him 1,000 yuan in cash in February 1959 as a part of the royalties for his translation of Balzac's *César Birotteau*, while the book was not even in the press's publishing plan.[32] During the time he had the rightist cap on his head, his books were still available in bookstores and some of them were even advertised in the newspaper.[33]

Fu's case was not unique. At all levels of the CCP's cultural affairs offices there were cadres whose political convictions were intertwined with their conscience and integrity, which led them to play on the borderline of party policies to maintain some equanimity. Thus, the restriction on publishing the works of rightists was not as absolute as has been commonly thought.

Here are a few more cases in point. The writer Ai Qing (1910–1996) was labeled a rightist and expelled from the party in 1957, but nevertheless, his edited book *Poems of Dai Wangshu* (1905–1950) was published in the same year and sold well: The first print run was 7,000 copies; the next year the reprint run was 18,500 copies.[34] The historian Xie Defeng (1906–1980), who was known for his translations of world history classics, had his best works published after he was labeled a rightist in 1957, including his translations of Thucydides's (460–395 BCE) *History of the Peloponnesian War* (published in 1960) and Appian's (c. 95–c. 165) *Historia Romana* (published in 1963).[35] The philosopher Zhang Dainian (1909–2004), under the pen name Yutong, published his magnum opus, *An Outline of Chinese Philosophy*, after he was branded a rightist in 1957. Chen Hanbo (1914–1988), then the editor-in-chief of the Commercial Press (one of China's most prestigious publishers), single-handedly supported the publication. Chen, a Communist veteran who joined the party in 1936, later served as the head of the Publication Bureau of the PRC's Ministry of Culture.[36] In this regard, party cadres – some of whom were intellectuals themselves – chose to ignore the political labels imposed on authors and often found ways to publish their works.

For Fu Lei, the royalties were an important, but not the sole, source of his income. In the early 1960s, Fu Cong sent cash and food worth about 200 yuan annually to his parents, not including books and music tapes.[37] After he settled in London, Fu Cong regularly sent a bi-monthly stipend worth 100 yuan to his parents. All this allowed Fu and his wife to maintain a standard of living much higher than that of average Shanghainese. The couple's monthly expenses included 55.25 yuan for rent, 48 yuan for food, and 40 yuan for utilities, telephone, and the maid's wage.[38] Fu unquestionably benefited financially from having a son abroad. In a letter Fu's wife wrote in April 1961 to Fu Cong, which is perhaps the most candid letter the couple wrote to their sometime absent-minded son in London about their daily life, the mother tried to let the son know that they needed his financial support. Still, the Fu family admitted that "our life is better than that of the public; what we have is far more than what other people have.... In general, we are happy and cheerful, and we also have music, calligraphy, painting and so on for our spiritual enjoyment, and we have the contents from work as well."[39] In another letter, in 1964, Fu told his son "we live a stable life, better than the great majority of people."[40]

Fu Lei's main complaint at the time was his health. He had various chronic ailments; nothing seemed life-threatening but everything was painful and depressing nonetheless: Trigeminal neuralgia, insomnia, nephroptosis, cataracts, chronic conjunctivitis, allergic rhinitis, and arthritis. He was treated at the Huadong Hospital, Shanghai's exclusive hospital for high-ranking CCP officials and senior intellectuals. Ding Ji'nan, a well-known doctor of Chinese medicine from Ruijin Hospital (Hôpital Sainte-Marie, established in 1907), regularly came to his home to conduct checkups and treatment.[41] Nevertheless, Fu's health was deteriorating in late 1965, which added to his medical expenses and made him less productive – hence his royalties fell. At the time of their death, the couple had a total of 1,466.39 yuan in cash and savings accounts.[42]

As Tenacious as the Grass on the Prairie

Millions of Chinese were extremely sympathetic to Fu Lei and his wife and took their tragedy "as emblematic of the fate of China's urban intellectuals."[43] Fu Lei stood for integrity amid a political storm that aimed to destroy it, and the mourning of his death, which at the time could not be expressed in public, represented the respect for such a character in the public mind. A woman named Jiang Xiaoyan (1939–), a total stranger to the Fus, hearing that the couple had no immediate family in Shanghai and their ashes would be discarded, took a great risk to claim to be Fu's nominal foster daughter and collected the ashes at the funeral home. She kept the ashes first at home then used Fu's old alternative name (*hao*) that few people knew to consign the ashes to the Yong'an Cemetery in suburban Shanghai. Jiang also wrote an anonymous letter to Zhou Enlai appealing to him to stop the purge of "patriotic personages" like Fu. The letter fell into the hands of Shanghai's municipal authorities and was listed as a grave assault on the Cultural Revolution. In June 1967, the authorities identified Jiang as the author and detained her. Fortunately, at the time when "the working class must lead everything," her interrogators were a group of simple factory workers, who apparently were sympathetic to someone collecting a stranger's ashes for a proper funeral, a good, moral deed in the Chinese tradition. After much probing and pondering, they concluded that Jiang was just a bookish young woman who did not know much about society and so acted recklessly, and let her go. The story became known after Fu was rehabilitated in 1979 and his ashes were moved to the Shanghai Cemetery of Revolutionary Martyrs, a privilege theretofore reserved only for high-ranking party officials. Although Jiang preferred to remain anonymous, in the post-Mao era her courageous act for a just cause became well-known.[44]

Yet the ways Chinese intellectuals coped with adversity in the Mao era were infinitely diverse. In their hardship, many intellectuals clung to the belief that where there is life there is hope. As an often-quoted Chinese proverb puts it, "As long as the green mountains are there, one need not worry about firewood." There were less forthright and unyielding ways than Fu's suicide to tackle Mao's tyranny.

Take Fu's friend Shi Zhecun (1905–2003), for example. Shi, three years senior to Fu, was a modernist writer noted for, among other things, his work as the founding editor of the journal *Les Contemporains* (*Xiandai zazhi*) in the early 1930s. His disagreement with Lu Xun (1881–1936) on some literary issues at that time put him in a difficult spot in the Mao era when Lu Xun had been elevated to the status of a saint. Shi never had the good fortune that Fu had with the party but shared all the misfortune. He was labeled a rightist in 1957, six months earlier than Fu; the cap was removed in September 1961, exactly the same time when Fu's rightist cap was removed.[45] His home was raided at the same time that Fu's home was searched. During the raid on Shi's home, he was dragged out to a denunciation meeting held in the alleyway of his home, humiliating him.

Shi's home was just around the corner from Fu's. As Shi was well aware of Fu's unbending character, he was concerned about how Fu would react to the unprecedented torment of the Cultural Revolution. In an evening in late August soon after the denunciation meeting – in his words, "my pillorying in the alleyway" – Shi took a stroll to the alley where Fu lived, hoping to find out "where Fu's anger led him." Standing in the alley looking at Fu's house, he could figure out little: It was quiet; big-character posters (*dazibao*) were pasted all over the door and on the front wall. Two weeks later, he learned about the couple's tragic deaths. "This was the last anger of 'Angry Hut,'" Shi commented on Fu's death twenty years later. "I almost in every way differed from Fu Lei; still, I respected him, as I respected a few others who took the same step at the time. Nevertheless, that Zhu Meifu would die with him was something I could not have imagined."[46]

Unlike Fu, Shi adopted an obsequious attitude after Liberation in a way known in Chinese as *tuo mian zi gan*, that is, "be spat on the face and let the spittle dry without wiping," a Confucian notion akin to the "turn the other cheek" in the Christian tradition.[47] For Shi, such passivity was not a matter of personality but a conscious choice based on his reasoning in coping with Maoist oppression; as he bluntly put it, "to live is a victory."[48] In other words, it was a strategy – or rather, philosophy – for surviving under tyranny. Shi triumphed with this philosophy and lived on to see not only his name rehabilitated but himself restored to the pantheon of Chinese literature. By the time he died at the age of ninety-eight, his literary works some seventy years earlier had regained the attention of scholars both in China and overseas.[49]

The life of Shanghai-based writer and translator Cao Ying (1923–2015) under Mao was another case of tenacity. Like Fu to French literature, Cao was well known for translating Russian literature into Chinese. His translation of Soviet writer Mikhail Sholokhov's (1905–1984) short story "Fate of a Man" and novel *Quiet Flows the Don* made him famous, but for that reason he bore the brunt of criticism after the Sino-Soviet split in the early 1960s when Sholokhov was condemned as the "forefather of revisionist literature." Cao, as the person responsible for introducing Sholokhov's work to Chinese readers, was denigrated as a "trumpeter of revisionism." During the Cultural Revolution, he was detained for a year. Cao was utterly tough and tenacious in facing his ordeal. When the radicals took him into custody, he whispered to his wife, "If anyone tells you that I committed suicide in the jail, never believe it, since I will never kill myself no matter what happens."[50] He exercised in his prison cell every day. Whenever sunlight streamed through the tiny window near the ceiling, he climbed up to the window to take in the precious rays, much like those Russian revolutionaries – the protagonists of some of the Russian novels that he has translated – did in the tsarist prisons.[51]

After one year of confinement in the prison cell, he was sent to a farm for "reform through labor." Heavy labor and malnutrition on the farm caused dreadful gastric bleeding and, in 1969, he had three quarters of his stomach removed to save his life. His ordeal was unending. In January 28, 1975, when he was assigned to work in a construction site, carrying 50-kilogram bags of cement, a bag carelessly unloaded from a truck hit his shoulder and fractured his twelfth dorsal vertebra. Cao faced the danger of being paralyzed the rest of his life. For six months, he had to lie motionless on a wooden board, eating and relieving himself on that narrow panel; it took him another six months of pain to get back to a normal life.[52]

In an interview in 2009 Cao was asked, "When you lay on that wooden board, did you feel unworthy – for just translating a few foreign novels, you nearly lost your life?" Cao replied, "Looking around, there were people whose lives were more miserable than mine. The sufferings I had cannot count as particularly awful; there were many people who suffered more than I did."[53] Such an outlook helped Cao survive the hardest time in Mao's era. Cao, whose real name is Sheng Junfeng, invented "Cao Ying" as his pen name, which literally means, "grass infant," inspired by the poet Bai Juyi's (772–846) famous lines about grasses on the prairie:

> The grass spreads out across the plain,
> Each year, it dies, then flourishes again.
> It's burnt but not destroyed by prairie fires,
> When spring winds blow, they bring it back to life again.

Cao explained that all his life he saw himself as an obscure but tough patch of grass as portrayed in Bai Juyi's poem, stepped on by many and burned by wildfires yet always surviving and reviving. Correspondingly, his favorite flower was the calyx canthus (winter sweet), which blooms in deep winter when the snow falls, symbolizing, in Chinese culture, toughness in harsh conditions.[54] Cao's persistence paid off. When "spring" finally came in the post-Mao years, Cao was already in his sixties but he became extremely productive and won a number of prestigious honors and awards, including the Gorky Prize in 1987 and the Shanghai Lifetime Achievement for Literature and Arts Award in 2014.[55] He was highly regarded to the extent that when he died at the age of ninety-two, Premier Wen Jiabao (1942–) handwrote a personal condolence to his wife, a rare expression of admiration from a top state leader.[56]

The Tale of Translating *Eugene Onegin*

The CCP's bombast and rhetoric are all too familiar images of Mao's China. Much less known is that underneath the turmoil, a sense of conscience and mortal integrity quietly existed. Cadres had to carry out what the party dictated; but deep inside, their sympathies at times still leaned toward the intellectuals, even if they were aware that such sympathies were not in line with the "party spirit" (*dangxing*) that they were supposed to uphold. This kind of dissidence usually expressed itself in some minor actions of cadres that subverted the party line.

Nor were oppressed people entirely submissive to autocracy; instead, they often passively resisted and wangled along to protect their intellectual interests and passions. The experience of East China Normal University professor Wang Zhiliang (1928–) translating Pushkin's *Eugene Onegin* from the Anti-Rightist Campaign to the Cultural Revolution reveals the maneuvering on both sides.

Wang was a Russian literature specialist in the Institute of Literature of the Chinese Academy of Social Sciences in Beijing. Life was fine for him until May 1958 when he was labeled a rightist and sent to rural Hebei (and later to the barren frontier of Gansu) for labor reform, all caused by his mild criticism of the Suppressing Anti-Revolutionaries movement of 1951. When his rightist verdict was announced, Wang was in the middle of translating *Eugene Onegin,* just starting on Chapter 2. He loved the job and was devastated that as a rightist he would not be able to continue the translation. In fact, his fascination with the book was taken as proof of his crimes. In a big-character poster posted at the gate of the institute criticizing him, he was caricatured in a cartoon image lying in a coffin, dying, with a copy of *Eugene Onegin* on top of his body.

On his last day in the office, Wang cleaned out his desk and, before leaving the building, went to men's room, not expecting that an obscure encounter there would change his life. No one was in the restroom; Wang was so miserable and hopeless that he stood in front of the urinal riveted to the ground. Then, he heard the door open and someone walk in, but he dared not look – being a rightist was like being condemned as a dangerously contagious disease carrier. Nevertheless, he sensed that man was He Qifang (1912–1977), the director of the institute. To his surprise, He Qifang stood behind him for a few seconds, then, in his heavy Sichuan accent, uttered: "You should still get *Eugene Onegin* done!" Before Wang could respond, He Qifang opened the door, looked around the hallway as if to make sure no one had seen him, and then quickly exited.

Wang was first stunned and then touched. Obviously, He Qifang deliberately took the restroom break to give him this message. Wang went back to his office and silently cried over the empty desk. Nobody would talk to him at the time, not even the janitor, let alone the head of the institute. The one-sentence encouragement meant so much to Wang that over the next twenty years, he brought *Eugene Onegin* with him in very harsh and uncertain conditions, continuing the translation, often on cigarette pack wrappers as they were the only paper available to him. Decades later, Wang wrote an essay titled "One Book, A Few People, and Dozens of Years" in which he gives details of his joys and ordeals with that "one book" and exclaims: "In retrospect, my emergence from confusion and chaos in life started in that restroom. It is the 'holy land' in my life [and] I shall forever remember it."[57]

Wang's story illustrates the fact that despite the anti-intellectual rhetoric in Mao's era, there was an undercurrent of sympathy for intellectual works among Communist cadres, even though such sympathy was not always readily apparent. He Qifang, an accomplished poet, was a Yan'an veteran and known in China's literary circles as an ardent proponent of Mao's policies. He was, for instance, a hatchet man in the mid-1950s campaign against the prominent literary theorist and critic Hu Feng (1902–1985).[58] Mao also personally knew He Qifang and once commented that He had two distinguishing characteristics: He was bookish and earnest. Mao regarded the former a shortcoming and the latter a merit.[59] As the head of the institute, He was under pressure to meet the quota for rightists imposed by higher-ups, and he might well have had some responsibility for labeling Wang a rightist. Yet, as an intellectual and poet, he rendered moral support to Wang's work – an action that was politically dangerous at the time. No matter how trifling his "restroom instruction" might sound, he certainly knew how significant it would be for his subordinate. More importantly, that a cadre of He's status would run the risk of showing support for a rightist reveals the kind of resistance to Maoist politics that was invisible but perhaps more common than people usually realize. Even Zhou Yang, the party boss in charge of cultural affairs and known for his heavy-handed purge of intellectuals, admitted that

it is a pain when a writer finds that his ideas are distant from the party's viewpoints. Any writer who loves our motherland and supports socialism should strive to keep his basic standpoint in line with the party's Central Committee. However, in some special situations when some deviations have occurred in the party's policy and work ... it is possible that the two are not in step with each other or harmonious.[60]

By the end of 1960, Wang managed to return to Shanghai for medical reasons. He was issued a Shanghai residence permit (*hukou*) and soon his rightist cap was removed. The whole process was almost miraculous in that Wang met a number of people including party cadres who ran the risk of helping this political outcast. First, his brother in Shanghai sponsored his return, providing a home for him. This meant that the brother's family had to share their already packed living space with a politically condemned relative, something most people would dodge in the Mao years. Wang's boss in Gansu, an editor who had a high regard for Wang's work, issued an official letter to verify the work unit's approval of Wang's resignation and urge "whomever it may concern" to make "an appropriate arrangement" for Wang. Such an approval, a key prerequisite for any employee to relocate, gave Wang a legitimate reason to stay in Shanghai for "medical treatment." In Shanghai, the neighborhood police officer, who knew nothing about Russian literature but sympathized with Wang for being a learned man in need, helped him to obtain a Shanghai *hukou*, something that had been severely restricted since 1958.[61] Neighborhood police officers were party agents under the Public Security Bureau tasked with surveilling the lives of ordinary citizens in residential areas, with the assistance of neighborhood organizations, the mass "self-government" units at the grassroots level in urban China (see Chapter 4). Despite their low rank in the bureau, these officers were carefully selected and indoctrinated.[62] Still, in this case, the time-honored culture of respecting literati trumped the party's anti-intellectualism.

Wang fell within the official category of "urban idle labor force," which meant he had no regular job in the city and did not belong to any work unit; hence he was under the supervision of the neighborhood committee. Through arrangements made by the committee, he worked as a middle-school substitute teacher and as a freelance translator for the Shanghai Science and Technology Information Institute, which paid at a rate of 2 yuan per 1,000 Chinese characters. The pay was fine but the job was unstable. To make ends meet, Wang also worked as a day laborer: He unloaded heavy planks from cargo ships on a dock south of the Bund, pulled cargo weighing over 200 kilograms dozens of times a day for an iron fabricator, and loaded bolts of fabric onto heavy machines in a bleaching and dyeing mill. Meanwhile, he continued his translation of *Eugene Onegin* in every spare minute.[63]

As a rightist, Wang seemed to have found a ray of light in his misfortune, encountering people who commiserated with him. The cadres who held the key to ameliorating his suffering – returning to Shanghai from the gulag-like factory in Gansu, removing the rightist cap, and getting a job in the city – gave him a helping hand. In doing so, they were playing on the borderline of what the party's policies allowed. Wang's fortune in misfortune tells us that there was resistance within the party system – even on major political questions such as stigmatization as a rightist. Some cadres, out of their own conscience, which was not always in line with the party's dictates, were willing to explore certain flexibilities in party policy to help those who had been condemned. Wang lived as a rightist in various locations – Beijing, Hebei, Gansu, and Shanghai – yet cadres in all these places shared a similar respect for *dushuren*, literally, "a person who reads books," a term commonly used to refer to intellectuals in general.

All the cadres who helped Wang along the way had little or no idea about the world of literature. Their sympathy for him, a person derided as the "dregs of society,"[64] was rooted in the long-standing Chinese tradition that held scholars in high regard. In the gloomiest anti-intellectual days of Mao's era, this tradition counteracted the rhetoric against "bourgeois intellectuals." Many years later, when Wang was in his eighties, he attributed all the kindnesses he had received during this difficult time to the power of literature. "Neither literature nor human affection has national boundaries," Wang said. "Poems filter everything else out of society, leaving only the most genuine affections among humans."[65] It is an idealistic notion, but no doubt even in the brutal years of Maoist class struggle, Wang's notion of humanity could still find justification.

By 1966 Wang had completed the first draft of his translation. In August, the Red Guards started the home-raid campaign, searching and confiscating everything associated with the so-called Four Olds.[66] Wang knew that as a former rightist his home would be raided. For him, the most valuable possession was the manuscript of *Eugene Onegin*. After much thought, Wang decided to hide it in a double-door bookshelf and seal it with couplets that read:

> The reed growing on the wall—top-heavy, thin-stemmed, and shallow of root;
>
> The bamboo shoot in the hills—sharp-tongued, thick-skinned, and hollow inside

As anticipated, the Red Guards soon appeared at the doorway; when they stepped into Wang's room and saw the couplets, they were outraged.

RED GUARDS: What do you mean to say? Who are you attacking?!
WANG: It's our great leader Chairman Mao who asked me to paste this in the room.
RED GUARDS: What a fart! Nonsense! Chairman Mao would ask you to write this? You're way too cocksure! Are you cursing our great leader Chairman Mao?! Do you want to die?

Facing the furious Red Guards, Wang calmly pulled out volume three of the *Selected Works of Mao Zedong*, China's bible in those days, and showed the young rebels an article titled "Reform Our Study," written in 1941, in which Mao quoted the same couplets as "an apt description of those who do not have a scientific attitude, who can only recite words and phrases from the works of Marx, Engels, Lenin and Stalin and who enjoy a reputation unwarranted by any real learning." Mao advises his audience, in a satiric tone, "If anyone really wishes to cure himself of his malady, I advise him to commit this couplet to memory or to show still more courage and paste it on the wall of his room."[67] Wang explained to the Red Guards that since he was an "intellectual who does not reform well," he pasted these couplets as an everyday warning to himself – exactly what Chairman Mao had instructed.[68]

It was a perfect defense. No Red Guard dared to argue with Wang or to tear down the couplets to search the bookshelf.

Old Fogies in New Society

Intellectuals like Fu Lei, Cao Ying, and Wang Zhiliang were not leftwing writers but they were sympathetic to the revolution prior to its victory and supportive of the party-state after 1949. The party's moderate leaders considered them friendly elements among the intelligentsia. Some of these writers, such as Fu Lei, had personal connections or long-time friendships with the party's cultural affairs cadres, which before the Cultural Revolution helped to put these intellectuals in a somewhat favorable position under the new regime.

There were also intellectuals who were generally apolitical and apathetic toward the revolution. They were not necessarily happy with the old regime nor the societal conditions under it, but their intellectual moorings and liberal mindset were at odds with Maoist ideology. When the Communists took power, many of those with financial means or overseas connections left the mainland, but most people had no choice but to stay. Some who remained were suspicious of the new regime, while others were inclined to believe its promise of a bright future for the people and the nation. The majority hoped for the best.[69]

Despite all their anxieties, they had to cope with the party-state and adapt themselves to socialist society. As the Maoists put it, "intellectuals from the old society" were particularly in need of thought reform in order to become "socialist new persons." Moderate party leaders, as we have noted, tended to have a realistic view of the intelligentsia and accordingly adopted sensible policies. In Shanghai's alleyway-house neighborhoods lived some well-known literati who were, in the pre-1949 era, too aloof from the Communists to be their beneficiaries in the post-revolution era; still the party intended to place them under the united front so long as their behavior did not raise suspicion. In the sweeping changes in post-1949 society, these old celebrities quickly faded out of the public scene. Most of them were middle aged at the time of the Communist takeover; the younger generation who grew up in the Mao era considered them passé. Their fame belonged to an age that seemed long gone, yet before the Cultural Revolution, many of them, who in the popular mind "had died a long time ago," managed to adapt to the new society and find a niche in it. Their stories again reveal both the relatively mild policies applied at the local level and the adaptability of learned people from a condemned era. Among them were two men whose post-1949 experiences illustrate prominent features of the intertwined party-intelligentsia relations in the early years of the PRC: The composer and songwriter Li Jinhui (1891–1967) and the writer and publisher Shao Xunmei (Zau Sinmay, 1906–1968).

"Cultural Demon" Li Jinhui

At the peak of his career, Li recorded and composed songs and instrumental music, founded music schools, and trained and helped launch the careers of Republican China's most notable singers, for which he was regarded as a forefather of modern Chinese popular music and music education. But he always had clouds of controversy over his head. He was attacked and criticized by people of all political convictions – from liberal May Fourth intellectuals, to the Nationalists, and the Communists – as a composer and lyric writer of unsavory music, earning him the reputation of creating "yellow" (that is, decadent and vulgar, even degenerate) music.[70]

Years of fame did not make Li a rich man. By the time of the Communist takeover, he could not even afford to pay a rental deposit on a place of his own in the city.[71] At the end of 1950, the fifty-nine-year-old Li and his wife and four young children moved to Siming Villa, a complex of new-style alleyway houses (in the style of British terraced homes – see Chapter 5) in west Shanghai, to share a unit rented under the name of his married daughter, Minghui.[72] The next year, Minghui left Shanghai for Beijing, but the Li family continued to live in that alleyway house for the next three decades.

The couple had a newborn son (the last of their seven children) in 1952. Li was able to continue his songwriting career at the Shanghai Film Studio, one of the most prestigious in the PRC. His job was to edit soundtracks of foreign movies, usually at home. He also was free to compose and edit popular music and lyrics in his "spare time" and publish them so long as they were politically acceptable. Such a lifestyle made Li very productive in these years: In 1950, he published twenty music booklets; in 1952, nineteen booklets; and the next year, thirty-three. An article in Beijing's *Guangming Daily* in 1954 criticized one of Li's music booklets but that did not prevent him from continuing to publish popular songs. The topics of the music and lyrics he composed or edited included traditional classics such as the *Butterfly Lovers* (*Liang Zhu*) and the *Tale of the White Serpent* (*Baishe zhuan*), propaganda songs for the campaign "to Resist America and aid Korea" during the Korean War, inspirational songs for children, and songs for promoting Putonghua (the "common language," or Mandarin).[73]

A major factor motivating Li was financial. His salary from the studio started at 119 yuan a month in 1950, based on the official standard for "literature and art personnel," grade 9. This was not low pay at all compared to average wages in the city, but Li had to support a large family and thus royalties from his music compositions became important to boosting his income. Remittances were delivered by the postal service, often in cash if the amount was below 30 yuan, to recipients at their residence. All transitions required a personal seal (instead of a signature). Li's children recalled that one of the happy moments in their childhood was when the mail carrier called their father's name at the doorstep, "Li Jinhui, affix a seal!" This meant a remittance had arrived. Often, when one of his children's birthdays was coming, Li would say, "Let me compose a song for the birthday cake." Soon a 12-yuan royalty would be delivered.[74] In 1956, word came down from a higher level – reportedly from Zhou Enlai – and the studio raised Li's salary to grade 5, which paid 215 yuan a month.[75]

The party's goodwill was expressed not only in pay but also political status – the latter was more important in the PRC. In July 1950, when the CCP's Shanghai Cultural Bureau, headed by Xia Yan (1900–1995), convened Shanghai's First Literature and Arts Conference, Li was one of the 531 invitees, all of whom were noted individuals in their respective fields. In March 1956, in an internal briefing at the Ministry of Culture, Liu Shaoqi declared: "Do we have a history of opera? Certainly we do.… It all started with Li Jinhui. Don't look down on the creative writings of the Li school."[76] In August, Li was invited to attend China's first National Music Week in Beijing as the guest of and art advisor to the president of the China Children Art Theater. At that meeting, Li was received by Zhou Enlai, who greeted him like an old friend – in fact, they had met four or five times in wartime Chongqing.[77] In 1956, he was elected (or rather, appointed) to the Shanghai branch of the CPPCC. In May of that year, he was also awarded a position as a special research fellow in the Chinese Institute of Music.

The encouraging environment in late 1956 and early 1957 inspired Li Jinhui to the point that he was thinking of reviving his ensemble, the Bright Moon Music Society, claiming that with such a step he could spread music to over 400 million people in six years. For a while, he was obsessed with the idea; in the words of his children, it was as if he was "possessed." Only after his levelheaded wife, Liang Huifang (1917–2008), who was twenty-six years his junior, kept warning him about the risk he would run that he calmed down and said nothing publicly about his plan.[78] Instead, during the Hundred Flowers Campaign, he wrote an article titled "Cutting off Poisonous Roots, Completely Destroy Yellow Music," fiercely condemning yellow music, of which he was the indisputable originator.[79] Li's strategy was clear: By preemptively condemning himself in the strongest possible terms, he hoped he might forestall further attacks. In the 1950 Literature and Arts Conference mentioned earlier, he took a similar step. The five-day conference was not really an occasion for self-criticism; in fact, the theme was "unity and creativity" and the list of invitees reflected the party's objective of building up a united front.[80] Li nevertheless made a speech at the meeting brutally criticizing himself: "I have composed many yellow songs. Since criminal ring leaders must be punished without fail, I deserve to be executed by shooting. Yet the party trusts me and has not penalized me. I will earnestly study and reform, and thoroughly remold myself."[81] Such self-imposed humiliation ran counter to China's traditional notion that "a gentleman ought to be executed rather than humiliated" (*shi ke sha, bu ke ru*).[82] However, in many of Mao's political campaigns, self-denunciation was likely to be taken as evidence that the person in question had a "good attitude." Denouncing oneself was a preemptive tactic to dodge a real purge. One had to be psychically strong, or at least thick skinned, to undertake such self-humiliation. Many intellectuals took precisely that course. In Li's case, at the time when his article on yellow music was published in the newspaper, he was happily playing with his children at home, totally flouting whatever he said in the article.[83]

The good attitude Li exhibited in public worked well. In October 1959, he was invited to attend the ceremony in celebration of the tenth anniversary of the founding of the People's Republic held in Tiananmen Square, a great honor for PRC citizens.[84] That year, a musical drama he wrote in 1924, *Three Butterflies*, was made into a color puppet animated film.[85] His salary was raised, he was offered a housing allocation, and encouraged to join the party, to which his replied: "I appreciate the raise. I am far from the standard of a CCP member. No need for housing."[86]

Li indeed quite enjoyed living in Siming Villa. His study on the second floor had a window facing east and a sizable balcony; both overlooked a big garden of the mansion of Sun Hengfu (1875–1944), a Shanghai banking mogul. No matter what the season, the trees and flowers in the garden infused the air of Li's room with their fragrance. Li daily stepped out of the room onto the balcony to enjoy the view, a rare treat in this crowded city of ten million. Whenever he had a visitor, he would show off the balcony view. Li often, almost weekly, went out with his family to concerts, movies, and performances of ballet and Peking opera.[87] In a letter to his elder brother dated February 3, 1960, Li wrote:

The Stinking Number Nine   77

In [the] past three years, I have been working as a music composer at the [Shanghai] Animated Films Studio. The leaders are solicitous in various ways, and the work is all within my capability. I have time to attend meetings organized by the city's Political Consultative Conference and I am encouraged to write cultural and historical materials. In addition, my chronic ailments are being gradually cured, so I am happy. I will enjoy the rest of my life and forever follow the party.[88]

There is little reason to doubt Li's sincerity in this private letter to his older brother, the closest of his siblings.[89] In November 1961, in his capacity as a CPPCC member, Li joined an inspection tour of colleges and universities in the city. After the trip he wrote to his daughter,

Figure 2.2 (a) *Left*, The vertical lines read "A Golden Age of Music Belonged to Him." The Mao era was certainly no golden age for Li Jinhui, a "cultural demon" of Republican China. Nevertheless, Li adapted to the new era and, in 1957, even felt comfortable enough to plan to revive his emblematic achievement, the Bright Moon Music Society (established in 1920). (b) *Right*, Inside Siming Villa, an upper-tier alleyway apartment complex on Yuyuan Road where the Li family had lived since 1950. Li's daughter Li Mingkang is standing in front of a huge portrait of Marx, Engels, Lenin, Stalin, and Mao, which was jointly painted by three of Li's children early in the Cultural Revolution. The slogan beneath the portrait reads "Long live Marxism-Leninism and Mao Zedong Thought!" Note also in the distance an antithetical couplet posted on the entrance of a house: "Listen to what Chairman Mao has said" (invisible) and "Follow the party's lead" (visible), one of the most popular antithetical couples in the Mao era. *Sources: (a) Hunan ren zai Shanghai* (Hunanese in Shanghai), www.hunaner.net/person/show.php?itemid=15; *(b)* Zhang Weiqun, *Siming Bieshu duizhao ji*, 461.

Mingyang, praising the accomplishments of the CCP as "magnificent, unprecedented, and making people truly rejoiceful," and claiming "the tour was very educational for me as it increased my understanding of the party's policies in the realm of culture and arts."[90] The "cultural demon" of old society obviously coped well with the new society. According to their children, both Li and his wife regarded the years they lived in Siming Villa after 1950 as the "most peaceful and stable time in their lives"[91] (Figures 2.2a and 2.2b).

"Rich Dandy" Shao Xunmei

The life of Shao Xunmei (Zau Sinmay) after Liberation is another case that reflects the complicated nature of the party's relations with "intellectuals from the old society." Shao was a poet and publisher well known for his advocacy for estheticism (*weimei zhuyi*), his role in the Crescent Moon literary society (1923–1931), his passion for the publishing business, and, not least, his extramarital romance with US journalist Emily Hahn (1905–1997), apparently with the acquiescence of his wife (Figures 2.3a and 2.3b).[92] Shao gave Hahn the entrée that enabled her to write a biography of the Soong sisters, "three women at the heart of twentieth-century China."[93] Hahn also wrote about Shao in her semi-autobiography, *China to Me*, and in a fictional memoir, *Mr. Pan*. Shao was among the few Chinese who personified the cosmopolitanism of the literati world of old Shanghai, as Jonathan Hutt has put it:

Aristocrat, millionaire, collector, playboy, socialite, dandy and businessman; Shao's numerous personae speak volumes on the true nature of literary fame in Republican Shanghai. Consequently, Shao's Belle Époque coincided with the golden age of China's first great metropolis. He was not simply a product of this city and a reflection of its aspirations; he was ultimately also a victim of its fickleness.[94]

At least three factors ensured that Shao would be in a disadvantaged position after Liberation. First, he came from one of the most powerful families in the late Qing government, which, in the CCP's class classification system, meant that he was a descendant of the "feudal bureaucratic class," the foremost target of the revolution.[95] Second, it was well known that on several occasions Lu Xun publicly attacked Shao, caricaturing him as a "rich dandy in the foreign concessions" (*yangchang kuoshao*) who achieved his fame only by wielding the wealth of his wife's family.[96] As pointed out before, Lu Xun was China's foremost literary saint in the Mao years. In all likelihood, anyone Lu Xun had criticized would be regarded as an enemy of the people. Finally, Shao's extravagant lifestyle and liberal writings during the Republican era made him a perfect fit with the party's definition of "bourgeois decadent writers."[97]

Figure 2.3 (a) *Left*, Shao Xunmei coped well with the new regime and was treated with respect until his letter to Emily Hahn in 1958 aroused suspicion of him being a US spy, for which he was detained in Shanghai's British-built Tilanqiao Prison without a formal charge for three-and-a-half years. (b) *Right*, Emily Hahn. *Source:* Shanghai Municipal Archives.

Yet Shao's trouble with the regime was far from immediate. With arrangements made by Xia Yan, deputy minister of culture (1954–1965), Shao was offered a full professorship at Fudan University in Shanghai, which he turned down because the position was not at the topmost rank.[98] Instead, he chose to be a freelance translator. His arrogance was tolerated. Again, thanks to Xia Yan, People's Literature Press gave Shao a monthly stipend of 200 yuan in the name of an "advance," although the advances were never deducted from the royalties for his translations.[99] Shao was productive at the time: His translation of Mark Twain's *The Adventures of Tom Sawyer* and Percy Bysshe Shelley's *Prometheus Unbound* were published in 1955 and 1957 respectively. He also translated Rabindranath Tagore's novels such as *The Home and the World*, *Two Sisters*, and *Four Chapters*.[100]

For years, Shao was known for his generosity to friends and his love for hosting literary gatherings at home, for which he earned the reputation of being a modern-day Lord Mengchang (d. 279 BCE, an aristocrat well known for welcoming all kinds of people to his home).[101] In late 1937 after the outbreak of the Sino-Japanese War, Shao and his family moved to Lane 1754 Middle Huaihai Road (formerly, Avenue Joffre), a cluster of twenty-eight upscale alleyway houses that were the homes of some of China's best-known celebrities, and lived there for three decades.[102] His home, Number Seventeen, became an important cultural site. After three o'clock, Shao usually held a tea party in his living room, attended by his literati friends. Among frequent guests were some of twentieth-century China's best-known writers and scholars, such as Shi Zhecun (1905–2003), Lin Huiyin (1904–1955), Sun Dayu (1905–1997), Xu Chi (1914–1996), Mao Xiaolu (1909–1988), and Zhou Xiliang (1905–1984).[103] The atmosphere was so relaxed, free, and unrestrained that it could be described by the Taoist phrase "drifting clouds and wild storks." The literati salon seems not to have been much affected by the change of the regime. After the war, more people came to Shao's living room for the afternoon tea and made themselves at home; the gatherings were so frequent and informal that sometimes guests gathered even when the host was out. Romance also developed among the crowd. One of the frequent visitors was Fang Ping (1921–2008), an English literature translator who specialized in Shakespeare. Fang fell in love with Shao's older daughter, Xiaoyu, and, after her premature death in 1956 at the age of twenty-six, married Shao's younger daughter, Xiaozhu.[104]

Meanwhile, Shao voluntarily took a course in a "spare-time university" (*yeyu daxue*, an institution providing a type of continuing education) sponsored by the Shanghai branch of the CPPCC to study "dialectical materialism and historical materialism," that is, Marxism. At the time Shao had just reached the age of fifty and already had the signs of pulmonary heart disease, which perhaps was caused by his years of opium addiction before Liberation, but he took the course seriously. According to his wife, the school was about three miles from their home and easy to reach by bus, but Shao always took a pedicab to class, a routine that suggested how earnest he was about the class (making sure to be there on time) and how his money-spending lifestyle continued (hiring a pedicab was easily ten times the bus fare). Shao was overjoyed when he "graduated" from the school with a certificate with his photo on it and the signature of Shi Ximin (1912–1987), the university president and secretary of the Shanghai municipal CCP committee.

Not only Shao but also his wife, Sheng Peiyu (1905–1989), was eager to embrace the new society. Sheng, who was born into one of pre-revolutionary China's most powerful and affluent families (she was the granddaughter of Sheng Xuanhuai [1844–1916], a Qing dynasty politician and business tycoon), was extremely active in the Communist neighborhood organizations that were established nationwide in the early 1950s. She was appointed a group leader of the Huaihai Road Number Two Residential Committee and served as director in charge of neighborhood health and hygiene.[105] She was energetic in carrying out numerous campaigns called for by the government: "Patriotic hygiene," verdurization, eliminating illiteracy, building "backyard furnaces" to make steel, and so on. She and Shao even volunteered the use of their family living room as a public canteen as part of the "urban people's commune" campaign in 1958. Like everything done by neighborhood committees, Sheng's work was voluntary and without pay, but it did enhance her political status. For her dedication, the Xuhui district government in 1957 and again in 1958 honored her as an activist.[106]

Shao's misfortune came in late 1958, unforeseen, like an accident. In 1957, to help with his brother's medical bills in Hong Kong, Shao wrote a letter in English to Emily Hahn (who was in the United States at the time), which he signed with his pen name "Pen Heaven," asking for US$1,000, the amount he had loaned Hahn some twelve years earlier. The letter fell into the hands of a government secret agency and aroused suspicion.[107] Through a family friend, party insiders contacted Shao a number of times, asking him to submit a statement listing all his "social relationships" to the authorities in order to save himself. Shao, however, did not take these warnings seriously: He was in the midst of translating Oscar Wilde's *An Ideal Husband* and decided he would complete it for publication before turning to an autobiographic report to the government. He was arrested in October 1958 as a "foreign agent." With no formal charges, he was detained for "investigation" in Tilanqiao, Shanghai's in-town prison built by the British in 1903. Three years later, in the relatively mild political climate of 1961–1962, Vice-Minister of Culture Zhou Yang and Vice Mayor of Shanghai Shi Ximin intervened in the case. Shao was released without charge and his 200-yuan monthly stipend was restored.[108]

However, the imprisonment ruined his already poor health; in particular, his asthma worsened.[109] Four years later, the Cultural Revolution started, and Shao's stipend was reduced to 120 yuan, then, 80, and finally eliminated. In poverty, Shao died of pulmonary heart disease on May 5, 1968. A few days before his death, his son noted that Shao was taking opioid pills at home. When he warned his father that the pills could kill people with heart disease, Shao just smiled but did not stop, as if he no longer cared. It was unclear if he took the pills to ease the pain or simply commit suicide; the source of the pills was also a mystery.[110]

Both Shao's fortune and misfortune after 1949 were odd: A well-known "rich dandy" and bourgeois cultural comprador of the Republican era was treated with respect under socialism, but a single letter sent overseas to collect a personal debt led to his downfall. The oddness is indicative of the complex relations between the party and old-timers of a bygone society. The following account, of Lu Xiaoman, further delineates the limits of the reductionism that characterized the absolute despotism of the Mao era.

Lu Xiaoman's Dual Identity

Few people were more representative of the elitist urban culture of Republican China than Lu Xiaoman (1903–1965), a well-educated and talented social butterfly, writer, and artist whose passionate and much publicized relationship with Xu Zhimo (1895–1931), one of the most renowned poets of twentieth-century China, became a tabloid legend in the 1920s. After Xu's tragic death in 1931, Lu lived in seclusion in a Shanghai alleyway house for decades but her fame endured. After Liberation, people with a background like Lu's seemed to be totally out of step with the new society. Yet her life under socialism did not lack political status and material comfort, and in a particular way, it illustrates the role personal connections played in Maoist politics.

A Former Social Butterfly

Lu was born into a wealthy family in Shanghai. Her father, Lu Ding (1873–1930, agnomen "Jiansan"), studied at the Imperial University in Tokyo and became a student of the Japanese statesman and first prime minister of Japan, Itō Hirobumi (1841–1909). When Lu returned home, he was appointed to several important posts in the government in Beijing (then known as Beiping), and thus Lu Xiaoman spent much of her youth in the capital. She studied at the École du Sacré-Coeur, a French-run convent school, where she learned to speak French and English, play the piano, and paint. This was Beijing's most exclusive elite school for girls; one alumna described it as "beautiful and very famous. All the children of diplomats and foreign dignitaries studied there. Tourists who came to Beijing visited the palaces, the Great Wall, Tien An Men [Tiananmen] Square, and our school."[111]

Lu stood out in such an environment. She was by any measure a talented young woman, fluent in English and French (she was the interpreter for Marshal Joseph Joffre [1852–1931] when he visited China in February 1922), and well versed in painting, calligraphy, and writing.[112] In 1920, when Wellington Koo (1888–1985), China's foreign minister, needed an interpreter for the government's diplomats, the trilingual Lu was chosen to work as a student intern, a job that involved socializing with foreign diplomats. She soon established herself as a bright

The Stinking Number Nine 83

and glamorous social butterfly in Beijing's high society. According to an eyewitness account,

> Xiaoman was a dancing buff. If she did not show up on any given day, almost everybody would be unhappy. Men, both Chinese and foreigners, were enchanted by her charm. But even women, both Chinese and foreigners, seemed to be dazzled by her and took great pleasure in just talking to her. She was poised, graceful, and spoke with gentle sweetness. Her charm was unmatchable.[113]

Wellington Koo once jokingly commented to a friend, in the presence of her father, "Lu Jiansan doesn't look smart at all, but his daughter is so pretty and smart!"[114]

Three years in Beijing's high society made Lu a national celebrity. Hu Shih (1891–1962), a key figure of the May Fourth movement and Chinese liberalism, made a well-known comment that "Lu Xiaoman is a part of the scene in Beijing that no one should miss." The writer and poet Yu Dafu (1896–1945), given to hyperbole, lauded her as "a Prometheus who shook China's arts and literature circles in the 1920s."[115] The prominent painter and educator Liu Haisu (1896–1994) praised Lu as "a smart woman of her time, a matchless beauty."[116] Lu was known as both beautiful and "talented in traditional Chinese literature, painting, calligraphy, and English, and skilled at socializing," and was a role model for parents, who encouraged their daughters "to learn from and act like Lu Xiaoman."[117]

In 1922, her parents arranged for the nineteen-year-old Xiaoman to marry Colonel Wang Geng (1895–1942), who served in the Beijing government after he graduated from the US Military Academy (West Point) in 1918. But Xiaoman was unhappy and the marriage soon fell apart. In 1925, she met the poet Xu Zhimo (1897–1931), one of her husband's friends, and the two fell in love. Xu came from an affluent family in Xiashi, a rural town in Zhejiang. He studied at a number of schools, including Peking University, before he went abroad in 1918 to study first at Columbia University and then the University of Cambridge, where he became fascinated with English Romantic poetry and decided to follow a literary career. Returning to China in 1922, Xu began writing poems and essays in the vernacular style and soon establish himself as a leader in the modern Chinese poetry movement.[118] In 1923, he founded the Crescent Moon Society, which was to become one of the most influential literary societies of twentieth-century China. By the time Xu met Lu, Xu had a son from his first marriage, with Zhang Youyi (1898–1989), whom he divorced in 1922, and had an unsuccessful romance with a noted architect and writer, Lin Huiyin (1904–1955), while both studied in England.[119] Lu divorced her estranged husband in late 1925 and married Xu the next year.

However, the marriage soon ran into problems. Xu's parents disapproved of the new couple's behavior. Moreover, they were so close to Zhang Youyi that they kept her at home as an "adopted" daughter; naturally, this caused discord in the family. To express his displeasure to the newlyweds, Xu's father largely cut off his financial support of the couple. Lu, on the other hand, continued to live the sort of extravagant life she had since childhood. The couple settled in a house on Avenue Foch in west Shanghai, facing the famous Hardoon Garden. Their neighbors were wealthy bankers and entrepreneurs.[120] They had fourteen servants, including maids, a chauffeur, and a chef. Lu spent much of her time dancing, partying, playing cards, going to the theater, and playing as an amateur actress. As just one indicator of her luxurious tastes, she only used handkerchiefs from Le Bon Marché, a rare commodity even in China's most Westernized city.[121]

Although Lu was still in her twenties, she had countless aches and pains, which she treated with massages and opium. In order to earn enough to keep up with his wife's free-spending habits, Xu taught at a number of universities in Shanghai and Beijing, commuting hectically between the two cities. In November 1931, at the age of thirty-six, Xu took a free ride on a postal plane bound for Beijing, but the plane crashed, killing Xu. Although this particular trip was not exactly job related, many people blamed his death on Lu's excessive spending, which, they believed, drove Xu to take multiple jobs, involving frequent travel.[122]

Xu's death struck Lu hard. As if in repentance, she quit all her social and leisure activities and wore only black or plain-color clothes for the rest of her life. Fresh flowers were always placed before a picture of Xu in her room. Still young – she was only twenty-eight when widowed – and attractive, she declined a number of offers from her social circle that might have led to an intimate relationship, including ones from Hu Shih and Chiang Kai-shek's brother-in-law, Song Zi'an (T. A. Soong, 1906–1969). Lu, however, had another man in her life, Weng Duanwu (1899–1960), who delivered therapeutic massages. Weng, son of a wealth bureaucrat from the city of Changzhou, was a friend of Xu. A man with multiple talents, Weng was the chief accountant in the Jiangnan Shipyard, one of China's earliest modern shipyards, but was also a painter, art collector, and amateur actor in Kun opera, one of the oldest extant forms of Chinese opera. Most of all, he was a qigong practitioner and knew how to use massage to treat pain. Even before Xu's death, Weng's relationship with Xiaoman was controversial and a favorite topic of Shanghai's tabloids.[123] After Xu died, Weng, a married man with five children, financially supported Lu and soon became her partner. For

Figure 2.4 For decades after her husband's death, Lu Xiaoman (*right*) had an illicit relation with a married man, Weng Tonghe (*left*; 1899–1960). Photo ca. 1957. The new regime knowingly overlooked this fact for the sake of promoting its united front work. *Source:* Shanghai Institute of Culture and History.

about a decade after Xu's death, he spent his days with Lu in her residence on Avenue Foch in the French Concession but in the evening, no matter how late it might be, he would return to his home on Medhurst Road (today's Taixing Road) in the International Settlement, a distance of about 2 kilometers. After the outbreak of the Pacific War in December 1941, Japan occupied Shanghai's foreign concessions and imposed a curfew. From then on, Lu's home essentially became Weng's primary residence, with his wife and children left at his Medhurst Road home. Weng's wife died in 1952, and thereafter he and Lu continued to live together in the Lu residence until Weng died in 1960 (Figure 2.4).[124]

A March-Eighth Red-Banner Pacemaker

The Communists viewed the Beiyang era (1916–1927) as a dark time dominated by repressive, anti-revolutionary, and traitorous warlords. That Lu Xiaoman was a socialite who mingled with top government officials could itself have been taken as a wrongdoing. In addition, her much publicized romance with Xu, her illicit relationship with Weng, and her opium addiction, all mirrored what the Communists condemned as the "decadence of the bourgeois lifestyle of the old society." Yet after Liberation, Lu was able to avoid any political trouble; in fact, she was treated with respect and kindness and allowed to continue her comfortable lifestyle.

Like thousands of other "old-society" celebrities and Nationalist officials, Lu was considered a united front personage. In her case, Chen Yi, the first mayor of socialist Shanghai from 1949 to 1958, played a direct role. When visiting an art exhibition in early 1956, Chen was struck by the elegance of a landscape painting by Lu. Looking closer, the mayor recognized the artist's signed name, and said, "I had a chance to attend Xu Zimo's lecture, he was my teacher, and I ought to regard Lu Xiaoman as my *shimu*."[125] *Shimu* is an old-fashioned and affectionate term for the wife of one's teacher or mentor – the word conjures up the image of a mother-like figure.

Watched over by Chen Yi, Lu became a member of the Shanghai Academy of Chinese Painting, the only institution of its kind for professional artists.[126] She was also appointed to a number of other prestigious positions. Starting from April 1956, Lu became a member of the Shanghai Institute of Culture and History, an organization created in June 1953 to honor experienced and acclaimed seniors (mostly, former Nationalist officials, intellectuals, and other notable old-timers) and put them in a position to have their memoirs and personal experiences in recent history disseminated.[127] In June 1956, Lu joined the Chinese Peasants and Workers Democratic Party, one of the eight officially registered "democratic parties" in the Chinese political system, and served on its Shanghai Xuhui District Committee.[128] In the CCP's terminology, she was now a "democratic personage" (*minzhu renshi*). In January 1960, she was appointed a member of the Counselors Office of the Shanghai municipal government, a post for high-ranking united front personnel.[129] None of these positions required day-to-day work but all of them conferred an important political and social status that the new regime granted to what it regarded as important personalities of a bygone era.[130]

Lu's salary came from the Shanghai Academy of Chinese Painting, starting at 55 yuan in 1956, and then increased to 60 yuan in 1960, and later to 80 yuan.[131] Lu found this income helpful but far from enough to meet her expenses. Financially, she had help from Weng and Weng's eldest daughter, Weng Xiangguang (1919–?), who lived in Hong Kong and sent her a monthly stipend of HK$300 (about 140 yuan).[132] In her personnel file at the Painting Academy, under the column of "family financial situation," Lu wrote, "Very difficult, sometimes [I] have a little copyright royalty income, absolutely no properties." She also identified her family background (*jiating chusheng*, that is, the class status of one's parents) as "petty bourgeois" rather than "bourgeois bureaucratic," which her family actually was.[133] Obviously, this was a little stratagem to protect herself in an environment where being poor made one less vulnerable politically. It could also have been an indirect plea for an increase in her salary. Regardless, with a monthly income of about 200 yuan, Lu's life continued to be comfortable compared to the lives of the vast majority of people in the city.

Lu lived in a new-style three-story alleyway house on Middle Yan'an Road (formerly, Avenue Foch), just a block west of the residence she had shared with Xu.[134] The house was a few minutes by foot from the bustling Jing'an Temple (known as Bubbling Well Temple among Shanghai's expatriates; see Chapter 5) shopping area (Figure 2.5), but the alleyway compound was peaceful and quaint: It was, as a Chinese phrase puts it, an island of tranquility in noisy surroundings. Lu did not have children, but her cousin Ahjin lived with her, practically as her maid and housekeeper. She had a telephone with a direct line.[135] As indicted earlier, less than 1 percent of Shanghai's households had a home phone at the time. All luxuries come with a price: In Lu's case, the monthly phone bill sometimes exceeded 20 yuan.[136] To put that in perspective, the monthly pay for a factory apprentice at the time was just 18 yuan.

88   Part I: The Condemned

Figure 2.5 Jing'an shopping area on Huashan Road (formerly, Avenue Haig), ca. 1960. The art deco style building on the left is the Paramount, built in 1932 and arguably Shanghai's most famous nightclub and dance hall. After 1953 it was converted into a 1,070-seat movie theater. Situated to the right, and not visible in the photo, is Jing'an Temple. *Source:* Shanghai Municipal Library.

Although Lu had quit opium before Liberation, she kept smoking cigarettes. In a culture where cigarette smoking was ubiquitous, the brand of cigarettes one consumed was an indication of one's social status. Lu's habit once again revealed the extravagant lifestyle to which she was accustomed. She smoked the very best brand, Zhonghua, a cigarette created in Shanghai in 1951, originally for Chairman Mao and a few other top Communist leaders. Using the best tobacco available in the country, the cigarette was in extremely limited supply. For thirty-seven years, from 1951 to 1988, it was classified as a "specially supplied cigarette" not available in the market. As the topmost brand created and produced in China, it was dubbed the "national cigarette," with Mao's calligraphy and an image of the Tiananmen rostrum printed on the packet.[137]

Ironically, the "national cigarette" was not for average citizens but for the most privileged: High-ranking officials, diplomats, united front personnel, and guests of upscale hotels. It was extremely expensive as well.[138] One might expect Lu would smoke such cigarettes with care. Well, she might have, but in a particular way. She smoked each cigarette only halfway, then extinguished it and stuck the remains vertically in an ashtray for Ahjin, who was also a habitual smoker, to relish the butts.[139]

Lu got her supply of Zhonghua cigarettes by virtue of being a member of the Counselors Office and the Institute of Culture and History, both institutions part of the CCP's united front apparatus. Another privilege of being a united front personage was receiving vouchers for meals at the exclusive club of the Shanghai division of the CPPCC.[140] The food at the club, prepared by chefs who specialized in either Chinese or Western cuisine, was among the best in the city. Wang Jingzhi, the scholar of Chinese classical literature and a friend of Lu's mentioned in Chapter 1, reminisced how Lu generously shared this privilege with him, a rightist in his twenties, warmheartedly ignoring his status as a political outcast:

Time: Three or four years after the Anti-Rightist movement.
Scene: In the dining hall of the Shanghai People's Political Consultative Conference Club located in the former Zhang Garden on Beijing Road West [formerly, Avenue Road], a rightist appeared as a frequent guest. He ordered Western dishes and enjoyed them immensely. That rightist was none other than me.

The Political Consultative Conference was a Communist united front organization for upper class glitterati. To be admitted to that club was a privilege accorded to those who were entitled to be "united front personages." How could I, a rightist, be allowed to enjoy such a privilege? It has to do with Lu Xiaoman – thanks to her generosity. After Lu Xiaoman became a united front personage, she received various kinds of "care." The Communists do everything according to rank. The united front has three ranks: the central, the municipal, and the district; each rank has its corresponding benefits. Lu Xiaoman belonged to the municipal level. During the so-called three years of natural disaster, people of this level received fifteen vouchers every month, which allowed them to have fifteen Chinese or Western meals at the club. At a time when the monthly ration was only a few ounces of cooking oil and a few ounces of meat for each person in the city, such treatment was the height of luxury.

Lu Xiaoman treated me as if I were her son or nephew. She often brought me there for something special to eat. Sometimes she even just gave me the vouchers and let me go there myself for a meal. For her, this was not just a personal sacrifice for my sake, but it also involved a political risk. At a time when most people would do all they could to avoid having any relations with a rightist, to bring a rightist to the club to enjoy privileges reserved for united front personages ran the risk of being denounced. But Lu did not care, and because she had an extremely good relations with everyone she knew, and no accusation was ever made against her.[141]

In an age of scarcity, famine, and constant political persecution, such generosity was not just a matter of sharing food; it was more an act of humanity. Lu was far from politically naive. She knew how to protect herself in the treacherous political climate and was astute in maintaining a subtle balance. An incident during the Anti-Rightist Campaign reveals how sophisticated she was in navigating Maoist politics. When Chen Julai (1904–1984), Lu's friend for thirty years and a colleague at the Academy of Chinese Painting known for his talent for seal cutting, got into trouble during the Anti-Rightist Campaign of 1957, Lu dutifully and actively criticized him. At campaign meetings, she made as many as eighteen denunciations of Chen's wrongdoings. That onslaught wounded Chen's feelings deeply. But later Chen realized that her accusations added nothing new to what he had already been accused of. Lu did not say a word about numerous conversations they had over the years in private that could be construed as politically reactionary and could be easily used as evidence against him. Such betrayal of friends was common in the Anti-Rightist Campaign (and virtually in all of Mao's campaigns against "class enemies").[142] If Lu had taken that road, in Chen's own words, "executing me by firing squad or burying me alive would not have been enough punishment in the political climate of the time."[143] No doubt Lu was putting on a show for the party, because without it, as Chen's longtime friend she would have had no way to keep quiet while surviving the devastating campaign.

In April 1958, soon after the Anti-Rightist Campaign, the CCP concocted a sub-campaign among intellectuals known as "submitting your hearts and minds to the party" (*xiang dang jiao xin*), calling on intellectuals to submit written reports on their thoughts.[144] Lu dutifully submitted thought reports to the academy but did not actually write them – Wang Jingzhi did. Lu apparently saw them as an annoying but unavoidable ritual and did not even bother to read what Wang had written. Decades later, Wang quipped that he, a newly convicted rightist, ghostwrote thought reports for Lu, a newly minted "democratic personage." Ironically, every thought report passed the scrutiny of the authorities.[145] In public, Lu was careful not to say anything more than she had to say. Once she advised Zhang Fanghui (1942–), a student who was taking a private tutorial in painting at her home, "Fanghui, this is an age in which one can't speak freely; the most important thing is never talk publicly about what you really think."[146] Lu's astute dealings with the regime worked. In 1959, the National Association of Artists awarded her the title of "March-Eighth Red-Banner Pacesetter," a major honor for China's working women.[147] Hers was a rare – perhaps the only – case in the Mao era where a flamboyant social butterfly from the Republican era was ranked with working-class idols.

The most substantial benefit for Lu from all the party's united front policies was that she qualified for medical care in the exclusive Huadong Hospital. It was originally the Country Hospital (also known in Chinese as the Hong'en Hospital), established by the Shanghai Municipal Council, the governing body of the International Settlement, in 1921.[148] To this day, the name of the donor who provided the funding, and who preferred to remain anonymous, is unknown. What we do know is that it was a foreigner who made his fortune in Shanghai and the donation was aimed at providing a place where patients, regardless of nationality and social status, would receive proper medical care. The hospital had state-of-the-art facilities and the best medical equipment of that era. Ironically, it was only after the revolution that claimed its goal was to create an equal society that this charitable institution was closed to the public and designated a medical center exclusively for the politically privileged.[149] The hospital (renamed Huadong in 1951) was only two blocks west of Lu's home. There she received the same high-quality medical care as high-ranking party cadres. In the CCP pecking order, Lu's qualification for the privilege came from her being a "democratic personage." To the often-sickish Lu, a particularly important benefit of that status was that she could get codeine, which was not available to patients in regular hospitals. Lu spent the last six months of her life at Huadong Hospital; she died there of emphysema on April 3, 1965, at the age of sixty-one, unable to fulfill her plan of hand-copying in standard Chinese calligraphy Mao's famous essay *On Contradiction*, a project she voluntarily started in the spring of 1964 as her gift dedicated to the fifteenth anniversary of the founding of the People's Republic.[150]

The Mayor of Shanghai and the Widow of a Poet

As we know, Lu's comfortable position in the PRC started with Marshal Chen Yi's acknowledgment of Xu Zhimo as his teacher and Lu, his *shimu*. But was Chen truly a student of Xu's?

From 1923 to 1925, Chen Yi studied at Voltaire College of ZhongFa University (L'Institut Franco-Chinois), founded in Beijing in the early 1920s by French-trained Chinese intellectuals. Chen might have attended some of the public lectures that Xu gave at the university, but Xu was not on the faculty. Chen's life in the college, in the words of Li Shuhua (1890–1979), then dean of Voltaire College and acting president of the university, "was using study as a cover for engaging in revolution."[151] In any event, Chen and Xu did not have a formal student–teacher relationship. The two, however, did know each other and, moreover, engaged in a heated and publicized debate.

92   Part I: The Condemned

In January 1926, Chen wrote a speech titled "In Memory of Lenin" for a Communist-organized rally at Peking University on January 21, the second anniversary of the Lenin's death. Chen sent the speech to the *Morning News Supplement (Chenbao fukan)*, one of the four major newspaper supplements in China at the time. Chen hoped that the article could be published before the meeting to help publicize the event.[152] Instead of publishing Chen's article, Xu Zhimo, who was the editor of the newspaper, wrote an editorial himself, published on January 21, using Chen's article as a starting point to criticize Lenin and Communism. Xu called Lenin a "fanatic" and dangerous, asserting that the Marxist notion of class did not fit Chinese reality. He argued that to claim a political theory is universal and applicable to all human societies, as the Communists do, is as dangerous as religious fanaticism. Xu called himself an "uneducable individualist" who would tremble before an iron-hearted man like Lenin. At the end of the article, Xu, who was five years senior to Chen, lectured Chen in a condescending tone: "Young man, do not eulogize the Russian Revolution. One should know that the Russian Revolution is the most miserable and painful reality in human history.… This is not a joking matter, not something like playing with water or fire to join in the fun."[153]

Chen Yi immediately punched back. On February 4, he published an article in the *Beijing News Supplement (Jingbao fukan)* to rebut Xu and defend Communism. In a caustic tone, Chen accused Xu of "doing everything in the article to drive a wedge between revolutionaries," that is, the Communists and the Nationalists, who at the time were forming a united front against the warlords. "Poor man, sitting on the grave of the bourgeoisie," Chen mocked, "you are tarnishing your whole life's worth of smartness!" Chen claimed, "I took some time tonight to write these words in an act to wake up Mr. Xu rather than to debate with him. It is worth the effort to lecture such an 'uneducable individualist' as Mr. Xu!"[154]

Thirty years later, the Communists had taken power and Chen Yi had become one of their top leaders: He was a member of the CCP Politburo, vice premier of the PRC, a PLA marshal (only ten men in the PRC had ever been awarded the title), and the mayor of Shanghai. Chen, like the other Communist leaders who had experience in Europe in their youth, such as Zhou Enlai, Zhu De, and Deng Xiaoping, was a moderate. No doubt Chen's time in Europe – he studied in France from the age of eighteen to twenty – helped him understand China's Western-trained "bourgeois intellectuals" better than the party's leaders with a rural background. After Chen publicly acknowledged Lu as his *shimu*, he also met her in person on a seemingly not prearranged occasion. In 1958, Lu was invited as a "patriotic democratic personage" to attend a municipal assembly meeting, which was attended by hundreds including the mayor. Lu arrived late; she was ushered to a front-row seat next to Chen Yi. The two had a good conversation during the meeting. Only when Lu left the meeting hall, however, did she learn that the man whom she had just chatted with was none other than the mayor.[155]

The goodwill for Lu might have come from an even higher level. Reportedly, Mao, while visiting the Shanghai Institute of Culture and History, had twice expressed a favorable opinion of Lu. The painter Liu Haisu recalled that in an inspection tour to Shanghai in the mid-1950s, Mao met Shanghai's high level "cultural personnel" and commented to the effect that "Lu Xiaoman is a senior figure in cultural circles, she was well-known in the 1920s, and she should be treated appropriately."[156]

The party had its reasons for placing Lu under the united front policy. One of them was her relationship with Hu Shih, who was a close friend to both Xu and Lu and was involved deeply in the Xu–Lu love saga and its aftermath.[157] Hu had known Lu before she met Xu, and the relationship between Hu and Lu was such that Hu's foot-bound and largely illiterate wife, Jiang Dongxiu (1890–1975), was fiercely jealous. On one occasion in summer 1926 right before Lu's wedding, she excoriated Lu and Xu and threatened, in front of Hu and his friends, that she would "reveal the true faces of you so-called intellectuals." Mrs. Hu had reason to be upset. In June 1925, Lu wrote three very intimate letters to Hu in English so Mrs. Hu would not be able to read them. Moreover, she deliberately wrote in "big messy letters" so the writing would look like a man's handwriting. In one of the letters, she signed as "yours forever rose" and wrote the letter "o" in the shape of a heart.[158] Hu and Lu also exchanged autographed photo portraits of each other, a gesture of close or intimate relations in those days (Figure 2.6).[159]

After Xu's death, Hu Shih offered to be "completely responsible" for Lu. Although Lu declined the offer and chose to live with Weng, her friendship with Hu continued. In 1946, fifteen years after Xu's death, Hu sent a letter to Lu, asking her to cut her relations with Weng and come to Nanjing, the then national capital, and let him "arrange a new life" for her.[160] Although Lu did not accept Hu's offer, her affection for Hu was clear. "You are the person who helped make our [Lu and Xu] marriage [possible]," Lu said in a letter to Hu in 1946, and continued in a slightly suggestive tone:

Figure 2.6 Two autographed photos (a, *left* and b, *right*) of Lu Xiaoman (ca. late 1920s) for her "teacher" Hu Shih, with whom Lu, in her early twenties, began an affectionate relationship that lasted for decades. After 1949, Lu became an important object of the CCP's united front policy in part because of her connection with Hu Shih. *Source:* Shanghai Municipal Archives.

I sometimes hate you, for you can be in love with me, but you cannot understand my hard-to-tell difficulties, blaming me like those people who do not know me well. Now I cannot let you misunderstand me anymore. I'll wait until you come, and then, would you allow me to vindicate myself in every detail? This is because down the road, in my most lonely time, I hope I can have one or two persons who can comfort me.[161]

Hu Shih left China in April 1949 for the United States and never returned to the mainland. Lu stayed in Shanghai, and the two lost contact.

In early 1960, unconfirmed news reached Beijing that Hu Shih might run for president of the Republic of China on Taiwan.[162] At the same time, united front cadres from both Beijing and Shanghai visited Lu frequently and often took her out for a fine dinner. In the conversation in a roundabout way, the cadres asked about her relations with Hu Shih, referring to him was "an intellectual and a patriot," not a reactionary demon as portrayed in official propaganda. They implied that she should not cut ties with Hu Shih and encouraged her to use her contacts in Hong Kong to get in touch with him. Lu was well aware of the government's intention and the reason behind it but did not take any action. In a private conversation, she told a friend that these cadres' visits indicated that the party's united front work was "getting into every nook and cranny."[163]

Despite the Maoist rhetoric in public against Hu Shih and the Western-inspired Chinese liberalism he advocated, the CCP had not stopped its united front effort to co-opt Hu since he chose to leave the mainland in April 1949 when the Communist victory was on the horizon. Mao, who in his early years regarded Hu as a mentor, knew the details.[164] In February 1956 in Beijing, at a dinner with intellectual delegates of the CPPCC, Mao cordially commented on Hu:

Hu Shih is stubborn. We have people who have sent messages to him trying to persuade him to come back. Who knows what has kept him there! As for our criticism of him: any criticisms would not be in kind words. To be honest, he did contribute to the New Culture movement. We should be truthful about that, and not deny his contributions. By the time the twenty-first century arrives, we should have already rehabilitated his reputation.[165]

Considering that just a few months earlier, an intense national campaign against Hu produced more than two million words of essays condemning Hu in the harshest terms, the tone of Mao's comments was remarkable.[166] Although Mao was disappointed about Hu's response to the CCP's olive branch, the efforts continued.[167] After Hu's second son, Hu Sidu (1921–1957), committed suicide during the Anti-Rightist movement, Lu Xiaoman was among the very few people in China whom the CCP could use for its united front effort to win over Hu Shih.

In a closed-door meeting of party leaders on March 8, 1957, Mao estimated that, at most, only 10 percent of China's five million intellectuals "believe in the Marxist world outlook," while the great majority "still resist the Marxist world outlook.... Most of these people don't say anything, resisting in silence, hoping always for the outbreak of World War III, wanting Chiang Kai-shek to return."[168] In other words, in Mao's mind, the great majority of Chinese intellectuals educated before Liberation were untrustworthy and ultimately hostile. They were, as a Chinese proverb describes it, "hidden dragons and crouching tigers." From a radical Maoist point of view, an important mission of the revolution was to clean up these "dregs of the old society."

However, Mao excelled in balancing party policies between ideology and realism. Just ten days before his secret speech that assessed intellectuals essentially as hidden enemies, in a State Council meeting of

February 27, 1957, Mao delivered a very different speech, claiming that the great majority of Chinese intellectuals supported socialism, and only a minority were leery of or disagreed with socialism. This speech was published in June 1957 under the title "On the Correct Handling of Contradictions among the People," and became one of the major published works of Mao during the PRC period. Apparently, the face the party presented to the public could be significantly different than that shown behind closed doors. Meanwhile, within the party there were moderate leaders, such as Zhou Enlai, Chen Yi, and Xia Yan, who leaned toward recognizing Chinese intellectuals as a productive part of society or, in the CCP's terminology, "a part of the working class." In principle, the party's united front policy applied also to accomplished intellectuals and socialites from the Republican era. Under this policy, the lives of the old-timers in the new society were still comfortable, at least materially, before the Cultural Revolution.

For centuries, two deeply internalized roles – as servants of the state and as critics of the ruler – characterized Chinese intellectuals. Now, under Mao, intellectuals became motivated by one thing: Sheer survival.[169] The people we have seen in this chapter lived in Shanghai's upscale neighborhoods, carefully pursuing their intellectual activities without challenging Maoist ideology. Many of the "intellectuals from the old society" were eager to adapt themselves to the party's demands and the new society, in large part for self-protection, and a few sincerely embraced the party. Regardless, they could never secure the full confidence of the party. Some of them, such as Fu Lei, Li Jinhui, and Shao Xunmei, did not survive the Cultural Revolution. Only in the reform era were they posthumously rehabilitated and transformed into cultural icons of China's post-Mao renaissance.

Part II

The Liberated

The Communist victory in 1949, dubbed "Liberation" in the People's Republic, was propagandized as the rescue of the people from the untold miseries of old China. In terms of age and gender, two groups were said to have particularly benefitted from the revolution. First was the generation that was born or grew up after Liberation, roughly equivalent to the baby boomers in the West. These people, the party declared, were blessed to be "born in New China and grow up under the Red flag." They were taught in childhood that they had the sacred mission to be successors to the Communist cause. In their youth they were organized into the Red Guards in 1966 to "defend Chairman Mao's proletarian revolutionary line." A half century later, the backbone of the regime's top leadership, including the party boss, Xi Jinping, and the premier, Li Keqiang, belonged to the Red Guard generation.

The second group consisted of women. The Marriage Law of 1950, proclaimed just a few months after the Communist victory, was a landmark in women's liberation from what the party called the four authorities – "the state, the clan, religion, and the husband" – that had oppressed women for millennia. Mao famously claimed that "women hold up half of the sky" and, in the new society, were capable of doing whatever men could do. By the end of the Mao era, nearly all working-age women in urban China were employed. The marked increase in gender equality is among the least controversial legacies of the Mao era.

This part of the book looks at a segment of each of these groups. The members of the generation that grew up under the red flag were educated in the Communist creed, yet the most popular titles on their reading lists were so-called bourgeois literature, in particular nineteenth-century European classics. Some party leaders themselves had been fans of foreign literature in their youth in the Republican era, and Marx and Engels had expressed their appreciation of European literature. This created a niche where translated foreign literature could thrive in the midst of pervasive anti-Western and anti-bourgeois rhetoric. Thus, paradoxically, in the Mao era more Western literature was published than at any other time in Chinese history.

Under the banner of "women's liberation," women entered the labor force in unprecedented numbers after Liberation. However, the state's reasons for promoting the employment of women involved more than their "liberation." A close look at Shanghai's alleyway factories reveals that women workers occupied the lowest rung of China's urban employment hierarchy, that the state was more concerned with minimizing labor costs and maximizing social stability than liberating women, and that the women themselves were more concerned with taking the opportunity to have some income to supplement the family budget and get on in the system than with being "liberated."

3   The Power of Balzac

The Maoist regime has been known for its tight political control and coercive ideological indoctrination of which anti-Western rhetoric was a hallmark. Paradoxically, classic European literature was widely available and enjoyed unprecedented popularity in the Mao era. Moderate party leaders in literature and cultural circles, many of whom were left-wing writers and voracious readers of European works in the Republican period, found justification in Marxist scriptures for consuming Western literature. During the Cultural Revolution (1966–1976), reading literature was one of the most common everyday deviations from Maoist orthodoxy, which condemned virtually all literature, save perhaps for Lu Xun's, to the category of *fengzixiu*, that is, feudalism (referring to China's imperial past and traditional culture), plus capitalism (referring to the modern West), plus revisionism (referring to the Soviet Union after Stalin). In the decade that followed the Cultural Revolution, millions of copies of Chinese translations of foreign (primarily, European) literature published before 1966 were circulated underground or semi-underground among youth.

As mentioned before, the act of reading banned books resembled what Michel de Certeau called the opacity of a "popular" culture manifesting itself as "a dark rock that resists all assimilation."[1] In this case, the assimilation – or the pressure for assimilation – came from the Maoist attempt to straightjacket Chinese society. However, the act of reading went beyond simple resistance to tyranny. It reflected an individualistic desire for an alternative "assimilation," that is, the longing to be Western. The reading of classic European literature in Mao's China constituted a bold crossover of time and space. The worn pages of forbidden books at the time influenced the hearts and minds of millions of Chinese youth, including the generation of intellectuals and political leaders who were born or grew up in the 1950s. Reading the classics of European literature became what Maurice Halbwachs has called a powerful "collective memory."[2] A Chinese reader concurred: "We had no utilitarian goals for reading forbidden books in those years, yet what we had read became deeply imbedded in our minds and penetrated our hearts. This is far beyond what those cultural dictators could have ever anticipated."[3]

Finding the "Emperor's Sword"

China started to translate and publish European literature late in the nineteenth century, in parallel with the introduction of Western ideas – in economics, science and technology, medicine, and a host of other fields – in an effort to know the West and thus cope with its encroachment.[4] Reformists such as Yan Fu (1854–1921), Liang Qichao (1873–1929), and many others regarded literature, in particular novels and other fiction, as an important means for enlightening the masses about the crucial need to save the nation.[5] Twentieth-century China's most prominent writer, Lu Xun (1981–1936), gave up his medical career for literature (including, in significant part, translations) in order to use writing as battle cry to stir up his fellow countrymen.[6]

At the popular level, foreign literature was considered exotic and trendy. By the early Republican period, as David E. Pollard has pointed out, "fiction as a whole was accepted as edifying reading, and the translation of fiction also recognized as a valuable, even noble, endeavor."[7] In the 1920–1930s, "fiction effectively swamped other forms of literature," and numerous Chinese writers started their writing careers by translating foreign literature. Translated literature inspired a generation of the so-called literature youth (*wenxue qingnian*) in the Republican era.[8]

Contrary to the image of an isolated and anti-Western China under Communism, in China after 1949 translated literature did not wither away, but instead flourished. In the first decade of the People's Republic, China published 5,356 translated works of foreign literature, more than a twofold increase over the preceding three decades. According to Chinese statistics on book publications, from 1949 to 1979, Chinese publishers issued 5,677 translated foreign literature titles by 1,909 authors from eighty-five countries.[9] Moreover, before 1949, a book of translated literature typically ran to 1,000–2,000 copies, but now, under the state-run publishing system, many more copies were printed to meet the demand of the nation's increasingly literate public.[10] In the first decade of the PRC, more than 110 million copies of books of foreign literature were printed, an average 20,000 copies per title.[11]

China's alliance with the Soviet Union in the 1950s meant that the great majority of the translated works published at the time were Russian and, to lesser extent, East European.[12] They dominated foreign literature classes in school, leaving little room in the curriculum for other readings. During the Hundred Flowers Campaign in 1957, Peking University students pinpointed the situation and grumbled about it:

Why do such great masters of world literature as Balzac, Byron and Shelley deserve only a two-hour lecture, whereas we had to study Pushkin alone for several weeks? Other excellent writers of world stature like Diderot, Hardy, Stendhal, Rolland, Dreiser, Twain, etc. ... do not even deserve to have their names mentioned! Alas, these great writers were unfortunate: they were not born in a Slavic nation![13]

Outside university classrooms, however, the popularity of European literature reached an unprecedented level.[14] Take Miguel de Cervantes's *Don Quixote* as an example. From 1922 to 1996, it had nineteen different translations in China, only three of which were published before 1949.[15] For another example, Stendhal's *The Red and the Black* (*Le Rouge et le Noir: Chronique de 1830*) was first translated into Chinese by Luo Yujun (1907–1988) and published in Shanghai in 1954; since then it has had at least eight translations in China and has been printed in the millions.[16] In an age of tight ideological control and for writers who were versed in a foreign language, translation was safer than creative writing. After all, translators of foreign literature were highly respected in twentieth-century China, perhaps more so than their counterparts in any other country in the world.[17]

The wide popularity of European "bourgeois literature" seemed to contradict the Maoist dictum that all literature and art should serve the "proletarian masses."[18] But Western literature could be justified on the basis that many writers in the West were critical of capitalist society and therefore could serve proletarian politics. Under the banner of "critical realism" endorsed by Maxim Gorky (1868–1936), the Russian writer revered as the forefather of proletarian literature, many European authors were regarded in China as progressive. Their works, according to party theorists, portray the reality of capitalist society and reveal the dark side of capitalism.[19] Chief among them were Stendhal, Balzac, Dickens, and Leo Tolstoy. There were also many other writers whose works do not necessarily fall within the realm of critical realism but are classics and, therefore, could be used, as Mao put it, for "making the past serve the present, making foreign things serve China."[20]

As in all Communist countries, in China, Marx, Engels, and Lenin were revered as saints. Their words were regarded as revealing universal truths and functioned as, in a Chinese metaphor, "a sword bestowed by [the] emperor" (*shangfang baojian*), that is, they were tokens of power or privileges given by the emperor. Using Marx and Engels's remarks on a particular work of literature was the most effective way to justify reading it. Party theorists who wished to wield the "emperor's sword" to validate Western literature turned to Marx and Engels's lengthy, and mostly approving, comments on authors of contemporary and classic literature.[21]

A few remarks of the Communist forefathers on literature were particular common in defense of reading European classics. A group of my informants, all of whom graduated from college in 1965 and none of whom majored in literature or a related field, could readily pinpoint a number of Marx's and Engels's comments on European literature.[22] These remarks were used to substantiate the merits of classic literature and justify their circulation. They were not as well-known as most of Mao's sayings in the *Quotations from Chairman Mao*, but the very fact that college students in the 1960s knew them and could recall them some fifty years later tells us that they were common knowledge among educated youth at the time.[23]

As early as in the Yan'an period (1935–1948), when armed struggle continued without respite, the party had already started to translate Marxist works on literature and the arts. Under the supervision of party theorist Zhou Yang, a volume of Marx, Engels, and Lenin on arts and literature was published in 1940.[24] Zhou himself also translated and compiled a volume titled *Marxism and Literature and Arts*, published in 1944.[25] To disseminate the work, the introduction of the book was published in the party's major mouthpiece, *Liberation Daily*.[26] These efforts were personally approved by Mao.[27] A revised edition of Zhou's book was published by People's Literature Press in August 1951, only three months after the press was founded, and a reprint was published in 1953. At least six books of Lenin's on art and literature were published between 1950 and 1960. The four-volume *Marx and Engels on Literature and Arts*, translated from Russian, was published in 1960–1966.[28] All these Marxist classics on literature and the arts laid the ideological foundation for publishing a large amount of Western literature in the PRC. In his essay "The English Middle Class," first published in the *New York Tribune* in 1854, Marx declared:

> The present splendid brotherhood of fiction-writers in England, whose graphic and eloquent pages have issued to the world more political and social truths than have been uttered by all the professional politicians, publicists and moralists put together, have described every section of the middle class from the "highly genteel" annuitant and fundholder who looks upon all sorts of business as vulgar, to the little shopkeeper and lawyer's clerk. And how have Dickens and Thackeray, Miss Brontë and Mrs. Gaskell painted them? As full of presumption, affectation, petty tyranny and ignorance; and the civilised world have confirmed their verdict with the damning epigram that it has fixed to this class that "they are servile to those above, and tyrannical to those beneath them."[29]

Since Marx contended that the works of British fiction writers delivered more political and social truths than were uttered by all the professional politicians added together, one could justify reading these works because they were a kind of sourcebook for studying capitalist society. Moreover, Communist theorists acknowledged that literature could be a powerful political weapon. The most prominent case was the work of the French writer Honoré de Balzac (1799–1850), who was politically conservative and sympathetic to the declining aristocracy of his time, yet his writings were considered by Engels to be a classic case of literary realism triumphing over political conservatism:

> That Balzac thus was compelled to go against his own class sympathies and political prejudices, that he saw the necessity of the downfall of his favourite nobles, and described them as people deserving no better fate; and that he saw the real men of the future where, for the time being, they alone were to be found—that I consider one of the greatest triumphs of Realism, and one of the grandest features in old Balzac.[30]

Indeed, Engels's words of praise for Balzac's works as valuable for understanding French society were among Engels's best-known statements and made Balzac one of the most popular European writers in China.

> Balzac, whom I consider a far greater master of realism than all the Zolas *passés, présents et à venir* [past, present, and yet to come], in "La Comédie humaine" gives us a most wonderfully realistic history of French "Society", especially of *le monde parisien* [the Parisian social world], describing, chronicle-fashion, almost year by year from 1816 to 1848 the progressive inroads of the rising bourgeoisie upon the society of nobles, that reconstituted itself after 1815 and that set up again, as far as it could, the standard of *la vieille politesse française* [old French refinement].[31]

Similarly, the Russian writer Leo Tolstoy (1828–1910) was seen in China as a "politically correct" author because Lenin had famously praised him as "a mirror of the Revolution."[32]

Realist works were favored by the party not just for their views critical of capitalist societies. In Marxist analysis of social class, a work that is disdained by the upper classes is likely to be a good one. Engels once pointed out that when Strauss's *Das Leben Jesu* was translated into English, "not a single 'respectable' book publisher wanted to print it.... The same thing occurred with translations of Rousseau, Voltaire, Holbach, etc. Byron and Shelley are read almost exclusively by the lower classes; no 'respectable' person could have the works of the latter on his desk without his coming into the most terrible disrepute."[33] This resonated with the Maoist logic that "We should support whatever the enemy opposes and oppose whatever the enemy supports."[34] No wonder all the authors Engels mentioned for causing their readers to come into "the most terrible disrepute" enjoyed a "respectable" status in Mao's China, and some were very popular.

In addition, a few Western writers won the party's approval because of their political stance. Victor Hugo (1802–1885) was famously known in China for his condemnation of the looting of Beijing's old summer palace, Yuanmingyuan, by Anglo-French troops in 1860. In a letter written in 1861, Hugo described the looting as "two robbers breaking into a museum, devastating, looting and burning, leaving laughing hand-in-hand with their bags full of treasures; one of the robbers is called France and the other Britain."[35] The writer also expressed his hope that "a day will come when France, delivered and cleansed, will return this booty to despoiled China."[36] His sympathy for China naturally engendered good feelings among the Chinese. In the ruins of Yuanmingyuan, now an 865-acre park that symbolizes China's "century of national humiliation," Hugo's words are inscribed in stone on the plinth that supports his bronze bust. For another example, Romain Rolland (1866–1944) was popular in China because of his political stance. His pacifism in World War I was in line with the Leninist view that the struggle was an "imperialist war,"[37] and his sympathy for the Bolshevik revolution, his denunciation of imperialism in general and of Japanese incursions into China in particular, all won him favor in China as a "progressive writer" and justified the circulation of his work.[38]

Another important reason for the spread of European literature in Mao's China was that party leaders in charge of cultural affairs were mostly moderates. Liu Shaoqi rebuked a censor in 1952 with remarkable firmness: "Banning a book is like shooting a person to death."[39] Many CCP key cultural officials were writers active in Republican-era Shanghai – particularly in its foreign concessions. Imbued with what they had experienced in a multicultural city, these cadres were much more familiar with and receptive to things Western than their comrades with a rural background.[40] To some extent, they were products of Shanghai's renowned cosmopolitanism. Deputy Minister of Culture Xia Yan once described how Zhou Yang was a somewhat awkward young hinterlander but loved what the city had to offer after he arrived in Shanghai from Hunan in 1927: Stylish clothing, dance halls, cafés, movie theaters, and so on. This environment apparently had an effect on Zhou, the future cultural tsar, as Zhou Yang was dubbed for his power over the PRC's cultural affairs.[41] Xia Yan himself started his writing career in Shanghai at the age of twenty-nine by translating (through a Japanese version) Maxim Gorky's novel *Mother*, published in 1929.[42] His tragicomedy play *Under the Eaves of Shanghai* (written in 1937), regarded as a classic of twentieth-century Chinese theater, is based on his own experience in the city's cramped alleyway-house neighborhoods.[43]

Like Zhou Yang and Xia Yan, various other party officials made their fame in Shanghai and wrote about the city. Mao Dun (1896–1981; the

PRC's first minister of culture, 1949–1965), was best known perhaps for his magnum opus, *Midnight*, first published in 1933, a realistic novel centered on an industrialist's family in Shanghai.[44] The novelist and deputy minister of culture Zhou Erfu (1914–2004), whose published works amount to about twelve million Chinese characters, was best known for his *Shanghai in the Morning*, a novel about capitalist experiences in socialist Shanghai in the 1950s. Many of these party leaders were versed in translating foreign literature. Zhou Yang was known for his translation, first published in 1938, of Leo Tolstoy's *Anna Karenina*.[45] Lou Shiyi (1905–2001), vice president of People's Literature Press, translated and published dozens of works of Russian and Japanese literature in the 1930s while he was a Shanghai-based left-wing writer.

When the Cultural Revolution broke out, party leaders in charge of cultural affairs, including those mentioned above, bore the brunt of the attack on "capitalist roaders within the Communist Party." In Mao's words, the CCP Propaganda Ministry, the party's highest cultural affairs organ, was the "headquarters of an underworld kingdom."[46] In a meeting in Shanghai in February 1966 with the Chinese military on literature and arts, Mao's wife, Jiang Qing (1914–1991), delivered Mao's accusation that for seventeen years following Liberation, China's theater stages had been ruled by "kings and princes, generals and ministers, scholars and beauties, dead persons and foreigners."[47] During the Cultural Revolution, nearly all literary classics were dismissed as feudalistic or bourgeois and were banned. Books were among the main items that the so-called revolutionary rebels (best known among them were the Red Guards) confiscated and, more often than not, burned in public. At the same time, the words of four Communist saints – Marx, Engels, Lenin, and Stalin – were lofted to a new level in propaganda, and Mao's words were revered as "supreme instructions."

Meanwhile, schools were closed and tens of millions of students had no classes for an entire two years (fall 1966 to fall 1968) before the great majority of them were sent to the countryside and remote border areas, in Mao's words, "to get reeducated by the poor and lower-middle peasants."[48] Under the circumstances, a strong undercurrent of reading "forbidden books" swept up Chinese youth to an extent the nation had never before seen. In Shanghai, rich cultural traditions – in particular, countless sources of books – had fed the movement.

Reading When "Reading Is Useless"

Before the Cultural Revolution, books in various categories, including casual reading, or what is called reading *zashu* (that is, "miscellaneous books" that are unrelated to one's study or work), were available in public libraries, school libraries, and bookstores. From 1952 to 1956, the city government established five municipal libraries.[49] By 1959, each of Shanghai's ten urban districts and ten suburban counties had a public library, all with a sizable reading room. At the end of the Mao era, these public libraries had a total collection of 10.8 million books, double the size of all library collections in Shanghai in 1950.[50]

Most students, however, got extracurricular readings from school libraries, where all enrolled students had borrowing privileges. In May 1966, when the Cultural Revolution began, Shanghai had 519 middle and high schools, each with a library and at least one full-time librarian.[51] In addition, every one of Shanghai's twenty-four colleges and universities had a sizeable library; many of them had hundreds of thousands of books on their shelves. Fudan University's library collections exceeded one million titles.[52]

Republican Shanghai was known for its booming publishing and bookstore businesses. The Communist takeover and the reorganization of the publishing business in the 1950s scared off many booksellers.[53] Still, early in 1950, Shanghai had 512 registered privately run bookstores, 2,399 roadside portable picture-book libraries, 133 rent-only bookshops, 59 used-book stores, and 251 used-book stands.[54] In October 1954, more than five years after Liberation, *People's Daily* reported that in Shanghai there were still 2,500 "yellow" bookstores, that is, stores selling or renting "feudalistic and superstitious books, including those with stories about banditry and sex."[55] The situation was ended by the Socialist Nationalization Campaign of 1956, in which virtually all bookstores, except for a few selling used books or otherwise singled out, were reorganized into the state-run Xinhua bookstore. By 1959, there were ninety-one Xinhua bookstores in Shanghai, sixty-one of which were in the city's ten densely populated urban districts. In the next three decades, they became the essential place, if not the only place, where people could buy new books.[56]

Students usually could not afford to buy casual readings in these stores. More sophisticated readers found the selection at Xinhua bookstores limited anyway and tended to search for less orthodox titles in the city's few remaining used-book stores, where not only were the prices typically 30 to 50 percent less than the original price, but the selection was greater. In addition, used-book stores were open shelf while Xinhua's stores were not.

In the 1960s when the social milieu became, as one Shanghainese put it, increasingly "sanitized" of anything that did not fit Maoist radicalism, in Shanghai's used-book stores, plenty of books not conforming to Maoist orthodoxy – what party radicals labeled "toxins" – were still available.[57] On Fuzhou Road, Shanghai's well-known "cultural street" since the late nineteenth century, used-book stores provided a haven for people who sought alternative readings (Figure 3.1). When the Communists took over Shanghai, there were more than 100 bookstores on this less-than-a-mile-long street and in small alleys adjacent to it. The new regime shut down most of them but kept open a few used-book stores and specialized bookstores selling Chinese classics, foreign language titles, art and music books, or old magazines. A few stores that specialized in the "four treasures of the study" (writing brushes, ink sticks, ink stones, and paper) remained open. Although far from the prosperity of its peak in the Republican era, Fuzhou Road kept its reputation as a cultural hub.

Figure 3.1 The largest used-book store on Fuzhou Road, Shanghai's well-known "cultural street" (ca. 1959). The banner above the entrance bears a popular slogan of the time, "Eliminate the seven pests [rats, sparrows, mosquitoes, cockroaches, bedbugs, flies, and water-snails], stress hygiene, eradicate disease, and ensure a great leap forward in production." *Source:* Shanghai Municipal Library.

Used-book stores were also found on the city's major thoroughfares. West Nanjing Road (formerly, Bubbling Well Road), North Sichuan Road, and Huaihai Road (formerly, Avenue Joffre) each had a sizeable used-book store in the busiest commercial section of the street.[58] Up to 1965, a few small used-book stores were allowed to run as streetcorner mom-and-pop shops. For instance, in the neighborhood of the Great Wall Cinema on Fuxing Road (formerly, Route Lafayette), a cluster of old bookstores remained open.[59] Curbside book vendors could still be seen in the busiest streets in the center of the city, selling old books such as *Gone with the Wind* and martial arts novels and works of the Saturday School (*Libailiu*) of the 1920s.[60]

These booksellers were oases in the cultural desert of Maoist China. Fudan University professor Zhou Zhenhe (1941–) used an expression from one of Mao's poems to describe Shanghai's used-book stores as a site of "endless awe-inspiring views."[61] Xiao Gongqin (1946–), a "public intellectual" in the 2010s, recalled that his broad interest in the humanities came from reading books in a large used-book store on North Sichuan Road every day on his way home after class when he was in middle school.[62] That particular bookstore also got Zhou first interested in reading:

In the summer of 1957 when I visited Shanghai for the first time, I was astonished by the wealth of used-book stores there. In the North Sichuan Road branch, bookshelves from floor to ceiling were filled with old books that I had never seen before. Browsing one translated book titled *The Love of Marriage* (*Jiehun de ai*) made me sizzle. I was just sixteen years old, and I wondered how this kind of book could be randomly put on the shelves for sale.[63]

As sex and sex-related subjects were taboo in public dialogue in the Mao era, sex education books like this one were categorized as "physical hygiene" to justify publication and circulation. A Shanghai resident, who preferred to use his pen name Tingyuwa (1943–), recalled that "medical books published before Liberation were filled with details; much of my knowledge of physiological diseases and puberty came from used-book stores."[64] Another Shanghainese, Fei Dinghan (1944–), recalled that when he was in college, a friend loaned him a used book called *Marriage Physiology* (*Hunyin shenglixue*). In the preface, the author quotes a speech of Deng Yingchao (1904–1992, wife of Zhou Enlai, and the then vice chair of All-China Women's Federation), on women and marriage to justify writing on the topic. Decades later, Fei had totally forgotten what Deng had said but could still recall the excitement of reading the book and how he relished a particular sentence in the book, "at the moment when genitals start in touch...." His excitement prompted him to hand copy the entire book. To ensure the best results, Fei used his meager pocket money to buy a nice notebook of buff glazed paper and a fountain pen for his little project – all that he regretted was that he was unable to copy the few illustrations of sexual positions in the book.[65]

It is pathetic that a young college student had to get some elementary information on sex in that way. By the time of the Cultural Revolution, even "physical hygiene" books were not available, as sex was regarded as "a shameful and forbidden act aroused by bourgeois ideology to seek the pleasures of flesh and thus weaken revolutionary resolve."[66] A few science and medical titles were still available, but sex education books disappeared. The only type of publication in which one could get a glimpse of the human body was an anatomy book. In 1969, the Shanghai College of Chinese Medicine compiled a widely used manual for barefoot doctors (healthcare providers with a modicum of basic medical training) that became a "unified medical reading" during the 1970s.[67] It has two pages of illustrations of male and female sex organs, and the pages were always most dog-eared in libraries or in used-book stores.[68] It was not uncommon in bookstores to see a young man looking at a book of female anatomy with intense interest while his face flushed with embarrassment.[69]

There was, however, considerable spontaneous resistance to state-imposed asceticism. Not only were published books hand copied, but underground writings also circulated among youth. It was estimated that between 1974 and 1976 alone, more than 300 different titles of hand-copied books by unknown authors were in circulation, and over 70 percent of urban youth had read or copied at least one of these unpublished underground manuscripts.[70] The basic content of these volumes produced and circulated in unusual social conditions, as Perry Link has noted, is not unusual at all, but reflects "what has interested human beings everywhere and at all times," including love and sex.[71]

One of the best-known hand-copied underground writings was a manuscript titled *A Maiden's Heart* (*Shaonü zhi xin*), which had an estimated 100 million readers across the country, including remote rural areas (Figure 3.2).[72] The manuscript is known for its explicit description of an erotic triangular love affair of a sixteen-year-old girl named Manna (the Chinese characters combine *man*, meaning "beautiful," and *na*, as in "Anna," "Diana," "Fiona," and so on, to convey the flavor of a Western name), her cousin, Shaohua, and a classmate, Lin Tao. The manuscript, which circulated from around 1974 to the early 1980s mostly among youngsters, existed in well over ten versions, since some readers exercised their creativity by adding to the story. An early version started with fewer than 5,000 Chinese characters but soon a "standard" version exceeded 10,000.[73] Although the descriptions of sex in the manuscript do not exceed what a standard sex education textbook would have, the manuscript has become, for those who experienced the age of Maoist abstinence, part of the collective memory of an entire generation.[74]

110   Part II: The Liberated

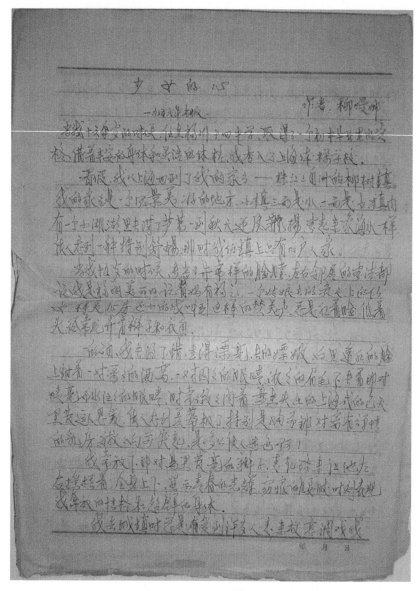

Figure 3.2 The first page of a hand-copied underground manuscript, *A Maiden's Heart* (*Shaonü zhi xin* or *Shaonü de xin*), ca. 1975. It claims to have been copied from a book of the same title published in 1956, although there is no evidence that such a volume was ever published.
Source: Courtesy of I-15.

The Power of Balzac

Sexual frustration sometimes was reflected in a low-down way: In public lavatory graffiti that took sex as its theme. In just about five years after Liberation, the CCP government had doubled the number of public lavatories in the city, from 400 in the late 1940s to 846 by the end of 1955. During the Socialist Nationalization Campaign of 1956, private-run lavatories were mostly closed, but the municipal government was able to keep the total number of public lavatories largely stable, at 822 in 1965. The Cultural Revolution set back these facilities; but, by the end of Mao era, 718 public lavatories were operated in the city. About half were open-air slab urinals, found along the city's thousands of alleyway neighborhoods (Figure 3.3).[75] Although nearly all public toilets had obscene and explicit graffiti, it was more common in poor neighborhoods, locally known as "lower corners." Periodically, as part of the "patriotic hygiene campaigns" throughout the Mao era, neighborhood committees used lime dust to whitewash the graffiti, but they never seemed to be able to obliterate all of it. Even some folk songs had obscene lyrics. One that circulated during the famine in the 1960s went like this:

> Little brother has a penis,
> slice it down piece by piece;
> deep fry them like oil nuts,
> five cents for two pieces;
> dip them in sweet sauce,
> dip them in hot sauce;
> yummy and delicious,
> yummy and delicious,
> come on and buy two more pieces.

The song was particularly popular among youth and children in their early teens.[76] As Emily Honig has noted, even during the Cultural Revolution when suppression of sex was at its severest, there was a "simultaneous proliferation of sexual activity and regulation," which "can be seen as the continual negotiation of sex and sexuality at the core of the Cultural Revolution."[77] Still, sex-related topics could be brought up "safely" if they were given the proper political slant. For instance, the interrogation of people accused of political wrongdoing, a common occurrence central to Maoist "proletarian dictatorship," often went astray in order to dredge up details of the accused's sexual misconduct, or, in official terminology, "bourgeois dissolute lifestyle," and interrogators often relished the lively particulars in lieu of pornography they had no way of getting.[78] Likewise, big-character posters, a common weapon in the CCP's political campaigns, particularly during the Cultural Revolution, were sometimes used to publicize sexual misconduct: "[P]eople used ink

Figure 3.3 An open-air urinal in a residential alley, ca. early 1980s. In a crowded city with limited private amenities, privacy and etiquette had to be compromised. Using a public urinal while pedestrians strolled by was not regarded as inappropriate. Limewash was commonly used on the walls for hygienic purposes. *Source:* Shanghai Broadcast and Television Station.

and brush to fill accusatory 'big-character posters' with details of sexual misdeeds."[79]

A survey of students assigned to factories in Shanghai in the early 1970s reported "random male–female relationships" among workers and frequent workplace talk about "obscene matters" or "dirty things between men and women," especially before and after meetings; in the toilets, showers, and dressing rooms; and during the night shift.[80] Toward the end of the Cultural Revolution, sexual frustration led to some extreme cases in which women were assaulted in public. During the National Day holiday of 1972, such incidents occurred on October 1 and again on October 3. Both were on the busiest streets in the city: One on the Bund and the other in front of the Xinhua Cinema on West Nanjing Road. In each of these incidents, a few men flirted with a young woman pedestrian and eventually started to peel off her clothes until she was totally naked. Hundreds of bystanders gathered, eagerly watching, yet none tried to stop the proceedings. The authorities soon identified

The Power of Balzac 113

the culprits and summarily executed them. However, this failed to stop such incidents. For a few years after the assaults in October 1972 similar attacks occurred every year till 1976, the year Mao died.[81] In an interview in 2011, the Cultural Revolution historian Jin Dalu described these kinds of incidents as "explosions when [sexual] repression was at its peak" and "the bigger the pressure [from the authorities], the bigger the rebound [from the masses]."[82]

To return to the subject of readings, for young people craving knowledge, the attraction of reading went far beyond sex. Most educated youths were fond of reading classic works in the humanities and social sciences. From these young people would emerge some of the best minds in the generation of Chinese who grew up in the Mao era. Chen Jianhua (1947–), a professor of literature at East China Normal University, recalled that in Shanghai's used-book stores before the Cultural Revolution, books that were antithetical to official ideology were like "the dregs of society floating up to gain the upper hand." Young readers like him, stumbling between the bookshelves in dimly lit stores, "cherished some hidden and nameless hope, and tried to smell and sense the legacy of sages and solons of the past." It was in the city's largest used-book store on Fuzhou Road that teenager Chen, who described himself as someone who "grew up under the red flag but had no desire to make revolution," found his solace in literature. Patronizing bookstores also led to making friends among the regular customers. In spring 1966, Chen met four like-minded young men in book-stores and together they established an informal reading group to discuss literature, translation, and creative writing.[83]

A few months later, the Cultural Revolution started. The city became a sea of red flags, big-character posters, and huge portraits of Mao. All schools were shut down so that students could "go into society to rebel against revisionism and carry out revolution." All libraries were also closed, and bookstores sold only Mao's works, Mao's portraits, and a few Maoist propaganda pamphlets.[84] Most books were labeled "feudal, capitalist, and revisionist" and banned. However, "surprisingly," Chen wrote, "although the movement was spreading like a raging fire, we had more literature to read. Many famous classics that could not have been found even in those used-book stores were now circulating among us through all kinds of channels."[85]

These books came from a variety of places, but two sources were most common. One was known as the "materials from home searches," that is, personal possessions Red Guards had confiscated in home raids, which occurred mostly from August 1966 to early 1967. Typically, confiscated books were kept in a warehouse of the work unit (*danwei*) where the victim was employed. Unlike other valuables, such as precious metals and jewelry, books were considered of lesser importance and often flowed out into the hands of individual Red Guards. Numerous books from private homes were burned or destroyed, but millions survived in warehouses and many others were scattered around among the "masses." In April 1967, the Shanghai Municipal Revolutionary Committee, the de facto city government, formed a group to "sort out books and cultural relics" that were confiscated from home raids. Two years later, the group handed over as many as 4,460,000 books to the Shanghai Library.[86]

The other source was the books taken (or rather, stolen) from libraries. Starting in September 1966, all secondary schools and colleges were closed for four to five years. Libraries were also closed and became targets of the Red Guards' search for "Four Olds." In the chaos, books were destroyed or sealed as "collections of feudalism, capitalism and revisionism," but theft was common.[87] Ironically, it was the Red Guards who had sealed the libraries and warehouses that availed themselves of these books. Many of them were hungry for learning and fascinated by the books. One elderly editor (b. 1930s) told historian Barbara Mittler in 2004, apparently in an annoyed tone: "The Red Guards, these 'little devils,' would ransack the homes ... and hit people for owning these books, but then they would take them home and read them."[88]

In the process, the Red Guards played a triple role. First, they were robbers of private homes in the name of revolution; then, they were thieves who stole these books from official holding places and put them into illegitimate circulation; and finally, they were the keenest readers of forbidden books. As former Red Guard Chen Jianhua confessed some forty years later:

These books were home-raid materials—the only reason they were circulating was that the Red Guards wanted to read them! We were all Red Guards, dressed in [imitation] green army uniforms with a red armband. Everything was suspended to make way for the campaign, but revolution cannot be a livelihood, much less can it resist the "weakness of human nature." Most of the time we were just idling around the whole day long, so reading came to be a major pastime. The situation echoes the [Chinese] saying, "No matter how persuasive good is, evil is still stronger." This is a huge irony of the Cultural Revolution.[89]

Studies of the Cultural Revolution have, inevitably, looked at the zealousness of the Red Guards. A much less-noted phenomenon was that after experiencing a few months of excitement at the beginning of the movement, most of the students became a so-called clique of the free and unfettered (*xiaoyao pai*), that is, they disengaged themselves from the upheaval. They had plenty of time on their hands during the most chaotic years of the movement, mainly from late 1966 when all schools were closed to the end of 1971 when millions of urban youth had been sent down to the countryside. Reading forbidden books, in particular foreign literature, filled the vacuum. Barbara Mittler has called the "idea that the Cultural Revolution negated foreign culture" one of "a great many myths" about the movement.[90] Although former Red Guard Chen Jianhua mockingly described reading forbidden books as a "weakness of human nature" or the "victory of evil," obviously, he is hinting that the basic human desire for knowledge is hard to quell.

Moreover, in this particular environment, reading was not just the usual practice of youth seeking knowledge or, more generally, trying to know the unknown. Reading gave a sense of pleasure and excitement that does not exist in ordinary conditions. It was what some social theorists call a type of "psychological reactance," that is, the human desire to eat the forbidden apple precisely because it is forbidden.[91] The seventeenth-century Chinese scholar Jin Shengtan (1608–1661) had famously declared that "reading a banned book behind closed doors on a snowy night is one of the greatest pleasures of human life."[92] Jin was in his early twenties when he made the statement. Some 300 years later, his posterity of similar age surely felt the same way.

Zhu Dake (1957–), a Shanghai-based culture critic, stated that in his youth:

Peeping into forbidden areas was a type of rebellion that spiritually excited me. It was the biggest drive that spurred my interest in reading. Inevitably, I was "being enlightened" by my own innocent sense of challenging [the authorities]. For example, my classmates and I took Romain Rolland's *Jean-Christophe* as the textbook for our lives. The protagonist of the book was my boyhood hero – my unrivaled idol.[93]

On another occasion, Zhu indicated how common this phenomenon was:

At the time, the talented life of Jean-Christophe was the light in my life. I turned the book that stayed in my hands for just one night into my bible. Perhaps it even became a shared guidebook for the music buffs throughout the west side of Shanghai. The romantic air of the book spread as if it were an epidemic. We all became sort of petty bourgeois, imitating in our talk and behavior the deportment of Christophe.[94]

Another Shanghai writer of the same age cohort, Chen Cun (1954–), reminisced that in the mid-1970s, in a house on Jiangsu Road (formerly, Edinburgh Road) just across the street from the home of the late Fu Lei, who had translated *Jean-Christophe*, he and his friends often got together to read Walt Whitman's *Leaves of Grass*, recite the "Song of Myself," and "take *Jean-Christophe* as our bible."[95]

This generation of urban youth might be the most widely read in foreign literature in twentieth-century China precisely because of the abnormal situation of the Mao era when a popular notion, promoted by

Maoist radicals, had it that, aside from Mao's books, "reading books is useless." Through their readings, however, these youth sensed the rhyme of life, the dignity of mankind, and the scope of the world. They found commonality in a great variety of readings in literature, art, and music. They were inspired by – to give just a few examples – the paintings of Théodore Géricault, the music of Richard Wagner, the philosophy of Friedrich Nietzsche, the novels of Prosper Mérimée, the short stories of Stefan Zweig, the music of John Lennon, the "Howl" of Allen Ginsberg, and the works of Herbert Marcuse. Even vice, eccentricity, and the heterodoxy in the outside world fascinated urban youth. As one of them put it, they were captivated by "the violence of New York City's mafia, the bohemian lifestyle, the ecstasy of cocaine addicts, and Che Guevara's gunpoint."[96] As de Certeau once described it, "I read and I daydream … The reader produces gardens that miniaturize and collate a world, like a Robinson Crusoe discovering an island."[97] By the end of the Mao era, young men who had not read *The Count of Monte Cristo* were mocked by Shanghai's "à la mode circle," that is, the city's self-imagined bourgeois community.[98]

The paradox was obvious. At the height of the Cultural Revolution, when it seemed that every student was abandoning learning, many were still reading; when it seemed that the Maoist radicals controlled what people read or did not read, this control had hidden loopholes; when the spread of a cultural desert seemed to be unstoppable, there were countless oases of literature in Shanghai's homes. Wang Anyi, who is now among the best-known writers of her generation, described the Cultural Revolution, when she was a teenager in Shanghai, as a time of "no education, no teachers, and no cultural facilities, but there were all kinds of books available and randomly circulating through society."[99] Wang Zheng (1952–), now a University of Michigan professor of women's studies, who had just finished her second year in middle school in Shanghai in 1966 when the Cultural Revolution erupted, recalled that "it was not until the Cultural Revolution that I had more security to read romantic stories leisurely."[100] She described her reading experiences during the chaotic years of 1966–1968 in an upbeat tone: "Except for a trip to Beijing to see Chairman Mao, I spent the first two years of the Cultural Revolution doing my favorite things at home, singing and reading. It was like a never-ending summer vacation. No school, no worries about math tests, and no homework. Books were plentiful."[101] Such a lifestyle infinitely clashes with the usual image of the Cultural Revolution as a miserable era, but Wang was certainly not alone in her cheerful recollection of the time. The writer Yin Huifen (1949–), who graduated from Xinhu Middle School in Shanghai in 1966 and became a factory worker in the Shanghai Automobile Gear Plant in 1968, had similar memories of her years in the late 1960s:

This was the period of time in my life that I read most. Leo Tolstoy, Anton Chekhov, Guy de Maupassant, Emily Brontë.... Books flowed through my hands like a river. When I was a child my family was poor and I could not afford books. Now I read with great pleasure like a fish in water. I read two hundred thousand characters a day.[102]

These books were quickly circulated among friends, classmates, neighbors, acquaintances, and others as a favor. Books usually stayed in one pair of hands for just a few days, sometimes just for one night, because they were precious and the owners of the books were always concerned that they would get lost in the flow, which in fact often happened. Although most of the time the authorities had more pressing things to deal with than checking up on young people's reading, in a politically oppressive environment, readers were still cautious. Borrowing and returning books were often done at night. Books would not be held in the hands but hidden inside the waist of trousers covered by a jacket. There might be patrolling workers' pickets on streets. If there was a suspicious person nearby, one would quickly move away and try to find a detour. At the destination – usually at the back door of an alleyway house – books changed hands in a few seconds while no one was watching, not unlike, as one reader jeered, "CCP underground activities" in the pre-Liberation days.[103] A person who was able to obtain books and circulate them among friends therefore was regarded as well-connected and resourceful – in the local slang, a person of the "broad way" (*ludaocu*).

Zheng Jian (1952–) was one of these "broad way" teenagers. He was a friend of Xu Yuanzhang, who lived in the garden house at Number Three Baoqing Road discussed in Chapter 1. Despite the family's bourgeois background, the Red Guards never searched Xu's house, and his father's rich collection of books remained intact and became a treasure trove for many hungry readers in his social circle.[104] Zheng, then only fifteen, helped to deliver books among friends. As a courtesy, Xu allowed Zheng to come to his home to read, usually after Xu took a nap in the afternoon and started practicing his oil painting. Decades later, Xu became an artist known for his oil paintings of Shanghai's European-style houses, and Zheng became a television journalist. For Zheng, in a recollection of his friendship with Xu, it was a scene of reading Western literature in that house that stayed in his mind:

He was sketching an image for an oil painting and I was reading *David Copperfield* on a sofa. We rarely talked, and the place was so tranquil that it seemed to be in a surreal world. Gradually, the sun began to set. It was too dim on the sofa, so I simply sat on the carpet near the window to read. After all these years, in retrospect, those were good long days, one after another. In those dream-like afternoons, the sunlight came into the room through the window shades unaccompanied by the stench of the outside world—after all, this was in the tempest-tossed time of 1967 after the "January Revolution."[105]

At the height of Cultural Revolution, in a home in the old French Concession once occupied by a German comprador, two young men regularly read classic European literature and perused prints of paintings by old-world masters – a scene in stark contrast to the usual image of this chaotic time. But even people who experienced the Cultural Revolution as relentlessly depressing have admitted that there was more freedom in reading at the time than has been generally recognized. Fudan University professor Chen Sihe (1954–) has called the years 1966 to 1970 a "gloomy time," but nevertheless, he has acknowledged that in those years, "reading among the people was never under real control."[106] In her fieldwork, historian Barbara Mittler recorded similar accounts. A musician who was born in 1942 told Mittler that at the time, except for "the eight model works" endorsed by Mao's wife, Jiang Qing, "the rest was all 'feudal, capitalist, and revisionist' [*fengzixiu*]. But we read all kinds of things that were *fengzixiu* anyway – Honoré de Balzac ... and Romain Rolland!" According to a historian born in 1957: "In the shops, I found Russian literature, Leo Tolstoy ..., and some French literature, too, especially after the 1970s. Nobody cared about us reading this."[107] Zhu Dake noted that he and many of his peers "grew up strong in a seemingly repressive and gloomy age, finding our souls through reading a multitude of books." In his words, "the cradle for my body was in the 1950s but the cradle for my spirit was in the brilliant years of the 1970s."[108] For this cohort of readers, the surreal contrast between the dream world of nineteenth-century Europe and the hard reality of Maoist China was both striking and fascinating. Many teenagers became nearsighted by constantly reading, often under a dim light (rooms in an average family's home were lit by light bulbs of only 25 watts), but, as one reader put it, "As my eyes drew closer and closer to the book, my heart and mind moved farther and farther from the world in which I lived."[109] Reading, in other words, was as much a retreat into an alternative world as a defiance of the revolution.

Mao had denounced the entire Chinese education system as dominated by "bourgeois intellectuals" and denied that a college education – aside from courses in science and technology – had any value.[110] The Communist Party's radicals stretched this notion by declaring that it is "useless to study," or more literally, "useless to read books" (*dushu wuyong*), a nihilistic doctrine that, at least ostensibly, pervaded society in the decade of the Cultural Revolution. But there was an undercurrent running against the party's nihilism, and youth who read books were a part of it. The Shanghai resident and scholar Wang Jingzhi regarded the circulation of banned and restricted books as a sign of the weakness of the regime. He described the situation in 1968:

> The machine of the Communist regime began to reveal numerous loopholes. A bunch of books that were designated for high-ranking officials and marked "restricted publication, circulation prohibited," somehow got to the common people, to the hands of a small potato like myself. I would read anything except for the little red book. Anytime someone loaned me a book, I was as happy as if I had picked up a piece of gold on the curbside.[111]

Wang was able to get a load of books in English from a Red Guard who saved them from the bonfires that were set to incinerate "bourgeois books" as he was curious about the contents of these books. Unable to read English himself, the young man loaned all the books to Wang on one condition, which Wang was happy to comply with: To brief him on the books. Not only did Wang read all the books but he also translated one of them, Ellery Queen's *The Greek Coffin Mystery*, in his spare time just for the pleasure of it.[112] It was at the peak of the Cultural Revolution that Wang read books like John King Fairbank's *The United States and China*, Richard Nixon's *Six Crises*, Herman Wouk's *The Winds of War*, and Robert Henry Stephens's *Nasser: A Political Biography*.

These books were published in the category of "for internal circulation only" and were commonly known as "gray-covered books" or "yellow-covered books" since the plain covers were in either of these two colors.[113] Before 1966, these books were printed mostly for party cadres ranked above grade thirteen.[114] During the Cultural Revolution, restricted books were published in the name of providing "negative materials that serve as a lesson" (*fanmian jiaocai*). From October 1949 to December 1986, China published 18,301 titles of books for "internal circulation," mostly between 1958 and 1976.[115] With huge numbers of restricted books published, implementation of the restriction varied over time and location, and people were able to find all sorts of ways to obtain copies.

Jiaotong University professor Jiang Xiaoyuan (1955–) recalled that it was a surprise that during the Cultural Revolution, when all Chinese classics were banned, his mother was able to purchase classic literature such as *Romance of the Three Kingdoms*, *Water Margin*, and *The Dream of Red Chamber*. The secret was that she was in charge of a program of training Vietnamese students. China exported these books to Vietnam and she asked her Vietnamese students to buy them for her.[116] Historian Zhu Xueqin (1952–) was a middle-school student in late 1967. His school, formerly Medhurst College, founded by the London Missionary

Society in 1898, had a collection of 40,000 books in its library. One day as Zhu was playing basketball on the school playground, a runaway basketball led him to a dump near the school library where piles of "Four-Old" books were discarded. Zhu took a bundle of the books back home and read them. This incident opened "the first celestial window of my spiritual reading," Zhu reminisced. From an old history book published before Liberation Zhu encountered for the first time a story of Russia's October Revolution that differed significantly from that in his school textbook. It was this book that prompted his interest in world history, which became his lifelong career.[117]

Beyond Shanghai

That Shanghai was a large city with a history of a strong Western influence no doubt played a role in the availability of books and in the social milieu of reading them during the Mao era. But was Shanghai unique in what we might call dissident reading, in particular, during the Cultural Revolution?

The answer is definitely no. In Beijing, for example, spontaneous reading groups among young people were common in the late 1960s and the books that circulated among students often came from an unlikely source: Recycling centers, which were ubiquitous in Chinese cities after the Great Leap Forward of 1958.[118] In late 1968, Wei Guangqi (1950–), then a middle-school student, found a trove of books in a recycling center in Haidian district in west Beijing. He and his fellow students each spent 10 yuan to fill up a big burlap bag of books at the rate of 0.26 yuan per kilogram. These books became his primary readings during his time in the villages as a sent-down youth. In 1978, when China reinstated entrance exams for higher education, Wei, who had no college education, passed the graduate school examination and became one of the first batch of master's students in the PRC. He credited this achievement to that burlap bag full of books.[119]

Another Beijing student recalled that in late 1966 or early 1967 he and three of his classmates once spent a whole day from eight in the morning till five in the afternoon in a recycling center east of Dongzhimen, selecting books from piles upon piles of volumes in the dust. By the time they finished their treasure hunt they "all looked like mineworkers right out of a coal pit," but their "hearts were filled with joy as if [they were] Christopher Columbus [and] had just found a new continent." They paid 0.27 yuan per kilogram for the books. They were so thrilled by the books that later they made another trip to the recycling center looking in particular for books of Western literature. These students came to see the readings as their "self-redemption in thought" during the ten years of the Cultural Revolution.[120]

Like Shanghai, many other cities, such as Beijing, Xi'an, Nanjing, and Guangzhou, also had some sort of youth reading groups in the late 1960s and much of the 1970s. Friends got together to discuss and exchange books, and formed what they called *shalong* ("salons"). The name was intended to convey some European flavor and the readings were almost entirely Western. A poem that was popular among youth in Beijing depicts the conversation of two friends – one a revolutionary and the other romantic, wallowing in the "spiritual opiate" of the eighteenth and nineteenth centuries – chatting in front of a fireplace:

> Oh, Tolstoy
> Gogol
> Dumas
> Stendhal
> Balzac ...
> they are the people I am yearning [to meet] day and night
> Oh, Julien Sorel [the protagonist of Stendhal's *The Red and the Black*]
> Prince Myshkin [the protagonist of Dostoevsky's *The Idiot*]
> Anna Karenina
> Eugene Onegin ...
> how many mornings and evenings they have accompanied me!

In the end, the two friends broke up. The person "poisoned" by Western values has no remorse but claims he would rather die as an ugly but happy and free fly than as the "comrade" of the revolutionary. And he vows to "devote his limited life to unlimited happiness in the world," a paraphrase of the revolutionary slogan of the time, "to devote limited life to unlimited service to the people."[121] Xi'an resident Ge Yan (1957–) recalled that he and a dozen of his friends in Xi'an's Number 71 Middle School formed an underground reading group from 1970 to 1974. They got their books by stealing them from the libraries of at least ten colleges and research institutes. The most popular readings among the group mirrored the underground readings elsewhere in the country – mostly foreign literature.[122] There was also a well-known music book titled *Two Hundred Famous Foreign Songs*, which, since its first publication in 1958, has become a music handbook for millions of Chinese.

A thousand miles northeast of Shanghai in the old Manchurian city Changchun, a young man named Qing Qiuzi (1952–) expressed almost identical feelings about his teenage years in the late 1960s as those of teenagers in Shanghai, although he was isolated in his activities: "1968, there were such wonderful days in that year. The [Red Guards'] factional wars had ended. Workers were still working, farmers were still farming, we students had nothing to do but relax, be carefree and bored. We still went to school every day, where we chatted, spread rumors, stole books from the library, or went swimming like crazy."[123] For Qing the good days ended in January 1969 when he and his classmates were sent down to a village 200 miles east of the city near the border with Korea. But the reading that started in 1968 continued and he benefited from it all his life. In his eight years in the Manchurian countryside, under the dim light of a kerosene lamp, Qing read extensively literary classics and other books that were stolen from the school library or were bought from roadside bookstalls. "With the seeds of literature sprouting in my heart, I felt some confidence," Qing reminisced. "Gradually, the spring of humanism touched my soul."[124]

In his semi-autobiographic novel *Balzac and the Little Chinese Seamstress*, the writer Dai Sijie (1954–) described how a box of "forbidden books," that is, Chinese translations of classic Western literature, completely changed the lives of two sent-down urban teenagers and an innocent and illiterate village girl. He remembered that when he started reading Romain Rolland's *Jean-Christophe*, he had intended the reading to be only a "brief flirtation," but it turned into a grand passion: "Jean-Christophe, with his fierce individualism utterly untainted by malice, was a revelation. Without him I would never have understood the splendor of taking free and independent action as an individual."[125] Of all the nineteenth-century European writers, it was Balzac that Dai was particularly fond of:

"Ba-er-zar-ke." Translated into Chinese, the name of the French author comprised four ideograms. The magic of translation! The ponderousness of the two syllables as well as the belligerent, somewhat old-fashioned ring of the name were quite gone, now that the four characters—very elegant, each composed of just a few strokes—banded together to create an unusual beauty, redolent with an exotic fragrance as sensual as the perfume wreathing a wine stored for centuries in a cellar.[126]

Melodramatic, but such admiration was generated by the power of the Chinese translation of the French author's works, and it was shared by many Chinese youths who grew up in the Mao era. "Picture, if you will," Dai Sijie guides readers back to his time, "a boy of 19, still slumbering in the limbo of adolescence, having heard nothing but revolutionary blather about patriotism, Communism, ideology and propaganda all his life, falling headlong into a story of awakening desire, passion, impulsive action, love, of all the subjects that had, until then, been hidden from me."[127]

As a sent-down youth during the Cultural Revolution, Chinese president Xi Jinping (1953–) had reading experiences similar to those of Dai Sijie and Qing Qiuzi. Liangjiahe, a village of about fifty households in

The Power of Balzac 123

northern Shaanxi where Xi spent seven years (1968–1975) as a sent-down youth, became famous after Xi rose to power in the 2010s.[128] The village was part of the North Shaanxi revolutionary base area, a cradle of the Communist revolution founded by, among others, Xi's father, Xi Zhongxun (1913–2002). But at the time Xi was sent down, his father had been purged by Mao and was kept in custody. Xi's experience in Liangjiahe played an important role in forging his character and outlook on life. Aside from hard labor on the barren land that toughened his willpower and gave him firsthand knowledge of peasant lives, reading was also an important part that experience. According to Xi himself, "The time we were sent down to the countryside was also the time for great exchanges of books." Lü Nengzhong (1932–), a Liangjiahe farmer who housed Xi for three years during Xi's seven years sojourn in the village (1969–1975), reminisced to a *New York Times* reporter in 2011, "He liked reading books.... They were thick books, but I don't know what they were about. He read until he fell asleep."[129] In 2016, *People's Daily* carried a long article about Xi's "love of literature" in which Xi provided details about his reading in the village:

We all carried books on our back when we went to the countryside; then in the villages, we exchanged books among ourselves. Even in that kind of environment, there was such a microclimate of book loving. I was even able to find a lot of good books in the possession of village schoolteachers, such as *The Red and the Black*, *War and Peace*, and some ancient textbooks of the Ming and Qing dynasties. I can say without exaggeration that I read all the classics of literature that were available to me at the time. To this day, what I can blurt out naturally comes from my readings of that time.[130]

One of the "thick books" was Goethe's *Faust*, which Xi got by taking a round trip of 30 kilometers on foot on rough country roads to borrow from a classmate who boasted of having the book but was reluctant to lend it.[131] Xi said that he loved the book too much to put it down and had kept it too long, forcing his classmate to walk all the way to his door to get it back. Decades later Xi recalled, "*Faust* is not easy reading; it is extremely rich in imagination. I mentioned to Chancellor Merkel, as well as to some German Sinologists, that at the time when I read *Faust* I did not understand it that well. They said neither do we Germans understand it that well. I said, so it seems it wasn't because I was too dumb."[132]

If *Faust* was a difficult book, then Nikolay Chernyshevsky's *What Is to Be Done?* proved to be inspirational for Xi. The protagonist of the book, Rakhmetov, who lived a sadhu type of life, sleeping on a bed of nails, had become a role model of Xi and his fellow sent-down youth. To imitate Rakhmetov, they took away the pad on the *kang* (a traditional brick platform used as bed in North China) and slept directly on the hard surface. On raining days, they went out to get thoroughly soaked; on snowy days, they took cold-water baths outdoors next to a raised platform around a well in the village. All this because they read the book in a cave dwelling in the village.[133]

Xi's generation of leaders commonly had some sort of book-loving experience. China's vice president Wang Qishan (1948–) was also a sent-down youth in the Yan'an area, living on a commune about 50 miles from Xi's. The future powerful deputy to Xi was also a book lover. Many years later, Xi would recall that Wang stopped by his place for a night and took away a book on economics.[134] Premier Li Keqiang (1955–) recalled that in his teenage years he benefited from the tutoring of an older neighbor named Li Cheng (1906–1977), a librarian who was erudite in classical Chinese. The courtyard house in which Li lived belonged to the Anhui Provincial Cultural and History Institute and a dozen of the institute's employees and their families lived there.[135] With schools and libraries closed after the Cultural Revolution broke out, for nearly five years Li Keqiang routinely went to Li Cheng's room at nine in the evening for an informal tutoring together with Li Cheng's son, who was about the same age. At 9:00 p.m. Li Cheng washed his feet in an enamel basin and then massaged them. This daily routine took about an hour. During that hour, Li discussed Chinese classics in history, literature, and geography. Such a teaching style resembled China's ancient home-schooling tradition and Li Keqiang had fond memories of it. The list of required reading for the tutorial included *The Historical Records (Shiji)*, *The Book of Han (Hanshu)*, *The Book of the Late Han (Hou Hanshu)*, *Comprehensive Mirror in Aid of Governance (Zizhi tongjian)*, and *Selections of Refined Literature (Zhaoming wenxuan)*, an eighteenth-century classic.[136]

All of the titles on Xi's and Li's reading lists were labeled "feudal, capitalist, and revisionist" and officially banned at the time. It would be intriguing and informative to know more about the influence of these reading experiences on China's leaders and their thinking. The effects of reading on an individual are usually impalpable and hard to articulate, but we may still detect a trace of influence. Soon after Xi became China's top leader he convened a forum on literature and art with the country's major writers and artists in attendance and delivered a speech at the forum on October 15, 2014.[137] In his speech Xi provided a long list of writers whom he regarded as representative of "world civilizations" outside China. Except for a few Indian authors, all on the list were Western writers, mostly nineteenth-century European authors whose books he read during the Cultural Revolution.[138] Premier Li was known for recommending to Chinese youth a few Chinese history and literature classics, most of which were drawn from his own reading in his younger years. In another case, at a CCP anti-corruption meeting on November 30, 2012, Wang Qishan, who had two weeks earlier been appointed head of the party's Central Commission for Discipline Inspection, recommended Alexis de Tocqueville's *The Old Regime and the Revolution* (published in French in 1856). When his recommendation went public, the publisher of a Chinese translation of the book had to run several prints in a few weeks to meet the market demand.[139]

The Tonya Complex

Not only "bourgeois works" like those of Balzac enlightened a generation of Chinese youth in love and sex but so did Communist literature that was intended to nourish the people's revolutionary spirit. The official ideology put sexual love as something, at best, subordinate to the revolutionary cause of Communism. Men and women were to be "comrades in revolution" first before they developed a relationship "one step further than comrades."[140] Still, under this principle, writers were able to wedge snippets of stories of love into the socialist-realist novels published in the seventeen years before the Cultural Revolution. In an era of abstinence, just a little romance or an inkling of erotic love in these novels provided the sort of enlightenment that had a long-lasting impact on young readers.

Among the most influential novels in that regard was *Bitter Flowers* (*Kucai hua*, also translated as *The Lettuce*) by Feng Deying (1935–2022). The novel, set during the Communist-led guerilla war against Japan, dealt with the lives of eight women in rural Shandong peninsula. The plot contains a few love stories, including one illegitimate love between the wife of a school principal and an illiterate village hired laborer with whom the author sympathized. Feng completed the manuscript when he had just turned twenty – perhaps many people would consider this too young to fully understand romantic love, yet the stories in the novel were both absorbing and sophisticated. Since its publication in 1958, over ten million copies of *Bitter Flowers* have been printed and the work has been translated into ten languages.[141] The Nobel Laureate Mo Yan (1954–) has regarded the treatment of love and sexuality in *Bitter Flowers* the best in all of Chinese literature published in the first seventeen years of the PRC.[142]

Qu Bo's (Chu Po, 1923–2002) *Tracks in the Snowy Forest* is another enormously popular novel with a love story that captivated many Chinese youth. The novel is based on the author's own experience of leading a PLA column in tracking down several Nationalist militiamen in Manchuria's snowy mountains during the Chinese civil war of the late 1940s. Published in 1957, more than 350,000 copies in numerous editions were printed.[143] The famous Peking opera *Taking of Tiger Mountain by Strategy* was derived from one of the story lines of the novel and it became one of the eight model plays favored by Madame Mao. However, this did not exempt Qu Bo from being purged during the Cultural Revolution, and the book was banned. The radicals' disfavor was in part due to a story of love between the PLA column head, code named Captain 203, and the only female soldier in the book, an army nurse named White Dove, modeled on the author's wife, who was also a military nurse.[144] The story traces all the subtleties of love and passion in the midst of warfare. In an age of mortification of the senses, the sideline story of love made the book "a chivalric romance novel" in the minds of a generation of Chinese readers.[145] Another popular novel, *The Song of Youth*, by Yang Mo (1914–1995), incorporated love stories set in the Communist-led student movement in the early 1930s, and provided a gripping account of love, family, and revolution among educated youth at the time.[146] Mo Yan summarized the significance of the love stories in these novels:

Looking back at the novels published in the seventeen years before the Cultural Revolution, my view is that the parts on love in these works are the most real. That is because when the authors wrote about love, they were applying their own ideas, not the ideas of society.... When writing about love, the writers partially and temporarily disremembered [the Maoist notion of] class and politics, and they gave free rein to their own beautiful feelings, hence naturally they depicted the beautiful feelings of the human. The plots of the novels in those seventeen years vary, but they all have just one thesis, and all the writers were striving to interpret something [around the thesis]. But in the few pages where the writers wrote about love, they forgot to interpret the leader's ideas. So, I believe these parts on love indeed represent whatever remained of the individual character of these authors.... Therefore these parts are unusually brilliant and remarkable.[147]

Perhaps no love story occupies a place more prominent in the hearts of youth who grew up in Mao's China than a translated work: Nikolai Ostrovsky's (1904–1936) *How the Steel Was Tempered* (hereafter, *Steel*).[148] The book is not a love story per se but a Communist saga about how the protagonist, Pavel Korchagin, an autobiographic character based on Ostrovsky, devoted his life to the Bolshevik revolution during the Russian Civil War (1917–1922). Korchagin grew up in a poor railroad worker's family and joined the revolution at age fourteen. He was wounded twice on the battlefield and suffered an accident when working on the railroad, which left him, still in his twenties, crippled and blind. In bed, he continued working for the revolution by writing. Pavel Korchagin's famous lines in the book were frequently quoted as a motto for the Communist philosophy of life: "A person should live his life thus: when he looks into his past, he would not regret time wasted in vain, nor would he be ashamed of having accomplished too little. When he dies, he should be able to say, I have devoted my entire life and all my energy to the most beautiful enterprise in the world – the struggle for the freedom of the human race."[149] This canonical book was hailed as a "masterpiece of socialist realism."[150] Reportedly, up to 1945 in the Soviet Union, *Steel* had been printed 246 times, for a total of ten million copies. In China, the CCP arranged for a party member named Mei Yi (1913–2003) to translate the book from a 1938 English edition; Mei's translation was published in Shanghai in 1942.[151] The translation was edited by Liu Liaoyi (1915–2001) based on the Russian original and republished in 1952. From that point until 1965, it was printed forty-six times and 1,369,000 copies were sold.[152] In September 1999, on the eve of the fiftieth anniversary of the founding of the PRC, Beijing conducted a public survey to select "the top fifty books that moved the People's Republic": *Steel* won out as number one.[153]

The Communists promoted the book to inculcate youth with a revolutionary spirit and devotion to the Communist cause. However, the part of the book about Pavel's first love, with a teenage girl, Tonya Tumanova, the daughter of the chief forest warden, caught the imagination of Chinese readers more than did his bloody revolutionary career. Millions of youths, girls and boys alike, were charmed by the image of Tonya in her first appearance in the novel (Figure 3.4): "She was wearing a white sailor blouse with a striped blue collar and a short light-grey skirt. Short socks with a colored edging clung to her shapely suntanned legs. Her chestnut hair was gathered in a heavy braid."[154] But the appeal of Tonya to Chinese readers came more from her character than her looks. Although a girl from a bourgeois family, Tonya gave more weight to a man's character than his social status, rejected the courtship of young men of her social rank, and fell in love with the son of a poor railroad worker. She had her own sense of justice and harbored Pavel at her home when he was a fugitive from jail. However, when Pavel's revolutionary zealotry infringed on her free spirit, she did not hesitate to protest and defend her individuality. Their final breakup in a dirty snow-covered little railway station on a stormy winter's day denoted the ultimate clash of social classes and outlooks on life of the two lovers. All of this captivated a generation of Chinese readers who grew up in the era of Maoist indoctrination.[155] As Mark Gamsa has noted, "Russian, and then Soviet, literature in China was identified with real life, its fictional characters with living men and women and its authors with teachers."[156] Russian and Soviet literature did not always serve as a conveyer of morality for building up revolutionary spirit that the party had hoped for; instead, as in the case of *Steel*, the imagination and imitation of figures in literature in real life were complicated.

128   Part II: The Liberated

Figure 3.4 Pavel and Tonya first met on a lakeside in a sunny afternoon while Pavel was fishing and Tonya was reading. The scene caught the romantic imagination of millions of young Chinese readers in the Mao era. *Source: How the Steel Was Tempered* (1964).

The writer Liu Xiaofeng (1956–) recalled that he first "got to know" Tonya when he was nine years old, reading through an abridged edition in Chinese for juveniles. He finished reading the book in the gunfire of the Red Guards' factional war in Chongqing. He saw teenage boys and girls die on the streets and could not help but imagine that if Tonya had joined

The Power of Balzac 129

Pavel in making revolution, they might have died together in love. By the time Liu was nineteen, the image of Pavel had faded but, in his words, Tonya remained "like spring drizzle, warmly cherished in my heart" and he started to "fall in love with Tonya." And, since Tonya first appears in the novel reading a book on a tree branch near a lake (Figure 3.4), he started to look for "a bundle of fiction that Tonya would have read": Hugo's *Les Misérables*, Dostoyevsky's *Humiliated and Insulted*, Dostoyevsky's "White Nights," Chekhov's "The House with the Mezzanine," Mérimée's *Carmen* ... "This is a private event that occurred in the autumn of 1975," Liu reminisced some twenty years later when he was a freelance writer in Hong Kong.

Not long ago, I read French composer Guy Ropartz's words, *Qui nous dira la raison de vivre*? ["Who would tell us the reason for living?"], which rekindled my empathy for Tonya's love, which had been ruthlessly destroyed. Still, I felt my heart was deeply touched: as if it were flying about with the striped blue collar of the sailor blouse that she was wearing. I dare not think about her – every time I think about her, I feel a dull pain in my heart.[157]

This might sound overly sentimental, but Liu's feelings about this fictional figure were definitively a collective memory among this cohort of Chinese, and numerous other youth echoed his romanticism. Tonya captivated youth not only in their fantasies but also in their real lives. Consciously or subconsciously, they acted as if "you are what you read." A reader named Wang Gang (1957–) recalled that he got a decrepit copy of *Steel* when he was thirteen and he immediately "fell in love with Tonya." The book was in a high school library where his mother worked. Although the stacks were sealed by the Cultural Revolution rebels, he was able to take home the dog-eared book, together with a brand-new copy of a book with a long title, *Selected Commentaries on Humanism and the Theory of Human Nature by Bourgeois Litterateurs and Artists from the Renaissance to the Nineteenth Century*. "Stealing these two books from the library," Wang said, "was my particular misdeed during the Cultural Revolution as well as a legacy I inherited from the Cultural Revolution." It was an important legacy in Wang's life: Five years later, he fell in love with a girl whom he had always fancied as Tonya. In his words: "My first kiss was bestowed on Tonya on a moonlit night."[158]

Railroad worker Liu Dazuo (1946–) recalled that in early 1969, he and his team were working in the bitter cold on a railway maintenance project in the city of Zhengzhou. Every time he saw a train passing through the station with passengers sitting in the warm cars, the scene of Pavel repairing railroad tracks on the frozen land when he encountered Tonya came to his mind.[159] Han Qiulin (1962–), who grew up in an isolated rural area in Helongjiang, read banned books that were circulated in his older brother's reading circle. Recalling his reading of "big books" in the 1970s, Han commented,

More than twenty years have passed, but to this day I can still vividly remember these books: *Steel, The Gadfly, The Story of Zoya and Shura, Notes from the Gallows*.... The first "foreign book" I had ever read was *Steel*. It was also the first book about love I had ever read; it touched my heart as no other book did.[160]

Mo Yan read *Steel* when he was a young boy in a village in Shandong. The love story of Pavel and Tonya, he wrote, "carried me away into a region of dreams as if I had become lovesick. Many years have passed, but I can still conjure up in my mind every detail of their story." Pavel was fishing, Tonya teased Pavel and annoyed him, and then apologized. "Like Pavel, I fell in love with Tonya at the moment when she apologized to him," Mo wrote. Was it a noble thing for a bourgeois girl to apologize to a poor working-class lad in rags? This was an age of class and class struggle, but in Mo's mind, "class barriers quietly fell" as he read. When he read the part in which Tonya "leaned ever so lightly against Pavel in a fleeting moment of sweet intimacy,"[161] Mo says "tears of happiness fell from the eyes of a silly country kid in Northeast Gaomi village [in Shandong]."[162]

For Mo Yan and his generation, emotions attached to fictional figures were an expression not of excessive sentimentality but the awakening of love. Memoirs about the deeply personal influence of Pavel and Tonya seem to have been primarily written by men, but women were no less interested in the story. Journalist Jing Fang (1968–) recalled that in her childhood, "Those heroic women [in party propaganda] with heavy eyebrows and loud voices make me feel respectful but I wanted to keep my distance from them." She started to like "bad women" in movies and children's books, who were always spies or "bourgeois girls." The most attractive woman in her world was *Steel*'s Tonya. "Tonya, either as a girl or as a young married woman ..., had such a graceful figure and beautiful face that it excited me and caused me to look up to her as a sort of goddess." Jing was ashamed about feeling this way, since a woman like Tonya should have been seen as a negative character in the party's teaching. Yet, despite her guilty conscience, Jing Fang remained, in her words, "secretly in love with Tonya" throughout her childhood.[163]

In his memoirs, Mao Yuyuan (1956–), a linguistics teacher, claimed that "in my life not only have I had a very strong 'Tonya complex,' but also I have had a 'Tonya' in real life, and I myself inappropriately played the role of 'Pavel.'" His first love affair, which resembled that of Pavel and Tonya's, was in 1972 when Mao Yuyuan, who came from a worker's family in Leshan, Sichuan, was a high school student. A classmate, the daughter of a PLA regimental command, fell in love with him and actively courted him, despite the gulf of their family backgrounds, much

The Power of Balzac 131

like Tonya chasing Pavel crossing the class divide in *Steel*. This might sound like no more than a romance of two high school sweethearts. But in a society where dating in college was banned and high school dating was scandalous, such a relationship required courage. According to the party dogma at the time, love and courtship should be take a back seat to the great cause of revolution. If not, the result was deemed bourgeois sentimentality or even decadence. Although Mao Yuyuan was also in love with the girl, his loyalty to the party complicated his feelings for his "Tonya." After much twisting and turning in their bittersweet relationship, the two broke up because of Yuyuan's sense of guilt over dating a girl while he should have devoted everything to the revolution.

Three decades later, Mao Yuyuan wrote a long memoir titled *Farewell Tonya* about this experience. In the memoir, he says: "She was a living example of a 'noble girl' (a Chinese Tonya) who always tries to retain and protect certain different things in the socialist revolutionary period; I was a 'brave fighter' (a Chinese Pavel) who always tries to deny and oppose nonconformities."[164] Mao admitted that the Pavel–Tonya story influenced his life more than he himself ever realized, and he regretted it. In an interview in 2011, he called *Steel* a "big poisonous weed," because it led young people to believe one should suppress romantic love for the revolutionary cause and imitate the behavior of fictional figures in real life.[165]

Overall, the young readers in those years were sympathetic to Tonya and, perhaps unconsciously, influenced by her character. They were disappointed or saddened that Pavel ended his relationship with her; at the same time, they started to appreciate the notion that she had her own free will. Tonya loved Pavel as "a person"' but once Pavel gave up "that person" (i.e., himself) to the revolution, her love was lost, and she would rather exercise her own will than bend it to "a person" who no longer existed.[166] Ostrovsky portrays Tonya as a bourgeois woman who eventually, in Pavel's words, was reduced to the "reek of camphor balls," but Chinese readers saw a streak of individualism in her character and admired it.[167]

No matter what character one chose to identify with, the impact of *Steel* on readers was enormous. Some psychologists have called this phenomenon "experience-taking": A situation where readers lose themselves inside the world of a fictional character and merge their own lives with those of the characters they read.[168] The Chinese Communists elevated early Soviet literature to a model for revolutionary spirit, "a moral example and manual of practice,"[169] but mortality and practicality did not always go in the direction that the party had designated. The story of Tonya is no more than a subplot of *Steel* intended to highlight the revolutionary spirit and class consciousness of the protagonist and, broadly, the Bolsheviks. Yet in the era of Maoist asceticism, it became an icon of youthful love and inculcated the dissident concept of individuality in the minds of millions of Chinese who read the book. In a society where the political authorities closely scrutinized individual lives, including what individuals read, the "experience-taking" in reading was a quiet but powerful force that molded thoughts and behavior that often diverged from party orthodox.

Reading and the Memories of a City

In a sense Balzac – if we can take the French author as an epitome of classic European writers who influenced readers in China during the Mao era – led an entire generation of young Chinese to wax nostalgic over a world in which they had never lived. Balzac's Paris seemed to fit particularly well the image of old Shanghai in the mind of these youths, even though the two cities were thousands of miles and more than a century apart.

The urban scene and architecture in Shanghai changed little in the second half of the twentieth century. For at least three decades after the Communist takeover, buildings and homes did not receive much care or maintenance; in their appearance, nearly all neighborhoods retained the atmosphere of the old city. The European-style buildings along the Bund still served as a kind of postcard symbol of the city. On the west side of the city, Avenue Joffe and Avenue Pétain were renamed but maintained their distinctive European character. The bronze bust of Pushkin at the heart of Shanghai's most elegant residential district stood until 1966 when the Red Guards pulled it down, leaving only a blank spot in a garden at a street intersection.[170] But all the stylish homes in the neighborhood, from those of Madame Sun Yat-sen and Madame Chiang Kai-shek to those of political bigshots, business tycoons, and gang bosses, remained untouched; only their occupants changed. Moreover, the city's alleyway houses – the half-breed terrace homes where the great majority of Shanghainese lived – housed more people than before and hence deteriorated faster, but their overall structure remained intact.

Shanghai in those years was like a city frozen in time. The buildings along the Bund, the emblem of city, remained virtually unchanged. In 1972 a US journalist noted that "the waterfront has changed remarkably little in its physical aspect since the days when the very name of the city became synonymous with shady dealing."[171] Streets remained much the same as they were in the pre-Liberation years, only their names were changed to eliminate the colonial imprint. Nearly all the city's streets, buildings, and other structures were built before 1949. For decades, they stood without adequate maintenance, subject to the ravages of rain and wind. Old street trees had grown taller and new ones were planted to shade bare sidewalks and back alleys, making China's largest metropolis a more walkable city.

Constant political campaigns and propaganda portrayed the city's past as decadent and wicked, but physically socialist Shanghai remained much like a poorly maintained living museum of old Shanghai, with touches and traces of every detail of the city's past. A Shanghainese who left the city in 1949 and returned in 1981 found that the alleyway where he used to live remained the same, only the buildings were now decrepit and crammed with more residents. He was even able to identify a crack on the pavement in the back alley where he used play marbles with the children in the neighborhood.[172] In another case, a resident who left Shanghai for the United States in 1947 and returned in late 1977 said that the city's streets and buildings seemed not to have changed much, for he had no problem at all in locating addresses: "Such a big city as Shanghai seemed to have been living under some malevolent spell over the past thirty years. The roads and streets were the same, the buildings were the same (except that these were older), and there were more people in all buildings."[173] It is therefore no surprise that visitors using a forty-year-old address could easily find the place they were looking for.[174] The physical stagnation of the city's streets and buildings was in sharp contrast to the great political and social changes during the same period (Figure 3.5).

Thus, before the building frenzy at the turn of the twentieth-first century that literally destroyed much of the old city, those who wished to indulge in sentimentality could give free rein to their nostalgia. In one case, a young man's obsession with old Shanghai led him to roam the city's old districts by bike on foggy winter nights. As the streets grew quiet and all the prewar buildings became clouded in mist – leaving the poorly maintained surfaces invisible but the skyline majestic – he imagined that these European-looking edifices were still in their heyday and that he was strolling through old Shanghai, which he had never personally experienced.[175]

It is ironic that most of those who were nostalgic about old Shanghai had little or no experience of it. As mentioned before, they were the first generation of children in socialist China, a cohort equivalent to the baby boom generation in postwar United States; in the Communist lexicon, they belonged to the generation "born in New China and raised under the Red flag."[176] All through school they had been told that they should be "Chairman Mao's good children" and become the "successors of the

Part II: The Liberated

Figure 3.5 At the center of Shanghai: The intersection of Nanjing Road and Tibet Road, ca. 1973. Western-style edifices built in the Republican era continue to dominate the skyline. Note the tall sentry box (*left*) from which a police officer manually controlled the traffic lights. But even here, in the city's busiest streets, automobiles were rare. Rickshaws had long been eliminated from the city since they were redolent of the old society, but pedicabs were plentiful. The tiny automobile on the left is a "turtle car," so called because of its size and shape. In the 1970s, such energy-saving vehicles were common. *Source:* Shanghai Municipal Archives.

Communist cause," yet by the time of the Cultural Revolution, when they were in their teens or early twenties, many of them were bored with what they had been taught and looked for an alternative. Reading the nineteenth-century European classics in the city's former foreign concessions seemed to be particularly suited to the mood of these youths. The imaginary bourgeois world of nineteenth-century Europe and the imaginary old "Paris of the Orient," as Republican-era Shanghai was dubbed, met flawlessly in the minds of Mao's teenagers.

Amid revolutionary posters and slogans, Wu Liang (1955–), who was a factory worker in 1971, cheerfully realized, "Balzac awakened me. Now I have been reminded that we had a totally different urban lifestyle right here in this city." With this new perspective, decades after old Shanghai had disappeared, he found that the material evidence of the old lifestyle still existed. The evidence was private and hidden away, burned in the streets, and discarded in trash bins. Still, in his home or in the homes of his classmates, he found objects of everyday life: Clothes, books, and photos of the past. "It was Balzac's eyes – sharp, caustic, even vulgar – that drove me to observe Shanghai," Wu said. He began to enjoy observing life in the city and gradually realized that Shanghai harbored many secrets: "They were inscribed in every brick of the walls, hidden behind every tightly closed window; they were inside the ruins of private gardens, cramped apartment buildings, grungy shantytowns, strictly guarded archives, and countless small attics and dark basements."[177]

Wu Liang recalled a little adventure he had in his youth after reading Balzac's short story "Gambara."[178] It was an early summer day in 1970, in an indolent afternoon, that Wu, who had then just turned fifteen, "found" an attractive woman in her thirties in a crowd of pedestrians on the streets of downtown Shanghai. He followed her block after block along Tibet Road toward the former French Concession, until she entered an alleyway-house neighborhood named People's Lane on Avenue Joffe, fantasizing that she was the baroness in the novel that he had just read.[179] Apparently the woman had noticed him, but she evidently concluded he was a harmless street urchin. In his fifties, Wu still remembered the occasion:

You would never imagine that nearly forty years later you could still clearly recall this tiny and absurd incident. It was seemingly unimportant, but yet, it was a weighty affair, as it connected you to an extremely turbulent and ruthless age and encapsulated a very private and warm memory: Balzac. A hundred and twenty years after his death, a short story he wrote was disseminated in Chinese in secluded Red China. On a random day of a turbulent age that differed entirely from the French Revolution, it affected a timid and sensitive youth. Balzac encouraged you, awakened you, regardless of how far apart these two countries were and how much they differed.[180]

The influence of Western literature on Wu was obvious. In 2016, he published a novel, *Sunglow*, based on his own experience living in Shanghai during the Cultural Revolution, and about a group of urban youth who came of age in the city at the time. Many of the characters in the novel have transliterated European names, such as Anna, Nora, Tirana, Tatiana, and Arnold; one of the protagonists is simply called Cousin Pons ("Le Cousin Pons," the protagonist of Balzac's eponymous novel). Although the backdrop of the story was Shanghai in the chaotic years of the Maoist revolution, some of the characters, as Wu put it, were "deeply sleeping in Balzac's novels."[181]

Sun Xiang (1957–), the only son of a working couple who were able to afford a more than comfortable lifestyle during the Mao years, wore an Omega watch worth 470 yuan when he was a teenage student at a three-year vocational school training medical personnel. After graduation he was assigned to a district hospital in Yangshupu in northeast Shanghai as a medical practitioner. The hospital was in an industrial working-class neighborhood but a number of his colleagues in the hospital came from the city's affluent residential areas where many still lived in old luxurious homes that had teakwood floors, cast iron bathtubs, and spacious rooms with wooden shutters on French doors leading to a balcony. In such surroundings, one might easily imagine "all the wonders of dreamlike old Shanghai."[182]

His like-minded colleagues had regular get-togethers as a reading group. They shared freshly made coffee from a teakettle and listened to elegant music played on a record player; sometimes Sun played the violin to entertain his friends. Exchanging "forbidden books" was something they all took an interest in. They all read, among others, *The Count of Monte Cristo, The Red and the Black,* and all the works of Ivan Turgenev translated into Chinese. Life in this homemade Arcadia was comfortable, enjoyable, and self-indulgent. Sun Xiang and his colleagues felt they were a cut above the average people in society, simply because – in their sense of superiority – they "owned the aroma of Shanghai coffee, the oomph of Maupassant's *Bel-Ami,* and the never-ending kaleidoscopic scene at the colonnade of an old balcony."[183]

Those who came from a "red" family background – the actual elite at the time – might not have shared this particular self-indulgence. After all, the goal of the revolution was to put an end to capitalism and bourgeois pleasures. Although the red families were the backbone of the regime, the children of the Communist elite were not immune to the influence of the bourgeoisie. Sun Peidong's studies on reading culture during the Cultural Revolution show that those who persisted in reading, including "illegitimate writings," and had the opportunity or privilege to do so were, first of all, children of Communist cadres and intellectuals.[184] In Shanghai, two prominent women writers of the Cultural Revolution generation, Wang Anyi and Chen Danyan (1958–), were both born into CCP cadres' families and were brought to Shanghai as children after their parents came to town, in a broad sense, as conquerors. Like most of the families of southbound cadres in the city after the Communist takeover (see Chapter 5), they too lived in affluent neighborhoods in the former French Concession. Growing up in a city tainted by Western-inspired bourgeois culture, the daughters of Communist cadres felt somewhat alienated and, as children of the new elite, looked down on the Babbittry of the city's petty urbanites. However, before long, this culture had overcome their "red pride." They became the most sentimental writers of the city's old culture and, at the turn of the twenty-first century when old Shanghai neighborhoods were ruthlessly razed to make way for skyscrapers, these authors established themselves as masters of "Shanghai nostalgia."

Wang Anyi was born in Nanjing and brought to Shanghai as a toddler by her parents, both of whom served in the PLA. She rose to fame in the 1980s primarily by writing about her generation of urban youth. Her award-winning novel, *The Song of Everlasting Sorrow*, published in 1995, depicts the third-place finisher in a 1946 Miss Shanghai beauty pageant who furtively clung to the glamour and lifestyle of old Shanghai until her tragic death in 1986.[185] Wang has been compared with writer Eileen Chang (Zhang Ailing, 1920–1995), who is regarded as "the author [who] best catches the feeling of old Shanghai."[186] However, unlike Chang, who was intimately acquainted with Republican-era Shanghai inasmuch as she spent the first thirty years of her life there, Wang and her generation of "Shanghai writers" can only draw faint images of old Shanghai based on fragments left in the city's avenues, alleyways, and slums. Wang, whose formal education was halted in 1966 when she had just graduated from elementary school, read extensively during the Cultural Revolution. The influence of classic European literature on her writing about the city is obvious. Wang acknowledged that in her "world of reading" there were two "huge mountains" (i.e., works from which one could constantly learn). One was *Les Misérables* and the other *War and Peace*.[187] In 1994 when Wang gave thirteen lectures on fiction writing at Fudan University, the foreign writers she selected to discuss were exclusively classic European writers, with only one exception, Colombian novelist Gabriel García Márquez (1927–2014).[188] As Xudong Zhang has pointed out, "Like her literary ancestors in early European and US realism (such as Honoré de Balzac, Charles Dickens, and Theodore Dreiser), Wang Anyi seeks to restore the city to human proportions, as she seeks to enter the soul of the city so as to dream its dreams and roam inside its unconscious."[189]

Chen Danyan also has sought to restore the city to human proportions. Born in Beijing, she was taken to Shanghai at age five in 1964 when her father, a CCP Yan'an veteran, was appointed the party boss of a Shanghai foreign trade corporation. Chen practically grew up in Cultural Revolution Shanghai.[190] But the horrors of the era did not affect her affection for the city: "I like Shanghai in the seventies. Then the city had experienced many vicissitudes, and because of this it was lovely. If I had lived in Shanghai in [its heyday in] the forties, I might not have liked it, because it was too arrogant and aggressive. I have always liked cities in decline. Such cities create emotions and sensitivities. In contrast to the glories of its past, there are many stories in its decline."[191]

One of the stories was the remarkable spread of Western literature among young people in one of China's most xenophobic ages. Chen's sentimentality is of course personal, perhaps derived from her middle-school years in the 1970s when her interest in literature began, which led her to a successful career in writing. Wang's and Chen's accomplishments in literature were exceptional for this age cohort, but many others of their generation were similarly inspired by literature. At the time when the sentiment fed by the Maoist ultra-left, "reading books is useless," was gaining ground, there were innumerable young booklovers whose spirit was nourished by the works of various "bourgeois intellectuals" – foreign and Chinese – all of whom were condemned. Readers' stubborn desire for the humanities in the most general sense was an unlikely yet true inheritance of Mao's China and one of the most telling stories of the concealed spirit of a city in its time of decline.

4   Alleyway Women's Detachments

Following its rise to power in 1949, the Chinese Communist Party identified "the core task of the party's work concerning women" as "mobilizing women to participate in socialist construction on all fronts."[1] Under the new regime, the overall trend of women joining the workforce meant that female employment rapidly increased. From 1949 to 1960, the number of nonagricultural and nondomestic women workers skyrocketed from 600,000 to over eight million.[2] By the 1980s, nine in ten ablebodied urban women were employed.[3]

A major boost to female employment occurred in the period 1958–1960 when the government launched multiple campaigns under the Great Leap Forward (GLF) banner. A major theme of the campaigns was "liberating women's labor power." In cities, women were organized into small neighborhood workshops for manufacturing, recycling, and other services. By April 1960, there were an estimated 3.75 to 4 million women employed in such workshops, in addition to the 8.25 million "regular" women workers and employees.[4] In other words, women workers in industry made up about a third of the nonagricultural female workers in the country.

Although a product of the GLF, the institution of neighborhood industry survived and prospered for decades after the GLF had failed. For most women, a position in a workshop was their very first job outside the home. Women who performed well assumed leadership positions and ended up practically running the workshops; indeed, the workshops came to be characterized as "a woman's army" (*niangzijun*).[5]

The GLF is seen as a major catastrophe, and justifiably so.[6] The famine that claimed tens of millions of lives during this period were without question a result of Mao's policy and even the CCP has acknowledged that the campaign was one of the key mistakes made by the party during the Mao era.[7] Yet, as far as women's employment is concerned, the GLF mobilized millions of women to take up work outside the home and established an irreversible trend of female employment in China's cities. There is unanimous agreement in China that it was the GLF, or simply "the year 1958," that gave rise to the new norm in urban China that practically all working-age women should work outside the home.[8] By the end of the Mao era, there were about twenty million women working in manufacturing, of which 8.48 million (or 42 percent) were employed in "collectives" that were largely developed from urban neighborhood industry.[9]

As the nation's largest city, Shanghai was at the forefront of China's neighborhood industry both in terms of the number of women who were employed and the way the industry operated. Between 1958 and 1960, the city had created 738,000 new jobs, of which 439,000, or about 60 percent, were performed by women.[10] By 1960, female employees in Shanghai numbered 665,000, a more than twelve-fold increase over 1952; of these, about 140,000, or more than a fifth of the city's total female employees, were working in neighborhood workshops.[11] These workplaces were operated by China's three-layer neighborhood organizations, which were introduced in the early 1950s. Shanghai was one of the first cities to establish this system. By the time the GLF was launched, neighborhood organizations had already become a fully functioning grassroots apparatus for governing the city's six million residents. Neighborhood organizations played a pivotal role in setting up neighborhood workshops, referred to as "alleyway production teams" (*lilong shengchanzu*; APTs), in the city's 11,000 alleyways. Over the following years, APTs became synonymous with urban neighborhood workshops throughout the country.[12]

As in the Soviet Union and East Europe, efforts to change the status of women in the PRC derived from ideological imperatives.[13] Based on the Marxist belief that women could not realize their productive potential unless they were freed from the drudgery of household labor, the party believed that women joining the workforce in "socialist construction" was a prerequisite for their liberation.[14] Behind this rhetoric, as we will see, was a sober calculation to employ women in low-paid jobs, with no fringe benefits, in order to supplement state-run industries. As Harriet Evans has pointed out, "The new communist government's policies on gender equality and female employment were fundamentally motivated by economic interests."[15] Unskilled women workers were regarded as a labor reservoir that was available in times of need but with no maintenance cost to the state.[16]

Nonetheless, the story of China's urban neighborhood workshops is not simply one of the exploitation of cheap labor. Women were not entirely passive in the process. They exploited the party's own slogans to legitimize their drive for financial independence, social status, and self-esteem. Yet, again, what was involved was not a simple dichotomy between exploitation and empowerment nor a confrontation between state and labor. Rather, the state and the workers had a shared common ground that made it possible to accommodate each other's interests. To be sure, in the Communist system the state remained the dominating force, but this did not preclude women workers at the grassroots level from actively pursuing their own interests. After all, APTs were not "typical" workplaces in state-owned industrial *danwei* (work units) that scholars have focused on,[17] but rather a novel institution of the GLF that turned out to be long-lasting and beneficial to both the state and the millions of women involved.

The Rise of Neighborhood Workshops

Neighborhood organizations were one of the major institutions established by the CCP after it took power. They were responsible for watching over every urban household and providing some community services. From the bottom up, the structure was (and still is) made up of three basic layers: Residents' small groups, residents' committees, and street offices.[18] As defined by the government, these were "self-governing mass organizations"; however, in reality they formed part of the party-state's top-down control mechanism, or the "roots of the state."[19] In the Communist partocracy, these committees constituted the lowest levels of urban administration, with each unit being a subdivision of an organ one step higher up in the bureaucracy. Staff members were appointed from above and were overseen by the CCP branch at each level.[20]

In less than a year after the CCP took control of the city in May 1949, Shanghai had started to set up neighborhood organizations in every part of the city. By the end of 1954, it had established 1,852 residents' committees, which supervised more than 36,000 residents' groups, staffed by 95,000 mostly unpaid women cadres.[21] During the GLF, these neighborhood organizations were responsible for setting up thousands of small manufacturing workshops and service facilities under the generic name "alleyway production teams" (Figure 4.1).[22]

In August 1958, Ma Wenrui (1912–2004), the PRC's minister of labor (1954–1966), called for "further liberating women's labor power," encouraging women, typically housewives between the ages of 25 and 45, to leave their traditional domestic duties in order to join "socialist construction" outside the home.[23] This call was met with great enthusiasm amid the frenzy of the GLF. Within days of Ma's announcement, Zhangjiazhai, a neighborhood in west Shanghai, founded the city's first ten APTs, which made toys, electrical devices such as lightning arresters, and clothing accessories.[24] In just a few months, 7,667 neighborhood

Figure 4.1 Downtown Shanghai at the intersection of Nanjing Road and Tibet Road prior to the Communist takeover in 1949. In the next half century, the city's architecture and landscape changed little. On the lower left is a typical alleyway-house neighborhood where APTs operated amid row upon row of homes. At the left top is the is the 24-story Park Hotel and, across the street from it, is the British racecourse. *Source:* Shanghai Yangpu District Library.

workshops were established and as many as 299,000 women were employed (Figure 4.2).[25]

Like many other things that emerged during the GLF, the mobilization and mass participation organized by the government involved not only widespread voluntarism but also excessive haste. The headlong rush to establish neighborhood workplaces reflected a herd mentality. According to the Shanghai Municipal Bureau of Statistics, at the end of 1959, 11,173 neighborhood workshops and service units had been established in the city. They employed 139,630 workers, nearly all of whom were women.[26] Another government survey of these "work units" (see Table 4.1) stated that in May 1960, Shanghai had 9,983 neighborhood workshops, which employed 278,000 women, or about 42 percent of the female employees in the city, a significantly higher figure than that mentioned earlier.[27] The discrepancy reflects the informal nature of the APTs in their nascent stage, as these workshops might come and go without entering the government's records.

Figure 4.2 A neighborhood sewing workshop in Zhangjiazhai, Jing'an district, Shanghai, December 4, 1958. The workshop is in a living room of a typical alleyway residence. Note that Mao's portrait is hanging on the wall, together with posters, slogans, and announcements. The colored paper streamers and paper flowers decorating the ceiling contributed to a celebratory atmosphere that was common during the GLF. All the sewing machines had been donated by residents in the neighborhood, and the workers had brought their own stools or chairs to work. *Source:* Xinhua News Agency; photo by Chen Meijuan, Xinhua News Agency reporter.

This dramatic trend did not last long. The GLF ended in disaster, including widespread famine in 1959–1961. To cope with this crisis, the government reduced investment in industry and called for a reduction in the urban population. Nationwide, tens of millions of urban-based employees were sent to rural and frontier areas. From 1961 to 1962, Shanghai laid off 312,000 employees of state-owned enterprises; 183,000 of them were sent to the countryside.[28] As a result, female employment in Shanghai experienced a major setback.[29] By the end of 1961, about half of the women who had been employed during the years of the GLF were laid off.[30]

Neighborhood workshops were not operated on the state budget, so presumably they would not have been affected by the cuts in state funding. However, these workshops had their own vulnerabilities. The downsizing of various industries meant that orders from state-run factories, which were essential to the existence of these workshops, were reduced. Given the informal nature of these work units, it was easy to shut them down. In March

Table 4.1 *Neighborhood organization-sponsored work units in Shanghai, December 1959*

Type	Number	
Production teams	4,600	Affiliated with 3,900 factories and produced 7,000–8,000 different products
Service points	3,274	Employed over 20,000 workers
Canteens	1,667	Had 400,000 registered patrons
Day-care centers	2,117	Enrolled 130,000 children under age 7
Elementary schools	643	Enrolled 150,000 first–sixth grade students, or 17% of the total elementary school enrolment in the city

Source: Survey conducted in March 1960 by the Shanghai Municipal Communist Youth League United Front Office. Zhonggong Shanghai shiwei dangshi yanjiushi, *Shanghai shehui zhuyi jianshe wushi nian*, 186.
Notes: According to what the government claimed to be "very incomplete statistics," in the year 1960 production teams produced, among other products, 29,740,000 toys, 1,700,000 umbrellas, 97,688,000 cartons, 6,826 straw hats, 3,400,000 woolen sweaters, 3,640,000 garments (other than woolen sweaters), and 5,680,000 scarves. SMA, B123-5-327-11.

1961, the number of Shanghai's neighborhood workshops fell to 7,572, with 242,983 workers. More than 6,700 were APTs, which employed 174,054 workers.[31] From late 1961 to the first half of 1962, neighborhood workshops underwent mergers, shutdowns, and reorganization. As a result, more than half of the workers "went back to the home kitchen."[32]

Yet, even after the widespread job cuts, more than 100,000 women still had jobs in the thousands of neighborhood workshops across Shanghai that survived the GLF. A number of the best-run APTs – 510 in total – were elevated to the category of "street factories" (*jiedao gongchang*). These were run, depending on their products, by various industrial bureaus that reported directly to the municipal government. These factories were known as "big collectives" and the level of compensation for their employees was second only to state-owned enterprises in China's industrial hierarchy. Employees received a monthly salary (rather than daily wages) as well as fringe benefits, including medical care and a pension.[33]

The remaining APTs (3,178 in total) were officially categorized as "small collectives." Their employees were paid daily wages, usually 0.60 yuan a day (later increased to 0.70 to 0.90 yuan), and received no fringe benefits except for an annual bonus of about 10 yuan which was distributed before the Chinese New Year.[34] In comparison, the average monthly pay for all employees in Shanghai in 1962 was 68.41 yuan.[35]

By the end of 1962, APTs employed 86,000 workers citywide.[36] In the following years, when the economy was recovering, the number of APT employees increased steadily. By 1965, APTs employed 127,000 workers, a 48 percent increase from 1962.[37] In fact, these neighborhood workshops became part of the government's solution for the unemployment problem. For instance, in July 1966 there were 53,000 unemployed youth in the city; 16,000 of them, mostly women, were assigned a job in neighborhood workshops.[38] In 1969, after the worst of the turmoil of the Cultural Revolution had subsided, APTs employed more than 190,000 workers. Over 80 percent of them were described as "toting shopping baskets, tending coal stoves, and taking care of the kids" before joining the workforce.[39] Overall, after the GLF, it became the norm for women to have a full-time job outside the home, and the decades following the GLF witnessed a remarkable shift toward the near universal employment of women in urban China.[40]

Types and Administration

Although all these workplaces went by the generic name of "alleyway production teams," they in fact varied widely in the products and services they provided as well as in their organization and role in production. Based on a citywide survey conducted at the end of 1965, the Shanghai municipal government listed twenty-one types of APTs, grouped into four categories. The categories included independent producers (5 percent), members of a production chain (67 percent), waste reclamation (12 percent), and services (16 percent).[41]

"Independent production" referred to workshops that produced their own merchandise, which consisted mostly of handicraft products such as various types of bamboo ware, embroidery, and wooden objects. These workshops were "independent" in the sense that they managed everything on their own, a working model known as *zichan zixiao*, or "production and marketing all by oneself." For instance, a workshop making bamboo ware was responsible for finding raw materials (i.e., bamboo) in the countryside, shipping it to the city, making the products and marketing them to retail stores. Many of these small workshops were in Nanshi district, the site of the old Chinese city and a center of family-run handicraft trades for centuries.[42] Needless to say, these APTs were not family-run businesses, although they bore some resemblance, and their "independence" reflected a certain level of flexibility permitted by the party's policy makers, who tended to acknowledge local conditions.[43]

The great majority of APTs formed one part of a larger production chain. These workshops took purchase orders from larger, state-run factories that outsourced parts and accessories for their products or else subcontracted the assembly of products. Commonly, APTs made or assembled items such as toys, clothing, pillowcases, scarves, shawls, embroidered apparel, shoe uppers, haberdashery (buttons, ribbons,

Table 4.2 *Types and sizes of APTs in Shanghai, 1965*

Type	Number of APTs	Number of employees
Clothing, shoes, and headgear	363	13,217
Knitting	64	2,408
Embroidery	88	4,214
Toys	132	8,186
Bamboo and wood products	71	2,601
Arts and crafts	16	256
Miscellaneous hardware	269	12,553
Cardboard boxes and paper bags	400	15,648
Stationery	23	938
Leather products	86	3,810
Plastic products	55	3,086
Glass products	11	461
Food processing	2	54
Gloves	137	4,392
Woolen sweaters	188	8,192
Cotton linters	69	2,535
Electronic parts	61	3,161
Blueprinting	3	45
Recycling	23	935
Waste processing	222	13,835
Services	477	19,144
Total	2,760	119,671

Source: SMA, B158-2-9-66.

zippers, etc.), cardboard boxes, brown bags, pins, safety pins, springs, stationery, school supplies, plastic products, and so on. Some workshops also helped larger factories make high-tech products such as radio parts, electric transformers, electricity meters, coils, and various tools (see Table 4.2).[44] The synergistic relations between APTs and state-run factories were crucial. The workshops soon became, as the government acknowledged, "an important force to supplement big industries and help many factories and enterprises to fulfill their production plans."[45] And, for APTs in this category, the purchase orders from big industries were essential for their survival.

"Waste reclamation" referred to the city's numerous waste recycling centers where residents could sell nearly all kinds of household waste for cash. Since China was still a poor country, every bit of *feipin* (scrap or waste material) delivered to recycling centers became source material for some type of industry.[46] Recyclable paper, such as books, newspapers, magazines, and wastepaper, were among the most common items sold, but there were many more. Worn-out shoes, rags, toothpaste tubes, broken light bulbs, fluorescent tubes, glass cullet, used electric wire, and

Table 4.3 *Waste reclamation depot rates, 1965–1979*

Item	Unit	Rate (in yuan)
Damp chicken feathers	*jin*	0.04
Damp duck feathers	*jin*	0.07
Pork bones	*jin*	0.01
Toothpaste tubes	tube	0.03
Newspapers (small)	*jin*	0.11
Newspapers (large)	*jin*	0.22
Books and magazines	*jin*	0.09
Used books	*jin*	0.24
Wastepaper	*jin*	0.02
Liquid medicine bottles (vials)	bottle	0.02
Scrap iron	*jin*	0.03
Ragged garments/rags/old cotton stuffing	*jin*	0.02
Broken glass (cullet)	*jin*	0.03
Worn-out shoes	*jin*	0.02
Orange peel (dried)	*jin*	0.10
Tortoise shells	piece	0.05
Plastic material	*jin*	0.34
Glass bottles	piece	0.09

Sources: Yang Lang, "Wo de jiesheng de waigong: wei ban'ge shiji qian de shimin shenghuo jianying"; Hu Weixing, "Laodizi feipin huishou ke jiejian"; I-12 and I-23.

used batteries were all recycled. In an age of scarcity, even food waste such as bones, chicken and duck gizzards (an ingredient used in Chinese medicine), and chicken and duck feathers were traded in. Human hair and nails were also traded in – barbershops routinely collected customers' hair to sell to the depots. A saying went that "there is no useless garbage, only misplaced resources."[47] By early 1960, there were 181 waste recycling centers in the city,[48] and, according to the Shanghai municipal government, by the early 1980s, the number reached 528. From 1957 to 1983, the Shanghai Waste Reclamation Company, the parent company of all recycling centers, purchased 23.62 million tons of waste materials with a total value of 4.83 billion yuan (about US$894 million).[49]

These depots were found in street-facing residential areas. The political slogans associated with these depots revolved around the notion that they would contribute to socialist construction by "repairing the old and recycling waste" and "turning waste into treasure."[50] Regardless, for residents it might have been a pleasant task to take a short walk to deliver scrap to a recycling center in return for cash. Although the sum paid was minimal (Table 4.3), people still found it worthwhile and in line with the traditional Chinese ethic that values frugality. Even well-off families did not casually put recyclables into the trash can. The writer Wang

Anyi once described a capitalist family that had a servant at home and could afford fresh milk every day (a sign of affluence), yet they had the maid keep every little piece of material that wrapped the top of the milk bottle – the cardboard lid, the paper cap, the string – and when a certain quantity had been accumulated, the family sold it to a recycling center. "The family's thinking was that milk and the maid were both needed for a quality life. On the other hand, scrap should not be wasted. Because [as the saying goes] 'the flesh of a mosquito is still a type of meat,' without accumulating savings however small, a high-quality life is impossible. This was the mentality in this city, which allowed its residents to live a leisurely and genteel life no matter what the circumstances."[51]

As for "services," neighborhood organizations ran day-care centers, canteens, manned telephone booths, and clinics, as well as what were called "service points" where people went to pay utility bills and get household goods repaired, clothes mended, laundry washed, and so on (Figure 4.3).

Figure 4.3 Manned public telephone booths, run by APTs as a public service, were on almost every block in the Mao era and into the 1980s. The attendant's job was to answer the phone, write down the caller's name and call-back number, and walk to the called party's home to notify him/her. For this, the called party was charged 3 cents. One could also make a phone call at the booth, as the man on the right is doing. This cost 4 cents. Since private telephones were virtually eliminated in the Mao era, these phone booths provided an indispensable service. *Source:* Shanghai Radio and Television Station.

Of these services, day-care centers were particularly important to women. China had a high birth rate of 2 percent in the early 1950s. Between 1950 and 1955, women on average bore more than six children. The next decade saw a slight decrease in fertility, to 5.61.[52] It was common in those days for mothers to have several small children at home. Neighborhood day-care centers were established, initially free of charge, to free women from child-care duties and encourage them go out to work.[53]

Each residents' committee had a clinic manned by one or two so-called barefoot doctors who were also on an APT payroll. These medical personnel typically received a few months of basic training in a district hospital and could treat minor illnesses, such as common colds, or minor abrasions. The barefoot doctor practice was first reported in suburban Shanghai in the mid-1960s; after 1968, it became a nationwide program, primarily in rural areas.[54] Periodically, the clinic gave vaccine shots to school children and residents for free as part of government drives. Clinic staff also made local house calls to administer prescription shots at a rate of 0.10 yuan per injection.[55]

The most important service launched during the GLF, and which continued throughout the Mao era, consisted of communal canteens. These public mess halls were run by the city's alleyway neighborhood organizations at a low cost. Mao regarded communal canteens a revolutionary step toward breaking with "bourgeois right" and challenging millennia-old customs and concepts. According to those close to Mao, he was long obsessed with the idea and overjoyed when it came to fruition.[56] Communal canteens widely appeared first in rural areas for free, but soon became a part of the "urban people's commune" campaign launched by the party in early 1960. By the end of 1960, in the urban districts of Shanghai (that is, exclusive of the city's ten suburban or rural counties; see Map 2), 7,266 communal canteens had opened, with 3,353,271 regularly registered patrons. This was 52.29 percent of the total population of Shanghai's urban districts (6,412,664). More than a third of these canteens (2,491) were run by neighborhood organizations. Regularly registered patrons (1,367,675) of neighborhood-run communal canteens accounted for over 40 percent of registered patrons of all the canteens in the city. The canteens employed 30,764 workers, nearly all of whom were women.[57] In the rural people's communes, public mess halls were proclaimed to be a "Communist utopia: all you can eat, three meals a day," but they did not last long.[58] In the city, public mess halls were not places for free food (patrons had to pay, see Table 4.4), but rather sites of women's liberation in the sense that they freed women from the family kitchen.

Table 4.4 *A typical alleyway communal canteen menu (prices in yuan), 1960s–1970s*

		Rice and Buns	
Steamed rice (500 grams)	0.14	Steamed bun (50 grams)	0.01
Bun with red bean paste	0.02	Bun with ground pork paste	0.03
Shandong-style bun	0.04	Rice porridge	0.02
	Beverages, Soups, and Noodles		
Sweet soybean milk	0.02	Noodle soup with green onions	0.04
"Love me" stewed noodles	0.06	Soybean soup	0.05
Fresh and salted pork with bamboo shoot soup	0.20		
		Vegetables	
Chinese greens	0.02	Stir-fried shredded bean curd	0.10
Stir-fried mixed vegetables and bean products	0.10	Various types of vegetable dishes	0.05 or below
	Meat, Eggs, and Fish		
Meatball with greens	0.15	Bighead carp braised in soy sauce with bean starch sheet	0.20
Stewed pork cubes in brown sauce	0.12 or 0.13	Small yellow croaker (two pieces served braised or steamed)	0.10
Large stewed pork loin in brown sauce with greens	0.15	Eight-treasure stir-fried in hot sauce	0.10
Braised pork chops with greens	0.20	Double-side fried egg	0.10
Thick soup of shepherd's purse with sliced pork and soft bean curd	0.10	Stewed trotters served in a crockpot	0.25
Boiled chicken with sesame oil and soy sauce	0.20	Various types of shredded meat dishes	0.10

Sources: I-6, I-13, and I-18; Xibo, *Shanghai wangshi*, 83; Yangchun san yue, *Jiyi zhong de shitang* (Canteens in memories), January 16, 2016, http://blog.sina.com.cn/s/blog_67c403500102vdxx.html.

Ironically, for the women who were hired to work in public mess halls, it was a matter of leaving the small home kitchen to work at a larger one "to serve the people."[59] These women brought their own recipes for all types for homemade dishes, which were not necessarily the sort of "downright bad food" that was commonly served in the mess halls of the rural communes (Table 4.4).[60]

The APTs came under the administration of two parallel structures. The street office had a management team that oversaw human resources and general day-to-day operations. Above it, the district's bureau of handicraft industries took care of purchasing and quality control. From 1973 onward, as part of the effort to carry out Mao's instruction to ensure "unified leadership" at all levels of administration, the street office party committee gradually took the leading role in all things related to APTs and was directly responsible to the district government. However, this change had little effect on the ground, where daily operations were run by a few team leaders appointed by the street office or the neighborhood committee. Virtually all of the team leaders were women and none of them were on the government payroll; they were, just like their co-workers, daily wage earners.[61] Few were party members, the most important emblem of social status in Mao's China. In fact, the party had a minimal presence in these workplaces. In 1969, at the high point of Maoism, less than 0.1 percent of APT employees were party members, the lowest proportion of membership among all types of urban work units in China.[62] The party's political neglect of APTs reflected its disregard for these women who worked on the bottom rung of urban employment.

Despite these administrative structures and their large number, the APTs cost the government virtually nothing. In 1968, a decade after the institution was established, the Shanghai municipal government undertook a general review of the workshops. In its report, it outlined four basic characteristics of APTs: APTs needed no investment from the state; they had no need for factory buildings or the kind of equipment that a regular factory would require; they were small, dispersed, and flexible in their operations; and they used spare or recycled materials to meet the needs of large factories. All of these characteristics were regarded as valuable, but the review made no reference to "liberating women's labor force," the rationale for creating these workplaces. Clearly, the government looked at the APTs from a self-serving perspective. While it was pleased with what the APTs had accomplished in the preceding decade, instead of rewarding them, it intended to keep them running as a place to exploit a subaltern workforce. The report concluded that "APTs are different from [state-run] factories and enterprises; they should not be detached from urban neighborhood organizations and take a so-called path to gradual elevation to become full-fledged work units."[63] This policy continued for the next ten years.

Meanwhile, these workshops had become not only a solution for unemployment but also a significant source of revenue for the government. Shanghai's toy industry, for instance, exported more than two-thirds of its output overseas, earning precious foreign exchange that China badly needed. Shanghai's APTs made up the great majority of the enterprises in the industry, and in 1965 alone, made a net profit of

US$5.2 million for the government through exports.[64] In 1972, the total annual output value of APTs reached over 140 million yuan, with more than 20 million yuan held in their collective reserve funds.[65] While the government assumed no financial responsibility for these enterprises, it raked in a handsome amount of taxes from them. Take, for example, Guangdong Street, a neighborhood in downtown Shanghai adjacent to Nanjing Road. The eleven workshops in the neighborhood employed 3,124 workers and, from January 1964 to September 1968, paid 939,700 yuan in taxes. This means that although China at the time did not have an individual income tax, on average each worker paid 300.80 yuan to the state, an amount that exceeded the average annual income of the workers.[66]

Professed Volunteerism

The Communist model of gender equality emphasizes the state at the expense of the individual.[67] In the beginning, the neighborhood workshops were established, at least purportedly, in the spirit of volunteerism and women's liberation in the great march to socialism. The premise regarding pay in these workplaces was "centralizing income, rationalizing distribution, promoting the Communist spirit, and the principle of distribution according to work."[68] Although having an income always helped (more on this later), at first most women were primarily motivated to join the workforce through government mobilization during the GLF. Among ordinary families in Shanghai in the 1950s, it was still customary for the wife to take on the role of homemaker; only about 17 percent of women were in paid employment.[69] The idea of working in a neighborhood workshop was not always welcomed by the women or their families.

Physically, all the workshops were located in residential neighborhoods, typically in a room or two on the ground floor of an alleyway house. These houses were usually two- to three-story Victorian/Edwardian terraced houses, introduced by the British in the late nineteenth century. About 80 percent of Shanghainese lived in such houses until the end of the twentieth century.[70] Since the houses shared a common wall, a few adjacent living rooms (typically around 20 square meters each) could be joined into one to create a workshop floor. Other rooms, such as kitchens and so-called pavilion rooms (a room above the kitchen originally designed as a study or guestroom), were also used for the same purpose.

These premises were mostly offered by residents, sometimes willingly, out of a sense of duty, but also because of the pressure to be seen as a good citizen of the socialist nation. People who had an extra room to spare would most likely have been families of former capitalists and well-paid professionals. They were mobilized to surrender their extra space to an APT at a time when the Socialist Nationalization Campaign had just ended. For them, contributing a room to a neighborhood organization was a way of showing their commitment to the socialist nation.

Sewing workshops may well exemplify the professed volunteerism in establishing APTs. At the beginning, residents brought basic furniture (chairs, stools, tables, etc.) and simple tools (e.g., scissors, rulers, tailor's chalk) from their homes to the workplace. These contributions often accounted for more than half of the primary equipment of the workshops.[71] Ma Liying, who joined a sewing workshop near Nanjing Road and worked there for decades, recalled her experience:

In 1958, Chairman Mao called for the liberation of women's labor. We all left home cheerfully, without hesitation. At that time, there was nothing to begin with, so we all voluntarily donated. This was called "starting an enterprise from scratch," with everyone contributing whatever they had. I had just bought a sewing machine for my home, but I donated it to the workshop. I wasn't alone in doing so; many people did the same thing. There was no need to persuade people to contribute.[72]

Treadle sewing machines were expensive (starting at around 150 yuan) but were in much demand, as sewing workshops were among the most common types of APTs. Other donations typically include a few old-fashioned square dining tables (known as a "table of the Eight [Taoist] Immortals" since it can seat eight people) and stools and chairs.

In the more affluent neighborhoods, the garages of private homes or apartment buildings were commonly turned over to APTs. Since private automobiles had been almost entirely eliminated from the city after 1949, most of these garages were unused; by removing the interior walls, they could be turned into sizable workshops. Various types of workshop sheds were also built at the entrances to alleyways, cul-de-sacs, or detached houses. These were meant for temporary use and were not authorized by the district's bureau of housing and real estate, which was responsible for issuing all title deeds in the area. Nevertheless, the legal status of these structures was uncertain since they were built by the neighborhood organization for APTs and often remained standing for decades. Frequently, the housing bureau accepted these buildings as they stood and would either provide a title deed retrospectively or else categorize the structures as "unauthorized constructions" but do nothing about it.[73] In addition, some of the air-raid shelters that were constructed in the early 1970s as part of China's preparations for a possible war with the "Soviet social imperialists" were used to house

APTs.[74] By the end of the Mao era in 1976, APTs in Shanghai had a total floor space of well over 8 million square feet and were dotted all over the city.[75] Nevertheless, since these workshops were all located away from the main streets among residential homes, casual visitors to the city rarely noticed them.

The Politics of Downsizing

The spirit of volunteerism and women's liberation that supposedly served as the foundation of the neighborhood workshop was fragile. Moral suasion, socialist devotion, and party propaganda during the GLF did boost morale and get the ball rolling, but ultimately it was pragmatism and utilitarian calculations of both the party cadres and the women workers on the ground that sustained the system. The politics involving the 1960–1961 downsizing and reorganization of the neighborhood workshops illustrates this point.

The reactions to the redundancies involved in this downsizing varied. Overall, workers complied with little resistance. Many women workers had not considered their job to be a serious form of employment to begin with and so being discharged was not particularly upsetting. Women in financially better-off families even felt relieved, since they had joined the workforce only because the government had called for it; now they could go back to a more relaxed lifestyle with their families and not worry about being seen by the authorities as politically backward or uncooperative.[76]

However, there was also a considerable amount of discontent and grumbling. Disgruntled employees confronted residents' committee cadres, some workers felt strongly that they had been mistreated, and some cadres charged that the upper-level party committee's decision was "after all, just for money."[77] One woman openly and frankly expressed her feelings to the neighborhood committee: "You mobilized us to go to work, you told us the factory wouldn't close, you said there was enough work for all us, and you said we shouldn't depend on our backstage boss [i.e., husband] for a living – why do you now ask us to return home?"[78] Some discharged workers went further by showing up at the workshop daily as if they had not been laid off, demanding to be paid out of the APTs' collective reserve fund, which was designated for emergencies. Such protests by women who desperately needed a job were understandable, yet the authorities were not sympathetic. The party wanted to limit the number of workers on the payroll and saw these complaints as an emerging demand among these workers for the government to take care of them. "The fact that some housewives who entered factories now should be dismissed but do not want to leave is in fact asking for the government to take care of them," one government report stated. "It is a demand that the state take care of the collectives and the collectives take care of the individual."[79] In the following years, the government frequently emphasized that APTs should remain under the administration of neighborhood organizations, that is, they should not in any way come under the government's budget.

Such an opportunistic approach to female labor contrasted sharply with the party's proclaimed principle of gender equality. This, however, should not come as a surprise. Just a few months before the launch of the GLF, with its huge demand for labor and consequent campaign to "liberate women's labor power," the party indeed recognized that housework is a type of "social work" and asked women to be content with being homemakers. In early 1958, top government officials publicly declared that "it is glorious [for women] to take care of household duties and hence the party's call for industriousness and thrift in managing one's household can be carried out by actual actions" and that "doing housework is a way to support one's husband and [adult] children in their workplaces, therefore it too is a contribution to the revolution."[80] On International Women's Day of that year, *People's Daily* carried an editorial suggesting that it would be more beneficial to the state if some women cadres retired and returned to taking care of their children so the government could avoid paying for childcare. It instructed the women that, "for the sake of the state, it would be better [for you] to resign and return home and attend to the housework."[81] Just four months later, however, Minister Ma totally changed the tone. In an article in *Laodong*, the Ministry of Labor's mouthpiece, he called for "further liberating women's labor power." This unleashed a frenzy of exhortations for women to work outside the home.[82] The swing of the pendulum seemed to be dramatic, but the forces at work in fact remained the same – that is, the party saw women as a reservoir of labor to be used at its convenience. China scholars have applied the concept of adaptive governance to explain the resilience of the regime after the Tiananmen crisis of 1989.[83] The CCP's adaptive governance, one may add, can also include rapid ideological fluctuations, justified by rationalizations in the vein of "Mussolini is always right" and an overweening sense of self-righteousness.

With regard to the layoffs, in determining who could stay – a decision left to street office and neighborhood committee cadres – women in their early thirties to early forties had priority. The rationale for favoring this age cohort was that older women "have a lot of household chores to do, they are physically weaker, get tired easily," and some of them had bound feet. "It would be bad," one internally circulated report claimed, "to let foreign visitors see women with bound feet working in a factory."

Younger women, on the other hand, were an unsettling force in the workshops, as they usually wanted to work for state-run or "big collective" factories; some of the more determined ones even wanted to apply for college.[84] In the minds of the cadres, a sort of culinary technique could, metaphorically, apply in this situation: Cutting off the two ends of a cucumber would leave the best part, the center.[85]

There were also detailed deliberations among cadres on the benefits of hiring middle-aged women. First, they were nearly all married and so had a husband with a regular job. Since the family did not necessarily depend on the wife's income to make ends meet, they were usually content with the meager income that came with workshop jobs. Second, married women tended to be stable. Most had a family to take care of and did not have any ambitions to move on to a state job. Third, these women were in good health and could do physically demanding

Figure 4.4 Moved by pedal power, date unknown, but similar scenes were seen in the Mao era as well as in the twenty-first century. A popular tricycle known as "yellow croaker car" is transporting a pile of used tires. The high-rise building in the background is the Broadway Mansions, a nineteen-floor art deco edifice that has been a primary symbol of Shanghai since its completion in 1934. Laundry hangs from a traffic light and a man carrying a ladder is riding a bicycle, another common way of transporting things around in the city. *Source:* Shanghai Radio and Television Station.

work, such as peddling a tricycle delivery cart known locally as "yellow croaker car" (the name came from the use of tricycles for shipping yellow croaker, a common fish in the lower Yangzi delta region), a popular way of moving goods in the city (Figure 4.4). This kind of work was often needed in neighborhood workshops, but older women were unable to do it and younger women were unwilling to do it. Finally, women in this age bracket typically had some schooling, which, it was argued, tended to make them fast learners.[86] Clearly, these cadres' calculations were hard-headed and differed little from the thinking of employers in a capitalist society; they had nothing to do with "women's liberation."

On Their Own Terms

Why, despite all the disadvantages, did hundreds of thousands of women in Shanghai (and millions of women elsewhere in urban China) work in neighborhood workshops? The simple answer is that since these women were poorly educated and largely unskilled (see Table 4.5), the job market did not offer them many choices. This explanation is by and large true but far from complete. Women had political and economic motives, as well as certain lifestyle concerns, for working in neighborhood workshops. In other words, when it came to the question of employment outside the home, these women were not entirely passive. Many worked in the same APT unit for years, seemingly content with their work life. There were several reasons for their satisfaction.

Politically, despite being at the bottom of China's urban employment hierarchy, women working for an APT had a work unit (*danwei*), which was "the locus of an individual's identity in urban China."[87] In such a milieu, APT workers were seen as occupying a level above housewives, as APTs provided a venue where housewives could be recognized as workers in a country that was ostensibly ruled by the working class. The sense of fulfillment and self-esteem that came with having a *danwei*, albeit the lowest one, played a role.

Economically, even though APT workers were at the lowest rung of the city's pay scale, the pay was sufficient to support the woman worker herself. Interviews with former APT workers conducted in 2011 found that working in neighborhood workshops definitely made them feel financially independent and provided a sense of satisfaction for being able to contribute to the household income. A woman who had worked as a childminder in a neighborhood day-care center recalled, more than half a century later, her excitement when she received her first month's pay packet of 10+ yuan, the very first pay

Table 4.5 *Level of education of 115,324 new women factory workers in Shanghai, 1958*

Level of education	No. of workers	%
Completely illiterate	31,781	27.56
Elementary school	66,568	57.73
Middle school	16,917	14.67
Two-year college	55	0.05

Source: Shanghai funü zhi bianzuan weiyuanhui, *Shanghai funü zhi*, 5:1:2.
Note: The level of education refers to the highest level of school that a worker attended but not necessarily completed.

she had ever received in her life. A woman worker in a garment workshop told of her feelings about her income: "It was fine if my husband had money, or my parents had money, but none of this counted when it came to me having my own money. Only when I was [financially] independent could I could really have my own status." Another woman was married to a seaman, a high-paid job at the time. On average, a sailor earned twice as much as a skilled worker and had other benefits.[88] Thus, financially speaking, this woman did not have to work outside the home, but she believed that "a woman who stays home and depends on her husband would not have political status." She joined a workshop that made shoe uppers. For her, "the 70- or 80-cent-a-day pay was the foundation of equality between men and women as well as the beginning for a husband and wife to be progressive together." Although her family was not at all under financial pressure, she often worked overtime in order to meet a goal she had set for herself: To earn 30 yuan a month. Later on, this hard work paid off when she was promoted to head of a street factory.[89]

Another attraction of APTs was that they offered women flexible working hours, an important consideration for women with small children and something that was not available in more regulated workplaces. When APTs were first set up in 1958, they had a somewhat unregulated schedule. As a former worker put it: "You brought a stool with you to the shop and started to work, and that was all there was to it."[90] Soon after, the work schedule was set at eight hours a day and six days a week, with daily work hours typically from 7:30 a.m. to 11:30 a.m. and 12:30 p.m. to 4:30 p.m., but a worker could take time off without pay largely anytime she wanted. The weekly day off could also be flexibly scheduled and did not necessarily have to be on Sunday.[91]

Some workshops had a piece-rate wage system, allowing workers to take assignments back home to finish. Thus, a woman could register in the workshop and have work assigned to her, but the whole family, typically children and the elderly in particular, could help with the work she took home. Safety pins, for example, were typically assembled at home (the clasp and the body of a pin was put together by hand for final permanent punching by a machine in a factory). Wages were based on the weight of the pins assembled. Assembling 500 grams of standard-sized safety pins (about 600 pieces) paid only 0.11 yuan.[92] But, since the assignments could be carried out at home, as long as the worker (or, rather, she and her family) could complete a good amount of work, the pay could still be significant. Another common take-home task was the joining together of machine-woven sweater pieces (i.e., bodies and sleeves). This practice of working in the home continued during the Cultural Revolution. In 1969, there were still about 40,000 such workers, known as "scattered households," in the city. Some earned as much as 60–70 yuan a month; in a few cases, their income exceeded 100 yuan a month. There were also reports of scattered households secretly delegating their quota to others and taking a commission.[93]

APT work required little skill and therefore there was no educational requirement or probationary period (most other jobs in Shanghai required a three-year apprenticeship). Jobs categorized by the government as work in the "handicraft industry" had a relatively light and physically less demanding workload in comparison to operating a machine or working on an assembly line in a regular factory, where the workers needed to keep up with the pace of the machine. There were also two breaks during the day. The morning one was for "radio broadcast exercises" – that is, exercises to music from the radio or, sometimes, a record player. The other break was in the afternoon for about fifteen minutes.[94] Most workplaces in the city had similar breaks, but the contiguity of the APT with the home apparently made the breaks more useful for workers.

Finally, these workshops were within walking distance or a short bicycle ride of home. Most APT employees rarely needed to walk more than a block or two to go to work; for many, the daily commute was just a matter of crossing the street or going to the other end of the alley. The short distance made it possible for most APT employees to return home to make lunch for their families during the hour-long lunch break and do a bit of shopping on the way, as most of the stores for daily necessities were within just a few blocks.[95] Some workers recalled that they lived so close to their workplace that they could run errands even during work hours. One might go back home to sign for a registered letter when the mailman came or, in the case of unexpected rain, take in laundry that was hanging on the line to dry.[96] A former APT worker recalled that she often spent the fifteen-minute break in the afternoon rushing back home to make a bowl of lotus root paste or some other light refreshment for her bedridden mother.[97]

Starting in 1973, APT employees who had worked for ten years or more were eligible for a retirement pension at the age of fifty-five, based on their years of service. For each year she had worked, an employee received a pension of 2 percent of her wages or salary, based on her pay rate in the year she retired. Retired workers also received near full coverage of their medical expenses. So, fifteen years after the APTs were founded, hundreds of thousands of workers finally received a benefit that was long overdue.[98]

The experience of a women worker, He Amao (1922–), reflects the "on my own terms" character that seemed to be common among APT workers. Amao was originally from Sichuan, where her father was killed in a Japanese air raid. With the help of her father-in-law, she got a job in a Shanghai cotton mill attending spindles, but soon the mill was destroyed in a Japanese air raid. To make a living, Amao and her husband worked as street peddlers on Middle Fujian Road, selling cotton cloth shoe vamps and homemade embroideries. During the GLF, the neighborhood committee recruited her to work in a newly founded workshop and made her a team leader. The workshop had grown quickly from three people to over 100. But Amao felt it was a bit too far from home and wanted to find a place nearby. She was offered a job in the neighborhood day-care center but declined it: at the time she was in her thirties but already had five daughters and two sons, which made her reluctant about taking care of small children as a job outside the home. Amao ended up working in the storehouse of a waste reclamation depot. One of the daily routines in the depot, as mentioned before, was transporting collected recycling materials to the storehouse by a yellow croaker tricycle. This was a chore the younger workers wanted to avoid, so Amao took the lead, making the round trip four times a day and using herself as a role model to prompt others to follow. She was proud that in her prime years she was able to transport about 1,100 pounds on a tricycle from Huaihai Road (Avenue Joffre) to the suburban town of Qibao, a distance of over 10 miles. After retiring from the station at age fifty-seven, Amao continued to work part time transporting goods by tricycle for a general store for another twenty years till she was seventy-eight. Years of riding probably contributed to Amao's longevity. In an interview in 2015 at the age of ninety-three, Amao, still hale and hearty, happily recalled her days pedaling a yellow croaker trike on Shanghai streets.[99]

"Liberating Women's Labor Power"

In reference to gender equality and women's role in society, Mao Zedong famously declared that "women hold up half the sky."[100] In the urban neighborhood workshops and services that were established during the GLF in the name of "liberating women's labor power for socialist construction," nearly all APT workers were female. In terms of sheer numbers, women in fact held up more than half the sky in these workplaces. These enterprises changed the traditional role of the woman as a homemaker. Despite the downsizing in 1960–1961, neighborhood workshops provided employment for hundreds of thousands of women for decades in the city of Shanghai alone.

Starting from 1973, these workshops and services became more than a workplace for women as they started to employ so-called sent-down educated youths who found a way – usually citing a medical reason or being the only child of the family – to return to the city and get their hukou status back after years of banishment in rural and frontier areas.[101] Since 1962 there had always been around 85,000 or more so-called social youth, mostly middle- and high-school graduates who, despite the authorities' call for youth to leave the cities and go "up to the mountains and down to the countryside," used the excuse that they had a medical problem to stay in the city, unemployed. About 70 percent of them were female.[102] These young people had been idle in the city for years and financially supported by their families; the government's solution was to assign them a job in APT, where they would earn 0.70 to 0.90 yuan a day. Although APTs therefore became more mixed in terms of gender and age, they still remained a workplace primarily for middle-aged women. As late as 1989, Shanghai's neighborhood workshops and factories still employed 157,000 workers – 72 percent of whom were women, with an average age of thirty-eight.[103]

Precisely because of the neighborhood workshops' low status in the employment hierarchy, it was relatively easy for job seekers to cross the threshold. In that regard, Mao's China differed from Stalin's Russia where industrial employment was almost exclusively a preserve of skilled workers. In the 1930s there were approximately one million unemployed in the Soviet Union, mostly unskilled women and teenagers, yet the labor exchanges were unable to meet 80 percent of factory managers' requests for labor. Stalin was well aware of the contradiction between persistent unemployment and the labor shortage, but refused to recognize that unskilled labor could be a reliable labor force, saying, "In any case, it is clear that these unemployed do not compose either a reserve or even a permanent army of unemployed for our industry."[104] The narrow definition of industrial labor derived from the regime's great emphasis on heavy industry. During the Soviet Union's first five-year plan, the government allocated as much as 78 percent of its investments to heavy industry.[105] Although the Soviets recognized both practically and politically that thousands of women labored in various branches of its industries, it held specific criteria for a "worker" in which the image was "the worker was not female."[106] While Mao's regime intended to imitate the Soviet model of industrial development and invested massively in heavy industry, the meager industrial foundation the regime inherited gave it little choice but to rely as well on light and handicraft industries, where women workers were indispensable.[107]

Although China could not indulge in a Stalinist refusal to acknowledge unskilled laborers (mostly women) as part of the working class, state-promoted employment for women was a shared experience in the Communist camp.[108] In her study of women workers in Eastern Europe, historian Susan Zimmermann has pointed out: "By comparison with many Western countries, under state socialism the inclusion of women into the world of paid employment was more advanced."[109] This was particularly evident in East Europe in the years parallel to the Mao era. In Poland, for instance, married women with children holding jobs outside the home in 1959 made up 30 percent of working-age women; in 1967, over 70 percent; and in 1970, 75 percent.[110] In East Germany, the state ended rationing, raised prices, increased the production of consumer goods, and lifted the lowest wages, all in order to mobilize married women's labor. As a result, the trend toward "double earning" (with both husband and wife in the labor force) increased after 1955 and jumped after 1958.[111] In Hungary, women's employment increased from 29 percent of all working-age women in 1949 to 44 percent in 1975; and by 1980 three out of four women between the age of fourteen and fifty-five were in paid employment.[112]

In China, APT workers were acknowledged as working-class people following the rationale that the monotonous repetitive work at the lower end of a production chain was suitable for women, and that the state could benefit significantly from their products and services. For policy makers at the grassroots level, women's liberation as a government dogma, or what scholars have called "socialist state feminism," had to be adapted to economic considerations and local conditions.[113] Ideological rhetoric asserted that entering neighborhood workshops entailed "women's liberation" and "working women are part of the proletariat," but ultimately in APTs' daily operations such proclamations faded into the background and became largely irrelevant.

Since the Communists largely denied social meaning to domestic work, for a woman who had never worked outside the home a job in a neighborhood factory signified a rise in social status. Thus, the institution of urban neighborhood workshops was an important landmark in labor history.[114] More importantly, because of women's employment in these workplaces during the GLF, women going out to work became expected, as something women were entitled to and the government was responsible for. As China scholars have noted, "one important legacy of the era of revolution is a residual sense of entitlement" that extends all across the country to people of diverse backgrounds.[115] A common saying regarding having a job in socialist China was that, at the end of the day, "The government has to find a way to give us a bowl of rice to eat" (*zhengfu zongyao gei kou fan chi ba*), and this included men and women alike.[116] This was not limited to Shanghai but was equally the case across China's cities, and continued into the post-Mao era.

The call for women's participation in paid labor in general and the introduction of neighborhood workshops under the banner of "women's liberation" in particular did not necessarily mean the authorities were genuinely concerned about women's rights or interests. As we have seen, officials were calculating both in initiating the institution and in reorganizing it. Even the official categorizing of various types of neighborhood workshops was designed to fit certain stereotypes. Chinese policy makers believed that some types of work were "more suited to women than to men because of the nature of their physique, degree of physical strength and physical characteristics."[117] The following policy statement referred to the division of labor in rural areas, but cadres in the city had the same mindset:

Physically, some people are strong while others are weak; some heavy manual farm jobs fit the stronger sex better. This is a division of labor based on the physiological features of both sexes, and is appropriate. We can't impose the same framework on female and male commune members alike in disregard of the former's physiological features and physical power. In some kinds of work, women are less capable than men but in others they are better.[118]

Communist Party cadres in Shanghai frequently expressed similar views regarding certain types of work they deemed fitting or unfitting for women. Purportedly, the differentiation was based on good intentions, that is, to take into consideration the physiology of women workers.[119]

Whether one agrees or disagrees with such an assessment, this kind of practical concern was the basis for organizing a huge throng of unskilled and poorly educated women into the handicraft sector of the economy that defined neighborhood workshops. For Chinese policy makers at the grassroots level, women's liberation as a government dogma, or what scholars have called "socialist state feminism," had to be adapted to board economic considerations and local conditions.[120] During the GLF, ideological rhetoric asserted that working for such neighborhood workshops entailed "women's liberation" and "working women as part of the proletariat" but, ultimately, such proclamations faded into the background and became largely irrelevant in the daily operation of these workplaces.

To the women who went to work in an APT, the new social status conferred by working outside the home was a motivation, but more practical factors such as the income (small but still meaningful), the easy commute to work, the flexible work schedule, the option of doing some of the work at home, the opportunities of manipulating the system to earn extra money, and so on, all figured in their deliberations over whether to work for an APT.[121] When the workshops were set up, no one could predict their future. In the end, not only did the institution survive but it thrived, greatly contributing to the near-universal employment of urban women in China and helping to foster a strong sense of job entitlement among them.[122]

There was an undercurrent of maneuvering and calculating during the GLF and its aftermath that was not readily visible but nonetheless was very powerful. In their analyses of state–labor relations in authoritarian states, scholars have developed the concept of "shades of authoritarianism" in which "a 'shade' is an ideal-type of manifestation of authoritarian governance exhibiting a distinct approach to state–labor relations that is nevertheless blurred at the edges."[123] To paraphrase, we may say that "liberating women's labor power" during the GLF was a shade of high socialism.[124] It was a distinct approach by the Maoist state to labor and gender issues, yet it had its blurred edges that allowed the state to wield the slogan in times of need and fade it out at will. Likewise, in times of need, women would use the slogan as a basis for political legitimacy to seek an occupation, gain status, and protect their lifestyle – in short, to pursue their own interests.

"Liberating women's labor power" has always been the CCP's proclaimed policy, and the GLF did not mark the beginning of such an effort. But, of all the political campaigns launched under Mao – and there were as many as fifty-five according to one account – the GLF was the only one that included a program specifically intended to emancipate women from their traditional role as homemaker so that they could work outside the home.[125] The GLF is regarded as an outrageously irrational campaign, yet a close look at the neighborhood workshops indicates that a certain rationality was alive and well. The APTs are an example of the "sense and sensibility" of both the party-state and grassroots society at a time of madness and chaos. The GLF "ended not with a bang but a whimper," but at least it left one positive bequest.[126] As far as the abiding effect of women's participation in workforce is concerned, liberating women's labor force during the Mao era turned out to be a win-win situation for both the state and society.

Part III

Under the French Parasol Trees

After Liberation, the Communists set about cleansing Shanghai in both the moral and physical senses. In just a few years, social vices notoriously associated with old Shanghai – drug addiction, gambling, prostitution, gangsterism, and so on – had disappeared. Tens of thousands of rickshaw pullers, "running like cattle and horses" (*niumazou*), and mendicants who rambled along the streets disappeared. A horrendous slum built along a fetid creek bed on the immediate outskirts south of the former French Concession was replaced by a tree-lined boulevard with a landscaped walkable median stretching for 3 kilometers. Another squalid shantytown near the railway station north of the former International Settlement was replaced by a "workers' new village," touted by the government as a glorious achievement. Aside from these showcase projects, mass campaigns orchestrated by the party for greening (most noticeably, adding parks and avenue trees) and "patriotic hygiene" lent the city a new and clean aspect.

However, the incessant political campaigns of the Mao era meant the economy was not a top priority, leaving the municipal government few resources for city planning and urban development. Shanghai's large edifices and residences that once had earned it the epithet of "an architectural museum of ten thousand nations" were poorly maintained for decades. Instead, as the population grew, they became overcrowded and were put to uses for which they were unsuited. As if a blessing in disguise, the underdevelopment helped ensure that the city's urban layout from its capitalist heyday remained more or less intact. The city thus became a strange mixture of the new and revolutionary and the old and bourgeois. In a way, the tree-lined boulevards together with ubiquitous political slogans – on posters, placards, banners, streamers, window displays, and so on – that adorned the imposing yet aging European edifices in the city symbolized this concoction.

For years the expression "French parasol-tree-lined streets" was not only a description of Shanghai's scenery but also a term that emblematized the city as a whole. Under these trees, the "Paris of the East," as

167

the city was dubbed in the Republican era, had become scruffy, but, in the midst of Maoist revolutionary paroxysms, life went on. Most importantly, the people of Shanghai did not always follow the will of an all-intrusive party-state. When and where they could, they followed their own individual paths, not necessarily with the intention of defying the party-state, but for the sake of survival and in search of comfort, whether that came from daily essentials such as food and clothing or simple pleasures such as tending a flowerpot on one's windowsill or cultivating a mini-parterre on a flat rooftop. Since private life was respected neither by the Communists' ideology nor practice, insisting on one's personal tastes and individuality amounted to contesting public space with the partocracy in the arena of everyday life.

5   Everyday Flora

Shanghai in the first three decades of Communist rule experienced so little urban development that its appearance remained largely unchanged from the pre-1949 era. There were a few public projects in the 1950s, most noticeably turning the site of old British racecourse into People's Square and People's Park, building the Sino-Soviet Friendship Hall (now the Shanghai Exhibition Center) on the site of the deserted Hardoon Garden, home of wealthy Jewish businessman Silas Aaron Hardoon (1851–1931), and improving the conditions in the worst shanty areas.[1] The revenue generated from the city's industry and commerce was mostly transmitted to the central government and was used to support "brother provinces and cities," causing Shanghai's infrastructure development to lag behind.[2] One visible achievement in terms of urban development under Mao was verdurization.

Verdurization (*lühua*) is a heavily loaded phrase in China. Like many other words in modern Chinese, it originated in Japan in the late nineteenth and early twentieth centuries, when Japan coined numerous words using *kanji* (Chinese characters) to convey new ideas and concepts derived from the West.[3] In the mind of progressive Chinese in the early twentieth century, verdurization was a sign of modernization and an essential step in nation-building.[4] Since then the country has been frequently torn apart by war and revolution, making the goal of greening the environment a remote luxury; but the concept and dream lived on.

Verdurization gained momentum in the 1950s when the newly established Communist regime, following the Soviet model, vigorously promoted a "garden landscapes" campaign as a part of so-called socialist construction.[5] Along with the campaign, *lühua* became very much an everyday term.[6] Tree planting and park building also became an important buttress of the state's claim to legitimacy and a mechanism for extending its control of public space. Verdurization was taken as a yardstick of Communism – widely proclaimed in Marxism as the ultimate goal of mankind. It became an emotive concept and relentless practice in Mao's China. The Chinese state used various verdurization campaigns as part of its project of building a socialist state and as a way of exercising ideological control, particularly in cities.

As part of its aspiration for a new society full of "socialist vigor," the PRC government sponsored numerous verdurization programs – planting roadside trees, building parks, renovating promenade gardens, creating public green spaces, and so on – from the 1950s through the 1970s to make China's cities, including Shanghai, "garden like."[7] Although the purpose of these programs was more political than ecological and many of them were not well planned or implemented, they did make Shanghai significantly greener.

On the other hand, ordinary people had their own ideas about the role of greenery in their daily lives – ideas that were often different from, and sometimes counter to, those of the state. The city's residents cared more about whatever foliage they could manage to have at home than the government's streets and parks program. Home gardening in the city was not just a matter of aesthetics and recreation but also a retreat from the harsh political reality of the Maoist revolution and, in some instances, a form of resistance to an all-pervasive state.

"Our Motherland Is a Flowering Garden"

Despite its reputation as China's most modern city, Shanghai in its heyday in the Republican era was a city with little public green space. Along the Bund and Nanjing Road, the area that served as an emblem of the city, there were hardly any trees or other greenery. In May 1949, when the Communists took over Shanghai, the entire city proper, an area of about 32 square miles, had only 18,600 street trees.[8] Public green space per capita in the city was just 0.16 square meters (0.19 square yards). There were 361 acres (1.46 million square meters) of private green space in the city, 2.2 times the public green space, but that space was very unevenly distributed: over 65 percent was in west Shanghai, mostly in private compounds in the city's affluent residential neighborhoods.[9]

The new regime promised the people a bright future and a just society and, as physical evidence of a "socialist paradise on earth," China would become a gigantic garden. In the words of a song composed in 1954,

> Our motherland is a flowering garden,
> Where the flowers are wonderfully bright-colored
> The warm and gentle sunlight shines upon us
> And every face has a broad smile.
> Wa-ha-ha and Wa-ha-ha,
> Every face has a broad smile.[10]

The song – the music was based on a Uyghur folk ditty while the lyrics are entirely in Mandarin Chinese – became one of the most popular children's melodies in China.[11] However, to turn China into a "garden" was not merely a fantasy in children's songs but a serious part of the government's strategic planning. In Shanghai, the municipal government had endeavored to add foliage to the city and the progress was impressive. Citywide, by the end of 1957, the municipal government had added 116,100 street trees to the city's urban districts.[12] By February 1958, the government had built twenty-eight parks and planted 120,000 street trees. In less than eight years following May 1949, public green space in the city had been increased by a factor of 5.8.[13]

Shanghai under socialism became a significantly greener city than it was before 1949. Huangpu district, the central part of the city, for example, in 1949 had 22,600 square meters of green space; by 1957, that had increased to 200,900 square meters, nearly a nine-fold expansion in eight years.[14] By the late 1950s, along four main streets in the downtown area – Yan'an Road, Tibet Road, Nanjing Road, and Jinling Road – 657 trees were planted. By 1963, every street in the district was tree-lined.[15]

The GLF of 1958 added momentum to the verdurization. One of the sub-campaigns of GLF was to "turn the earth into a garden." The CCP Central Committee passed a resolution late that year outlining a long-term plan to turn two-thirds of China's farmland into "garden landscapes" of trees, lawns, and lakes.[16] Such a plan sprang directly from Mao's mind. Before the resolution was adopted, in an extended CCP Politburo meeting in the seaside town of Beidaihe in August, Mao, explicitly linking the task of verdurization to the ultimate goal of building Communism:

We must make the mountains and rivers of our motherland entirely verdurous, reaching such a level that every place is landscaped as beautifully as a garden. The wild must be tamed. Trees must be planted well, to certain specifications, and not be planted without follow-up care. The spacing between rows of trees as well as the types of trees must be appropriately matched. Everywhere the landscape should look like a park. To achieve this means meeting the requirements of Communism.[17]

With Mao's call for "garden landscaping" or, more specifically, afforestation, almost immediately tree planting became a countrywide mass movement.[18] In Shanghai, the municipal government called for the planting of 155,000 trees, which exceeded the total number of trees planted in the city since 1949. However, the plan was immediately dwarfed by the number of tree plantings pledged by the "masses" during the GLF: an absurd target of 120 million. The slogan of the day was "every family

Table 5.1 *Public green space per capita in Shanghai, selected years of significance during the Mao era*

Year	Significance	Population	Public green space (square meters)	Per capita green space (square meters)
1949	PRC founded	4,189,400	662,000	0.16
1958	GLF launched	5,781,300	2,570,000	0.44
1965	Eve of the Cultural Revolution	6,430,700	3,721,800	0.58
1976	Death of Mao	5,519,100	2,573,800	0.47

Sources: Compiled from data in Shanghai tongzhi bianzuan weiyuanhui, *Shanghai tongzhi*, volume 3, chapter 1; Shanghai yuanlin zhi bianzuan weiyuanhui, *Shanghai yuanlin zhi*, 384.

should plant trees, every home should plant flowers, everyone should take care of plants, and every plant should survive." Drawing an analogy, the government promoted "using every bit of space, as long as a needle can be squeezed in, for greenery."[19]

There are no data on the actual results of the pledges, but given the irrationally inflated numbers reported all across the country during the campaign, one can rest assured that most of these pledges did not materialize. According to Shanghai municipal government data, from 1958 to 1962 the city planted 319,000 street trees, of which 119,000 survived, a rate of 37 percent.[20] The rate was not good; still, adding over 100,000 street trees in just about four years was an admirable accomplishment. Another survey found that by the end of 1962, Shanghai had more than 148,300 trees growing in green spaces that were affiliated with 6,850 work units; among them, 112,000 were sizable trees, with a trunk diameter over 13 centimeters.[21] At any rate, Shanghai in the early 1960s was a city significantly greener than it had been a decade earlier (see Table 5.1). Arthur W. Galston (1920–2008), a US botanist who visited China twice, in 1971 and 1972, keenly noted that on Shanghai streets, "trees are never far away."[22]

The most commonly planted street trees in Shanghai were London plane trees, or platanes, a type of hybrid that accounted for 87 percent of all street trees in Shanghai in the early 1950s.[23] Shanghai started to plant trees, mostly willows, along the Bund and Nanking Road in 1865 right after the Taiping Rebellion, which several times threatened the city. In 1887, the French Concession authorities spent 1,000 taels of silver to purchase plane trees from France, and the trees soon became very popular.[24] By 1902, the trees planted in upscale residential areas along

Avenue Joffre (present-day Huaihai Road) in the French Concession were almost exclusively plane trees. This French connection contributed to the tree's popular, albeit misleading, name, in Chinese, *Faguo wutong*, or "French parasol tree."[25] The name led people to think the tree was somehow European, and it became an enduring emblem of the Shanghai street-scene beloved by writers. For instance, Zhou Erfu starts his famous *Morning in Shanghai* simply by depicting street trees in the former French Concession in the early 1950s:

> Its tires hissing softly over the asphalt surface of the road, a little black Austin car was approaching in the distance. The avenue was lined with neatly-spaced plane trees, the lime-wash applied last winter already beginning to flake off the bottoms of their trunks, and their broad, rich-green leaves fluttering in the breeze. The avenue was almost deserted and not a sound disturbed its tranquil calm. From a clear, cloudless sky the afternoon sun threw the shadows of the plane trees on the roadway in a neat pattern. Passing over an intersecting avenue, the little Austin slackened its pace and came running across the shadows of the trees.[26]

To this day, the words "French-parasol-tree-lined streets" still conjure up nostalgia for old Shanghai.[27] The trees were also brought from Shanghai to Nanjing after the Nationalist government established the latter as China's national capital in 1928. Major thoroughfares in present-day Nanjing are still lined with them.[28]

However, in the anti-Western atmosphere of the late 1950s, the foreign origin of the plane tree was deemed politically incorrect. In Shanghai, there was an attempt to get rid of it in favor of the white poplar, which commonly grows in the Loess Plateau of northwest China and was regarded as not only an "authentic Chinese tree" but also a type of "revolutionary tree." This symbolism was promoted by the celebrated left-wing writer Mao Dun (1896–1981), whose essay "Eulogizing the White Poplar" (*Baiyang lizan*), written in 1941 right after the author visited Yan'an, the Communist heartland on the plateau, glorifies the tree as an icon of the spirit behind China's "national liberation." After the Communist victory, the essay was included in middle-school textbooks as a required reading, and hence was extremely influential. A well-known Shanghai writer, Ru Zhijuan (1925–1998), added to the imagery: She dedicated her first anthology to the tenth anniversary of the founding of the PRC and named it *The Tall White Poplars* (*Gaogao de baiyangshu*).[29] In late 1958, in some districts white poplars comprised 76.4 percent of newly planted street trees. By 1964, there were 45,600 white poplars on Shanghai's streets, or 48.69 percent of all the roadside trees in the city.[30]

However, it was soon found that white poplars cost more to maintain and provided relatively little shade. The trees also tended to attract a type of moth known as *cimaochong* ("bristle insects") whose bristles can float in the air and irritate human skin, something that children were particularly vulnerable to.[31] By the early 1970s, poplars were no longer the choice for street trees and London plane trees were once again the preferred type.[32] For instance, as part of the preparations for Richard Nixon's visit in February 1972, all the poplar trees on both sides of Shanyin Road (formerly Scott Road) were replaced by London plane trees to impress the visitors, although the street was far from the itinerary of Nixon's delegation.[33]

Overall, since the early 1970s the selections of street trees became more diverse. A survey in 1990 found there were twenty-nine main types of roadside trees in Shanghai. Among them, London plane trees remained the majority (60.8 percent), followed by camphorwood (camphor laurel) (15.4 percent) and others (23.8 percent), including southern magnolias, gingko trees, Chinese ash trees (*Fraxinus*), paulownias, and ailanthuses (tree of heaven).[34] In addition, a survey conducted in February 1982 found that 1,398 "ancient and precious trees" – of which 225 were over 300 years old – survived in the city.[35] By no means did the Communist regime turn Shanghai into a "garden," but it is undeniable that the city became noticeably greener under its rule.

Parks

Parallel with the tree planting projects, building parks was another important part of the socialist verdurization program. The Shanghai municipal government made significant progress on that front in just eight years: In May 1949, there were fourteen parks, covering about 163 acres (658,800 square meters) in total.[36] By 1958, the number of parks increased to fifty, and the total acreage to 568 (2.3 million square meters).[37]

Like tree planting, park building was highly political. In a city where for decades the main parks excluded the Chinese, opening parks to the public was palpable evidence of Mao's proclamation that "the Chinese people have stood up."[38] It was also a concrete measure for fulfilling the party's promise that "the people's government is for the people." The following description of three parks along the Bund and Nanjing Road provides a glimpse of park building that epitomized the party's use of parks to promote nationalism and socialism.[39]

Since its establishment in 1868 as "the Public Garden," Huangpu Park (also known as the Bund Garden before 1946) was embroiled in decades of controversy over its rule excluding "Chinese and dogs" from entering.[40] Originally a fallow beachhead of about 5 acres at the confluence of the Suzhou Creek and the Huangpu River, the park was the city's first "public garden" – as its original name indicates – albeit it was exclusively for use by Western expatriates. The Shanghai Municipal Council spent 10,224 taels of silver from both Chinese and foreign taxpayers for the project. Although the rule excluding "Chinese and dogs" was lifted in July 1928, in the decades that followed, the park continued to symbolize China's national humiliation. The Communist regime was keen to use the park to demonstrate that the party was at the vanguard in the struggle to protect and promote China's national interests. On June 9, 1949, just two weeks after the Communist takeover, the newly established city government cleaned out all the landmines that had been placed in the park by the Nationalist army during the civil war and opened the park to the public. Over the next thirty years, the appearance of the park changed little, except for the addition of a flood-prevention wall, a pavilion for viewing the river, and a 9-meter-high manmade hill with a waterfall and spray fountain. As a showcase for the city, the park had flowers in bloom in all seasons. A survey in 1986 found there were 3,546 trees of 111 species in the park. A 200-meter-long shelterbelt on the north divided the park from the Bund.[41]

Before 1949, if one walked from the Bund along the famous Nanking Road westward for a mile, one reached the British racecourse, later transformed into People's Park and People's Square. The project of turning the racecourse into a park at the center of the city was unquestionably the most significant urban reconstruction for public recreation after the Communist takeover. The British racecourse was established in 1850.[42] Over the ensuing century, it became home to Shanghai's largest casino and, in the minds of Chinese nationalists, was associated with vice brought by Westerners. The decision to turn the northern part of the racecourse into a park was made in September 1951 and construction started in June 1952.[43] In just four months, a 47-acre (188,500 square meter) park was built. By any measure, the park was impressive. It had 73,700 square meters of greenswards and 13,400 trees. There was a manmade river 1.2 kilometers long, 3 to 5 meters deep, and 12 meters wide, with a waterside pavilion and five stone and wooden bridges. In 1956, in the southwest part of the park through which the river passes, an area was designated for fishing; it often attracted hundreds of anglers. In 1958, a 13-meter-high hill occupying an area of 250 square meters was made at the southern end of the park. The hillsides were decorated with 1,500 plots of bright yellow and purple chrysanthemums dotted with a hundred plots of scarlet sage. The park also featured bamboo pavilions, corridors, and pergolas. From the central lawn of the park, a few famous buildings can be seen on the skyline: The Park Hotel, the Shanghai Library Tower, Grand Theater, the Pacific Hotel, and others, much like viewing Fifth Avenue high-rises from New York's Central Park (Figure 5.1).[44]

Strolling from the People's Park further westward along West Nanjing Road (formerly Bubbling Well Road) for 1.5 miles, one reached the small

Figure 5.1 People's Park, Shanghai. Photo taken from the Shanghai Municipal Library tower (originally the Shanghai Race Club tower built in 1933), ca. 1965. Many of the Shanghai's famous landmarks from the Republican era are visible in the background, including the Grand Theater (built 1928), Park Hotel (1934), Pacific Hotel (1926), the Sun (1936), Wing On (1918), and Broadway Mansions (1934). *Source:* Shanghai Municipal Library.

yet stylish Jing'an Park, which was built in the early 1950s based on the same nationalistic agenda as the Bund Park and the People's Park. The place was originally the Bubbling Well Cemetery, built for Europeans and US citizens by the Shanghai Municipal Council in 1898.[45] Western expatriates regarded it the "best cemetery" in Shanghai. Over the years, with few exceptions it was reserved for the richer segments of the foreign population.[46] By the time the Communists took over the city, the cemetery had been expanded to 8.3 acres (33,600 square meters). Although by then most foreigners had left the city, the cemetery still had 6,214 graves, of which 5,353 were occupied.[47] In 1954, with the approval of China's Ministry of Foreign Affairs, the Shanghai municipal government invested 180,000 yuan (about US$73,170) to remove most of the coffins and turn the cemetery into a park named after Jing'an Temple, a nineteenth-century Buddhist temple located just across the street. The

Figure 5.2 (a) *Top*, The marble pavilion inside the Bubbling Well Cemetery (*left*), built in 1898 for Shanghai's European and US expatriates, survived when the cemetery was reconstructed into Jing'an Park in 1954. (b) *Bottom*, It remains the only marble pavilion in Shanghai's parks. *Source:* Shanghai Municipal Library.

entrance of Jing'an Park featured a 100-meter-long 27-meter-wide trail with thirty-two London plane trees that had been planted when the cemetery was built. A huge oil painting of the same type of London plane trees was placed at the end of the trail; looking from the park entrance, it seamlessly extended the view of the tree-lined corridor.[48] On the western edge of the park stood an ancient gingko tree from the middle of the eighteenth century with a girth of 162 centimeters.[49] Numerous maidenhair trees, peonies, calyx canthus, southern magnolias, and fragrant osmanthuses made this 8-acre park into a sort of mini-resort. An ancient Greek-style milky-white marble pavilion, which was originally built as a resting place for cemetery visitors, survived and stood as a reminder of the park's European past (Figures 5.2a and 5.2b). That the former "foreigners' hill cemetery," as the place was dubbed by Shanghai locals, was turned into a park for "working people to relax" and was touted as a notable achievement of the new government.[50]

Except for a few years in the early 1950s when they were free, most parks charged an entrance fee of 2, 3, or 5 cents, depending on the size of the park.[51] Starting from July 1956, a monthly pass with unlimited entrance to all parks in the city was available for 50 cents.[52] Recall that the average monthly pay for all employees in Shanghai in 1962 was 68.41 yuan and remained roughly the same throughout Mao's time, which means that the monthly pass cost just about 0.07 percent of the average pay.[53] In 1963, a total of 312,500 monthly passes were sold and a third of park visitors in that year were monthly pass holders.[54] The cost of visiting parks was considerably lower than in the Republican era, when entrance fees typically were 20 cents, which was about the average wage of a factory day-laborer at the time.[55] At that time, park visiting thus was part of a middle-class lifestyle, and not a recreation available to the great mass of the population.[56] The affordability of park entrance fees in socialist Shanghai led to park visiting becoming a common and for many people a daily activity. The city's parks attracted close to a million visitors annually in the early 1960s; by 1990, the number exceeded three million.[57]

In a quiet residential neighborhood north of the old Hardoon Garden in Jing'an district, there were two mini-parks free to the public: Nanyang Park (0.92 acres), opened in 1922, exclusively for the children of Shanghai's expatriates, and Xikang Park (1.37 acres), opened in 1951. They were so tiny and located in out-of-the-way back streets that few people knew of their existence. However, precisely because they were little known, they became havens for those who did know. According to Cheng Naishan, whose home was just a block east of the parks, summer nights in the parks were particularly pleasant. In the lush growth of trees and grass, flickering fireflies danced in the air, distressing dating lovers who were whispering to one another in deep groves. Using pocket nets made of gauze, boys caught fireflies and put them in wide-mouthed glass jars that originally contained Bright brand powdered milk. In the dark of the night, the fireflies looked brighter than usual. "In our imagination, they were somehow connected to Cinderella's crystal shoes," Cheng reminisced. "My older brother once brought home a bottle of about fifteen to sixteen fireflies; it looked like he had picked stars from the sky and put them in a jar."[58]

Aside from their usual function as sites for recreation, Shanghai's parks (Figure 5.3) frequently held seasonal flower shows of various types and sizes. The chrysanthemum show, in particular, was a long tradition. Beginning as early as 1875, a chrysanthemum show had been held regularly in Shanghai's walled Chinese city in the middle of the ninth month in the lunar calendar (usually October).[59] Among Shanghai's Western expatriates, flower shows were customarily held in the Bund Garden.[60] During the Republican period, Shanghai's Chinese municipal government sponsored a number of chrysanthemum exhibitions and horticultural shows.[61]

The Communist government certainly wanted to carry on this tradition and turn it into a showcase for the claim, as mentioned before, that "the people's government is for the people." With government funding, Shanghai's first chrysanthemum show after Liberation (held on November 10–28, 1954, at People's Park) was spectacular. It had more than 60,000 flowerpots with 250 different types of chrysanthemums. Dozens of unusually large chrysanthemums called *daliju*, or "great standing chrysanthemums," were the jewel of the show: One of them had 217 flowers, each about the size of a rice bowl, blooming from a single stem.[62]

To celebrate the tenth anniversary of the founding of People's Republic, a two-week event called a Hundred Flowers exhibition was held in October 1959 in Xijiao Park, a former British golf course of about 70 acres in a western suburb.[63] There were nearly 200 different species of flowers in bud or in bloom, including more than fifty that were blooming out of season. In simply equipped nurseries, the botanical gardeners took painstaking efforts to create this unseasonal blooming, and they succeeded remarkably well. Plants that typically do not bloom in late September and early October, such as the pear (which naturally blooms in early spring), peonies (in mid-spring), and the red plum and wintersweets (in deep winter) all bloomed around National Day (October 1). These experiments were considered not merely scientifically successful but also politically important since they added to the imposing celebration of the tenth anniversary. The exhibition lasted two weeks and attracted some 300,000 visitors.[64] And in November, immediately after the show, a huge chrysanthemum exhibition was held in People's Park.[65]

Figure 5.3 Paintings of parks in Shanghai during the Cultural Revolution by Zhang Nianchi (1942–). (a) *Top*, teahouse in the Fuxing Park (formerly, the French Park), with its grape trellis and surrounding parasol trees, was a popular place for relaxation in summer (painting date: July 1972); (b) *Bottom*, sunset on a summer day in People's Park, with people enjoying the cool shade of the trees (painting date: June 1972). *Source:* Courtesy of the artist, Zhang Nianchi.

Table 5.2 *Major chrysanthemum exhibitions in Shanghai's parks, 1954–1977*

Date	Venue	Size	No. of Visitors
Nov. 10–28, 1954	People's Park	400 types in 60,000 pots	600,000
Oct. 1–15, 1959	Xijiao Park	Over 190 types	300,000
Nov. 1959	People's Park	800 types	n/a
Nov. 2–24, 1973	Fuxing Park	400 types in 30,000 pots	1,030,000
Nov. 1974	Zhongshan Park	40,000 pots	1,000,000
Nov. 6–30, 1975	Hongkou Park	700 types in 80,000 pots	1,500,000
Nov. 1976	Fuxing Park	n/a	670,000
Nov. 5–29, 1977	Fuxing Park	500 types	400,000

Sources: Compiled based on data in Shanghai yuanlin zhi bianzuan weiyuanhui, *Shanghai yuanlin zhi*, 360–4.
Notes:
All numbers have been rounded.
The October 1959 exhibition in Xijiao Park, entitled "A Hundred Flowers Bloom," was dedicated to the celebration of the tenth anniversary of the founding of the People's Republic, and included over fifty types of plants that usually do not blossom in autumn.
The 1976 exhibit at Fuxing Park was a combination of "A Hundred Flowers Bloom" and a chrysanthemum exhibition in celebration of the downfall of the Gang of Four.
All the exhibitions were organized and sponsored by the Shanghai Municipal Park Management Office. Flower exhibitions in district parks are not included.

Flower shows were suspended in the early years of the Cultural Revolution, only to reappear on an even larger scale after Nixon's visit in 1972.[66] For almost the entire month of November 1973 there was a chrysanthemum show at Fuxin Park, Shanghai's "French Park" of about 18 acres in the former French Concession. Choosing this venue symbolized openness to the West. More than 30,000 chrysanthemums were on display, making the show an extremely popular event in the autumn of that year. Daily visitors averaged more than 44,000 and by the end of the show, about 1.3 million people – nearly all were residents of Shanghai – had visited the exhibition. The population of the urban districts of Shanghai in the early 1970s was around 5.5 million, which means about a quarter of the population visited the exhibition.[67] Such large chrysanthemum shows continued to be held every year in various parks in the city in the remaining years of the Mao era, each attracting about one million visitors (Table 5.2).

Home Gardening

Neither the amount of public green space per capita nor the greenery in Shanghai's parks adequately reflected the full picture of foliage in the city. What official statistics ignored, but was important to the verdurization of the city, was greenery at home. For Shanghai's residents, a few ceramic pots of flowers and plants in a tiny space at home constituted a garden much more relevant to their daily life than street trees and city parks.

In comparison with the usual urban jungle of a modern metropolis, Shanghai in much of the twentieth century had fewer tall buildings and the great majority of the residents lived in two- or three-story terraced alleyway houses.[68] There were typically three places where flowers could be raised outside such buildings: A front dooryard leading to the living room on the first floor, a balcony connecting the second-floor bedroom overlooking the dooryard, and a flat roof at the back of the third floor.[69] The dooryard and balcony were designed for outdoor activities a step away from the rooms, and the flat roof was primarily for drying the laundry. Although none of these places was big enough for a garden in the usual sense, to Shanghainese, they were spaces for creating a mini-Eden. As the city became increasingly crowded in the twentieth century, even the windowsill of an attic room could be used for a box garden (Figure 5.4b). Balzac once jeered at Parisians' appreciation of a little urban greenery, saying that only the "Paris townsfolk, who, emerging from the stony abyss in which they are buried, would find something to admire in the flats of La Beauce [an agricultural region near Paris]."[70] The Shanghainese' appreciation of a little greenery at home came from urbanites' craving for nature, something shared by residents of other large cities such as Paris or New York, but in Shanghai it had its own cultural roots and, moreover, political implications (see later and Figure 5.4a).

Contrary to the common image of the Taoist-like recluse living in the remote countryside or deep in the mountains, far from human contact, an age-old Chinese maxim has it that "the great hermit seeks retreat in the marketplace."[71] Here the "marketplace" (*shi*) refers to any busy urban setting, and the idea is that in such a place an individual life would be easily submerged or go unnoticed – exactly what the hermit wants. More philosophically, the saying implies that the hubbub of a bustling city should not affect one's ability to find inner peace, and only those who live in the midst of urban dissipation while resisting its temptations are true hermits. Cities from this perspective were an ideal place to seek asylum from adversity – not in the sense of street people surviving on the curbside, but in the traditional Taoist sense of rising above reality, especially in times of political repression.[72]

A tangible if simple way of seeking peace of mind in the city was through bonsai-type gardening in one's residence. As is commonly

Everyday Flora 183

Figure 5.4 Gouache paintings by Zhang Nianchi (1942–). (a) *Left*, *Poinsettias* (painted January 1, 1976), flowers known in China as "Christmas red" (*Shengdan hong*). The artist's note reads: "My wife and I immensely love Christmas flowers. We have bought such flowers every year to celebrate the New Year, placing our hope in the coming new year." Note that the painting was executed on New Year's Day of 1976, the last year of the Mao era – the artist's hope is self-explanatory. (b) *Right*, *A Windowsill Garden* (painted March 19, 1979). An unpublished note the artist wrote about the painting reads: "During the Cultural Revolution, even planting flowers was considered bourgeois and therefore anathema. Thus, in Zhongnanhai, flowers were pulled up so vegetables could be planted. Nevertheless, I still planted a lot of flowers on my windowsill. Look, they are full of life." *Source:* Courtesy of the artist.

known, in Beijing's courtyard houses (*siheyuan*, or quadrangles) three items formed the classic scene in the courtyard: A pergola, a fish tank, and a pomegranate bonsai.[73] The yard of an alleyway house was substantially smaller, but the flavor and style were similar. Indeed, the Beijing style was said to have been brought by southerners from the lower Yangzi delta region, in which Shanghai was by far the biggest and most important city.[74]

The front dooryard of an alleyway house was usually walled and known as a "sky well" – viewed from the bedroom on the second floor, the square or rectangular patio does look like a well.[75] The size of the sky well varied, but most were around 10 square meters. They were designed as an open-air space immediately outside the living room for outdoor activities – typically, gardening. A Shanghai resident who left the city for San Francisco in 1981 recalled a common use of alleyway house front yards:

> Walking in through the gate is a tiny dooryard where a leisure-minded household would have a ceramic tank for raising goldfish and a few potted plants. In a corner of the yard, there might be a begonia. Although there wasn't enough sunlight for the plant, it still blossomed every year. The flowers didn't last long; they dropped in the rain and wind, leaving plenty of petals on the ground, and making the viewer a bit sentimental.[76]

Such sentimentality was common. In another case, Ye Shengtao (1894–1988), a prominent educator and publisher, extensively planted around his Shanghai alleyway home and even hired workers to break up the pavement in his front dooryard for gardening, leaving only a strip for access to the house. The patio thus became a mini-garden with wisteria, wild rose, peony, and calyx canthus; in Ye's own words, he had created a small world to let the plants compete according to the Darwinist principle of "survival of the fittest."[77]

Mao's Politicization of Flower Planting

The common and simple pleasure of having a little flowerbed in one's dooryard was ludicrously politicized in the pan-politicization age of Mao, especially after the mid-1960s when the dogma of class struggle regained its grip over Chinese politics after a few years of respite in the wake of the Great Leap famine. As mentioned earlier, in the 1950s the government promoted tree and flower planting as part of its "turning the earth into a garden" campaign. At the height of the campaign in 1958 gardening was encouraged as a way of "making our motherland a socialist great garden." In praising the enthusiasm of the masses for the campaign, *People's Daily* mentioned particularly that in densely populated central Shanghai, where there was little space for outdoor plants, people "have started to plant flora along streets and alleys and grow all kinds of potted flowers, climbing plants, and the like on their balconies and flat roofs."[78] The newspaper also reported that in Shanghai's working-class neighborhood of Zhabei, where the Japanese devastating bombing in 1932 and 1937 created notorious shantytowns, "residents tilled all the land that was deeply damaged by the gunfire of the Japanese imperialistic aggressors. In the shanty areas, working people are filling up stinking creeks and, atop them, planting beautiful flowers."[79]

However, Mao's vision of "garden landscaping," as indicated earlier, was essentially a dream of afforestation rather than flower planning. If there was an aesthetic component of his vision, it would be a uniform landscape under socialist state planning, as James Scott put it, "a perfectly legible forest planted with same-aged, single-species, uniform trees growing in straight lines in a rectangular flat space cleared of all underbrush."[80] The failure of the GLF along with the Great Leap famine of 1959–1961, led to another type of Maoist extremism. Flower planting, in particular at private homes, was criticized as bourgeois, and Mao personally endorsed such criticism. In July 1964, in a conversation about gardening with the head of his bodyguard detail, Wang Dongxing (1916–2015), Mao explicitly expressed his aversion to potted flowers:

Displaying potted flowers is the stuff of the old society. It is the pastime of the feudal gentry class and pampered sons of the bourgeoisie who [characteristically] hold a caged bird in their hands. Only those who stuff themselves with food but have nothing else to do would plant and display flowers. The country has been liberated for years, but the number of people who plant flowers has not been decreasing; instead, it is increasing. We must change this situation. I for one do not like to have potted flowers in my room—there might be some benefit in having them during the day but they are harmful at night. On my order, the flowers in my house were removed long ago. After that, I also asked them to remove the flowers in the yard.... All the nurseries ought to be eliminated and most of the gardeners should be laid off, leaving just a few to take care of the courtyards.[81]

Mao's remark was in reference to Zhongnanhai, the 100-hectare (247-acre) compound in central Beijing where China's top leaders lived and their offices were located. It may have seemed unusual for Mao to issue instructions on an ostensibly trivial matter such as potted flowers, but clearly, it was not a random comment. Among top leaders who lived in Zhongnanhai, two were known for loving flowers: Marshal Zhu De (1886–1996) and Premier Zhou Enlai. Zhou was fond of crabapple blossoms and had many crabapple trees in the courtyard of his Zhongnanhai residence known as the West Hall of Flowers (Xihuating). These were considered fruit trees, which may explain why they survived Mao's dictate.[82] But Zhu was not so lucky.

A principal founder of the Red Army and for years its commander-in-chief, Zhu played only a secondary role in the party leadership after 1949. For well over a decade following the Communist victory, he indulged in planting orchids at his residence and in the nursery of Zhongnanhai. He was very knowledgeable about the plant and often compared notes with orchid gardeners in Beijing and elsewhere. The orchid, one of the "four gentlemen" plants in the Chinese literati and art traditions, symbolized a specific virtue: Its elegant appearance emblematized aloofness from politics and material pursuits. Probably because it is often found in deserted shady valleys, in Chinese culture the orchid represents the gentleman who remains refined and upright no matter what the temptation. Moreover, the orchid is said "to enjoy its own lonely charm."[83] As a result of this reputed connection with the Chinese gentry, the CCP disdained those who were attracted to the flower as "feudal" or "bourgeois." Zhu no doubt was aware of this danger and hence justified orchid planting by its economic value, that is, the flowers were in demand in Southeast Asia and Japan, and exporting orchids overseas could earn precious foreign currency for China's socialist construction. Zhu also believed that orchids could "enrich working people's cultural lives." Thus, he often gave orchids as gifts to parks and nurseries across the country for public exhibition.

However, despite Zhu's careful defense of orchid planting, given his status in the party, politics was inevitably involved in this seemingly harmless hobby. Soon after Mao's comments on flowers, Zhu had to give up all the orchids in his courtyard and at the nursery – about 6,000 orchids of 400 different types – to Beijing's Zhongshan Park. Zhu's docile surrender was praised as evidence of his strong "party spirit" (*dangxing*), but the Communist veteran was not happy. Reportedly, as Zhu watched his favorite flowers being moved out of Zhongnanhai he muttered, "Orchids are not bourgeois."[84]

If Mao did not specifically mention the names of any individual leaders in his comments on flowers, in 1966, two years after Mao's criticism of people who kept potted plants, it could not be clearer that Zhu's orchids were part of the "situation" in Mao's mind that needed to be changed. In an expanded CCP political bureau meeting in Beijing on May 23, 1966, Zhu, Mao's lifetime collaborator in revolution, was accused of opposing Mao's leadership. As evidence, it was claimed that Zhu had once said, referring his orchid hobby, that in China's history, a politically frustrated person often found solace by planting orchids.[85]

Mao's instruction had its targeted audience. For that reason, it was circulated internally within the party and was not publicized until late 1966, when the Red Guards published it in their newspapers, accusing the leaders of Beijing's Department of Agriculture and Forestry of blocking a "supreme instruction of the great leader Chairman Mao."[86] Nevertheless, even without official publication of Mao's speech, his accusation that planting flowers was "bourgeois" was widely known and taken seriously. One author recalled that after Mao's remark, "thousands of potted flowers were put on the sidewalks," apparently abandoned by people who were afraid of the consequences of keeping flowers.[87] The writer Jung Chang (1952–) described how Mao's words affected her life in Chengdu, the capital of Sichuan province in southwest China:

In 1964, Mao had denounced cultivating flowers and grass as "feudal" and "bourgeois," and ordered, "Get rid of most gardeners." As a child, I had had to join others in removing the grass from the lawns at our school, and had seen flowerpots disappear from buildings. I had felt intensely sad, and had not only struggled to hide my feelings, but also blamed myself for having instincts that went against Mao's instructions, a mental activity I had been brainwashed to engage in like other children in China.[88]

Also in Chengdu, journalist Li Chengpeng (1968–) recalled a similar experience in his childhood. Li and his parents lived in a courtyard house that was the home of Li's extended family. There were Nationalists and Communists in the family, but the different political affiliations did not prevent them from living in peace together for decades, including in the most difficult time during the War of Resistance against Japan (1937–1945). However, after the Communist takeover the little clan was divided by a seemingly trivial matter: How to use the courtyard. "Those who liked to plant flowers in the yard were seen as bourgeois, while those who proposed using the space for storage of scrap iron and copper [for the GLF] were regarded as revolutionaries." The divide lingered for years and eventually turned to a bitter political fight within the family during the Cultural Revolution, replete with struggle meetings where family members condemned each other over potted flowers.[89] It all sounds mad. Years later, even those who experienced the time firsthand called it absurd and surreal. An author who wrote for *People's Daily* exclaimed: "Now when we talk about the politics related to flowers and plants at the time, we cannot help but laugh about it. Nevertheless, it was indeed what we had once experienced!"[90]

Back Alleys in Color

Yet there were deviations and variations that were not readily noticeable in the widespread absurdity of Mao's China. Unlike in Beijing, Chengdu, or other inland cities, in Shanghai flower planting continued to thrive even when it was criticized as bourgeois. It seems that people were aware of the danger involved, but few took it seriously. Besides, despite its ups and downs, the call for *lühua* initiated in the 1950s remained valid throughout the Mao era, giving people two kinds of political correctness concerning flower planting to consider: To condemn it as bourgeois or to justify it as an act of verdurization. In Shanghai at least, the latter prevailed.

On November 2, 1956, during the Socialist Nationalization Campaign, the Shanghai Flowers and Plants Company was founded as a municipal organ in charge of parks and greening-related businesses in the city. Under its administration, on October 1, 1959, a large store, the Shanghai Flower and Bird Store, was open on West Nanjing Road in the center of the city. It occupied sixteen storefronts in the city's busiest commercial district; no store in Shanghai had ever occupied such a long strip of street frontage. Its 600-square meters of floor space and 600-square meter nursery at the back of the store regularly carried over 1,000 types of plants, flowers, bonsais, birds, and fish as well as garden merchandise such as flowerpots, seeds, fertilizer, birdcages, fish tanks, and various kinds of gardening tools and books. The store remained open during the Cultural Revolution, although its merchandise was reduced to little more than gardening tools and fertilizer. There were also forty-seven flower stores at the district (*qu*) level all over the city, including five stores that, up to 1965, were still privately run.[91] Political correctness was used to justify having flower shops in the city against the accusation of flower planting being bourgeois. In the justification, the Shanghai Flower and Bird Store was established as a tribute to the celebration of the tenth anniversary of the founding of the PRC, and all the flower shops across the city were in business for the purpose of "promoting mass verdurization" and "enriching working people's cultural lives."

It was certainly true that people loved to have a little greenery at home to enrich their "cultural lives." For instance, in the neighborhood of Shanyin Road (formerly, Scott Road), a 712-yard-long back street in northeast Shanghai, almost every household had planted flowers and trees in their dooryards, or on their balconies or flat roofs. Da Qizhen (1952–), a resident for over forty years, had fond memories of the urban greenery in her neighborhood. According to Da, there was such a variety of plants in the area that walking down the street was like strolling through a little botanic garden. Among the most common plants were palms, camphor trees, pines, cypresses, magnolias, loquats, cherry-apple trees, and plantains (dwarf banana plants). There were also conifers, broadleaf plants, tropical plants, and plants from the frigid zone. Late spring and early summer were the most beautiful seasons, when lianas were colorful and full of life. Pink and bright red rosebushes bloomed together with lilac wisteria in spring; in summer, tangerine-colored Chinese trumpet creepers and purple morning glories were most striking. The tough Boston ivy needed just a little dew and sunlight to grow vigorously, "as if it was delighted to wrap itself around buildings in a thick layer of green velvet." Da reminisced that such an environment "put the residents of the houses in a good mood and [soothed their] emotions and pedestrians felt mellow and carefree."[92]

Da was among many Shanghai residents who cherished memories of growing flowers at home during the Mao era. One resident named Zheng Jian (1952–) recalled that in his childhood, every year when "the morning glories bloomed, it brought me joy. Was this because this is the season I could swim in the river? Or because it presaged that Children's Day [June 1] was coming? Neither of these seems right. I just like this flower."[93] Li Qing (ca. 1965–), a US professor of mechanical engineering who published her memoirs about her life in China under the pen name Hanyan, grew up in a Shanghai alley called Marks Terrace, a cluster of European-style apartments built by Wing On Company, one of the "big four" department stores in Shanghai, as mentioned earlier. Hanyan recalled that at the end of the gated alley there was a tiny strip of unpaved land adjacent to the alleyway's bamboo fence. On that strip of land bloomed roses and jasmine, among others. This was due to the efforts of a retired worker, whom the neighbors called Old Uncle Wu, and his wife. The couple had moved from a shantytown to a vacant garage in Marks Terrace as part of the government's effort to improve working people's living conditions. They were the first working-class people of Subei origin to have moved into this relatively affluent neighborhood.[94] It was predictable that their behavior at times annoyed the other residents, but the little greenery they created was a welcome addition to the alley. Decades later when Hanyan returned to visit Marks Terrace, she found that Old Uncle Wu, now a ninety-four-year-old widower, still lived in that garage, but the little parterre had disappeared and a banal cement wall with a newly built high-rise behind it had replaced the bamboo fence. It was a depressing visit. Hanyan remarked that Old Uncle Wu's "rosebushes of yesterday," as she affectionately called them, symbolized the things she missed most about the neighborhood.[95]

Zhang Da-Peng (mentioned in Chapter 1) recalled that he took much pleasure in the tiny garden in the front yard of his alleyway home in west Shanghai. The yard once had an iron gate with a pretty inlaid running deer but, like thousands of other iron objects in the city, it was dismantled during the GLF to feed the "backyard furnaces," leaving just a gap in the wall.[96] Around 1963, when the economy was improving, the district housing administration sent workmen over to set up a crude wooden gate. Zhang began to plant flowers and vegetables in the yard and soon he specialized in roses. He studied how to grow roses and searched everywhere for varieties that he lacked. The rosebushes grew luxuriantly. In the late spring of 1965, they burst forth in bloom in all colors at one time. The blossoms numbered about 1,000, and many were as big as a rice bowl. In Zhang's words, "the scenery had more beauty than one can take in"[97] (see Figure 5.5).

The writer Wang Anyi provided a similar description of a plant that was prevalent in Shanghai's residential areas: "Fragrant oleanders reach out over the courtyard walls, as if no longer able to contain their springtime passion." During the famine of spring 1960, "even the scent of the oleanders aroused hunger." For a lonely Shanghai girl sitting in her room, it felt like "oleanders grow in other family's courtyards and pink clouds fill their sky; outside her window is a lonely parasol tree." The popularity of the plant prompted Wang to use it as a background – in contrast to a murder scene – to end her most renowned novel, *The Song of Everlasting Sorrow*, about Shanghai: "The potted oleanders on the balcony across the way were beginning to bloom, opening the curtain on yet another season of flowering and decay."[98]

It should be noted that for Zhang Da-Peng, gardening went beyond being a simple pastime to being a way get through the hardship and survive the political persecution of the time. After graduating from a college of geology in Beijing, Zhang refused to take a government-assigned job in a factory in the city of Lanzhou, in the barren province of Gansu in northwest China. He returned home to Shanghai in fall 1963, unemployed. Zhang became one of the "urban idle labor force," a government category for the unemployed, an object of suspicion and discrimination. He was subjected to the supervision of a middle-aged woman dubbed by the neighbors as Big Sister Hu, who was the head of the neighborhood committee and lived on the upper floor of the same building where Zhang lived. It turned out that gardening helped Zhang get along with Hu. Hu thought a young man like Zhang who stayed home and gardened could not be a troublemaker. Better yet, whenever the roses bloomed, he always cut some for her. Zhang and Hu thus maintained a cordial relationship. Over the years, the little front yard became Zhang's retreat in the midst of political upheaval: When the spring of 1966 arrived, as Zhang reminisces in his memoir in the third person voice, "the glorious sunshine gently touched [his] garden. The roses were in full bloom and 'one hundred flowers contended in beauty.' It was all peace and tranquility, his own desert isle. Outside, the world was very different," as the Cultural Revolution was looming.[99]

Although people might not openly connect gardening with Maoist politics, Zhang Da-Peng raised plants as a way of coping with political trauma. We have encountered, for instance, the writer Fu Lei and his rose garden in Chapter 2. Another well-known case was the painter Liu Haisu who, like Fu and over half-a-million other intellectuals, was labeled a rightist in 1957 and persecuted during the Cultural Revolution. Liu himself was not particularly fond of gardening but his wife, Xia Yiqiao (1918–2012), also an artist, was a flower lover and, in the years of her husband's political trouble, managed to keep the family's little yard flourishing. The rose, calyx canthus (winter-sweet), plum, camellia, and goji (wolfberry), all found their way into the yard.[100] Even during the most chaotic years of the Cultural Revolution, there were small gardening communities among neighbors and friends in the city. For instance, through their shared love for roses, both Xia Yiqiao and Zhang Da-Peng knew Fu Lei's gardener, Ahxiao; and after Fu's tragic death in September 1966, Xia hired Ahxiao to tend her garden.[101]

While obviously not everyone had enough leisure time to raise flowers at home, flower planting went much beyond the few noted people mentioned above. Tan Yingzhou (1966–), a professor of foreign literature at Fudan University, recalled that his childhood was full of flowers and plants associated with average people, even though he grew up in the chaotic years of the Cultural Revolution and its aftermath. Tan's granduncle (his paternal grandmother's younger brother) planted over 100 plants on the flat roof of an alleyway house – typically such terraces are about 10 to 15 square meters – literally turning it into a little garden. His garden also extended to his windowsills. Every morning he would get up at five to water or fertilize his plants and admire the view. He took pleasure from giving away flowers to friends and relatives and serving as a volunteer "plant doctor." Often, he would take sick plants from friends and after "intensive care" on the roof garden return the plants rejuvenated. Tan was particularly amazed how a dying pomegranate in the dooryard was transformed into a vigorous shrub under Granduncle's care. His pastime perhaps contributed to Granduncle's longevity: He lived to ninety-eight.[102]

The pomegranate was not the only highpoint in Tan's childhood memories about gardening at home. His grandaunt (unrelated to the granduncle) lived in the same house with the Tans and planted all sorts of annuals on the roof. Among them, the cypress vine was most impressive. The delicate, pentagram-shaped little red flowers with white pistils climbing along the wall became a bright spot in Tan's childhood.[103] The plant, which originated in Central America, has a poetic name in Chinese, *niaoluo*, a term from the *Classic of Odes* that can be loosely translated as "a feminine touch." The cypress vine was a common climbing plant in Shanghai. Da Qizhen also recalled that in summer her balcony was constantly full of colorful climbing plants and flowers: Red cypress vines and marvel-of-Peru (also known as the "four o'clock flower"), blue morning glories, yellow towel gourds, and silver-gray houseleeks, not to mention the multicolor heronsbill, all making for a kaleidoscopic scene on the little balcony.[104]

Many people recalled that a little greenery served as an oasis in the Maoist cultural desert during the Cultural Revolution. To return to the case of Chengdu resident Li Chengpeng, although Li's neighbors had their spats over flower planting, the flowers never disappeared. During the Cultural Revolution Li's childhood home still had a porch with a fretwork decorated with chrysanthemums and spider plants.[105] Lu Zhiming (ca. 1960–), a journalist in Xiamen (Amoy), recalled that some of his most joyful moments as a young boy were spent picking marvel-of-Peru (locally known as "rouge flowers"), which were ubiquitous in the city. "Early in the morning, we followed the grownups to go out to pick rouge flowers," Lu reminisced. "We children like to suck on the pistils to taste the sweet nectar; this was our happiest moment." The custom was to throw half of the picked flowers up onto the roof and leave the other half at home – legend has it that this makes the women of the household beautiful.[106]

These portraits do not readily correspond with the usual image of the Cultural Revolution as a dark age, full of misery and bloodshed, but neither do they necessarily contradict it. Rather, they reveal the complexity of life under Communism and remind us that it was multifaceted. In a city that was the heartland of Mao's last revolution, the much-condemned bourgeois lifestyle – exemplified here in flower planting – persisted, or even flourished. In a way, as we have seen in a number of cases cited above, precisely because of the hardship people endured during Mao's time, they had all the more reason to take up some sort of recreation or pastime such as gardening as a way to retreat from the harsh reality surrounding them.

An example is Sheng Aiyi (1900–1983), a daughter of Sheng Xuanhuai (1844–1916), late Qing China's most prominent bureaucrat, entrepreneur, and educator. Aiyi, a celebrity in her own right, pursued and won China's first lawsuit over the right of women to inherit family property.

In 1932, she cofounded the Paramount, a famous nightclub and dance hall in Shanghai (see Figure 2.5), and became the first woman entrepreneur in modern China's entertainment industry.[107] Her futile love affair with T.V. Soong (1894–1971), Chiang Kai-shek's brother-in-law who served twice as the premier of the Republic of China, was public knowledge. After the Communist takeover, her husband, Zhuang Zhujiu (born 1897), a banker, was accused of being a counterrevolutionary and was thrown in prison, where he died in the late 1950s. Sheng was forced to leave her upscale home with a garden on Huaihai Road and live in a garage on Wuyuan Road (formerly, Route Mgr. Maresca), facing a septic tank – every few days a truck came to pump out the contents – and a messy roadside food market.[108] The change in her living conditions was dramatic, and perhaps traumatic as well, but she soon found some consolation in simple things. A little red flower growing out of a crack in the pavement near the garage door caught her attention and she started to collect wild flowers nearby and replanted them in all kinds of containers she managed to find. Sheng was an amateur painter and calligrapher, and these flowers were to become the subjects of her art. Over the next twenty-plus years, the trinity of gardening, painting, and calligraphy added some comfort to her life in a shanty. "The story of her life," one writer has commented, "was not her dramatic downfall into a living hell but rather her ability as an elite woman to live in hell with grace and dignity."[109]

Such grace and dignity could be seen as a modest protest against tyranny. An old capitalist's self-confinement amid greenery was precisely such a gesture. Nie Chongbin (1957–), a Shanghainese who now lives in the United States, recalled how the plants on the flat roof of her home became a haven for her grandfather during the Cultural Revolution. In 1947, her grandfather Nie Qijun (b. 1906) paid seven gold bars (312.5 grams each) to purchase a permanent lease on a three-story alleyway house called Rongkang Villa, built in 1939 on Changsu Road (formerly, Shanzhong Road) in west Shanghai. In 1967, part of his house was forcibly occupied by "revolutionary rebels," an action justified by Mao's call to attack the bourgeoisie. For seven years, Nie refused to leave the building in protest of the unlawful occupation of his home. "The flat roof on the third floor of the house thus became his world, where he planted all sorts of morning glories in riotous profusion," Nie Chongbin recalls. "In the summer, while playing in the alleyway, we children often raised our heads toward the flat roof calling: 'Grandpa, grandpa, throw some morning glories down,' then we would see an abundance of morning glories flying down like numerous colorful parachutes descending from the sky."[110]

194 Part III: Under the French Parasol Trees

Figure 5.5 Shanghai's various types of European-style houses were generically referred to as "foreign garden homes" (*huayuan yangfang*), since they typically had a fenced-in front yard and were mostly built in the city's former French Concession. After 1949, many of these homes got new occupants, as, for the most part, wealthy businesspeople moved out and CCP cadres moved in. Pictured here is a young man telling stores to a group of children as a neighborhood service in such a garden home with lush flora (ca. 1964). *Source:* Qin Feng lao zhaoxiang guan, comp., *Shanghai zhizhao*, 115.

Urban Farming

Everyday flora, no matter how pathetic it might be in the eyes of people who have no experience of the Maoist era, provided aesthetic and psychological relief from fear and despair, but it went beyond that. The Mao era was an age of scarcity of virtually all consumer goods. From 1955 on, most daily necessities, especially food, were rationed. Thus, it is understandable that bonsai-type gardening often turned into mini-farming, and thus helped put food on the table.

The practical use of green space appeared soon after 1949 in the city's most affluent neighborhoods where most residents were Western expatriates and Chinese elites. The Communist takeover of Shanghai involved "southbound cadres" (*nanxia ganbu*) from the "liberated areas" in rural North China (in particular, Shandong and northern Jiangsu). In May 1949, when Shanghai was liberated, 7,282 southbound cadres took over the city. In the next two years, they were joined by hundreds more from the same areas.[111] The soldiers stationed in the city were also mostly from the rural north. In a CCP internal meeting held in Nanjing on September 17, 1949, Deng Xiaoping announced that southbound cadres of the PLA, not the CCP's underground organizers and activists in the city, were to be the backbone of the Communist leadership after the takeover.[112]

A considerable number of the city's elegant European-style houses now had new occupants, and they, like Mao, had little appreciation for flowers and trees. For them, land not planted in crops or vegetables was simply land that was wasted.[113] One observer noted that the new denizens of these premises were "numerous children who spoke northern dialects ...; or entire houses full of their relatives from the north. The gardens of these houses were no longer for flowers; instead, they became vegetable plots."[114] A resident who lived in such a former Nationalist official's house on Panyu Road (formerly, Columbia Road in the French Concession) for nearly thirty years with three other families including one of a southbound cadre, recalled how he and his neighbors had turned the garden into a mini-farm. This 495 square meter (5,328 square feet) plot had originally had a lawn and a variety of trees, flowers, and climbing plants. The garden was kept largely intact, although it was poorly maintained before 1966 when, in the chaos of the Cultural Revolution, the Shanghai Foreign Trade Company turned most of the garden into an open-air warehouse. The residents then turned the rest of the garden – about 100 square meters – into a vegetable plot for the four families that lived in the house. This tiny urban farm supplied food in all four seasons: Chinese baby cabbages all year around except for midsummer; water spinach, towel gourd (loofa), and cowpeas in summer; hyacinth beans and bok choy in autumn; and spinach and white radishes in winter. Homegrown sweetcorn, sword beans, and tomatoes were also frequently on their dining tables. A fig tree in the corner of the garden produced fruit every year, thanks to an old formula for a fertilizer offered by the man's grandmother: Bury pig lungs or intestines around the roots of the tree every winter. Edible wild herbs such as Indian asters (*malantou*) and shepherd's purse (*jicai*) did not need much care but grew lavishly in the garden. Together with mincemeat, these wild vegetables made a perfect filling for wonton dumplings.[115]

Most Shanghai residents were denied the luxury of having such a garden at home, yet the spirit of making gardening practical, which could be traced back to the Republican era, was common. Lu Xun's son Haiying (1929–2011) recalled that in his childhood, he and his mother planted pumpkins in the dooryard of their alleyway house on Shanyin Road, a lot of just about 50 square feet. His father gave a homegrown pumpkin to a family friend, Mrs. Uchiyama, who used it in a Japanese-style stewed dish and shared it with Lu Xun's family. In return, Lu Xun's wife made dumpling soup with pumpkins and shared them with the Uchiyamas.[116] Watermelon was another plant that one might not expect to find in the middle of a city, but taking advantage of the ample sunlight on the flat roofs of alleyway houses, some residents planted watermelons. This was more for fun than for the fruit, as the watermelons were usually only fist size and hardly edible (not to say that in summer watermelons were the cheapest fruit in the city, typically 5 cents per *jin*). Still, planting watermelons had a practical purpose in summer: The sprawl of its large leaves on the flat roof made the room underneath it – the so-called pavilion room – cooler.[117] In the same vein, the comic artist Zhang Leping (1911–1992), who is best known for the cartoon character Sanmao ("Three Hairs") he created in 1935, had in the yard of his residence on Wuyuan Road a shaddock tree that every year in mid-autumn produced numerous fruits. They were too sour to eat but the Zhangs used them as an air freshener and were always happy to share the fruit with anyone who came to the door asking for them.[118]

Climbing plants such as towel gourd, cucumbers, and balsam pear were among the most popular plants in the city. With their bright yellow flowers, towel gourds were often planted with purple or lilac morning glories and red cypress vines to form a pleasant scene; but planting towel gourds was more than just for viewing pleasure. Fresh towel gourd is a popular vegetable in Chinese cuisine. Two dishes, towel gourd stir-fried with garlic and with dried shrimp, were served in many households. Fully ripened towel gourds also were used as sponges. Balsam pears, also known as bitter melon, were believed to reduce "fire" in one's body (a notion of inflammation in Chinese medicine). The popularity of the plant led a Shanghai writer, Zhou Peihong (1951–), to recall that her strongest childhood memory was of row upon row of balsam pears that her grandmother planted on the flat roof of the family's alleyway house near Jing'an Temple.[119]

The flowers of the garden balsam, the marvel-of-Peru, and the cypress vine – all common in Shanghai – were used to make paste rouge. Girls used the flowers to dye their nails at home but would wash the dye off before going out in public. In a political environment where aesthetics in daily life were condemned as bourgeois, such use was politically incorrect. Students were taught in school that coloring one's nails was decadent, something that the "exploiting class," human parasites living without working, did out of boredom. However, it seemed that the human desire for beauty, even if it was as petty as this one, was hard to suppress. A harmless use of the flowers among children, like those in Xiamen mentioned earlier, was to suck the pistils.[120]

For centuries, the lower Yangzi delta region has been known as China's premier silk and silk production area, but few might imagine that there was a plan to plant mulberry trees and raise silkworms right in the city. In April 1958, the Chinese National Silk Company made a formal proposal to the Shanghai municipal government, calling for mobilizing "household labor" in both urban and suburban districts of the city to plant mulberry trees and raise silkworms to supply the silk reeling industry. According to the plan, mulberry trees were to be planted and serve as natural fences in all the city's "scenic areas," such as parks and street intersection gardens; by 1962, Shanghai would be self-sufficient in raw silk; by 1968, there would be about twenty million mulberry trees in the city and its suburbs.[121] Like many other radical ideas that emerged during the GLF, the plan did not entirely materialize, but it nonetheless reflected the belief that urban greenery ought to serve utilitarian purposes. Although planting mulberry trees in the city proper for that purpose was not practical, in Shanghai's suburban counties, mulberry farming did increase substantially, from 80 mu (13 acres) in 1956 to 4,633 mu (763 acres) in 1975.[122]

At the same time, raising silkworms became a popular pastime in the city, especially among children and young adults. Shanghainese called the little creatures "silkworm babies" (*can baobao*), and a shoebox was usually all one needed to start to raise the babies.[123] Silkworms were available from street peddlers for one cent each and mulberry leaves, one cent for three pieces.[124] But peddlers did not always have fresh leaves for sale and silkworms were big eaters (on average a silkworm consumes three to five leaves a day), so picking leaves from mulberry trees in parks and on the streets was prevalent, often causing damage to the trees and their surrounding greenery. To cope with the situation, the Shanghai park authorities simply hacked off the branches of many mulberry trees in public spaces.

Shanghai culture critic Zhu Dake recalled that in his childhood he often traded his precious candies for information about where to find unmolested street-side mulberry trees and would walk long distances to collect the leaves.[125] Another Shanghai resident, Chen Jianxing, recalled that in order to find mulberry trees, he and his schoolmates searched all of Zhongshan Park (a 50-acre park in west Shanghai built in 1914 as Jessfield Park), but could not find any. Later, they found that there was a mulberry tree in Lane 476 of Changning Road, a few blocks east the park. Unfortunately, that tree was inside a walled residential compound. Prompted by the urgent need to feed their "silkworm babies" at home, Chen and his friends climbed over the wall at night and reaped their harvest. In a hurry, Chen fell off the wall and nearly broke his leg.[126] Hunting for mulberry leaves was such a shared memory that the Shanghai painter Chen Danqing, who also enjoyed raising silkworms in his childhood, exclaimed: "In retrospect, life then was not a typical urban life; in fact much of our space was semirural."[127] This "semirural space" allowed the generation of children who grew up in the Mao era, when the city was "stuck in time," to experience a slice of pastoral life that was rare in a densely populated city. In an interview in 2014, a Shanghai resident, Ms. Lei, recalled that she had never worried about having mulberry leaves for her silkworms in her youth as she had a mulberry tree in her backyard. In fact, she often shared the leaves with her silkworm-raising neighbors. Decades later she wanted to resume the hobby but mulberry trees by then were so rare in the city that she had to drive over 40 miles to Chongming Island to get some or pay for shipping, which cost more than the leaves themselves.[128]

Much less common was raising bees as a hobby – and for honey. There is at least one documented case in Shanghai. In spring of 1971, when rape flowers were turning yellow the fields in suburban Shanghai, Zhang Da-Peng, then an electrician in a zipper factory, brought two wooden beehives by chance from two bee farmers of Yiwu, Zhejiang, with the notion of raising bees at his home in west Shanghai. It seemed like an unrealistic plan yet it went well. The day Zhang placed the hives in his tiny front yard, the bees diligently buzzed in and out. He soon saw bees flying back with the fuzzy upper part of their legs covered with yellow pollen about the size of tiny grains of rice, proving that the area around their new home could support them. One month later, Zhang began his first honeycomb cutting. Zhang recalled how happy he was the first time he saw the honey flowing down the sides of the bucket of the centrifuge. In the next eighteen months, the bee population grew and Zhang was able to collect about 6.5 pounds of honey every two months. He then could afford to add some honey to the milk for his baby daughter (born in August 1970). He also gave some to his relatives and friends.

Zhang was so encouraged that he even had a plan to develop as many as seventy beehives and relocate part of them to the suburban village where he first bought the hives. However, before he was able to turn his little enterprise into a profitable business, it came to a sudden end when one of his neighbors, an old woman who had a severe allergy to bees, was stung and hospitalized. The incident made it clear that in a crowded city like Shanghai, where every window was open during the summer, bee raising was not really viable. The fact that Zhang was able to raise bees at all and harvest honey indicated there were sufficient sources of nectar and pollen in the area.[129] Moreover, in a small way Zhang's plan to profit from an amusement at a time when making money outside a regular government-assigned job was almost a crime tells of the hidden resilience of the capitalist spirit in the city.[130]

In 1958, at the height of the GLF, Mao asserted that if Chinese landscapes everywhere looked like a park, China would have reached the stage of Communism.[131] By 1964, the GLF had proven to be a failure; still, Mao reiterated the point, only figuratively prolonging the time needed: "Take two hundred years to achieve verdurization, that is Marxism."[132] China's state-sponsored "reshaping the mountains and rivers" (*gaizao shanhe*) often caused ecological disaster at the local level and went down in history as failed schemes to improve the human condition (to paraphrase James Scott's words).[133] However, the campaign for verdurization, despite its ups and downs during the Mao era, did make China's cities greener.[134] In the case of Shanghai, when Mao's army took the city in 1949, the per capita green space (0.16 square meters) was barely enough to put a pair of shoes; by the time of Mao's death in 1976, it had increased threefold to 0.47 square meter, or about the size of a newspaper.[135]

However, greenery was politicized. The party-state proclaimed the afforestation of public spaces in the city to be patriotic and evidence of the benevolence of Communist rule, but condemned home flower planting as a manifestation of a bourgeois lifestyle. Ordinary urban residents cared little about the ideologies "planted" in verdurization but used them for their own purposes. Despite Mao's condemnation of flower planting as "feudal" (the standard Maoist label for China's imperial past) and "bourgeois" (the standard label for modern Western values), in Shanghai homes gardening for pleasure remained alive and well throughout the Mao era. A flowerbed in the dooryard, or potted plants on the balcony, windowsill, or flat roof, served as little islands of greenery in the midst of the urban jungle of concrete. More significantly, they represented a spirit that was deemed unorthodox, if not rebellious. In a seemingly trivial but pragmatic way, Chinese lives under Mao were more colorful – both metaphorically and literally – and diverse than has usually been thought.

At the height of the Cultural Revolution, when Chinese society seemed to have completely lost its moorings, Mao whined in private to his confidants about what he regarded as the ineffectiveness of his revolution, that is, that life still goes on: "What's all this talk about the Cultural Revolution? ... Aren't people still getting married and having babies? The Cultural Revolution is very remote from most people."[136] Apparently Mao was unhappy about the mundanity in Chinese life that, in his mind, hindered the march toward a Communism. On a short note to his comment, what Mao may not have known was that, against his wishes, people were still growing flowers at home. What would have outraged Mao even more was that ordinary people gardened at home to assuage their anger, smooth human relations, and express their discontent with his rule.

The story of public green spaces and private gardening in Shanghai thus reveals a split politics that goes beyond the simple matter of flora or greening. For the state, verdurization was a strategy to enhance socialist morality and political legitimacy. The city's residents did not always accept the party's dictates, much less invariably comply with them. In general, they cared less about politicized greenery on streets and in parks than whatever foliage they could manage to have at home. Moreover, for some victims of Mao's political campaigns, private home gardening was not only a recreation but was also, explicitly or inexplicitly, a refuge. Home gardening thus became a circumspect maneuver for coping with tyranny and part of the grassroots pragmatism that eventually triumphed over the state's rhetoric.

6 In the Eyes of Foreign Onlookers

The poet Bei Dao (1949–), who was born and grew up in Beijing, recalled his first trip to Shanghai in the summer of 1957 when he was eight years old: "The level of prosperity [in Shanghai] was astonishing. Compared with Beijing, it was a totally different world; there seems to be something hidden behind its prosperity." Bei Dao grew up to become one of the most acclaimed writers of his generation. Half a century after the trip he ruminated on its impact on his life: "Later in life I have been traveling like crazy all over the world; it can all be traced back to that trip to Shanghai." The city was in fact at a low point in its history when the boy from Beijing visited, with its once vibrant commerce and industries hermetically sealed in socialism and its infrastructure in disrepair. Yet Bei Dao's awestruck impression of the city was not just part of a child's excitement on seeing a fascinating city for the first time but was shared by many seasoned visitors to the city, including a number of top-notch journalists from the West. "Every story is a travel story – a spatial practice," Michel de Certeau once claimed.[1] In a few decades after 1949, foreign visitors' observations of Shanghai and its people coincided surprisingly with the little boy's impression of the city. It would be an exaggeration to say "onlookers see most of the game" (as a Chinese saying puts it), but the fact that a sophisticated journalists' reaction to Shanghai dovetailed with that of a child tells us that something made Shanghai stand out during the murkiest period of the nation's recent history.

Mao's China was a closed country. For three decades, it had few foreign visitors and even fewer foreign residents. This was in sharp contrast to the situation in Shanghai in the century leading up to the Communist takeover in 1949 – a century when foreigners of all walks of life lived in the city and could be encountered every day on its streets. In late 1948, when the Chinese Communist army was approaching the Lower Yangzi delta region, many foreigners left Shanghai. Still, by the time of the takeover in May 1949, there were 32,049 foreign expatriates in the city, the great majority Europeans and US citizens. By the end of 1955, the number of foreigners had dropped to 2,185 and continued to fall to a few hundred in the early 1960s. In December 1965, in a city of six million people, Shanghai's Euro-US population was statistically negligible: Twenty-five Britons, seven Frenchmen, six US citizens, five Germans, and three Italians.[2] Starting from the summer of 1966, the chaos of the Cultural Revolution drove most of the remaining foreigners away; by the end of 1976, Shanghai's total foreign population was just over 100. Also, very few foreigners visited the city. In the entire year of 1969, for instance, only 774 foreigners visited or stopped over in Shanghai – on average, about two visitors a day.[3]

However, despite the paucity of foreigners in Shanghai, the city remained one of the most popular destinations for foreigners visiting China. In the early 1970s when China softened its stance on "American imperialism," foreign visitors to Shanghai, most of whom were from the West, increased tenfold in five years, from 4,742 in 1971 to about 50,000 in 1976.[4] Those who had a chance to visit Shanghai in the Mao era and wrote about it unanimously commented on the vitality of the city and noted that its people enjoyed a level of comfort that exceeded that in other Chinese cities they visited, including the capital. Despite their limited access to everyday life in China, many visitors at the time were not exactly tourists but rather careful and mindful observers of a closed country. Their accounts of Shanghai are thus a metaphorical album of snapshots of the city and its people – an album that is in many ways richer than anything the Chinese themselves put together. Piecing together these snapshots yields a picture of the tenacity and vivacity of the people of Shanghai in an age of continuous revolution, international isolation, and material shortage.

Before the Cultural Revolution

In October 1955, six years after the Communist takeover, *Boston Globe* correspondent Dennis Bloodworth (1919–2005) sent a report from Shanghai describing the city as "far from being a reformed character." The most notable aspect of the city's character, according to Bloodworth, was the spirit of its people: "Along the Bund, below the solid skyscrapers with their lingering, if deceptive, stamps of Big Business, the pavements are crammed with lively careless crowds who have nothing in common with the purposeful plodders elsewhere." Bloodworth noted that the "local administration finds it no simple matter to cut Shanghai's cloth to Peiping's [Beijing's] ideological pattern," and "even the state department stores, damning evidence of the people's taste in Peiping, are full of a wide range of excellent goods in Shanghai, including materials of deviationist elegance."[5] The British journalist James Cameron (1911–1985), who spent two months in China in late 1955 reporting for the *News Chronicle* of London, made a similar observation: "Shanghai and Peking were in different worlds.... The difference showed up in small ways – a richer individuality of dress, a brighter splash of neon lighting, a certain uncowed anarchy among the pedicab-drivers, a glimpse of lipstick here and there – but also in the biggest possible of ways: Red Shanghai was still, and of design, one of the most considerable capitalist cities of Asia."[6]

Considering these reports appeared just a few years after the Communist takeover of China's foremost hotbed of capitalism, some deviations from Communist orthodoxy might not be entirely unexpected. Besides, the street scenes they depicted, after all, were before the sweeping Socialist Nationalization Campaign of 1956, which essentially eliminated private businesses and led to decades of poor economic performance, not to mention the GLF of 1958–1960, which caused widespread famine and nearly destroyed the economy. However, even after all of the economic hardship and devastation, foreign visitors continued to find the city and its people dynamic. Individuality of various sorts observed on Shanghai's streets was frequently mentioned in journalists' reports. For example, David Chipp (1927–2008), a British journalist and the first non-Communist reporter posted to the PRC, wrote in late 1957 that after the nationalization campaign, vibrant consumerism was still visible in Shanghai: "The stores, although they now nearly all [are nationalized], give the impression that they are there to sell things. They are better stocked with everything from daily necessities to luxury goods and the sales people have about them a professional air which is lacking elsewhere in China."[7] Old foreign-made goods – relics of offices and homes of a begone age – were sold in secondhand stores at reasonable prices. These stores, "where the supply of such goods and the memory of the bourgeois lifestyles of pre-1949 China were strong," remained open throughout the Mao era.[8] In the streets, "the many hawkers, selling everything from coat-hangers to fountain pens, and the loud-voiced newspaper boys still have the capitalist 'vice' of trying to attract customers."[9] Chipp also noted that in Shanghai "many of the people in the streets look far better dressed than in other cities. This is particularly true of the women, who have kept their grace and dress well. There is an air of individual prosperity."[10] A major goal of Mao's revolution was to eliminate individualism, yet what impressed foreign visitors to the city was precisely people's distinctiveness, which itself can be taken as sign of dissidence. Danish writer-photographer Jørgen Bisch, who visited China in 1958 for twenty days and then again in May 1964 for six weeks, wrote in his report: "Shanghai's seven millions, so individualistic as to be called 'untamed' by their rulers, struggle to toe the Party line."[11] Paolo Alberto Rossi (1887–1969), the Italian consul general in Shanghai from 1948 to 1952, wrote in his memoir that when the Cultural Revolution started, "One would be wrong to think of Shanghai, the New York of the Far East, as nothing more than an imposing array of buildings, a complicated display of business, cultural, and religious organizations. There is the indomitable spirit there which Chinese Communism has not yet been able to destroy."[12]

Part of the indomitable spirit was commerce and, among the people, a conviction that "business is business," which of course clashed with the Maoist "politics in command" dogma. French journalist Robert Guillain (1908–1998) reported on Shanghai in October 1964, after fifteen years under Communism: "The many socialized shop-windows are decorated with a thousand products of China's light industry, which is being stimulated again after the crisis of 1959–1961." In the eyes of Guillain, who had lived in Shanghai in the late 1930s, "Socialist clerks appear to be just as keen to make their fingers fly over their beloved abacuses as they were in the days of capital."[13] W.J.F. Jenner ([William John Francis "Bill" Jenner] 1940–), a Briton who worked for China's Foreign Languages Bureau in 1963–1965, described Shanghai of the time as "physically little changed since the 1940s," with its streets still pulsating with energy (Figure 6.1). The city, in his words, "felt like a slightly outdated version of the modern world where people walked briskly instead of ambling as in Peking."[14] Dick Wilson (1928–2011), an English journalist and writer who specialized on China, wrote after his 1964 trip to China: "Politically and economically … the middle class is restricted to a humiliating minor role. It is only when one visits Shanghai that one realizes the extent of its inner resistance to the Communist kiss of death."[15] If one bears in mind that these reports were made when the country had just come out of the worst famine in the world's history, the normality, if not prosperity, of the city was impressive.

The briskly walking Shanghainese were not a homogenous crowd either. An attentive visitor could not miss that they came in every variety to constitute the "inner resistance." K.S. Karol (1924–2014), a France-based journalist who spent four months in China in 1965, reported from Shanghai that the "uniformity of the Chinese crowd ('the blue ants') has been very much exaggerated by Western journalists – there is a great variety of colors and styles in people's clothes."[16] Likewise, Dutch writer Hans Koningsberger (1921–2007), who visited Shanghai in 1965–1966, described the city as lively and dynamic. Koningsberger's first impression of Shanghai came as he was walking out of the Zhaibei railway station across a square, facing the city to the south: "It looks impenetrable;

Figure 6.1 The annual Buddha Bathing Festival and temple fair around Jing'an Temple in west Shanghai, 1958. The festival was held from 1881 to 1963 to celebrate Shakyamuni's birthday, traditionally observed on the eighth day of the fourth month of the lunar calendar. The city government issued permits to hundreds of traders to set up tents at the festival, with tramcars running in the middle of the street. The temple fair usually lasted three to four days and attracted millions of visitors (an estimated four million in 1961). *Source:* Shanghai Municipal Archives.

it is teeming; puddles in the street and the low clouds reflect unseen neon signs; it is the capital of an unknown world."[17] Later he caught a glimpse of the lives in that capital of an unknown world on the Bund, the waterfront boulevard that, in some eyes, epitomizes the city:

The Bund was and still is one of the great streets of the world, like Fifth Avenue, Nevski Prospekt, and the Ginza. People stroll through the park at the water front, children roll in the grass, vendors of ices knock on wood, and young men take pictures of their girlfriends. This picture taking is different from the Western pointing-like-a-gun approach: a tripod is set up, a smile arranged, all with great patience and care. Bystanders watch with neutral expressions on their faces. And while the posing girl leans over the stone balustrade and stares at the waves with a little smile, a junk goes by within ten feet, a man and woman working a side oar with a furious effort against the stream, while a naked baby sits on deck, tied to a mast against falling overboard, and smiling back at the girl on the balustrade.[18]

A scene like this seems incongruent with the political climate of the time. Three years earlier, in October 1962, Mao called for the entire nation to "never forget class struggle," his way of signaling that he was returning to power in full force after a brief political seclusion following the failed

GLF. At the time of Koningsberger's visit, China was heading toward another calamity, the Cultural Revolution.

A Glimpse of Shanghai during the Cultural Revolution

In the fall of 1966, Shanghai, like the rest of the nation, was caught up in a Maoist revolutionary frenzy. Billboards were full of Cultural Revolution slogans, handwritten big-character posters were haphazardly pasted on the walls of old European-style edifices, and mobocracy ruled the streets. But even in the most chaotic time of what was to become Mao's last revolution, Shanghainese still maintained some style and flair. Neale Hunter and his wife Deirdre – both were from Australia and taught English at the Shanghai Foreign Language Institute from 1965 to 1967 – noted that at the peak of the chaos in late 1966, "The girls still wore their hair long, and we saw styles in trousers and footwear that would not have survived in the capital."[19]

Very few foreigners visited China in the first five years of the Cultural Revolution, but those who did could not help noticing, like the Hunters, that Shanghai was different. In November 1970, the *New York Times* reported from Shanghai that "the people generally appear well dressed, often favoring gray cloth over the blue that is most common in Peking. Clothes seem more trimly cut.... The women take some trouble with their appearance and hair. Many are beautiful, often quite startlingly so. That, at least, has not changed." Shanghai also appeared animated: "It is a city of people – bustling crowds in Nanking Road's department stores, buying food at well-stored shops and stalls."[20] The Associated Press reporter John Roderick (1914–2008), who was regarded as the "AP's No. 1 China-watcher" and had lived in Shanghai in the late 1940s,[21] had a similar impression when he revisited the city in 1971. In commenting on "the great department stores like Wing-On," Roderick noted that "although their inventories are smaller, they still have a wide variety of goods on display. Many are out of reach of the ordinary worker, but articles such as clothes, shoes and other essentials are cheap and well-made."[22] Roderick easily found places he was familiar with from his first visit though the names had been changed. The YMCA had been transformed into a hotel for overseas Chinese; the Palace Hotel, a name totally unfitting a revolutionary "People's Republic," was renamed the Peace Hotel; and the Broadway Mansions Hotel was redubbed the Shanghai Mansions – but they "continue[d] their original functions of accommodating travelers comfortably."[23]

Therefore, it is no surprise that in 1972 when the Nixon delegation and its media team came to town, "the Americans found Shanghai a pleasant change after the austerity of Beijing and Hangzhou," the two cities they had visited prior to Shanghai. "Even in 1972 Shanghai women dared to wear lipstick and bright clothes," one of Nixon's press team wrote. Shanghai's "streets bustled with crowds and its shops had a richer variety of goods than those in Beijing and Hangzhou."[24] A US journalist's diary entry of February 27 – the day before the Shanghai Communiqué was signed – clearly reflected the excitement of the Americans:

> SUNDAY: This is Communiqué Day in Shanghai. After Peking and Hangchow, it is a joy to be back in what most of us consider a *real* city. Noisy crowds throng the sidewalks and bicycles fill the streets near the magnificent waterfront. A touch of lipstick and rouge, plus an occasional bright blouse or kerchief, make the women stand out. There are specialty shops for clothing, cutlery, bicycles, electrical and photographic equipment, toys, wine and liquor, bedding, and food. At the number-one Shanghai department store, which looks like Macy's, I checked some prices. Hot-water bottles are 4 yuan; blankets are 32 yuan; a bicycle is 100 yuan; a long-playing record of the music for *Red Detachment of Women* costs 9 yuan; a couple of lipsticks are 2.5 yuan.[25]

China in those days was notorious for allowing foreigners to visit only a few officially designated places where good things were displayed to impress them. The Shanghai municipal government undertook extraordinary preparations for Nixon's visit, going so far as to call on residents to remove all their laundry drying on balconies and apartment windows facing the street. In the neighborhoods where Nixon's motorcade would pass, even runny-nosed children were kept off the streets.[26] Nevertheless, the streets at large were open to pedestrians and stores welcomed anyone who walked in. The authorities were unable to turn an entire city of ten million people into a Potemkin metropolis, even if they had wanted to do so. One widely known story of US citizens witnessing poverty in the city – at least from the Chinese point of view – was about a street peddler. In the trip to China in January 1972 to make arrangements for Nixon's visit, Alexander Haig (1924–2010), the president's chief of staff, and a few other members of the US delegation walked by an open-air food market in Shanghai and stopped at a stall where an old woman sat on a low stool, with green onions and ginger root spread out on a white sheet of cloth on the ground for sale.[27] The US citizens asked the woman why she was doing this on a freezing cold winter morning. Instead of giving a standard politically correct answer, such as Mao's famous quote, "To serve the people," the woman's response was blunt: "*Meiyou banfa ah!*" ("It can't be helped"), meaning she had no choice if she wanted to eke out a living. The tale of this little encounter circulated among Shanghainese to exemplify two points: That Haig was unfriendly to China (i.e., he deliberately embarrassed China by talking to a poor peddler) and despite the authorities' careful preparations, China still "lost face" to the Americans.[28]

The Chinese – in this case, Shanghainese in particular – apparently had a much too rosy image of the United States and did not know that in comparison with the thousands of homeless people in US cities, an old woman selling some vegetables on the street was something US citizens would find far from disgraceful. Quite the contrary, the Americans on that trip had an overall favorable impression of Shanghai. Zhang Hanzhi (1935–2008), a confidant of Mao's and one of the interpreters for Nixon, paid particular attention to US journalists' reports on Nixon's visit to Shanghai and founded that "none of them were ill disposed."[29] Soon after Nixon's visit, the *Washington Post* reported from the city in a very upbeat tone:

The sidewalks teem with people. Some perch on railings and watch the world go by. Others lounge in wickerwork chairs and read, and still others squat on the sidewalk to play games of poker and chess. A mother sits on the curb and breast-feeds an infant. Older children do their homework by the dim light of the street lamps. Other children gather round the adults as they play their games, or start games of their own. Some drift into the all-night eating-houses along the way to buy a bowl of ice cream.[30]

After the PRC was admitted to the United Nations in 1971, foreign embassies mushroomed in Beijing. However, it was a common knowledge among China's foreign expatriates that it was not the capital but Shanghai that was China's "real city" for shopping and relaxation in their otherwise rather drab sojourn: "Foreigners living in Peking look forward to the occasional trip to Shanghai. Apart from the city's intrinsic fascination, it is by far the best shopping center in China, its stores well stocked with consumer goods of quite remarkable range and quality." Shanghai apparently beat all other Communist countries in that regard: "Diplomats who have served in Eastern Europe say they saw nothing like it there – not even in the showcase stores in Moscow."[31]

Overseas Connections

Aside from shopping, it was the city's more open and amiable environment, connected with Shanghai's international experiences in the past, that foreigners found attractive. This legacy never entirely disappeared after 1949. Journalist Edgar Snow, who had lived in Shanghai in the 1930s, revisited the city in the autumn of 1960 and stayed in the historic Cathay Hotel (now the South Building of the Peace Hotel), a property of Victor Sassoon (1881–1961), a legendary tycoon of old Shanghai. For

35 yuan (about US$14.50) a day, Snow chose to stay in Sir Victor's suite in order to, in his words, "wake up in the morning knowing how Victor Sassoon felt when he owned Shanghai."[32] To his dismay, he did not sleep well. After tossing around in bed, he ended up on the living room couch, only to wake up early in the morning. At seven o'clock, Snow went down to ramble on the Bund, which was already populated with people of all ages playing tai chi, practicing sword dancing, singing, or strolling (see Figure 6.2). Encouraged by the pleasant atmosphere, Snow randomly said hello in Chinese to an old man on a bench. It turned out that the man could speak "stilted but animated English," and the two had a pleasant chat about family, politics, and the *China Weekly Review*, a Shanghai-based English language newspaper that Snow worked for in pre-Liberation days.[33]

That a foreigner could have a lively conversation with a perfect stranger on the street might be seen as odd in Mao's China. There were stories about people who got into trouble simply by talking to foreigners. But China is a big country – even a government as domineering as Mao's could not control every person every moment. Besides, for nearly a century the Shanghainese had been accustomed to interacting with foreigners in public places; this led to a sense of familiarity and ease that never entirely died out. In another case, when K.S. Karol visited Shanghai in 1965, he and his friend the photographer Marc Riboud explored the city at their leisure, without the presence of an interpreter or government-assigned guide. By chance they came across the Great World, an amusement arcade on the corner of Yan'an Road (formerly, Avenue Edward VII) and Tibet Road established in 1917, walked in and mingled with the locals there.[34] Even during China's most isolated and anti-foreign years, it was possible for foreigners to take such self-guided tours. Colin McCullough, a Canadian newsman who visited China in late 1969, wrote that in Shanghai any visit to a factory or a commune had to be prearranged but, "One can, of course, simply go walking. And this is what I did – in the morning, afternoon and even late at night. At no time was I stopped or bothered in any way."[35]

Through their long-standing familiarity with *yangren* ("ocean people," as Westerners were called), the people of Shanghai had a historical connection with the outside world. But they also had a present connection. As it had been China's most cosmopolitan city, Shanghai had a high concentration of people who had relatives, friends, or other connections abroad. In the Mao era, Shanghai was second only to the southern provinces of Guangdong and Fujian in terms of the value of overseas remittances sent to its residents.[36] In those years, having an overseas connection could be

Figure 6.2 Tai chi on the Bund, 1979. The two high-rises in the background are Shanghai landmarks: *left*, Sassoon House (once the Cathay Hotel, now the Peace Hotel), built 1926–1929; *right*, the Bank of China Building, built 1936–1937. Photo by Alain Nogues (1937–). *Source:* Gettyimages.

condemned during political campaigns as a sort of crime, but, ironically, overseas remittances were always welcomed and indeed encouraged. During the famine of the early 1960s, the party, through its local cadres, urged people who had relatives in Hong Kong or elsewhere abroad to reach out for financial help.[37] In order to encourage overseas remittances, starting from June 1961, for every 100 yuan sent from "capitalist countries or the Hong Kong and Macao regions," the payee was entitled to receive ration coupons for purchasing goods in shortage: 6 kilograms of food grains (rice and wheat), 10 *chi* (about 3.3 meters) of cotton cloth, 1 kilogram of cooking oil, 1 kilogram of sugar, 1 kilogram of fish, 500 grams of meat (usually pork), and 500 grams of cake products. By September 1962, the types of ration coupons awarded for each 100 yuan in foreign remittances were expanded (for example, cigarettes and bar soap were added) and the amount doubled, and for certain types of goods, trebled.[38] In July 1961, a store – the Overseas Chinese Store – was opened specially for people to use these coupons (Figure 6.3).[39]

Even in the most repressive years of the late 1960s, when any overseas connection was highly suspicious and could put one in jeopardy, overseas remittances were never discouraged and the ration coupon rewards continued. There was a tacit understanding that it was all right for someone who had been politically denounced to receive remittances from family or friends abroad. Although China was nearly completely isolated from the rest of the world and was subject to spasms of xenophobia, overseas remittances to Shanghai fell just slightly at the beginning of the Cultural Revolution but then steadily increased after 1970. By the end of the Mao era in 1976, overseas remittances were more than double what they had been a decade earlier (Table 6.1). The policy of welcoming money from abroad was no doubt pragmatic but its justification was ideological: Foreign currency helped support "the socialist construction of the motherland."

The ration coupons or vouchers awarded to people who received foreign remittances could be used at the Overseas Chinese Store on Nanjing Road, which had been specially designated for accommodating the shopping needs of foreign remittance recipients.[40] Only those who held overseas remittance vouchers were allowed to enter (see Chapter 1). The Overseas Chinese Store was one of Shanghai's most exclusive emporiums, exceeded in its exclusiveness only by the Friendship Store, which was open only to visitors who held a foreign passport (Figures 6.4a and 6.4b). The existence of these privileged places in the center of the city further enhanced the Shanghai people's long-standing approbation of things foreign – as the locals cynically put it, "Having an overseas connection was like stinky tofu: it smells bad but tastes delicious."[41]

Figure 6.3 Shanghai Overseas Chinese Store, ca. 1975. Opened in July 1961 and later moved to this skyscraper at 727 Nanjing Road adjacent to the Wing On department store (to the right, connected by two enclosed bridges). Constructed in 1932 as the New Wing On Tower, the building was known for its famous dance hall and rooftop garden, the Seventh Tier of Heaven, run by the Wing On Company. The building also served as Shanghai's first television tower from 1958 to 1974. *Source:* Zhihu (Question and Answer website), www.zhihu.com/question/333940741.

Table 6.1 *Overseas remittances to Shanghai residents, 1953–1982 (US$1,000)*

Year	Sum	Year	Sum	Year	Sum
1953	897	1954	781	1955	807
1956	562	1957	471	1958	490
1959	409	1960	455	1961	474
1962	562	1963	678	1964	784
1965	844	1966	760	1967	679
1968	700	1969	740	1970	780
1971	856	1972	1,032	1973	1,317
1974	1,500	1975	1,620	1976	1,650
1977	1,763	1978	2,075	1979	2,563
1980	2,814	1981	3,026	1982	3,248

Source: Shanghai qiaowu zhi bianzuan weiyuanhui, *Shanghai qiaowu zhi*, 165.

Thus, in Shanghai, interest in the world outside China (particularly, the West) was not easily curbed. A few months after Nixon's visit, a US journalist described what a foreigner could encounter on Shanghai's streets:

In most Chinese cities, a foreigner strolling around at night is someone to stare and wonder at, but not someone you'd want to talk to. But in Shanghai, a foreigner strolling down Nanking [Nanjing] Road can expect to collect an instant throng of persistent inquisitors.

"Where do you come from? What do you do? How do you like China? Have you seen our Chinese leaders?"

After more than a year of perfunctory contact with the man-in-the-street in Peking, it is an exhilarating experience.[42]

This inquisitiveness about the world outside reflected a spirit that did not fit with the party's propaganda, which peddled platitudes that portrayed China as a happy land while outside it, "two-thirds of the people in the world live in an abyss of misery."[43] With China's international isolation and constant watching over people's lives, keenness about the West itself was a deviation. To the dismay of the authorities, there was plenty of it, and there was little they could do about it. A Chinese American who visited China for a month in 1974 was impressed by the people she met in Shanghai, saying "they were very knowledgeable and knew a great deal about big events happening outside the country; they were not at all closed up without information."[44]

What these visitors observed in the city were flashes of a tenacious spirit. Perhaps Dick Wilson came closest to describing a fundamental

Figure 6.4 (a) *Top*, The Shanghai Friendship Store, 353 Nanjing Road (opened on February 26, 1958; photo ca. 1960). The building was originally constructed in 1931–1932 on a lot owned by the real estate mogul Silas Aaron Hardoon (1851–1931). The portrait of Lenin with the sign "Long Live Leninism" in the window display on the right, suggests that the majority of the patrons were from the Communist bloc. (b) *Bottom*, In January 1970, the first floor of the building was used as a Xinhua bookstore while the Friendship Store was relocated to the Bund 33 inside the former British consulate. The sign atop the roof repeats the famous call from the *Communist Manifesto*, "Workers of the world, unite!" *Source:* Shanghai Municipal Library.

reality of Shanghai when he commented that "superficially the Shanghai middle class has submitted dutifully to the egalitarian, idealistic direction of the Communist Party, but in the struggle of the mind it is not so clear which force is the stronger."[45] At times this struggle of the mind might appear trivial or something that could be simply dismissed, yet it reflected the fact that lives in Mao's China were more complex and livelier than is usually portrayed or understood. In people's homes, daily life involved a constant maneuvering and shifting to cope with the ideological uniformity imposed by the party and the material scarcity caused by its policies. Few foreigners had a chance to walk into these neighborhoods,[46] but the lives there were the sources of what they observed on the streets, and only through the lives there can the vitality on the streets be appreciated. Chapter 7 focuses on what the Chinese called *yishi* (clothing and food), the basics of life, to illustrate how people endeavored to attain some level of contentment in a difficult time.

7   The Essential Does Not Change

The Chinese term *yishi* (clothing and food) is in a somewhat odd order. While food and clothing are both essential to human life, for obvious reasons, food is more vital than clothing. Yet in Chinese, clothing always goes ahead of food, as in *yishi, yishi fumu* (parents of clothing and food, a metaphor for sources of livelihood such as one's customers, patrons, or employers), *yishi zu er zhi rongru* ("only when the people have enough of clothing and food, they will know what is honor and disgrace," a famous quote from the seventh-century BCE Chinese philosopher and politician Guan Zhong), and so on. Perhaps the concept here is that, while food is essential for life, clothing distinguishes humans from all other forms of life.

Regardless, it is undeniable that food and clothing are essential for human existence, and "the essential doesn't change," as Samuel Beckett (1906–1989) famously declared. This chapter, following the word order in the term *yishi*, explores how people acquired, consumed, and deployed daily necessities, and in the process confronted the government's rationing and also the Communist Party's interference in everyday life.

Clothing

Clothing is of course both distinctly individual and highly social. What someone is wearing is often a display of their tastes, habits, and status. Society can be judgmental about such things, which in turn affects the individual's choice of attire. Hence the choice of what to wear in public, or fashion, involves a certain amount of deliberation that reflects an individual's social behavior as well as the social milieu of a given time. As Michel de Certeau and others have argued, through a pedestrian's steps, the walker engages in dialogue with the city.[1] Therefore, clothing can be a contentious element in public space, whether or not people who wear the clothes are conscious of it.

In a free society, as social theorists such as Lefebvre and Certeau seem to agree, "fashion helps explain why at a given time groups of people are moved to do some things in roughly the same way," and "to think about fashion is to think about how we go from one configuration of daily existence to another."[2] In the Mao era, however, two elements complicated this otherwise common pattern. One was the party's policing of people's daily lives, and thus how "at a given time groups of people are moved to do some things in roughly the same way" was subject to the party's policies. The other was the frequent shortage of fabric and other materials for making clothing, a situation that greatly limited fashion in its conventional sense but opened the way for clever, and idiosyncratic, solutions.

From the very start, Mao's China was known for the monotony of its clothing, which was largely imposed by the party. Immediately after Liberation, one of the first things Western expatriates in Shanghai observed was the radical change of people's attire on the streets, how "the beautiful clothes, the elegant fashions, were replaced by the forerunners of unisex blouses and trousers."[3] This was not just a matter of a change in individual lifestyles, nor was it, at least at the beginning, imposed by the government, but it was a political statement: It was an unmistakable act of compliance with the new regime and with a changed society. Those who loved fashion and individuality in their dress must have been bewildered by the sudden imposition of an inseparable link between clothing and politics. In such circumstances, following one's own tastes came at great price.

One such person was the writer Eileen Chang, who found fame in Shanghai during the Japanese occupation (1942–1945) and stayed in the city after Liberation. The party reached out to her by inviting her to attend the Shanghai's First Literature and Arts Conference, held on July 24–29, 1950 (the same conference Fu Lei attended; see Chapter 2). The more than 500 attendees were dressed in blue or grey "people's wear" (a variation of the Zhongshan suit that is commonly known in the West as the Mao suit, which comes in both men's and women's styles).[4] Chang sat silently in the back row of the meeting hall, but the anomaly of her attire was nonetheless obvious. Thirty years later, Ke Ling (1909–2000), a senior editor and writer who helped published some of Chang's works that made her famous, recalled that Chang was dressed in a qipao – the body-hugging dress prevalent in the Republican era – with an ivory wool knit mesh sweater on top of it. "Even though Chang had changed her style of dress from the splendid to the prosaic, she still stood out from others at the meeting," Ke reminisced. "In fact, I cannot image how she would have looked if she had worn a Zhongshan suit."[5]

Chang, who was known for her distinguished style of dressing (she often designed her own clothes and made her own patterns), had tried to adapted to the new society. For instance, her first full-length novel was published in installments in a Shanghai newspaper in the early 1950s and it has a cheerful ending in line with the Communist spirit of the time.[6] But in July 1952 Chang left Shanghai for Hong Kong and three years later went on to the United States.[7] She left quietly; before her departure, even her only brother did not know she was leaving. He described the day he got the surprising news from their aunt whom Chang had lived with: "I left her apartment crying. On the streets, pedestrians here and there all wore the people's dress. I remember that Sister once said that 'the people's dress is too stiff, I can never wear it.' Perhaps that is why she left. She left to find a place far away, and never came back."[8]

Chang, like others with financial means and overseas connections, could walk away.[9] But, most people could not. Yet the story about the clothing of the people she left behind was not one of the total surrender of individuality to the dress code of the Communist Party. The party itself was also subject to swings of the political pendulum, which affected fashion. Although the overall trend of clothing in Mao's China was toward thrift, simplicity, and uniformity, and the party touted the concept of "inner beauty" or "labor is beautiful" in regard to clothing, there were occasional shifts in the party's aesthetics. For instance, in the mid-1950s, the party encouraged young women to wear colorful and flowery dresses (*huayifu*). *Youth News*, the official newspaper of the Communist Youth League (Shanghai branch) and the PRC's first newspaper aimed at youth, called on young people, especially women, to dress up. "Now we have the ability to dress up a bit prettier, but girls' clothing is mostly still 'one dress fits all,'" the newspaper wrote. "We should not only make our country like a garden of hundreds of flowers, but also dress up our girls like fresh flowers and precious jades. Girls, be brave, dress in flowery clothes!"[10] One item of the flowery clothes that the party encouraged women of all ages to wear was a Russian-style frock known as the *bulaji*, the Chinese transliteration of the Russian word *platje*.[11] This baggy one-piece dress, usually, but not always, short-sleeved, had a long skirt that flared out at the hem and was fabric-costly to make. It did not suit a time of fabric shortages, but the political message was clear: Wearing the *bulaji* was a way to show China's solidarity with the Soviet Union. By the late 1950s when Sino-Soviet relations soured, the *bulaji* faded away.

However, the idea that people should have stylish clothing or, more generally, an affluent life, continued, and was also justified by the party's ideology. In March 1958, the Shanghai Clothing Company, the sole government-run enterprise of its type in the city, published a manual titled *Clothing, 1957–1958*. It includes examples of 180 different types of clothing in eleven categories, including the qipao, women's one-piece dresses, skirts, men's suits, overcoats, children's clothes, and so on. The editors carefully avoided using the phrase "fashion" (*shizhuang*), and instead chose a more generic word, "clothing" (*fuzhuang*) as the title of the manual but, in any case, the handbook is an authoritative guide to fashions of the time. In the preface, the editors claim that "clothing is a cultural symbol, as well as a very specialized ... art. One of our responsibilities is to serve the aesthetic needs of the working masses, and provide them with materials about clothing styles, as well as [features] adapted to men and women's natural attributes" (see Figure 7.1).

Even the most radical in the party supported the pursuit of material well-being. In 1958, Zhang Chunqiao, arguably the staunchest Maoist in the party, published an article praising the thrifty spirit of the Good Number Eight Company of Nanjing Road (*Nanjing lu shang hao ba lian*), a PLA unit stationed in Shanghai: "Does this mean we don't want to have an affluent life? No, no, and the third answer is still 'no,'" Zhang wrote. "Our socialist country led by the working class should not only have clothing, grain, poultry and fish, and all kinds of things for daily use, but also have an extremely great variety of them."[12] Zhang was a leading apostle of a frugal, Communist puritanical lifestyle as a bulwark against the corrosive influence of the bourgeoisie. Yet he did not in principle deny that material well-being was a goal of the revolution. Even during the most radical years when people's clothing was at its dullest, there were ardent revolutionaries who attempted to add some color and style. In 1974, Mao's wife Jiang Qing commissioned tailors from Beijing, Tianjin, and Shanghai to design a one-piece women's dress that supposedly incorporated characteristics of traditional (in particular Tang dynasty) women's clothing. More than 100,000 of these so-called Jiang Qing dresses were produced in just a few months in late 1974 and early 1975. Jiang Qing wore the dress at international events such as the opening ceremony of the 1974 Asian Games in Tehran and on other diplomatic occasions. However, the Chinese public was indifferent to the dress. In big cities, the retail price of the dress started at 20 yuan but, because of poor sales, was quickly reduced to 4 yuan. Yet that still failed to boost sales. In the post-Mao era, the unpopularity of the dress was attributed to the unpopularity of Jiang Qing herself, but the actual reasons had to do with practicality rather than politics: The skirt was both too fabric-costly to make and too cumbersome to wear.[13] Thus the Jiang Qing dress lasted for about a year and had died out before the political downfall of Jiang in October 1976.[14]

No doubt the brief interlude of the government's promotion of "flowery dresses" was politically motivated. The people had their own tastes, sense of practicality, and lifestyles, all of which did not always follow the dictates of the party-state. This was particularly clear during the Cultural

Figure 7.1 The cover of a fashion guide, *Fu-Zhuang*, published in 1958. The editors claimed that one of the purposes of periodically publishing fashion manuals was to "enrich the working people's sartorial knowledge." *Source:* Shanghai Municipal Library.

Revolution when the state could not have been more intrusive in everyday life in the name of waging continuous revolution against revisionism (a tag for the Soviet Union after the Sino-Soviet split in 1960). One of the sub-campaigns of the Cultural Revolution involved attacking so-called bizarre dress and outlandish clothing (*qizhuang yifu*), condemned as a remnant of the decadent bourgeois lifestyle that eroded the spirit of revolution. The campaign started on August 20, 1966, two days after Mao received hundreds of thousands of the Red Guards in Tiananmen Square and called on the entire nation to "smash the old ideas, old culture, old customs, and old habits of all exploiting classes" – known in short as "smashing the Four Olds."[15]

Although no written dress code was promulgated during the campaign, Maoist radicals strictly watched over what people wore. The bottom of trouser legs was mandated to be not narrower than seven *cun* (about 9 inches; 1 *cun* = 1.3 inches) for men and six *cun* (a little shy of 8 inches) for women. The rise on a pair of trousers was to be no shorter than eight *cun* (10.5 inches).[16] The idea behind these regulations was that clothing should not reveal the outlines of the human body, lest it be sexually provocative and lead to bourgeois debauchery. On and off throughout the Cultural Revolution decade – depending on the political sub-climate in any particular time and place – picketers patrolled the main streets of cities solely for the purpose of policing what people wore. Occasionally, they had a professional tailor as advisor. With a tape measure and scissors in hand, they stopped pedestrians and measured their trousers. If the trousers did not meet the required specifications, the bottoms would be cut as a warning. In lieu of a ruler, which was not always available, the 500-milliliter beer bottle, commonly found in Shanghai households, was used to measure the width of trousers: The picketers would let the person go if the bottle could be insert into the trousers with no difficulty; otherwise, the trousers would be cut. Pointed leather shoes were another target. At the height of the campaign, one often saw men and women rushing home helter-skelter, barefooted or wearing socks, with a pair of cut-up leather shoes in hand.[17]

However, even under this sort of invasion of everyday life, people's desire for the basic freedom of choosing their own clothing did not bend entirely to the will of the state. People persisted, dragged their feet, and frequently followed their own wishes but in a roundabout and discreet way, which was every so often tolerated, making what cannot be said can be done. Whether it was done consciously or not, asserting one's personal proclivities was a form of political resistance to the power of an all-intrusive state. Ultimately it was more a manifestation of the human need to express individual identity and tastes than a political statement.

Indeed, it was during the Cultural Revolution decade, when political control of daily life was at its height, that resistance to state-imposed uniformity became most subtle and innovative. At a time when some Western observers saw only a "vast ocean of gray" and a sea of monotonous Mao suits or, to use a derogatory term, millions of "blue ants," in fact there existed some choices and even innovative clothing designs in terms of color, style, and material. Here are just a few examples, perhaps pathetic but nonetheless real:

1. A jacket with three or four buttons could be worn instead of a jacket with the standard five buttons. People who had grown tired of the Maoist button-to-the neck jacket could wear a casual jacket with a V-collar, conveying a natural and unrestrained air.
2. Choice was also possible in the number of pockets. Unlike the Mao suit with its four standard pockets, the three-button jacket had two pockets at the bottom. Various modifications to the Mao suit were possible as well. This included removing the two upper pockets, removing the upper right pocket, changing the shape of the pocket covers, or simply removing the covers.
3. A further relaxation of the jacket was to replace the buttons with a zipper, remove all pockets from the front, and have a pocket on each side. This sort of jacket was a forerunner of the signature outfit of Kim Jong-il (1941–2011), the North Korean leader, who often wore a zip-up tunic with matching trousers in khaki, gray, or black.[18] China's post-Deng leaders also wore this type of jacket on less formal occasions such as inspection tours of factories or villages. The various modifications of the Mao suit brought about new types of clothing known as "youth jackets," "student jackets," "dual-purpose jackets," and so on.
4. The style of the neck of woolen sweaters conveyed various images: The V-neck sweater was conventional and formal, the polo neck gave an impression of comfort, the crew neck looked old-fashioned, and the turtleneck had a cute and school-student-like air.
5. A woman's fashion statement was to wear a light-colored shirt inside a three-button jacket and turn the collar of the shirt outside to overlap the jacket collar. This fashion seemed to be officially acknowledged. For a time, women interpreters, women cadres, and wives of top government leaders dressed in this way when they received foreign visitors.
6. Since Chinese-style cotton-padded jackets cannot be washed, and since they are typically worn for many winters, to keep them clean, they were worn with a dustcoat on top. Men's dustcoats were usually

blue or grey, while women's dustcoats or blouses were much more colorful, to the point, as an author put it, of "vying with each other for glamour."[19] In addition, a women's fashion was to turn the shirt collar outside the cotton-padded jacket to protect the jacket's collar from getting dirty while at the same time allowing for a variety of false collars to play an important role in fashion (more on this later).[20]

7. Although miniskirts were banned and no skirt was supposed to rise above the knees, it was not considered improper for young women to wear shorts that revealed much of their legs. Shorts were extremely common among both men and women in the summer.
8. An imitation of the PLA uniform, known as the "casual military uniform," was a symbol of "political correctness" and was considered fashionable.

It should be pointed out that although Shanghai had long been China's fashion capital, and although it may have continued in this role in the Mao era, the maneuvering to style clothing to suit individual tastes was not limited to Shanghai but was national phenomenon. The writer Qing Qiuzi's description of people's outfits in the northeastern city of Changchun in his youth in the late 1960s gives a glimpse of fashion in an inland city that mirrors what was happening in Shanghai:

At that time clothing came in basically two colors: blue and green. But when it came to the details, there was a lot going on behind all this. Let's first look at the yin [female]. How girls got their allure, how young men showed their handsome side—there were particulars about being conscientious. Girls wore a small Chinese-style cotton-padded jacket with a mandarin collar and button loops, on top of which was a cotton dustcoat in a floral pattern that added a feminine touch. Who said that time was an age of dreary gray? No two girls would have dustcoats with the same floral pattern. Then there was a scarf—huge and 100 percent pure wool, soft and warm—covering a girl's neck up to her ears and nose, leaving only her vibrant winking eyes and her bangs falling across her forehead—full of feminine charm.

Moving on to the yang [male]. The winter outfit for young men also had its particulars. It was a cotton-padded overcoat worn on top of a thick sweatshirt. The fashion was that the overcoat should have a brown mohair fleece collar and the sweatshirt should be a cardigan type with a metal zipper in front. The zipper should not be zipped up to the neck but left half-way open "to present a handsome curve." Even the heavy cotton-padded trousers had their charm. The subtlety was that one left light-colored thermal underwear "peeking out" at the bottom of the trousers, which was regarded as a sort of risqué fashion.[21]

The significance of the picture depicted here was not in the details of what people wore but the concept of fashion behind the details and the energy people devoted to pursuing them. The pursuit had no commercial motivation, unlike in a capitalist society, but the desire and appreciation for aesthetics were largely the same.

By the early 1970s, there was a reaction to narrow trousers in the West and Shanghainese quickly followed. This reaction resulted in bell-bottom pants, long and loose enough to cover a pair of wing-tip leather shoes. Since Nixon's historic visit to China resulted in an increasing number of visitors from or via Hong Kong to the mainland, fashion magazines brought in by visitors played an important role in introducing the latest fashions to the Chinese. There were also other channels that gave the then shut-away Chinese public a glimpse of Western attire. One of them was Glenn L. Cowan (1952–2004), a US table tennis player who enjoyed a moment of fame thanks to the "ping-pong diplomacy" of 1971 that led to Nixon's visit to China in 1972. After the thirty-first World Table Tennis Championships in Nagoya in 1971, the US ping-pong team was invited to China. Their visit was filmed and much publicized. Cowen and Premier Zhou Enlai's conversation on hippies made the headlines all across the world.[22] The big bell-bottom pants the visitors wore caught the attention of the Chinese and, in the words of an author who was a teenager at the time, "made Red China panic." Many years later, when recalling the fascination with the pants that the Shanghai youth had, the author quipped: "Cowan once asked China's wise premier Zhou Enlai, 'what do you think of the hippies in the West?' What he really intended to ask was, 'what do you think of the bell-bottom pants I am wearing?'"[23] For most Chinese, Cowen's bell-bottom pants and long, long hair were their first exposure to hippies.

Another source of inspiration for clothing was Cambodia's Prince Norodom Sihanouk (1922–2012), who was exiled to Beijing after being overthrown by a military coup in March 1970. Sihanouk was treated as a personal "guest of Chairman Mao" during his sojourn in Beijing (1970–1975). Often with top Chinese leaders, Sihanouk and his wife, Monique (1936–), frequently appeared in Chinese news. As "friends of the Chinese people," the couple made numerous trips to various parts of China during their exile and after each trip, a documentary of the trip was released to the public. From 1956 to 1975, the year Mao last received the prince, the Chinese Central Newsreel and Documentary Film Studio had made thirty-five documentaries of Sihanouk's visits and tours in China, most of which were filmed after 1970.[24] The documentaries, each about thirty minutes, were among the very few films available in Chinese cinemas in the 1970s. They were shown at the beginning of a feature movie as a sort of bonus. Sihanouk *qinwang* (prince) and Monique *gongzhu* (princess), as they were popularly called, became household names and rare celebrities at the time when Mao was China's sole idol.[25]

On one occasion Monique wore a ski suit with a fur collar turned out of the suit. Soon the same style of collar appeared on Shanghai's streets. It was not a fur collar – few could afford fur – but a knitted one. However, the imitation was, as the locals put it, "a vivid perfection."[26] More than three decades later, many Chinese still recalled the image of "Sihanouk standing in a convertible, gracefully waving his hand and heartily smiling, and by his side was his beautiful wife. The crowd filled the sidewalks on both sides of the street, waving flowers and chanting slogans of welcome. Sihanouk was indeed like the most dazzling movie star."[27] A journalist wrote that in these public appearances, "the always changing outfits of Princess Monique were a bright spot in an era of murky gray. For girls who love to dress up, these images constituted their awakening."[28]

Whatever the sources of inspiration were, at a time of tight political control of people's daily lives, the drive for fashion or attire that diverged from the party-imposed norms was very much alive and manifested itself whenever there was a slight relaxation in the political climate. After the CCP held its ninth National Congress in April 1969, the chaos and most violent factional fights of the Cultural Revolution subsided. In Shanghai, the clothing people wore on the streets was a subtle yet visible sign of that trend. A foreign journalist's report on China in late 1969 gave a glimpse of a street scene regarding women's clothing: "People in Shanghai are well-dressed.... I noted that many of the young girls were wearing rather stylish low-heeled shoes made of leather. Most women in Peking wear black velvet or corduroy slippers. There were also quite a number of women wearing skirts. In Peking, nearly all women wear trousers."[29] In fact, about the same time, "outlandish clothing" quietly came back. A list of outfits and hairstyles observed on the streets of Shanghai year-by-year reveals fashion trends at the time:

> 1969: The "wonton collar," the "*shumai* [a Cantonese open dumpling] collar," black yoga pants, Dutch-style leather shoes.
> 1970: "Rockets" (wing-tip leather shoes), handlebar moustaches, sunglasses.
> 1971: Wide cuffs, elastic waists, Buddhist nun's shoes, lean-to-one-side hairstyles.
> 1972: Big sharp V-collars, big patch pockets, big buttons.
> 1973: Semi-transparent female nylon blouses, bell-bottom pants, windblown hairstyles.[30]

China's improved relations with the United States in the early 1970s resulted in a relatively mild political environment insofar as everyday life was concerned. In his 1971 visit to China, the Nobel laureate Yang Zhenning noted that about 30 percent of the women in Shanghai dressed in skirts, of which about a third were in colored patterns.[31] The colors on the street reflected the sort of relaxed milieu the city had not seen since the beginning of the Cultural Revolution. Two months after Nixon's visit in February 1972, *People's Daily* carried a commentary titled "The Service Industry Should Be Better at Serving the Workers, Peasants, and Soldiers," giving the stamp of approval for people's quest for material well-being. The article quoted Stalin as saying, "In the view of Marxism, either in the socialist period or in the Communist period, individual tastes and needs are different in quality and quantity; it cannot be that all are the same and all people are equal." Accordingly, the commentary goes on to say that it is absolutely wrong to interpret "revolutionization" (*geminghua*) to mean that everyone "eats one type of food, wears one kind of clothing, has one type of hairstyle, and strikes one posture in photos."[32] The proposition of the commentary was in line with Zhang Chunqiao's 1958 article quoted earlier. Apparently, after years of denying the legitimacy of people's need for material well-being and dismissing the longing for a better life as "bourgeois," the radicals in the party were compromising and presented – even if slightly – a benign side of government policies.

The Lin Biao incident of 1971, in which Lin allegedly plotted a coup against Mao, marked the beginning of the end of the Cultural Revolution, although the official end would not come until the death of Mao five years later.[33] Disillusionment with Mao's revolution and skepticism of its dogma were widespread, if not openly expressed. As a result, the Cultural Revolution became largely a spent force, and it seemed now that everyone belonged to the so-called unfettered clique and disengaged themselves from the revolution and devoted their time and energy to reading (as discussed in Chapter 3) and pursuing material comfort within their limited means. The 1970s was a do-it-yourself time in the city. Many people, especially young people, including urban sent-down youth who managed to return to the city with or without permission, had plenty of time on their hands. To kill time as well as save money, people learned how to use firewood to make furniture, assemble a radio with materials from a junk shop, use unrationed spare parts to put together a bicycle, and so on. But, far more commonly, people learned how to sew, and amateur tailors were found everywhere.

Homemade clothes cost about half of store-bought clothing and could be made to suit a person's tastes and means, more so than clothing ordered from a professional tailor shop. Although it is impossible to know how many amateur tailors the city had, in general everyone knew someone who was an amateur tailor in the neighborhood or was able to place an order through acquaintances with such a tailor.[34] Determining how much to pay for the services of an amateur tailor was a matter of decorum or social protocol, but it was always less than a tailor shop would charge.

Some of these amateur tailors were in fact not really amateurs at all but professional tailors in state-run shops moonlighting to earn some extra money. This was certainly a "capitalist tail" that the party radicals aimed to cut off. Nevertheless, the service met people's needs and few, either among the "masses" or party cadres, bothered to complain about it.[35]

Tailor Shops

This "capitalist tail" was connected to small tailor shops that had been ubiquitous in the city for decades. Zhong Fulan, who grew up in the 1950s and 1960s in Xujiahui in southwest Shanghai, recalled that despite their limited means, his mother had always managed to keep the family of six children fairly well dressed. The secret was a little shop run by an old tailor at the entrance of the alleyway where the Zhong family lived. Zhong, who is now a folklorist, drew a portrait of the tailor in his childhood neighborhood that typifies the old tailors who survived after the Socialist Nationalization Campaign:

The old tailor named Yang originally came from a village in rural Subei. He was the fifth child in his family and thus was known by others as "Yang the Fifth Kid," but my mother insisted that we should call him "Yang the Fifth Master." He was a man of medium height, quiet and kind—I have never seen him annoyed with anyone since the time I started remembering things. Years of working with needles and thread led to his habit of always narrowing his eyes. His tailor shop occupied just a single room at the entrance of the alleyway where we lived. The only things in the room were just an ironing board, an old sewing machine, a bamboo ruler, a pack of chalk, an iron, and, of course, a coal-dust-ball stove. Yang the Fifth Master often had a leather ruler hanging over his shoulders; the over-sleeves he wore were faded, and there was a pair of large square-shaped glasses resting on his nose.[36]

Tailor shops like Yang's were found all over the city. According to the Shanghai Textile Industry Bureau, in 1949 Shanghai had "over 6,600 tailor shops and vendors that were located on street corners and alleyway entrances everywhere and employed close to 40,000 people."[37] The key equipment for these family-run businesses was a sewing machine – US-made Singer machines were common. However, the US embargo in the 1950s prompted China to develop its own sewing machine industry.[38] The Butterfly brand, made in Shanghai, replaced Singer as the "invincible" ("butterfly" in Chinese is a homophone for "invincible") sewing machine in the market. By 1957, Shanghai employed 6,377 people in the industry and turned out as many as 176,400 sewing machines a year.[39] As a result, the number of tailors with sewing machines increased markedly, from 727 in 1950 to 2,229 in 1954.[40] (See Figures 7.2a and 7.2b.)

Figure 7.2 (a) *Top*, An artist's impression of an alleyway tailor shop in Shanghai. (b) *Bottom*, Wang Qianguo (1930 –), a native of Ningbo who stated to learn tailoring at age 14 and came to Shanghai in 1952, ran a shop at the entrance of Lane 424, Shunchang Road (known as Xiangshun Li or "Auspicious Alley," built in 1928) for four decades. *Sources*: "Kandong Shanghai" (Understanding Shanghai), https://kknews.cc/news/pp5jvqj.html, archived April 12, 2019.

A sewing machine cost about 150 yuan, a great deal of money for most families, since an average factory worker earned about 30 to 40 yuan a month at the time.[41] However, for a tailor this was a worthwhile, even necessary, investment. With a sewing machine as the "means of production" at home, a modest living could be made. There were 16,881 clothing vendors in Shanghai in 1954–1955; most of them were retailers for big clothing factories but there were also tailors who made clothing to sell in their own little shops. The Socialist Nationalization Campaign in 1956 did not completely change this situation. At the time, there were 23,490 clothing (including shoe and hat) shops in the city, with 56,472 employees. These businesses were organized but not entirely nationalized. Small privately run tailor shops like Yang's were organized into a city-wide cooperative association but by and large continued to operate in the same fashion that they had before the campaign.[42]

For residents in Zhong's neighborhood, having clothing made in Yang's shop had some attractions. First of all, was the quality. Every part was meticulously sewn by machine or stitched by hand, or both. Yang's workmanship came from years of training and experience and, not least of all, a strong work ethic that was standard among tailors. In addition, Yang charged very reasonable fees, almost always within a customer's budget. Finally, if a customer was short of cash, he or she could have clothes tailored on credit. "No worries; whenever you have the money" – that was Yang's watchword when customers could not put cash on the counter. Needless to say, tailors like Yang were very popular.[43]

As they had done for decades, more affluent customers turned to high-end fashion shops that employed some of the city's best tailors. Shanghai had produced a number of famous brand names in the fashion industry in the Republican era, such Hongxiang (founded in 1917), Baromon (founded in 1928), and the Siberian Fur Store (founded in 1930).[44] These shops trained and retained the best tailors in the country and represented the zenith of fashion in Republican China. After the nationalization campaign of the mid-1950s, many highly skilled tailors (mostly men) went to work in large factories. But old brand-named fashion shops remained open, only now they were state-run. Tailors in these shops had loyal customers who patronized them almost surreptitiously. When tailoring was needed, a customer would send a postcard to a tailor with a simple line, "Drop by our home tomorrow evening for a chat." Moonlighting tailors charged a few yuan for a garment (for instance, 4–5 yuan for a women's dress) – it did not take many pieces plus their salary in state-run shops (around 60–70 yuan a month) to assure them of a handsome income.[45]

False Collars

One of the most common pieces of clothing made by both professional and amateur tailors was the so-called false collar.[46] This was a dickey or bib collar, without sleeves and body. Thus, strictly speaking, the name was misleading – the "false collar" was a fake shirt but a true collar. Shanghai was known as the birthplace of this little garment, although it is not exactly clear when it emerged. It could have first appeared in the city's slums in the Republican era. In any case, the false collar was likely to have been inspired by the Western dickey, which would be entirely understandable since Shanghainese had lived cheek by jowl with Westerners for generations.[47] But it was not common until the 1960s. Clearly, this was because of the severe shortage of cotton fabric after the Great Famine caused by the GLF. In 1961, at the height of the famine, the annual ration per person of cloth in Shanghai was 2.6 *chi* (2.8 feet) of a standard 2.4 *chi* (2.6 feet) wide fabric, a piece barely enough for making a set of adult underwear.[48] In commenting on false collars, a Shanghai local writer noted that "only those who were cornered into a life and death situation could be inspired to tailor such a collar."[49]

In Shanghai – and in most cities elsewhere in China – people typically wore a long-sleeve cotton jersey, then, depending on the season, a shirt and a jacket on top of it. For most of the year, from mid-autumn to late spring, the shirt was worn in between the jersey and the jacket. At a time when fabric was rationed, it seemed extravagant to wear a shirt when only the neckline could be seen. The false collar was a product of a time of fabric scarcity. It required only about an eighth of the fabric needed for a regular long-sleeve shirt, and it could be made of remnants, which were not rationed. In addition, false collars were easy to wash thus saving soap, another rationed item. When stores sold false collars, they called them, for good reason, "thrifty collars."[50]

At first, people outside Shanghai considered the false collar a curiosity and evidence of Shanghainese stereotypical stinginess. In the late 1960s, when false collars were brought by Shanghai youth sent-down to Manchuria, at first glance local people mistook them for a woman's brassiere: "You Shanghai men also wear bras?"[51] The little invention nevertheless was quickly welcomed nationwide and, somewhat melodramatically, was regarded as "Shanghainese' outstanding contribution to the history of Chinese costume."[52] Undoubtedly, the functionality, aesthetics, and economy of false collars fitted people's everyday needs. A Beijing woman named Xu Xiaodi (1953–) recalled her generation's fascination with this little garment: "We were young and our femininity was like an inextinguishable fire and our desire for pretty things could not be repressed." Among these "pretty things" were false collars: "young people often had a number of false collars of various colors as a fashion statement."[53] In the south, people of Xu's generation echoed that feeling, as reported in the *Southern Daily*:

In that most difficult environment, one still was driven by the desire for attractive things. The false collar represented a spirit of forging ahead. Nowadays shirts are no longer a luxury and the false collar has long been seen as a "relic." Young people may laugh at this kind of "man's bra" or "gunstock." But those of us who have lived through that era, we have absolutely full respect for it.[54]

Peng Zuji (1940–), a biologist who had worked in the Shanghai Institute of Biological Products since 1956, recalled how a false collar helped enable a real marriage. A colleague of his in the institute was a college graduate who hailed from rural Shandong, which meant he had moved from being a villager to a highly regarded professional. They played soccer together in their leisure time and became good friends. When the man had his first vacation and went to visit his family in Shandong, he borrowed Peng's jacket and a false collar so he could present the best face possible to his family and girlfriend. This staging was effective. His parents were delighted by their son's new look and gasped in admiration that he had now become a "city person." And his girlfriend and her parents were also impressed. In fact, her parents, who had not been happy about their daughter's choice of boyfriends, completely changed their tune and gave their approval to the relationship. Peng exclaimed in his memoir decades later: "It was something I could never have imagined: A set of clothes – one genuine, and one fake – helped pave the way to a real marriage. It was entirely worth it! So, I gave the clothes to my colleague as a souvenir."[55] Was the story overly dramatic and the parents too shallow? Perhaps. But only those who lived through a time when every scrap of fabric was precious could understand the seemingly extraordinary appreciation of the little device called a false collar.

Knitting

Although no statistics are available on the gender ratio of amateur tailors, it is generally believed there were more men than women, especially among those who made formal outfits such as Mao suits and Western-style trousers.[56] However, there was another do-it-yourself way of making clothing that was extremely popular and entirely female – knitting.

In the Mao era, nearly all Shanghai women knew how to knit. Knitting sprang from the long-standing concept of *nühong* (women's needlework) in which needlework is regarded part of a woman's virtue and household duties.[57] However, the popularity of knitting in Shanghai had a more recent origin. Worsted wool fabric was first imported to China, mainly to Shanghai, around 1880, and by the early twentieth century Shanghai had become the center of worsted in China. Xingsheng Jie, a street in the French Concession shorter than a hundred meters, with dozens of worsted stores, both retail and wholesale, was the epicenter of China's worsted business. The business on this single street accounted for more than 90 percent of the trade in all of China.[58] By the 1940s, a few women in Shanghai had successfully built a career as a designer of knitted goods. Among the most famous was Feng Qiuping (1911–2001), whose knitting program was a hallmark of the prosperity of fashion at the time. The trend continued in the 1950s. Just three days after Liberation, Feng was invited to the municipal radio broadcast station, which had just been taken over by the PLA, to teach knitting over the radio. The program was a hit. Feng was able to turn the scripts of the program into a book, *Common Knowledge of Worsted Knitting*, which was published in 1959 and ran in numerous prints; the fourth edition alone had a print run of 841,500 copies.[59]

Knitting was so common among women that many of them carried some knitting work with them all the time, including on their daily commute to work. Since during the rush hour buses were always packed, knitting needles could be a hazard. Hence a sign was posted on buses: "No knitting!"[60] However, knitting at the workplace was acceptable. A middle-school teacher recalled that, when society was locked in the pressure cooker of Maoist "class struggle," cooking up tension and suspicion in human relations, the most relaxed time she and her colleagues enjoyed was when they gathering in the office to knit and chat.[61] It was also common for women workers to knit during "political study" sessions, which in theory constituted the most important activity in a work unit during the Mao era, when the byword was "politics in command."[62] These sessions were the major channel by which the party's documents were announced and newspapers (typically *People's Daily* and *Liberation Daily*) were read aloud to the assembled workers. Typically, study sessions were held once a week, but at the height of a political campaign, unscheduled sessions could be called at any time. The Chinese classic literature scholar Wang Jingzhi, who was assigned to work in a machine shop in January 1971, described a conversation of the sort he often heard at work when the head of the shop was going to convene an unscheduled meeting:

CADRE (announcing): "We will have a study session today."
WORKER (whining): "Gee, I didn't bring my knitting today. Why didn't you tell us earlier?"
CADRE (apologetically): "Just a quick meeting, just a quick meeting...."⁶³

Clearly, knitting in political study sessions was so acceptable that workers felt entitled to grumble without fearing that they would be accused of neglecting political study, and cadres were accommodating.

Depending on its quality, 1 *jin* (catty, 1.1 pounds) of pure woolen yarn in the 1960s and 1970s cost around 17 to 20 yuan. In general, the 1.3 *jin* of woolen yarn needed to make a medium-size man's sweater cost 22 yuan; 1.1 *jin* for a medium size woman's sweater cost 18.5 yuan. The cost could be cut in half if one used a wool mixed with polyester yarn.⁶⁴ Either way, considering that an average worker's monthly pay at the time was just 30 to 40 yuan, a sweater, even without taking into consideration the cost of labor, was expensive. But a handmade sweater had a number of merits. It was durable: It could be worn for more than a decade. And it could be unraveled back to yarn to be reused to make a sweater in a different style. Even when the sweater was worn out, it could be unraveled and the yarn used to make a few smaller items, such as gloves, hats, high collars, and scarfs.⁶⁵

Aside from all this, one could get some yarn by engaging in a little larceny. Many factories periodically provided workers with white knitted cotton gloves for the purpose of "labor protection." It was a common practice for workers to save the gloves or, in some cases, simply spirit extra gloves out of the factory. When one had accumulated enough gloves, they could be unknitted, dyed to a desired color, and knitted back into a cotton sweater, usually, but not always, for children.⁶⁶ Knitting was practiced on such a massive scale that the Shanghai Knitting Crafts Factory was able to assemble 500 different styles of commonly knitted objects and publish a manual of knitting styles, of which 12.27 million copies were sold.⁶⁷

It was the hands of Shanghai's self-made tailors and semi-underground professional tailors that produced the clothing the party considered outlandish. Paradoxically, the authorities themselves provided some legitimacy for this clothing, or at least this was what the people who wore "outlandish styles" tried to argue. On September 27, 1974, Mao received Imelda Marcos (1929–), then the first lady of the Philippines. This made the headlines of every Chinese media outlet (Figure 7.3). The news reports featured a picture of Mao (reports on Mao always included a picture) with the modish Imelda. Just a week after the meeting, in Shanghai's former French Concession a young woman dressed in a long white skirt in the "Imelda style" walked down the street, attracting thousands of gawkers. The dress was an imitation of the *terno* (*filipiniana*) dress worn by Mrs. Marcos as seen in her photo with Mao. That was the woman's justification for wearing such "bourgeois clothes." She was detained by patrolling militia and charged with "hooliganism," but at the end of the Mao era, her story became a legend.[68] This was not an isolated case of how the people of Shanghai could create and exhibit their own individual lifestyles – in this instance by challenging the party's all-pervasive dress code.

Figure 7.3 In a rare courtesy, and perhaps also on an impulse, Mao performs a Western rite by kissing the hand of the Philippines' first lady Imelda Marcos when he received her in Beijing on September 27, 1974. Marcos's *terno* caught the imagination of China's younger generation who had never before seen such an outfit. *Source:* Xinhua News Agency.

By the end of the Mao era, clothing had become a visible sign of the failure of the Cultural Revolution. On July 19, 1975, the CCP authorities in the clothing (including shoes and hats) business conducted a survey by sending observers to watch and count what women pedestrians wore on Shanghai's five busiest streets. The report indicated that in just two hours, there were 1,095 women pedestrians who wore skirts. Of those 1,095, 204 skirts covered the knees (19 percent), 102 reached the knees (10 percent), 580 were one to two inches above the knees (55 percent), and 169 were "super short," that is, three to six inches above the knees (16 percent; in a similar survey conducted in 1973, super-short counted for only 2–3 percent).[69] A few months before Mao's death, the Shanghai Municipal Communist Youth League Committee conducted a survey on lifestyle trends as seen on streets. According to its report, on July 28, 1976, in just fifteen minutes, at the corner of Nanjing Road and the Bund, over forty young pedestrians dressed in "outlandish" clothes and "weird" hairstyles passed by. The report summarized the features of "bourgeois decadent clothing" in a four-syllable pattern typical of the Chinese language.[70] First, "long" (*chang*) – tops covered the hips, like a cut-off qipao, and the sleeves of what was supposedly a short-sleeve shirt stretched all the way down to the elbows. Second, "sharp" (*jian*) – such as a swallow-tail coat and notched triangle collar. Third, "explosive" (*lu*) – for example, using semi-transparent materials for shirts and skirts; wearing a dark-colored bra; cutting skirts short so that they ended two or three inches or more above the knees. Fourth, "sensational" (*yan*) – such as clothing in "strange" colors, like dark coffee. What the authorities found most worrisome, the report warns, was that these young people were proud of having such clothes and took pictures in the outfits on the Bund with its European-like skyline in the background.[71] Ten years earlier, the Cultural Revolution started with the Red Guards cutting trousers and shoes on the streets (in Shanghai, it started on Nanjing Road and the Bund). People were fearful and compliant, and before long the so-called bourgeois lifestyle seemed to have been eliminated. Ten years later, Chinese youth, many of them former Red Guards, dressed in clothing the party considered outlandish and kept abreast of fashions in the decadent West, thus exposing the failure of the party's policy of policing people's lives.

Moreover, by the late years of the Cultural Revolution, there were clear signs of growing indifference and irritation among the public over the party's meddling with what people wore. Since the party's "dress code" was highly subjective, Red Guards who policed "outlandish" clothing on the streets were often confronted by those being checked, in part because the Red Guards themselves might wear things that were deemed strange, and passersby would often express sympathy for the hapless prey. In a few extreme cases, the prey became the predator and attacked the Red Guard pickets. Perhaps one young woman worker's reaction when being stopped on the street for her short skirt hits the point: "There aren't enough ration coupons for cloth; that's why I have to wear a short skirt!"[72]

Some of those who dressed in Westernized apparel or led a perceived Western lifestyle were members of the so-called old class (*laokele*), the dignified remnants of the city's colonial past, discussed in Chapter 1. *Laokele* as a colloquialism first appeared in the early 1960s when the economic disaster of the GLF brought shortages of virtually everything needed for daily life and clothing was hard hit. The old rich and their families, though politically tainted, took advantage of the old clothing in their closets and could, with or without alterations, wear them. These outfits were made of good-quality fabric – a rarity in the Mao era – and were in the styles of the good old days of pre-1949 Shanghai. Soon they were denounced by the party as "bizarre clothing" and became one of the first targets of the Cultural Revolution. Unlike the old rich, the majority of Shanghainese did not have a wardrobe full of quality clothing, although they admired and imitated the old class whenever they could. Together, the old class and its imitators were unintentional rebels who added color and style to the streets of Mao's Shanghai, and in the process unconsciously yet stubbornly – and sometimes shrewdly – dissented from the party-imposed social norms in clothing.

Food

Daisy Kwok, a daughter of George Kwok Bew (1868–1932), co-founder of the Wing On department store, grew up in one of the city's richest families and married a successful Chinese businessman who had graduated from the Massachusetts Institute of Technology. Kwok lived an extraordinarily privileged life until 1958 when her husband was arrested for fraud and for keeping a pistol at home, a counterrevolutionary crime. He died in prison three years later. Inevitably, after his downfall, Kwok encountered a great deal of adversity. Kwok, an English teacher at the Shanghai Foreign Trade Company's part-time college, was sent to farms in suburban Shanghai for labor reform. Her daily tasks were digging fish ponds and cleaning toilets. In 1968, she was allowed to return to the college but her salary was reduced from 148 yuan to 24 yuan. After providing support for her son, who was still in college, at 12 yuan and spending 6 yuan for her monthly bus pass, she had only 6 yuan left.

To eke out a living, Kwok usually skipped breakfast and had lunch in the college mess hall. One day, with the Red Guards incessantly jeering at her, she simply couldn't bear another minute in the mess hall and walked out of the school looking for another place to eat, and here is what she found:

I found a cheap restaurant near the old city wall, which served noodles. The first time I went there I looked at the menu pasted on the wall:

Shredded meat with noodles   23 fen [cents]
Salted vegetables with noodles   13 fen
Plain noodles   8 fen

My mouth watered at the first item. Too expensive. The second item wasn't too bad and [was] cheaper. After reflecting a moment, I realized I couldn't even afford that, so I settled for a bowl of plain noodles for 8 fen.[73]

From that day on she often had plain noodle soup at the restaurant. Kwok reminisced that the meal of noodles was an antidote to her hardship during the Cultural Revolution. In China, food, especially in connection with hardship and fortitude, occupies a central place in reminiscences about life. Jia Zhifang (1916–2008), a writer and a professor at Fudan University who had been branded a "class enemy" in 1955 and was imprisoned for twelve years and then subject to "supervisory control' for thirteen years, made a rule for himself during the Cultural Revolution. He usually smoked a cheap band of cigarettes called Production, which cost 8 cents for a pack of twenty cigarettes, and spent just a few cents on a vegetable dish at the university canteen. However, every time he was denounced at a public "struggle sessions" (*pidouhui*), instead of feeling angry or depressed, he would reward himself by smoking Warrior (Yongshi) brand cigarettes, which cost 12 cents a pack, and ordering a meat dish – either pork ribs for 14 cents or braised pork for 13 cents. By the time the Cultural Revolution had become a spent force, he was allowed to leave campus to shop and get a haircut. He would then go to Wujiaochang (Pentagonal Square), a shopping center near Fudan University, where he would treat himself to what he called a "banquet": Three *liang* (150 grams) of liquor (which cost 24 cents), pork head meat (20 cents), and five *liang* (250 grams) of plain noodles.[74]

For Daisy Kwok, a "Shanghai princess" (as her biographer called her), eating plain noodles was a memorable event. Despite their poetic name, "sunny spring noodles" (*yangchun mian*) are no more than plain noodles, and certainly were not regarded as a delicacy, but if carefully prepared, they could be tasty. The noodles were usually thin, about millimeter in diameter, and were freshly made from wheat flour: Overnight stock was considered stale and no dry or preserved noodles were used. The noodles, usually in the quantity of one or two bowls, were cooked in a huge wok of boiling water until they were just soft enough to eat, then placed into a bowl of soup. The key to making authentic sunny spring noodles was the soup, which was made from the bones of pigs, cattle, or chickens, things otherwise regarded as waste. The bones had little meat, but since they were protein-rich and meat was rare enough to be considered precious, they could not be wasted. The cook put the bones in a large wok and submerged them in cold water, and then heated the water to the boiling point and kept it near boiling temperature for at least five hours (ideally, overnight), adding liquor to mask the strong flavor of the bones. The water thus became a kind of broth, which was then filtered through cotton gauze to remove the impurities. Or, if the restaurant could afford it, the broth was clarified with egg white and then filtered. A vegetarian soup could be made in the same way by substituting bean sprouts and roots of dried brown mushrooms for the bones. This was cheaper and bean sprouts and mushrooms were readily available. Other key ingredients, added just before the noodle soup was served, were a drop of lard and a teaspoon of light soy sauce, both of which were put at the bottom of the bowl before the soup was poured in. Then, just before serving, green onions and garlic leaves, sliced into small bits, were added for flavor and color.[75]

Sunny spring noodles are a classic example of how Shanghainese used the limited resources available to them to add a little comfort to life. In 1996, when Chinese were much more affluent than in the Mao years, Kwok spoke about the sunny spring noodle soup she had nearly thirty years earlier in a definitely positive tone. As the interviewer describes it, she gently inhaled as though sniffing the scent of a rose and said: "Oh, it smelt so good, with chopped-up shallots floating in the clear soup in a big steaming hot bowl. I always finished it. I would sit there in the small shop which was always warm in winter. Then I'd go home to my little attic."[76]

As is commonly known, a standard Chinese meal has two main components, *fan* (the staple food; in Shanghai and much of South China, steamed rice) and a few dishes called *cai* (mainly, meat and vegetables).[77] The critical importance of *fan* in Chinese life is reflected in a widely known colloquial expression, "eat this bowl of rice," a synonym for "job," "profession," or "livelihood." In the rice-centered dietary culture of Shanghai, noodles, like jiaozi or wonton dumplings and steamed buns, were regarded as a type of dim sum – a steamed dumpling snack – rather than a proper meal. However, since noodles, especially noodle soup, combines *fan* (the noodles) and *cai* (meat, vegetables, and soup) in one bowl, it was considered to be a perfectly fine and affordable substitute for a standard meal. Noodles were thus served everywhere in the city.

In May 1949, when the Communists took over Shanghai, there were more than 15,000 restaurants of all types and sizes in the city, ranging from upscale establishments to roadside food stalls, serving Chinese food of all regions, including various types of dim sum as well as European cuisines. The great majority of these restaurants served noodle soup. This included *puluo* restaurants (a name derived from the Chinese transliteration of "proletariat"), known for their affordable menu.[78] During the Socialist Nationalization Campaign of 1955–1956, restaurants, like other businesses, were merged and reorganized. Privately run eateries, mostly small street stalls serving freshly cooked foods (noodles, wontons, buns, steamed rice, and stir-fried dishes) were organized into government-run collectives. By the end of 1965, Shanghai had 4,095 restaurants – which employed 37,432 workers – less than a third of the number of restaurants in 1949.[79] However, most restaurants in the pre-1949 era were small (what the locals called "husband and wife shops"),[80] while the government-run restaurants were sizable, generally having nine or more workers. Socialist Shanghai continued to be known for its variety of eateries that served street food, or "little eats" (*xiaochi*).

The majority of these eateries were what Daisy Kwok called "cheap restaurants," which had things like plain noodles for 8 cents on their menu. They were often located on back streets or at the entrance of alleyways, and most of their customers lived on the same block or just across the street. These restaurants opened long hours, typically from 6 a.m. to 2 a.m. Some of them were pubs as well, serving beer and cheap white spirits and a few small dishes to go with the liquor, but plain noodles were always on the menu. For 29 cents, one could have a "wine dinner" that included two liang (100 grams) of kaoliang liquor, one dish selected from of a variety of stir-fried dishes, and one bowl of spring noodles.[81] Shen Jialu (1956–), who worked in one of these restaurants on Yunnan Road in downtown Shanghai in the early 1970s, recalled:

Yunnan Road at night was a fairyland for drunkards. Early in the evening, drunkards had already occupied seats in numerous restaurants along the street. These people did not have much money but came every day, and here was the usual order: a bottle of liquor known as Little Firework, a dish of chili sauce or spiced bean curd, and a bowl of plain noodles. They would sit in the restaurant from 4 p.m. to midnight or even early in the morning. The most troublesome thing, however, was that once they got drunk, there was a ruckus: they fought, overturned tables, and threw beer bottles at each other. The most eye-catching lines on the wall of the restaurant were a quotation of Chairman Mao, "Develop the Economy and Ensure Supplies," and, below it, the phone number of the neighborhood police station.[82]

Yet, according to Maoist class analysis, these unruly customers were "authentic proletarians" who represented the "most advanced class in human history." Their alcoholism tarnished the sage-like image that the party had painted of them for years, but there was not much the restaurant management could do to stop their rowdiness.

Amid the violence of drunkards, scenes of romance might also be played out in these restaurants. For young men with limited means, these eateries were also places where they could treat a date to an affordable bowl of plain noodles. In vulgar Shanghai slang, should this kind of dating lead to sex or marriage, the woman might be mocked as having been "knocked down by a bowl of plain noodles" (*yiwan yangchunmian dadao*), that is, won over on the cheap.

The ubiquity of these small eateries caught the attention of China's then very few foreign visitors. Australian historian Ross Terrill (1938–), who visited Shanghai in 1971, noted that "these neighborhood eating houses are full of interest," and he had a chance to eat in one. "It is in the middle of a shopping district," Terrill wrote. "People come in with bags and bundles – food, textiles, and now and then a camera, radio, or watch. Noodles (boiled or fried) are the specialty of the house.... A hearty restaurant, a carrefour of gossip, noisy with chatter and laughter."[83] Terrill noted that the restaurant's décor was "at the level of a public toilet," but there were no flies and, most of all, "the food is excellent." Even in the very anti-Western environment of the Cultural Revolution, Terrill and his Australian friend were able to sit and mingle with the locals in that "proletarian restaurant," and engage in some people watching:

> The range of diners reflects the relatively prosperity of Shanghai, with its sophisticated industry and higher wages. Here are four men, colleagues it seems, who take their noodles swimming in soup (*t'ang mien*) and already have four empty beer bottles in front of them. Beside us a quiet couple, intellectuals carrying books whose titles I can't catch, who eat fried noodles (*ch'ao mien*) and later hefty slices of the universally popular watermelon.... To remember what dishes to bring to what table, waiters fix a numbered clothespin on a bowl in the center of the table: "7" is "noodles with fish," "16" is "chicken soup." No writing down is called for, and the evidence of what you've eaten and will pay for sits there was a row of pins; "7," "7," "16," "11," "4": total, Y2.90.[84]

By Western standards, a five-dish meal for two for under 3 yuan or little over a dollar was dirt cheap, yet the cost was equivalent to a few days' wages of a factory worker, such as those in the neighborhood workshops discussed in Chapter 4. Even plain noodle soup was not as affordable as it might sound. A Shanghai family of five or six typically spent about 50–60 yuan a month on food, and usually both husband and wife needed to work to put food on table. Rice and wheat flour ranged from 14 to 17 cents per *jin*.[85] It was common for such a family to spent 20–25 yuan a month on rice and flour and about 25–28 yuan for meat, vegetables, fruit, and everything else (cooking oil, sugar, condiments, seasonings, etc.). This meant that the family's daily budget for *cai* was 0.80–0.90 yuan, and if the family paid 8 cents per person for a bowl of plain noodles, it would have used up half of its budget for *cai* that day.

More to the point, the good variety of items available in the city's food markets provided the ingredients for home-cooked dishes that made plain noodles in restaurants seem too plain. The daily dishes of Shanghai families were more nourishing and diverse, and sometimes even cheaper than plain noodles in restaurants. Back in the Republican era, Shanghai was known as for the abundance and variety of foods available in its markets. In 1940, for instance, one of Shanghai's major food markets at Baxianqiao (literally, Bridge of the Eight Immortals) carried more than 2,700 daily items, evidence of the wealth of the city's food culture.[86] As one author has put it, even the human excrement of Shanghai was "considered superior and especially fertile thanks to the rich diet of the people."[87]

Stating from 1953 with the institution of a state monopoly on the purchase and sale of grain (known as "unified purchase and sale"), the supply and selection of food were drastically reduced. For nearly four decades (1955–1993), food grain and cooking oil were rationed. On average, monthly rations were about 28 *jin* (14 kilograms) of rice and 0.5 *jin* (250 grams) of cooking oil per person.[88] Most of the time during the Mao era, other common foods such as pork, fish, eggs, soybean products, and sugar were also rationed.

The party was well aware of the importance of the food supply to the people and, consequently, to the stability of the regime. Since the ration of staple food grain (primarily rice) was fairly sufficient, there was no outright starvation in the city. However, undernourishment did exist and frequently there were shortages of non-staple foods, mainly meat and eggs and to some extent aquatic products. Pork, by far the most popular meat in the Chinese diet, was constantly in demand and, off and on, it too was rationed. But overall pork consumption increased steadily during the Mao era. The average annual pork consumption per person in Shanghai was 9.83 kilograms in 1950, 12.03 kilograms in 1964, and 26.52 kilograms in 1976.[89]

The supply of vegetables also increased. In the early 1950s, the city's daily supply of vegetables stood at 1,000–1,400 tons. This jumped to 3,000–3,600 tons in 1961 and 1962, providing 0.47–0.58 kilograms (1–1.3 pounds) of vegetables per capita per day. This was the highest level of vegetable consumption in Shanghai's modern history. Vegetables remained the main source of nutrition afterward and supplies were mostly adequate. On average from the late 1960s to the 1970s, the vegetable supply in the city remained at 2,300–2,500 tons per day (or around 0.40 kilograms per person).[90] Also, vegetables were affordable. For decades the average retail price of twenty-seven of the most commonly consumed vegetables was just about 5–6 cents per *jin*.[91] These vegetables – such as green beans, broad beans, and sweet peas – were extremely important as sources of protein since meat, eggs, and dairy products were in short supply. In addition, inexpensive aquatic products such as sea snails, mussels, eels, and loaches were unrationed and commonly available (see Table 7.1).

Table 7.1 *Prices of non-staple foods in Shanghai, 1963–1977, cents (fen) per* jin *(500 grams)*

Vegetables

Chicken-feather-shaped little greens, 3	Shanghai bok choy, 5
Cabbage, 3	Chinese cabbage, 7
Three-colored amaranth, 7	Toothed medicks, 8
Chives, 8	String beans, 10
Local broad bean pods, 5	Broad bean pods, 7–8
Sweet beans, 12	Tomatoes, 5–8
Potatoes, 10	Celery, 7–8
Eggplant, 5–8	Spinach, 7
Soybean sprouts, 6	Green bean sprouts, 7–13
Fresh soybean pods, 8	Cucumbers, 4
Wax gourds, 7	Pumpkin, 6
Tofu (soft), 11	Dried bean curd, 5/piece; 4/piece (spicy)
Sweet potatoes, 3.5	Salted potherb mustard, 10

Meat and Eggs

Pork, average, 85	Pork rib back, 80
Lean pork, 103	Small pork ribs, 56
Chicken eggs, 78–85	Duck eggs, 77–82

Aquatic Products

Cutlass fish (small), 15–21	Cutlass fish (large), 22–27
Cutlass fish (extra-large), 31–35	Yellow croaker (small), 21–25
Yellow croaker (large), 35–40	Shad, 70
Pomfret, 50	Cuttlefish, 26
Yangtze River saury, 60	Finless eels, 40
Loach, 20	Common winkle (regular), 8–10
Common winkle (small), 5	River snails, 12
Clams, 18	Mussels (pumpkin-seed shaped), 35
Blood clams, 20	Carp (live; 150 grams or more), 74
Crucian (live; 150 grams or more), 82–84	Tullibee (live; 200 grams or more), 47
Bighead carp (live; 500 grams or more), 54	River fish average, 63.43
Sea fish average, 38.72	

Cooking Oil and Sugar

Soybean oil, 88	Peanut oil, 88
Rapeseed oil, 81	Sesame oil, 102
White granulated sugar, 78	Brown Cuban sugar, 68

Sources: Shanghai jiage zhi bianzuan weiyuanhui, *Shanghai jiage zhi*; Shanghai fushipin shangye zhi bianzuan weiyuanhui, *Shanghai fushipin shangye zhi*; Shanghai sucai shangye zhi bianzuan weiyuanhui, *Shanghai sucai shangye zhi*; I-27; I-30; I-31; I-33, and I-46.

The standard container that every family used for shopping for uncooked food was a braided bamboo basket with a handle on the top (Figure 7.4). The government used a colloquial expression to describe its efforts to improve the food supply for urban residents as "bamboo basket projects."[92] These efforts included such things as subsidizing vegetable farmers, and, in the city's suburbs, expanding vegetable farmland and increasing its productivity. The government also allowed a small number of tiny private foodsellers to continue to operate after nationalization, mainly so these people could eke out a living; but this also gave the city's consumers some options when it came to buying food. Before 1966, there were 1,984 licensed peddlers in the city. Even the radical "cutting off capitalist tails" during the Cultural Revolution did not eliminate them. By the end of the Mao era, Shanghai still had 882 private peddlers, including 700 selling green onions and ginger root (like the one Alexander Haig allegedly had met) and 133 selling aquatic products such as finless eels, river snails, and clams.[93]

Aside from eleven indoor food markets, the rest of Shanghai's food markets were open-air. Each occupied a 250-meter or so stretch along a back street. One exceptionally big open-air market along Julu Road (formerly, Rue Ratard) stretched for nearly a kilometer and occupied an area of over 8,000 square meters. In most of these markets, tents were permanently set up on sidewalks on both sides of the street. Shoppers walked down the middle of the street, and automobile traffic was blocked, making these streets practically the city's only car-free pedestrian zones. The markets sold all kinds of uncooked foods and, occasionally, deli products. In 1954, Shanghai had 250 such food markets, most of which had originated as spontaneously formed open-air farmers' markets in the preceding century. Like all types of commerce, these markets were socialized in the late 1950s. By 1966, the number of food markets had been reduced to 149; but all over the city, the government set up more than 500 "supply network points" (*gongying wangdian*), that is, small shops or clusters of tents that were, for administrative purposes, considered part of a larger food market. To make shopping convenient, the plan was that on average every 0.2 square kilometers and 2,100 households would have a food-sales point.[94] In practice, such a precise goal was hard to achieve, but food and grocery shopping was always just a short walk from home.[95]

Part of everyday life in Shanghai was shopping for fresh food in a nearby market. Every so often this was a daunting task, as there were always long lines in front of the tents that sold popular items or things in short supply. The markets opened at six in morning, but people lined up one or two hours earlier to improve their chances of getting what they wanted. Because each tent sold only one type of food, it was hard to get

244   Part III: Under the French Parasol Trees

Figure 7.4 A queue in front of the entrance of an indoor food market (built in 1928–1930) at the intersection of Fuzhou Road and Zhejiang Road in downtown Shanghai, 1956. The market was known for the great variety of its aquatic products, which were frequently unrationed. Note the bamboo basket that almost everyone carries. Note also the store on the far left had just added four characters, *gong si he ying* (joint state–private ownership), handwritten with a writing brush on its original carved shop sign, indicating that the ownership of the store had been changed. *Source:* Shanghai Municipal Library.

more than one or two items before the food was sold out. By 8 a.m., the market's morning hours had largely ended, and all that remained were only a few less popular items.

To try to make shopping fair, the market administration often limited the amount of any particular item in demand (unrationed fish, pork ribs, fresh eggs, etc.) each customer could buy. Since market shopping involved hours of waiting in line early in the morning (a particularly unpleasant task in winter and on rainy days), some families hired a maid to do the shopping. These maids were mostly middle-aged housewives who, to make a little extra money, did the shopping for their neighbors. Sometimes these women also brought their children to help. To get the job done, a woman simultaneously took a place in multiple lines, using a ragged bamboo basket or just a broken brick to mark her spot. People in general would honor this token, but if her leave of absence took too long, this courtesy was not always forthcoming and disputes inevitably followed. Cursing sometimes led to jostling but rarely developed into a fist fight. The early morning shopping therefore required energy and some level of aggression. It is estimated that by the end of the Mao era every morning nearly one million people were shopping in Shanghai's food markets, making them the liveliest as well as the noisiest and most contentious places in the city.[96]

The various bamboo basket projects did not solve the overall problem of a shortage of food but they did ease it. The very existence of such efforts and other measures to cope with the food supply problem indicate that the party was sensitive to – and, to some extent, effective in handling – real-life issues of the people. Except for the Great Famine years of 1960–1962, there was generally a good variety of seasonal vegetables and aquatic products available in the market at low and government-subsidized prices, and most of the time they were not rationed. At the same time, the people of Shanghai were creative in using limited food supplies to put diverse dishes on the dining table. It should be noted that the city has been known for its culinary tradition that was sustained by women and men alike. Unlike the conventional image of men working to support the family and women taking care of home cooking, Shanghai men were known for cooking frequently, if not daily, at home, which sometimes made them a laughing stock of people outside the city – particularly among northern Chinese, who were frequently stereotyped as male chauvinists – and earned them the not so flattering reputation of being "less-than manly men."[97] No matter who took care of cooking, within a budget of about 50 cents, a Shanghai family was able to prepare a meal for four to five. Such a budget was not enough to cover steamed rice, but for cooks steeped in China's renowned food tradition, it was sufficient for turning out home-cooked dishes (*jiachang cai*) that were often nutritionally balanced and flavorsome. A group of my informants, three women and one man, easily came up with a list of dishes they used to cook within this budget. A menu typically included three dishes and one soup, such as:

> Sautéed spinach stir fry with tofu
> Dry braised string beans
> Stir-fried sea snails with soy sauce and ginger
> Tomato and egg soup

or

> Stir-fried three-colored amaranth with red preserved bean curd sauce
> Shredded pork stir fry with dried bean curd and chili pickled mustard
> Steamed eggplant with garlic bits
> Purple seaweed and dried shrimp soup with green onions

There were also many alternatives. For instance, dishes like stir-fried Shanghai bok choy or bean sprouts, shepherd's purse with ground pork, or a soup of brined potherb mustard with broad beans could replace any of the items on the menus. Obviously, these dishes did not provide much animal protein. Pork, poultry, and eggs were expensive and often rationed, meaning they were used in small quantities, such as shredded pork or ground pork for stir-fry dishes and egg drops for soup.[98]

A major challenge with cooking vegetable dishes was that they usually require a certain amount of cooking oil to be tasty, but the monthly ration for oil – and oil was always rationed – was just 0.5 *jin* (250 grams) per person.[99] Pork fat therefore was a popular substitute. Canned lard was among the most common items that Hong Kong families sent to their mainland relatives in the early 1960s. The meat supply improved significantly after 1961, when the party introduced economic reforms in the wake of the GLF disaster. By September 1, 1965, pork sold in Shanghai for 0.85 yuan a *jin*, which included a 10 percent government subsidy. This price remained unchanged until October 1979. Moreover, for over twelve years (from June 1, 1964, to July 15, 1976), pork was "available without restriction" (*changkai gongying*), meaning it was not rationed.[100]

Still, for most families, a substantial meat dish was a treat they could afford only once or twice a month, and poultry was a rare luxury. The most common meat dishes were pork-based, such as red braised pork belly, stewed pork chops, sweet-and-sour pork ribs, and so on. Red braised pork belly, in particular, was not only said to be Mao's favorite dish but was so popular among the public that it was almost a synonym for meat.[101] Among commonly consumed aquatic products were cutlass fish, yellow croaker, and river catfish, usually lightly fried or steamed with green onions and ginger; more elaborate cooking added tofu, fermented broad bean sauce, or salted cabbage. Meat soups were also popular. A local delicacy known as "pickled fresh" (*yanduxian*), which was introduced in Republican-era Shanghai and became a well-known homemade dish in the lower Yangzi delta area (generally known as the Jiangnan region), was a soup of cured pork plus fresh pork with bamboo shoots or sheet bean curds (dried tofu folded into the shape of a knot). Another local favorite was "Russian soup." In the mid-1930s, there were about 30,000 Russians and East Europeans living in Shanghai – local people dubbed them all "White Russians."[102] They had a significant influence on the city's food culture. "Russian soup" – a borscht made of cabbages, carrots, tomatoes and, most importantly, beef – became a popular dish in many households.

As noted earlier, to prepare meals within a tight budget and in the face of a short supply required waiting in line to buy the ingredients. Until they were in their forties or fifties, people who were born or grew up in the 1950s never experienced a life without the need to line up at the market. In Karl Gerth's words, "queues became an iconic image of shopping life."[103] A woman born in 1951 once asked her father if there was a time when people did not have to wait in line to buy groceries. The father, a middle-school teacher, told her lining up daily at the market did not exist until after Liberation.[104] Queuing up became such an omnipresent part of daily life that people had to find ways of coping in order not to be consumed by it. The early morning markets were a place for neighbors to get to know each other and, once acquainted, to help each other secure a spot in line. Waiting in line, people often talked about all kinds of subjects, even unsanctioned political news. Rumors from the marketplace – prefaced by the words "people in the food market said that ..." (*xiaocaichang li de ren jiangde*) – were something that people paid attention to because, based on experience, they were up to date and usually accurate.[105] In the teeming food markets children often got their first lesson in the fundament fact that life can be competitive: Cutting in line and shoving to get ahead were frequent. Yet, standing in line could also bring some unlikely gratification, according to one Shanghai resident.

The charm of these lines is that once you queue up, you will feel a kind of collective enthusiasm for a certain type of food and an odd sense of assurance that "once I am in line, the final victory—that is, getting the food—will come." While in line, one smells the food. In front of the Harbin [bakery], one smells the cream

248   Part III: Under the French Parasol Trees

cake baking; in Bright Village [a restaurant/delicatessen], one smells smoked herring; in front of the Number Two Food Store, one smells oil-scented crispy moon cakes. Middle-aged women are chatting about what they are going to fix for dinner; a man with glasses is reading; and little children are nagging for candies. What a colorful and delicious thing it is to stand in line to buy some food![106]

Such good cheer amid the daily tedium of standing in line for groceries reminds us of the so-called coolies' fun in old Shanghai, with rickshaw pullers winding their way through the traffic that hampered bigger vehicles, and then laughing and joking with – and teasing – the traffic cop. Despite their exhausting work, these men found moments of mirth.[107] The contexts of the two were unalike, but the spirit of finding contentment amid hardship was similar. It was this kind of optimism and vitality that helped sustain people through the hardships of the Mao era.

Conclusion

Although Mao's regime was one of the most contentious in history, one could argue that its accomplishments were remarkable. Since the mid-nineteenth century China had been torn apart by constant warfare, political turmoil, and natural disaster, but under the Communists it was united. The revolution instilled in the Chinese people a sense of unity and national rejuvenation. Life expectancy at birth grew from 35–40 years when the Communists took power to 65.5 years by the end of the Mao era, one of the most rapid sustained increases in documented global history.[1] The regime also presided over what has been described as "perhaps the single greatest educational effort in human history."[2] In 1949, China's illiteracy rate stood at roughly 85–90 percent; by 1979, this figure had dropped to about 25 percent.[3]

On the other side of the ledger, Mao's China was one of the most repressive and disaster-ridden nations in the world. Acting according to the principles of Communism, the state seized all land and largely eliminated private property. The CCP apparatus was established in every village, urban workplace, and neighborhood, policing every aspect of people's lives to a level unprecedented in history. It was the only country that had tens of millions of people who starved to death not because of war or natural disaster but because of the government's policy failures during the GLF.[4] It purged hundreds of thousands of intellectuals during the Anti-Rightist Campaign, and condemned many so-called rightists and their families to decades in "labor reform" camps. Nearly twenty million urban youths were involuntarily sent to border regions and barren rural areas to be "reeducated" by "poor and lower-middle peasants," imposing tremendous hardship and causing countless tragedies to both the urban and rural populations.[5] Finally, in the final ten years of Mao's rule, catastrophic destruction of culture and social values under the aegis of the Cultural Revolution brought the country to the verge of collapse and bequeathed a legacy of destruction and violence to generations of Chinese to come.

Looking at the Weberian tripartite classification of political authority – rational-legal, charismatic, and traditional – it is clear the Mao regime successfully rolled the first two into one but failed to encompass the third.[6] The establishment of the PRC provided the Communists legal-constitutional authority that throughout Mao's time (and indeed to this day) met no effective challenge. Mao excelled at what Daniel Leese has called "charismatic mobilization" as a way either to implement the party's policies or to circumvent the party as an institution by appealing directly to the masses.[7] His extraordinary qualities and personality cult accounted for his charismatic authority. Mao's revolution attempted to challenge and ultimately eliminate traditional authority (i.e., one where power derives from long-established culture, customs, and social structures), but in the end largely failed.[8]

The Maoist party line condemned anything and everything that did not meet its "proletarian" values as "bourgeois" or "feudal." Such "reactionary" remnants were to be attacked, purged, and eliminated. The political and ideological goal, especially in the last decade of the Mao era, was to spark "a revolution deep in one's soul," with the impossible mission of ridding human nature of "selfishness."[9] But the standards were arbitrary, often rendering the political climate of a given time contradictory with that of other times. This kind of contradiction was not acknowledged as an error or insistency, but rather was rationalized as in line with "Marxist dialectical materialism." Maoist ideology became a conglomeration of terms and symbols that were wielded as a weapon in factional infighting, spouted as a testament to loyalty, and manipulated by individuals scrambling to get ahead. On the ground, competent party cadres were not those who were ideologically rigid but those who knew how to cut and fit party policies to suit diverse situations and individuals.

Scholars have pointed out that in their daily operations CCP cadres had become bureaucratic technocrats who responded to and attempted to modify or change the "structure," which is "broadly defined to refer to everything that lies outside a political actor and sets limits to what is politically possible at any particular time through dynamic manipulations."[10] In such manipulations, as Aminda Smith has noted, cadres and officials recognized "the limits of simplistic solutions to complex social problems, and they frequently meditated on the tensions between the theory and the practice of ideological remolding."[11] Sociologist Erving Goffman called this type of maneuvering "a working understanding."[12] As this study has revealed, even when purges and "class struggle" were most severe, there were local cadres who commiserated with people who had been politically condemned, obeyed age-old cultural enactments, followed common sense, or blended party policies with old values and practices. In other words, functionaries at various levels of the party-state apparatus found ways to practice political tai chi, so to speak.

The most formidable force opposing Maoist ideology, however, was not something that was organized or confrontational – rather, it was the sheer indifference of the people. Tai-chi type circuitousness and wangling were more commonly found among ordinary people at the grassroots level than in officialdom. It was not carefully planned but instead was extemporaneous. The Shanghai way of coping with Communism depicted in this study had no established ideology, no perceptible organization, no given agenda. At one level it was a spontaneous struggle for survival; at another, it was a clever and persistent pursuit of comfort and pleasure. Either way, it constituted a pattern of unintended and also informal resistance against Maoist heavy-handed interference in everyday life. "The general pattern of life is important," sociologist William Foote Whyte once wrote, "but it can be constructed only through observing the individuals whose actions make up that pattern."[13] What the preceding chapters have provided is precisely such observations of individual actions and behaviors that constituted that pattern.

As we have seen in this study, Mao's era was marked by a constant shortage of virtually every daily necessity. To get by, people devised ways to put extremely limited resources to best use. In an age of material scarcity, creativity and ingenuity were often reflected in trivial ways, ways that might be thought to be insignificant and might be easily overlooked. But as Georg Hegel said, "The familiar, precisely because it is familiar, remains unknown."[14] It would take effort to discern fashion in a time when every inch of fabric was rationed, to know how fine food could be when every drop of cooking oil was controlled, to appreciate a little flowerpot culture when aesthetics were condemned as bourgeois – in short, it would require an attentive eye to see colors and individualities in the vast ocean of monotony and uniformity and to recognize the significance of the insignificant.

These small manifestations of individuality reveal a type of everyday resistance to party-dictated norms in private life. At the private level, Shanghainese, from the old rich and best minds to common people living in crowded back alleyways, struggled to keep their lifestyle intact as much as possible, using the party's own policies and programs to maintain a way of life that the party might well condemn as "bourgeois decadence." The essence of such a lifestyle – for some it was no more than the pursuit of a simple pleasure – never died out during Mao's time, but instead became a powerful undercurrent beneath the surface of Communist asceticism. There were colors among the humdrum and monotony, interests that diverged from official doctrine, and individuality hidden in uniformity.

Elizabeth J. Perry has pointed out that central to Maoist mass mobilization was "the role of cultural positioning, or the strategic deployment of a range of symbolic resources (religion, ritual, rhetoric, dress, drama, art, and so on) for purposes of political persuasion."[15] There was another side of cultural positioning as well, one where people were apathetic toward official mobilization while in subtle and savvy ways they circumvented Maoist norms and, in daily life, "positioned" themselves with their own deep-seated cultural norms. This was done informally, in the way that "people employ various forms of action that are not premade" but are created ad hoc to "make the most of the possibilities in given circumstances."[16]

The tai-chi type of resistance that this study has explored found fertile ground in Shanghai largely because it could be enacted in everyday life where "being informal" was the order of the day. If there is a "tyranny of informality," as a social theory on contemporary cultural practices has argued, then the power of informality applies perfectly to daily life in Shanghai in the time of Maoist tyranny.[17] As we have seen in this study, the power of informality was typically executed quietly and often invisibly. It was like "an underground movement of secret freedom fighters, each acting individually and independently to ignore, evade, resist and thwart the increasingly heavy hand of government power."[18] The informality and invisibility exerted a subtle but sure influence on one's character without one being consciously aware of it. In silence, people crafted an insurgence to defend the city's character.

By the end of the Mao era, the legacy of the city's capitalist spirit and its associated bourgeois lifestyle survived just below the surface of Maoist socialism (Figure C.1). A percipient observer could almost smell the remains of the past after decades of revolution. Historian Ross Terrill, who visited China in 1974, exclaimed, "It is amazing how often socialist Shanghai talks about capitalism, how insistently a visit to Shanghai evokes thought about the bitch-goddess of capitalism. Twenty-five years of Liberation, yet not quite liberated from this specter. You see no sign of capitalism, but it remains a psychic dragon, to be looked in the eye and slain."[19]

Shanghai was not alone in preserving old values and practices that undermined the Maoist dictatorship and cultural positioning. Scholars have noted that a "second society," underground and mostly invisible, existed nationwide by the end of Mao's rule.[20] Mao famously proclaimed that in the struggle for Communism, "Either the East Wind [Communism] prevails over the West Wind [capitalism] or the West Wind prevails over the East Wind; there can be no compromise."[21] Mao apparently was too categorical in his claim. Even in the most radical years of Mao's revolution – in what Michael Dutton described as "the years that burned" – the wind did not always blow in one direction.[22] Less than a

Conclusion 253

Figure C.1 Shanghai shortly after the Mao era. Photo taken from the Shanghai Television Tower looking east by Bruce Dale in 1980. Note that the thin shadow of the tower (on the right pointing upward) is pointing east to the Shanghai Library and People's Park and People's Square, which were the British racecourse before Liberation. *Source: National Geographic*, vol. 158, no. 1 (July 1980): 28–9.

decade after the close of the Mao era, anthropologist James L. Watson pointed out: "There is often a discrepancy between the expressed goals of political campaigns and the practical consequences of social engineering. In this China is by no means unique."[23] In more recent research, scholars have noted that "heterogeneity, limited pluralism, and tension between official and unofficial cultures were persistent features of grassroots society during the Mao years."[24] In that regard, Shanghai was not a unique case of deviation and resistance.

Nevertheless, the city did possess some exceptional qualities that made the tai-chi type of nonconformity possible. Most notably, its culture of openness and inclusiveness – both of which derived from its history since late imperial times – stood in sharp contrast to the stultifying, rigid, and dogmatic atmosphere of the time. Shanghai was vibrant long before the arrival of foreigners. Decades before Europeans set foot in town, Shanghai was noted for its culture of openness and receptiveness, to the extent that its folk customs were regarded as "soft" and newcomers often overshadowed native people so much so that they changed the economic landscape.[25] When the British arrived in Shanghai after the Opium War, they found a striking difference between Guangzhou (Canton), where they had had at least a century of business experience with the Chinese, and Shanghai, a town new to them. These foreigners found Shanghai's people more amicable and the city and its environs more accessible to strangers from afar.[26] This kind of openness was a long-standing norm, and the British were merely another type of "guest merchants," as businesspeople from out of town were called.[27]

The story of the century of Western domination of the city that followed has been often told. It was largely because of Shanghai's semi-colonial status – with foreigners acting as both exploiters and guardians – that the city's receptiveness continued. And, in this semi-colonial atmosphere, the phenomenon of newcomers from elsewhere in China triumphing over Shanghai's natives became even more striking. It was an expanded version of what local historians described as Shanghai's softness.[28] This led to a distinctive culture known as *Haipai* – "Shanghai style" – in contrast to "indigenous" culture represented by Beijing (*Jingpai*, or "Beijing style").

While the Beijing style has been regarded as orthodox, earthbound, and conservative, the Shanghai style has been perceived as new but unorthodox, innovative but commercially driven – in the eyes of Communist revolutionaries, quintessentially capitalist. It was also perceived as liberal, open, and, in particular, receptive to Western influences.[29] Although this is true it is also incomplete. The role Chinese migrants played in the century after the Opium War was equally, if not more, important. After all, with foreigners accounting for only 3 percent of Shanghai's residents even at the peak of the foreign dominance in the city, Shanghai was essentially still a Chinese city. Around that time, 80 percent of the city's Chinese population was born outside Shanghai.[30] This phenomenon can be summed up by the Chinese metaphor "presumptuous guests usurp the host's role." The rapid growth of Shanghai in the late nineteenth and early twentieth centuries was orchestrated, promoted, and carried out almost entirely by outsiders, that is, either foreign expatriates or migrants from elsewhere in China. Shanghai's celebrated cosmopolitanism prior to 1949 was in large part derived from that tradition.

The return of Shanghai's old cosmopolitanism in the post-Mao era is a testament to the vitality of the city's character, in particular its cosmopolitan tradition. "Shanghai would have been a great city had there never been a foreigner in the place," a Western expatriate in Shanghai wrote in 1926 when Chinese nationalistic fervor was at a high point. "It would continue to be a great city even if the foreigners should vacate their modern buildings and go home." Quoting the statement decades later, at the time when the Communists had just taken power and foreigners were driven out China, historian Rhoads Murphey declared: "While the first sentence is an overstatement of the case, the second sentence is undoubtedly accurate."[31] Today it is clear that neither of the sentences is accurate.

It might be questionable to declare that foreigners were an indispensable force driving Shanghai's development, but it is clear that the greatness of the city lies in its openness and cosmopolitanism, the most critical ingredient of which is receptiveness to the ideas brought by newcomers, be they foreigners or not. Western influences, even when they came in the form of an aggression and were protected by gunboats, have been a great stimulus. As Marie-Claire Bergère has pointed out, in Shanghai "the customary xenophobia took the form of a modern nationalism that aimed to take up the Western challenges on its own terms: It aspired to economic modernization, material prosperity, and social progress."[32]

Shanghai's receptiveness to Western influences made it seem abnormal in the eyes of the multitudes in the vast expanses of earthbound China. Eventually, after 1949, Shanghai's old cosmopolitanism was condemned and, as a consequence, the city stagnated, at least in its infrastructure. However, as this study shows, old ways of life and the "bourgeois" spirit lived on, sometimes in private homes, sometimes surfacing in back alleys and major thoroughfares, contesting with the party for public space. Overall, the people of Shanghai during the Mao era developed an art of being ruled. In time, this hidden legacy prepared the way for the dramatic and widespread resurgence of "bourgeois" pleasures after Mao.[33]

In the post-Mao era, especially since the early 1990s, the party has called for a return of the spirit of capitalism, and bestowed it with political legitimacy. In one of his speeches during his historic 1992 southern tour,[34] Deng Xiaoping made a rare self-criticism regarding Shanghai:

In the areas of talented personnel, technology, and administration, Shanghai has an obvious superiority, which radiates over a wide area. Looking back, my one major mistake was not including Shanghai when we set up the four Special Economic Zones (SEZ). Otherwise, the situation with regard to reform and opening to the outside in the Yangzi River delta, the entire Yangzi River valley, and even the entire nation would have been different.[35]

The party, in a sense, unleashed Shanghai so as to stimulate the "socialist market economy," its top priority after Tiananmen.[36] What Deng was unwilling or unable to admit in public was that the city's bourgeois spirit and Westernization, which had been denounced by the party for so long, now were useful.[37] Shanghai's post-Mao boom has been celebrated, in Wen-hsin Yeh's words, as "the return of the banker," so that the city could "reclaim a genealogy."[38] Such a genealogy can be traced back to the city's not so distant ancestry, in the late nineteenth century and first half of the twentieth century when receptivity and creativity were in the city's DNA. This has made the decades of Maoist isolation seem like an unfortunate but easily forgotten interlude in the city's long history of openness and adaptation.

To paraphrase General MacArthur's famous words, Maoism has not died, it has only faded away. While one cannot be certain whether it will be revived someday or in some way, one can be certain that should it return to China in full force, it will be met with the kinds of accommodation, deviation, and manipulation delineated in this study – particularly at the grassroots level. This is because resistance arising from common human needs and a sense of dignity or, more generally, basic humanism, although not always readily visible, is nonetheless tenacious and, to the dismay of any autocrat, all-powerful.

Appendix

List of Informants

No.[a]	Sex	Year of birth	Occupation[b]	Location	Date
I-1	M	1942	Radio factory manager	Shanghai	6.25.2015
I-2	M	1938	Enamel plant worker	Shanghai	8.17.2016
I-3	M	1943	Middle-school teacher	Shanghai	8.17.2016
I-4	F	1949	Shop clerk	Shanghai	8.17.2016
I-5	M	1939	Hospital worker	Shanghai	6.21.2007
I-6	F	1945	School teacher	Shanghai	8.17.2016
I-7	M	1943	College professor	Shanghai	11.20.2015
I-8	M	1944	Senior accountant	Shanghai	11.20.2015
I-9	F	1945	High-school teacher	Shanghai	11.20.2015
I-10	M	1944	Textile company manager	Taipei	1.14.2012
I-11	M	1939	Office worker	Hong Kong	9.12.2014
I-12	F	1950	Recycling center worker	Shanghai	3.18.2013
I-13	F	1938	Neighborhood canteen worker	Shanghai	7.31.2013
I-14	F	1946	Schoolteacher	Shanghai	6.29.2014
I-15	F	1946	Factory office worker	Shanghai	6.29.2014
I-16	F	1925	APT worker	Shanghai	7.3.2014
I-17	F	1939	APT worker	Shanghai	7.3.2014
I-18	F	1936	APT worker	Shanghai	7.3.2014
I-19	F	1944	"Barefoot doctor"	Shanghai	7.20.2017
I-20	F	1922	APT worker	Shanghai	7.12.2004
I-21	F	1925	APT worker	Shanghai	7.12.2004
I-22	F	1936	APT worker	Beijing	7.27.2013
I-23	F	1939	APT worker	Shanghai	5.31.2014
I-24	F	1953	APT worker	Tokyo	7.2.2016
I-25	F	1936	"Barefoot doctor"	Shanghai	6.5.2016

(cont.)

No.[a]	Sex	Year of birth	Occupation[b]	Location	Date
I-26	F	1941	APT worker	Shanghai	6.5.2016
I-27	F	1941	APT worker	Shanghai	6.5.2016
I-28	M	1951	Carpenter	Shanghai	7.25.2017
I-29	F	1949	Bank clerk	Shanghai	7.1.2015
I-30	F	1938	Domestic maid	Shanghai	6.21.2013
I-31	F	1940	Domestic maid	Beijing	8.15.2011
I-32	M	1945	Tramcar conductor	Shanghai	11.202015
I-33	M	1952	Factory worker	Shanghai	7.3.2014
I-34	M	1943	Yangzi River boat attendant	Shanghai	12.20.2015
I-35	F	1949	Tailor	Singapore	6.12.2016
I-36	F	1940	Physician	Berlin	5.30.2017
I-37	F	1947	Factory worker	Shanghai	3.20.2013
I-38	M	1943	Bus conductor	Shanghai	7.20.2017
I-39	M	1944	Accountant	Shanghai	6.30.2019
I-40	F	1950	Restaurant worker	Shanghai	7.17.2014
I-41	F	1953	Office worker	Shanghai	7.24.2014
I-42	F	1948	Factory worker	Shanghai	7.17.2018
I-43	F	1947	Factory worker	Shanghai	7.17.2018
I-44	F	1945	Factory worker	Shanghai	3.21.2013
I-45	M	1954	Noodle house cook	Taipei	1.19.2012
I-46	F	1948	Shop assistant	Shanghai	6.25.2013
I-47	F	1951	Librarian	Brisbane	5.25.2012

[a] Informants are cited in the text by code, such as "I-1." Some of the interviews conducted in Shanghai were arranged by the Institute of History and the Institute of Sociology, Shanghai Academy of Social Sciences, and the Shanghai Research Center, Fudan University. The interviews were conducted with the understanding that the names of informants would not be divulged, with a few exceptions where the interviewees had no qualms about disclosing their identity.

[b] The column "Occupation" shows each informant's occupation of longest duration during the Mao era.

Character List

afei 阿飛
Ahjin 阿锦
Ai Qing 艾青 (1910–1996)

baoliu gongzi 保留工資
Baromon 培羅門
Bei Dao 北島 (1949–)
buke 補課

Appendix

cai 菜
cailanzi gongcheng 菜籃子工程
can baobao 蠶寶寶
Cao Ying 草嬰 (1923–2015)
chang 長
changkai gongying 敞開供應
Chen Cun 陳村 (1954–)
Chen Danyan 陳丹燕 (1958–)
Chen Hanbo 陳翰伯 (1914–1988)
Chen Jianhua 陳建华 (1947–)
Chen Julai 陳巨來 (1904–1984)
Chen Sihe 陳思和 (1954–)
Chen Yi 陳毅 (1901–1972)
Chenbao fukan 晨報副刊
chi dingxi 吃定息
chi qiaohui 吃僑匯
choulaojiu 臭老九

Da Qizhen 達奇珍 (1952–)
Dai Sijie 戴思傑 (1954–)
Dai Wangshu 戴望舒 (1905–1950)
dangxing 黨性
danwei 單位
dashi 大師
dazibao 大字報
Deng Yingchao 鄧穎超 (1904–1992)
dushu wuyong 讀書無用
dushuren 讀書人

falü 法律
fan 飯
Fang Ping 方平 (1921–2008)
fanmian jiaocai 反面教材
feipin 廢品
Feng Deying 馮德英 (1935–)
Feng Qiuping 馮秋萍 (1911–2001)
fengzixiu 封資修
Fu Cong (Fou Ts'ong) 傅聰 (1934–2020)
Fu Lei (Fou Lei) 傅雷 (1908–1966)
Fu Min 傅敏 (1937–)
fuqi laopo dian 夫妻老婆店

Gao Mingkai 高名凱 (1911–1965)
Gaogao de baiyangshu 高高的白楊樹

gaoji zhishifenzi 高級知識分子
Ge Yan 葛嚴 (1957–)
geminghua 革命化
gong si he ying 公私合營
gongying wangdian 供應網點

Haiying 海嬰 (1929–2011)
Han Qiulin 韓秋林 (1962–)
He Amao 何阿毛 (1922–)
He Qifang 何其芳 (1912–1977)
heideng wuhui 黑燈舞會
Hongxiang 鴻翔
Hu Feng 胡風 (1902–1985)
Hu Shih 胡適 (1891–1962)
Hu Sidu 胡思杜 (1921–1957)
Hu Xueyan 胡雪巖 (1823–1885)
Hu Yanyi 胡延溢
Hu Yaobang 胡耀邦 (1915–1989)
Huang Jiguang 黃繼光 (1931–1952)
Huang Jinrong 黃金榮 (1868–1953)
huayifu 花衣服
hukou 戶口

jia lingtou 假領頭
jia lingzi 假領子
jiachang cai 家常菜
jian 尖
Jiang Xiaoyan 江小燕 (1939–)
Jiang Xiaoyuan 江曉原 (1955–)
jiating chushen 家庭出身
jicai 薺菜
jiedao gongchang 街道工廠
Jin Shengtan 金聖嘆 (1608–1661)
Jing Fang 荊方 (1968–)
Jingbao fukan 京報副刊

kanji 漢字
Ke Qingshi 柯慶施 (1902–1965)

laokele 老克勒
laoxiu 老朽
Li Jinhui 黎錦暉 (1891–1967)
Li Keqiang 李克強 (1955–)
Li Lihua 李麗華 (1924–2017)

Li Qing 李清 (ca. 1965)
Li Shenzhi 李慎之 (1923–2003)
Li shi ba jun 黎氏八駿
Li Shuhua 李書華 (1890–1979)
Liang Huifang 梁惠芳 (1917–2008)
Liang Qichao 梁啟超 (1873–1929)
Libailiu 禮拜六
lilong 里弄
lilong shengchanzu 里弄生產組
Lin Huiyin 林徽因 (1904–1955)
Liu Dazuo 劉大作 (1946–)
Liu Haisu 劉海粟 (1896–1994)
Liu Liaoyi 劉遼逸 (1915–2001)
Liu Shaoqi 劉少奇 (1898–1969)
Liu Tsing-kew 劉靖基 (1902–1997)
Liu Xiaofeng 劉小楓 (1956–)
Lou Shide 婁師德 (630–699)
Lou Shiyi 樓適夷 (1905–2001)
lu 露
Lu Ding 陸定 (1873–1930, agnomen "Jiansan" 建三)
Lü Nengzhong 呂能中 (1932–)
Lu Xiaoman 陸小曼 (1903–1965)
Lu Xun 魯迅 (1881–1936)
ludaocu 路道粗
lühua 綠化
Luo Ji'nan 羅稷南 (1898–1971)
Luo Yujun 羅玉君 (1907–1988)
luoshi zhishifenzi zhengce 落實知識分子政策

Ma Liying 馬麗英
Ma Wenrui 馬文瑞 (1912–2004)
malantou 馬蘭頭
Malu tianshi 馬路天使
Manna 曼娜
Mao Dun 茅盾 (1896–1981)
Mao Yuyuan 毛喻原 (1956–)
Maodun lun 矛盾論
Mei Yi 梅益 (1913–2003)
Meiyou banfa ah 沒有辦法啊
minjian ziliao 民間資料
minzhu renshi 民主人士
Mo Yan 莫言 (1954–)

Nanjing lu shang hao ba lian 南京路上好八連
nanxia ganbu 南下幹部
niangzijun 娘子軍
niaoluo 蔦蘿
Nie Chongbin 聶崇彬 (1957–)
niumazou 牛馬走
Nu'an 怒安 (Angry Peace)
Nu'an 怒庵 (Angry Hut)
nühong 女紅

pidouhui 批鬥會
Peng Zuji 彭祖基 (1940–)
po sijiu 破四舊

Qing Qiuzi 清秋子 (1952–)
qingke 請客
qizhuang yifu 奇裝異服
qu 區
Qu Bo 曲波 (Chu Po, 1923–2002)

Sanetō Keishū 實藤惠秀 (1896–1985)
shang zhi jiao 上只角
shangfang baojian 尚方寶劍
Shao Xunmei 邵洵美 (Zau Sinmay, 1906–1968)
Shao Youlian 邵友濂 (1840–1901)
Shaonü zhi xin 少女之心 or *Shaonü de xin* 少女的心
shehui xiansan laodongli 社會閑散勞動力
Shen Jialu 沈嘉祿 (1956–)
Sheng Aiyi 盛愛頤 (1900–1983)
Sheng Junfeng 盛峻峰 (1923–2015)
Sheng Peiyu 盛佩玉 (1905–1989)
Sheng Xuanhuai 盛宣懷 (1844–1916)
Shengdan hong 聖誕紅
shi 市
shi ke sha, bu ke ru 士可殺不可辱
Shi Ximin 石西民 (1912–1987)
Shi Zhecun 施蟄存 (1905–2003)
shihui 實惠
shimu 師母
siheyuan 四合院
Song Zi'an 宋子安 (1906–1969)
Sun Hengfu 孫衡甫 (1875–1944)
Sun Xiang 孫翔 (1957–)

Appendix

tianfan difu 天翻地覆
tongzhan duixiang 統戰對象
tuo mian zi gan 唾面自幹
tuomao jiamian 脫帽加冕

Wang Anyi 王安憶 (1954–)
Wang Dongxing 汪東興 (1916–2015)
Wang Gang 王剛 (1957–)
Wang Jingzhi 王敬之 (1933–)
Wang Qishan 王岐山 (1948–)
Wang Xianguo 王賢國 (1930–)
Wang Zheng 王政 (1952–)
Wang Zhiliang 王智量 (1928–)
Wei Guangqi 魏光奇 (1950–)
weimei zhuyi 唯美主義
wenxue qingnian 文學青年
Weng Xiangguang 翁香光 (1919–)
Wu Liang 吳亮 (1955–)
Wu Tongwen 吳文同 (1908–1966)

Xia Yan 夏衍 (1900–1995)
Xia Yiqiao 夏伊喬 (1918–2012)
Xiandai zazhi 現代雜誌
xiang dang jiao xin 向黨交心
Xiao Gongqin 蕭功秦 (1946–)
xiao shimin 小市民
xiaocaichang li de ren jiangde 小菜場裏的人講的
xiaochi 小吃
xiaokai 小開
xiaoyao pai 逍遙派
Xiaoyu 小玉
Xiaozhu 小珠
Xie Defeng 謝德風 (1906–1980)
Xingsheng Jie 興聖街
Xu Xingye 徐興業 (1917–1990)
Xu Yuanzhang 徐元章 (1946–2015)
Xu Zhimo 徐志摩 (1895–1931)

yan 艷
Yan Fu 嚴復 (1854–1921)
yanduxian 腌篤鮮
Yang Mo 楊沫 (1914–1995)
Yang Zhenning (Yang Chen-Ning) 楊振寧 (1922–)

yangchang kuoshao 洋場闊少
yangchun mian 陽春面
yangren 洋人
Ye Lingfeng 葉靈鳳 (1905–1975)
yeyu daxue 業余大學
Yin Huifen 殷慧芬 (1949–)
yishi 衣食
yishi fumu 衣食父母
yishi zu er zhi rongru 衣食足而知榮辱
yiwan yangchunmian dadao 一碗陽春面打倒
Yongshi 勇士
Yu Zheguang 虞哲光 (1906–1991)
Yutong 宇同

zashu 雜書
Zhang Dainian 張岱年 (1909–2004)
Zhang Fanghui 張方晦 (1942–)
Zhang Zugan 張祖淦
zhaogu 照顧
Zheng Jian 鄭健 (1952–)
zhengce 政策
zhengfu zongyao gei kou fan chi ba 政府總要給口飯吃吧
zhengzhi guashuai 政治掛帥
zhishifenzi 知識分子
Zhong Fulan 仲富蘭 (1950–)
Zhonghua 中華
Zhou Erfu 周而復 (1914–2004)
Zhou Peihong 周佩紅 (1951–)
Zhou Xuan 周璇 (1920–1957)
Zhou Yang 周揚 (1908–1989)
Zhou Yunqin 周韻琴
Zhou Zhenhe 周振鶴 (1941–)
Zhou Zongliang 周宗良 (1875–1957)
Zhu Dake 朱大可 (1957–)
Zhu Meifu 朱梅馥 (1913–1966)
Zhu Xueqin 朱學勤 (1952–)
zhua geming, cu shengchan 抓革命, 促生產
Zhuang Zhujiu 莊鑄九 (1897–)
zibenjia jiqi dailiren 資本家及其代理人
zichan zixiao 自產自銷
zifang dailiren 資方代理人
zongyao tianli renqing jiangde guoqu 總要天理人情講得過去
zujie 租界

Notes

Introduction

1 The only other countries with still-existing Communist regimes of comparable age are Vietnam and North Korea. But unlike the PRC, in both countries Communist rule was significantly interrupted by war.
2 Allison, *Destined for War*, Harvard Kennedy School, www.hks.harvard.edu/publications/destined-war-can-america-and-china-escape-thucydidess-trap.
3 Xiong Yuezhi, "Lishi shang de Shanghai xingxiang sanlun."
4 *All About Shanghai and Environs*, 43.
5 Snow, *Red China Today*, 504.
6 Historian Xiong Zhuzhi devoted an entire chapter in his multivolume general history of Shanghai to the issue of Shanghai's images in modern times; see Xiong Yuezhi, *Shanghai tongshi*, 1: 91–116; see also Gaulon, "Political Mobilization in Shanghai," and Braester, "'A Big Dying Vat,'" on how Communist propaganda immediately after the Liberation and in the 1960s may have contributed to the notion of Shanghai's decadence.
7 Cao Cheng, *Yi huan bei chang ji*.
8 From 1849 to the Japanese occupation of the city in December 1941, Shanghai was divided into three administratively separate areas: the International Settlement, the French Concession, and the Chinese district. Hanchao Lu, *Beyond the Neon Lights*, chap. 1.
9 MacFarquhar and Fairbank, *The Cambridge History of China*, 15:682.
10 Shen Zhihua, *Sulian zhuanjia zai Zhongguo*, 50.
11 Wang and Barr, *Shanghai Boy and Shanghai Girl*, 192–3.
12 Tata, *Shanghai 1949*, 13.
13 Ibid., 30.
14 Barber, *The Fall of Shanghai*, 147.
15 Robert Guillain, "Shanghai Has Fallen without a Fight," by cable for *Le Monde* (May 27, 1949). On another occasion Guillain wrote: "On the spot it was a remarkable event. Shanghai, citadel of capitalism and of the West in Asia, fell into the hands of her conquerors. And who were these latter? Peasants, peasant-soldiers from the river, poor, badly armed, wearing grass-colored sackcloth. Their army did not fire a shot, and one did not even hear the tramp of their marching feet – they wore slippers. These rustics had undoubtedly never seen a city; they craned their necks to gawk at the unbelievable skyscrapers. They neither stole nor raped; and if occasionally they made a purchase, they paid in cash. This had never been seen before

in China." See his preface to Roger Pelissier's book, *La Chine entre en scène* (Paris: Julliard, 1963), 127, quote from Karol, *China*, 127n80.
16 Karol, *China*, 125.
17 *Chicago Daily Tribune*, January 27, 1950.
18 Karol, *China*, 125.
19 *New York Times*, November 20, 1950.
20 Terrill, *Flowers on an Iron Tree*, 74.
21 Zhang Hongming and Pang Yuan, *Zhongguo fangdichan guanli yuanli*, 557–8. Shanghai was not much behind the national average of urban housing during the Mao era. In 1949 the average per capita floorspace in urban China was 6.25 square meters; by 1962 this figure had shrunk to around 3 square meters. The massive campaigns to reduce the urban population thereafter brought per capita floorspace back to around 5 square meters by the end of the Mao years. Kirkby, *Urbanization in China*, 165; Wilson, *Anatomy of China*, 34; see also Chao, "Industrialization and Urban Housing in Communist China," 382, Table 1.
22 Rossi, *The Communist Conquest of Shanghai*, 13.
23 "Finding and Using Grassroots Historical Sources from the Mao Era (by Jeremy Brown)," *Chinese History Dissertation Reviews*, December 15, 2010, https://dissertationreviews.wordpress.com/2010/12/15/finding-and-using-grass roots-historical-sources-from-the-mao-era-by-jeremy-brown/. Scholars have also long been aware of the exceptional availability of newspapers and other sources of data in Shanghai and, in part because the city administration had considerable experience in statistical work, it is likely that the accuracy of data on Shanghai is above average for urban areas. Howe, "The Level and Structure of Employment and the Sources of Labor Supply in Shanghai, 1949–57," 219.
24 Perry, "Trends in the Study of Chinese Politics."
25 See, for example, Roderick MacFarquhar, *The Origins of the Cultural Revolution* (in three volumes) and *Mao's Last Revolution* (co-authored with Michael Schoenhals); Andrew Walder, *China under Mao: A Revolution Derailed*; Felix Wemheuer, *A Social History of Maoist China: Conflict and Change, 1949–1978*; and Frank Dikötter's trilogy chronicling Mao's China: *The Tragedy of Liberation*, *Mao's Great Famine*, and *The Cultural Revolution*.
26 See the "Resolution on Certain Questions in the History of Our Party since the Founding of the People's Republic of China," adopted at the Sixth Plenary Session of the Eleventh Central Committee of the Chinese Communist Party, June 27, 1981.
27 A number of recent edited conference volumes on the Mao era reveal various aspects of the complexity of Maoist politics and society within the one-party system. See, for example, Eyferth, *How China Works*; Brown and Pickowicz, *Dilemmas of Victory*; Brown and Johnson, *Maoism at the Grassroots*; and Veg, *Popular Memories of the Mao Era*.
28 Geertz, *Interpretation of Cultures*, 3–36. Jeremy Brown and Matthew Johnson have used the term "high socialism" to refer to the period from the mid-1950 to 1980 in China, a term that captures the nature of the era. Brown and Johnson, *Maoism at the Grassroots*, 6.
29 "Introducing *The Communist*," in the *Selected Works of Mao Tse-tung*, 2:285–96. For an analysis on the "three magic weapons," see Apter and Saich, *Revolutionary Discourse in Mao's Republic*, 209–10.

30 Historians have debated whether the CCP carried out the transition to socialism quickly, slowly, or not at all in the early 1950s. See Cochran, *The Capitalist Dilemma in China's Communist Revolution*, 2–6. For its part, by the end of 1956, the Chinese government was able to declare that the socialist transformation had been largely completed.
31 Van Slyke, *Enemies and Friends*, 258. A few researchers have noted the role of the united front in the CCP's policies since 1949; see, for example, Miller, *The CCP's United Front Tactics in the U.S.*; Wickeri, *Seeking the Common Ground*; and U, "Dangerous Privilege" and *Creating the Intellectual*.
32 Even during the turbulent times of Cultural Revolution, people who worked in the CCP's United Front Department survived longer than most others in the CCP bureaucracy since they were not a target of Mao's. And, with Mao's prompting, Premier Zhou Enlai was able to protect some prominent united front personalities. See MacFarquhar and Schoenhals, *Mao's Last Revolution*, 96 and 118.
33 Mao, *Selected Works of Mao Tse-tung*, 5:332–49.
34 See the CCP Central Committee report delivered at the party's Ninth National Conference, *Renmin ribao*, April 28, 1969.
35 Mao's definition of *zhishifenzi* (intellectual) was broader than the term is generally used in the West. It could include teachers at all levels, administrative personnel in government and the PLA, commercial banking personnel, engineering and technical personnel, design personnel, news reporters, and physicians. As Timothy Cheek has indicated, it includes "what we would generally consider both intellectuals and professionals (or technical intelligentsia)." Cheek, *The Intellectual in Modern Chinese History*, 161.
36 The point was first raised in Mao's essay "The Chinese Revolution and the Chinese Communist Party" (December 1939), Mao, *Selected Works of Mao Tse-tung*, 2:305–34. This aspect was reiterated by Mao after Liberation; see for example, "Guanyu tonglu ren de yiduan hua" (A talk on fellow travelers), *Hongqi* (Red Flag), no. 19 (1959).
37 Goldman, *China's Intellectuals and the State*, introduction and chap. 9, "Thought Workers in Deng's Time" (by Lynn T. White III), 253–74.
38 The Hundred Flowers Campaign refers to a period of a few months in early 1957 when people were encouraged to openly express their opinions of the Communist Party. The campaign was named after a couplet quoted by Mao in 1956: Let a hundred flowers blossom together, let a hundred schools of thought contend. By the summer of 1957, however, Mao turned the campaign into an ideological crackdown known as the Anti-Rightist movement, which persecuted at least 550,000 alleged "rightists."
39 The question was asked by Luo Ji'nan (1898–1971), who was best known for translating Franz Mehring's biography of Karl Marx into Chinese. Huang Zongying, "Wo xinling Mao Zedong Lu Ji'nan duihua"; Chen Kun, "Wo de bofu Luo Ji'nan." For an empirical study of the Mao-Lu conversation, see Chen Mingyuan, *Jiaru Lu Xun huozhe*.
40 Huang Zongying, "Wo xinling Mao Zedong Lu Ji'nan duihua." On Lu Xun as a Maoist icon, see Goldman, "The Political Use of Lu Xun."
41 Nearly half a century later, when the Mao-Luo conversation became a known fact, there were lively discussions on the conversation and the role of

intellectuals as political critics in the PRC. See Chen Mingyuan, *Jiaru Lu Xun hai huozhe.*

42 Bo Yibo, *Ruogan zhongda juece yu shijian de huigu,* 2:1006; Zhonggong zhongyong zuzhi bu and Zhonggong zhongyang wenxian yanjiushi, *Zhishifenzi wenti wenxian xuanbian,* 48–9.

43 Yu Guangren and Ji Yibing, "Zhishifenzi jieji shuxing rending de jiannan lichen"; Wang Laidi, "Mao Zedong de zhishifenzi zhengce." Despite the party's efforts at law making and its propaganda about law (see Altehenger, *Legal Lessons,* Parts I and II), in the Mao era (and to some extent to this day), it was the often-fickle party policy (*zhengce*), rather than the law (*falü*), that affected people's lives.

44 Mao, *Mao Zedong sixiang wansui,* 498–9.

45 Yan Ming, *Yimen xueke yu yige shidai,* 236–51.

46 Sun Peidong, "Jingshui shenliu."

47 The Great Leap Forward was a radical economic and sociopolitical campaign launched in 1958 in an attempt to achieve Communism before the Soviet Union. Among the catastrophic results of the campaign were widespread famines from 1959 to 1961 that reportedly claimed tens of millions of lives.

48 Kirby, "Continuity and Change in Modern China."

49 Pantsov, *Mao,* 477.

50 Mao, *Mao Zedong xuanji,* 3:846, 4:1112.

51 Premier Zhou Enlai and other moderate leaders within the party quickly promoted the policy and made it politically legitimate. Keizo Okubo, a Japanese economist, noted that signs bearing the slogan "Strive for the Revolution and Increase Production" were seen in every plant he visited during his three-month trip across China in late 1966 and early 1967. Trumbull, *This Is Communist China,* 120.

52 *Renmin ribao,* September 7, 1966, October 10, 1966, and February 21, 1969. For the politics of publishing these editorials, see Tang Yanming and Tang Yaming, *Mao Zhuxi yulu de dansheng ji qita,* 239–46. For the original document of the Chinese Communist Party Central Committee's "Ten-point decision on grasping revolution and promoting production (draft)," December 9, 1966, see https://ccradb.appspot.com/post/84. For Mao's view that the Cultural Revolution should serve as a powerful engine for raising economic productivity, see Mao, *Jianguo yilai Mao Zedong wen'gao,* 12:83, 141. See also Wang Li, *Wang Li fansilu,* 616.

53 Gerth, *Unending Capitalism,* 4.

54 Dikötter, "The Second Society," 183–4.

55 Scott, *Weapons of the Weak.*

56 de Certeau, *The Practice of Everyday Life,* 18.

57 Huntington, *The Clash of Civilizations,* 153.

1 The Upper Crust

1 The campaign officially started in January 1952 and ended in October of that year, but the most intense period was from January to April; by May 1952, the final assessments for businesses under investigation had been announced. Renmin chubanshe, *Sanfan Wufan yundong wenjian huibian,* 37–9.

Notes to pages 21–24   269

2 Zhonggong zhongyang dangshi yanjiushi, *Zhongguo Gongchandang lishi*, 2:165.
3 In old *renminbi* (the Chinese currency before 1955), equivalent to three billion yuan or US$1.25 billion. See Wu Xiaobo, *Lidai jingji bian'ge deshi*, 181. Estimates of the total provided by other sources vary from US$500 million to US$1.25 billion. See Gerth, "Wu Yunchu and the Fate of the Bourgeoisie and Bourgeois Lifestyles under Communism," 194.
4 Mao Zedong, *Mao Zedong xuanji*, 5:57–8. For a detailed account on the campaign in Shanghai, see Gardner, "The Wu-fan Campaign in Shanghai."
5 After the Five-Anti Campaign, central leaders had policy recorded in formal party documents, such as the "Common Program of the Chinese People's Political Consultative Conference," legitimizing a level of continuity in the private economy. State capitalism was initially considered a way to develop the private sector under planned guidance, not to nationalize it altogether and at once as most Western literature has supposed. See Bennis Wai-yip So, "The Policy-Making and Political Economy of the Abolition of Private Ownership in the Early 1950s." On the other hand, the pressure of paying off the fines levied in the Five-Anti Campaign did help accelerate the pace of industrial nationalization. See Richman, *Industrial Society in Communist China*, 895–6; and Willy Kraus, *Private Business in China*, 58.
6 Mao Zedong, *Mao Zedong wenji*, 231.
7 Walder, *China Under Mao*, 79.
8 For the government's rationale of adopting the redemption policy, see Liu Shaoqi's speech of November 16, 1955, in *Liu Shaoqi xuanji*, 2:176–83; for Stalin's policy against private businesses, see Ball, *Russia's Last Capitalists*, 60–82.
9 The pace of the nationalization of private businesses was much faster than the CCP's top leaders had anticipated. Even Mao expressed pleasant surprise in a State Council meeting over the unexpected speed of the transition. See *Renmin ribao* (People's Daily), January 26, 1956.
10 Mao personally knew the situation and, on that basis, he emphasized that the redemption policy should be used primarily for pacifying big businesses. Mao Zedong, *Mao Zedong wenji*, 7:174–83.
11 Smith, *Revolution and the People in Russia and China*, 1.
12 Zhonggong Shanghai dang zhi bianzuan weiyuanhui, *Zhonggong Shanghai dang zhi*, 537.
13 According to a Red Guard account, in August and September 1966, at the height of the campaign, 150,000 homes in Shanghai were searched. In those two months, 32,500 kilograms of gold, 900,000 pieces of gold or silver jewelry, 300,000 pieces of jade, 2.4 million silver dollars, and foreign currency worth millions were confiscated. *Shanghai hongwei zhanbao* (Shanghai Red Guard battlefield report), May 15, 1968. Another report gives the figures of "3.3 million in US dollars, 370 million yuan in cash and bonds, and 2.4 million yuan in silver dollars" and an unspecified number of gold bars, gold and silver jewelry, all confiscated from Shanghai's homes in August and September. Jennifer Lin, *Shanghai Faithful*, 209. See also Xu Jilin and Luo Gang, *Chengshi jiyi*, 227.
14 An example of a portrayal is Robert Loh's *Escape from Red China* (New York, 1962), which has become such a classic in US readings on China (the book was

reprinted in both hardcover and paperback as recently as 2010). More recently, Frank Dikötter's acclaimed "People's Trilogy" portrays the Chinese revolution as an endless tragedy. Shao and Dikötter, "History as Humanity's CV."

15 Since the term *zichan jieji* can mean both "bourgeoisie" and "capitalist class," I use "bourgeois comfort" in this study to refer to the material well-being of former businesspeople. These people were not necessarily "middle class" in the sense the term is typically used; in view of Chinese standards of living at the time, *zichan jieji* was regarded as upper class or the social elite.

16 This is, of course, not to overlook the research in the field that has identified various forces and elements that were at odds with the regime, including recent studies by historians of the PRC on such realities in everyday life beyond ideological rhetoric and elite politics. See Brown and Johnson, *Maoism at the Grassroots*, 1–15.

17 Jie Li, *Shanghai Home*, 16.

18 Three articles of Mao, revered as the holy grail of class analysis, served as the cornerstone for united front policy-making: "Analysis of the Classes in Chinese Society," "The Chinese Revolution and the Chinese Communist Party," and "On New Democracy." See *Selected Works of Mao Tse-tung*, 1:13–19, 2:305–31, 339–82.

19 The distinction could be arbitrarily drawn to fit the needs of the regime. A revealing case of such political pragmatism involves Liu Hongsheng, the "King of Matches and Wool." Liu was categorized by the Communist government as a "national capitalist" even though he had not only worked as a comprador for the British-owned Kailuan Mining Administration but also as a Nationalist government official, managing several state-owned or state-sponsored big businesses under Chiang Kai-shek. When Liu expressed his concern to Premier Zhou Enlai in person, Zhou explained that the party used one term to express its approval of one group of capitalists (the "national" ones) and another to indicate its disapproval of another group (the "comprador bureaucratic" ones). See Cochran and Hsieh, *The Lius of Shanghai*, 289–90. Historian Brett Sheehan has found that the attitudes toward capitalists in the PRC shifted back and forth – sometimes they were viewed as good and other times as bad (and sometimes "not so bad") based on the role of business in the polity and society. See Sheehan, *Industrial Eden*, 202–30. For a discussion on the epithet "red capitalists" and a few individuals who wore that hat in the early years of the People's Republic, see Leighton, "Capitalists, Cadres, and Culture in 1950s China."

20 Zhonggong Shanghai dangzhi bianzuan weiyuanhui, *Zhonggong Shanghai dangzhi*, 530.

21 Shanghai Municipal Archives, File Q194/1/285/2-12.

22 Shanghai gongshang shetuan zhi bianzuan weiyuanhui, *Shanghai gongshang shetuan zhi*, 486.

23 Shanghai Municipal Archives, File A33-6-13:33.

24 Retention pay was not exclusively for capitalists, but was also bestowed on various types of professionals whose pre-1949 salaries were above the wage scale set in the mid-1950s. By April 1962, Shanghai had about 151,000 state employees in industry receiving retention pay. Shanghai Municipal Archives, File B127-2-410.

25 Yang Shuming, "1978–1979: luoshi Dang dui minzu zichan jieji zhengce" (1978–1979: Fulfilling the party's policies on national capitalists), http://shtzb.eastday.com/shtzw/node1240/node1593/userobject1ai1752952.html; also, *Shiji* (Century), 1 (2011): 12–14. Following the usual practice in the PRC, all salary figures given in the study are monthly payments unless otherwise noted.
26 Shanghai Municipal Archives, File A33-6-13:42.
27 Shanghai laodong zhi bianzuan weiyuanhui, *Shanghai laodong zhi*, 339.
28 Ibid., 215.
29 Probably because of Wang's political prominence during the Cultural Revolution, the factory gave her a monthly bonus of 10 yuan; see Ye Yonglie, *Sirenbang xingwang*, 2:636 and 3:1047.
30 Pay varied slight according to geographic area; see Li Weiyi, *Zhongguo gongzhi zhidu*, 205–8, Table 6-4; Zhuang Qidong et al., *Xin Zhongguo gongzhi shigao*, 119–21.
31 Shaoshan Mao Zedong tongzhi jinianguan, comp., *Mao Zedong yiwu shidian*, 510; Long Jianyu, *Mao Zedong jiaju*, 152–3. The salaries, of course, did not reflect fully the standard of living of these leaders, as they typically had other privileges awarded to high-ranking cadres, such as furnished homes and personal physicians, chefs, and chauffeurs.
32 Bergère, *Shanghai*, 384.
33 Chen Danyan, *Shanghai Princess*, 117.
34 Ibid. There were various reasons for capitalists to leave, stay in, or return to China in the wake of the revolution. Nationalism played an important role but the decisions were never easy. For eleven case studies of how individual businesspeople made their decisions in this regard, see Cochran, *The Capitalist Dilemma in China's Communist Revolution*.
35 Xu Zhongni, "Fangwen Shanghai zibenjia Rong Yiren."
36 Liu's letter to his eighth son dated December 17, 1949; see Cochran and Hsieh, *The Lius of Shanghai*, 337.
37 Chen Danyan, *Shanghai Princess*, 115.
38 Cheng Naishan, "Nanjing Xi Lu Huayuan Gongyu."
39 Wang Jingzhi, *Lengdong sanshi nian*, Acknowledgments. Wang's mother was unable to write her book before her death in 1994.
40 Gu Zhenyang, "Baiquelin de gushi."
41 Richman, "Capitalists and Managers in Communist China."
42 *Los Angeles Times*, October 22, 1964, p. 2.
43 Wang Ju, *Jindai Shanghai mianfangye de zuihou huihuang*, 232–4.
44 Zhonggong Shanghai shiwei tongzhanbu, et al., *Zhongguo ziben zhuyi gongshangye de shehui zhuyi gaizhao*, 2:1225–42.
45 Shanghaishi difangzhi bangongshi, *Shanghai ming jianzhu zhi*, 339–42.
46 Shanghai Municipal Archives, File Q196-1-468.
47 Ibid.
48 Cheng Naishan, *Shanghai luomanshi*, 348.
49 Cheng Naishan, "Nanjing Xi Lu Huayuan Gongyu," 58–67.
50 Zhang Zugan, "Qing xi Huxiang." Zhang's home was in Lane 192, Shanyin Road, in the same alleyway-house neighborhood where Lu Xun resided during the last ten years of his life.

51 Qishi niandai zazhishe, *LiuMei Huayi xuezhe chongfang Zhongguo guangan ji*, 55.
52 Chen Danqing, *Duoyu de sucai*, 94–9.
53 Shanghai had numerous secondhand stores selling various kinds of home goods throughout the Mao era. The items these stores sold were mostly from pawnshops (officially known as "small loan banks" so as to avoid the negative image of pawnshops in the pre-1949 society), goods intended for export that were slightly defective and directed to the domestic market, and confiscated items from the home ransacking during the Cultural Revolution. They also sold goods for individuals on a commission basis. These stores were troves of things from the "old society." As Gerth noted, Huaiguojiu, a secondhand store on Huaihai Road, "served as an exhibition of material culture underlying the bourgeois lifestyles that many of the people who visited it had few opportunities to encounter" (Gerth, *Unending Capitalism*, 191). See also, Shanghai riyong gongye, comp. *Shanghai riyong gongye pin shangye zhi*.
54 Ibid.
55 Zhang Weiqun, *Shanghai longtang yuanqi*, 271–81.
56 According to data on Chinese library collections, from 1949 to 1979 China had translated and published 5,677 works of foreign literature by 1,909 writers from eighty-five nations; most of these books were published before 1967. Meng Shaoyi et al., *Zhongguo fanyi wenxue shi*, 278.
57 Although Hollywood movies quickly faded out in China after the outbreak of the Korean War and were officially banned in November 1950, Hong Kong movies soon filled the vacuum and, in Shanghai, remained the top draw until the early 1960s. Zhang Jishun, *Yuanqu de duoshi*, 282–4.
58 Sun Shufen, *Sheng si jie*, 185–8; Gu Meizhong, "Wo de pengyou Zhou Yi."
59 Zhang Da-Peng, *Life Under Mao Zedong's Rule*, 226.
60 Cheng Naishan, *Shanghai luomanshi*, 350.
61 Jiang Weimin, *Vogue Grandma*, 29.
62 I-1, see List of Informants. Kuoshu, *Metro Movies*, 29.
63 Zhang Da-Peng, *Life Under Mao Zedong's Rule*, 217.
64 Ibid., 266–9. During the Mao era, Chinese banks did not require personal identification for deposits or withdrawals. It was not until 1997 that personal identification was required for banking.
65 *Longtang shenshen shenjixu* (How deep are the deep alleyways), http://jiansu909.blog.163.com/, accessed December 16, 2014.
66 Shanghai Municipal Archives, File C48-2-2471-54. The file contains a collection of meeting minutes and speech transcripts of the All-China Federation of Industry and Commerce, Standing Committee of the Shanghai Branch, January–September, 1963. The sources quoted in this article are dated September 19–24, 1963.
67 Wakeman, *Red Star over Shanghai*, 110.
68 Shanghai Municipal Archives, File C48-2-2471-54. The Park Hotel was known in Chinese as Guoji Fandian (International Hotel).
69 Shanghai Municipal Archives, File C48-2-2471-54.
70 For a list of these restaurants, see Shanghai yinshe fuwuye zhi bianzuan weiyuanhui, *Shanghai yinshe fuwuye zhi*, 75–80.
71 Ibid., 85–6.

72 Ibid., 60–6.
73 Sun Yaodong and Cheng Naishan, "Hushang diyi meishijia Shen Jingsi."
74 Swislocki, *Culinary Nostalgia*, 210.
75 Shanghai yinshe fuwuye zhi bianzuan weiyuanhui, *Shanghai yinshe fuwuye zhi*, 70.
76 I-2, I-3, and I-4; Wang and Barr, *Between Two Worlds*, 177–8; Bai Hua, *Rumeng suiyue*, 173; Dong Zhujun, *Wode yige shiji*, 492–5.
77 Zhonggong zhongyang wenxian yanjiushi, *Chen Yun nianpu*, 95–6.
78 The Jinjiang Hotel was cofounded by Dong Zhujun (1900–1997), a businesswoman who worked closely with the CCP municipal government in establishing the hotel as the foremost in socialist Shanghai and hosted Richard Nixon during his historic visit in February 1972. See Dong's autobiography, *Wode yige shiji*.
79 Shanghai Municipal Archives, File C48-2-2471-54.
80 I-5.
81 Zhang Da-Peng, *Life Under Mao Zedong's Rule*, 328.
82 Shanghai Municipal Archives, File C48-2-2471-54.
83 Ibid.
84 Ibid.
85 Bai Hua, *Rumeng suiyue*, 179–80.
86 Wang Anyi, *Xunzhao Shanghai*, 44–5
87 Jia Zhangke, *Haishang chuanqi*, 20.
88 Zhang Da-Peng, *Life Under Mao Zedong's Rule*, 416, 455. It was estimated that from 1965 to 1975 on average every year close to 200,000 Shanghai residents reached the employment age of sixteen. The city constantly had at least 70,000 of what the government called "social idle labor force" (*shehui xiansan laodongli*), which included domestic servants. Shanghai Municipal Archives, Files B127-1-157, B127-1-131, B127-2-133-58.
89 Hanchao Lu, *Beyond the Neon Lights*, 110–16.
90 For a complete list of the architectural heritage sites, see Shanghaishi difangzhi bangongshi, *Shanghai ming jianzhu zhi*, 846–92.
91 Ibid., 510.
92 Ibid., 100. For an account of these "pigeon lofts," see Wang and Barr, *Between Two Worlds*, 200–1.
93 Shanghai zhuzhai jianshe zhi bianzuan weiyuanhui, *Shanghai zhuzhai jianshe zhi*, 106.
94 Shanghaishi difangzhi bangongshi, *Shanghai ming jianzhu zhi*, 413–16; Chen Haiwen, *Peace and Prosperity*, 147.
95 Yuan Rong, "Fengrenji yu Minguo shiqi Shanghai siying junzhuang gongye."
96 Incidentally, Bei Runsheng was the granduncle of the Pritzker Prize winning architect Ieoh Ming Pei (I. M. Pei, born in China in 1917).
97 Shanghaishi difangzhi bangongshi, *Shanghai ming jianzhu zhi*, 415. On Hudec's architectural works in Shanghai, see Poncellini, "Laszlo Hudec in Shanghai."
98 Cheng Naishan, *Shanghaijie qinghua*, 96. The Green House inspired Cheng Naishan to write a novel, *Lanwu* (Blue House), first published in 1983, with an English edition in 2005. It is generally regarded as Cheng's magnum opus.

274 Notes to pages 43–49

99 Ibid., 88. Cheng was able to provide the details of Wu's death because she was married to Wu's grandson, Yan Erchun, and had practically become a member of the Wu family. Cheng was in close contact with Wu's widow, Bei Juanlin (1903–1996), in Bei's late years.
100 Shanghaishi difangzhi bangongshi, *Shanghai ming jianzhu zhi*, 437–41.
101 Liu Sheng, "Left Behind."
102 Interviews with Zhou Zongliang's two grandsons, *Shilin* (Historical Review), 2004 supplementary issue: 70–2. Zhou had four wives and sixteen children.
103 Jiang Weimin, *Vogue Grandma*, 329.
104 The report is dated September 24, 1963; Shanghai Municipal Archives, File C48-2-2471-183.
105 Zhang Da-Peng, *Life Under Mao Zedong's Rule*, 228.
106 Ibid., 228–9.
107 Wang Weiming, *Shanghai qiqing liuyu*, 66–7.
108 Ibid.
109 Zhang Yihe, *Wangshi bingbu ruyan*, 207.
110 For a detailed account on Shanghai's dance culture before and after the revolution, see Farrer and Field, *Shanghai Nightscapes*, especially chaps. 3 and 9.
111 Liu Sheng, "Left Behind."
112 Jiang Weimin, *Vogue Grandma*, 331.
113 Interviews with Zhou Zongliang's two grandsons. "Shanghai de zhangli" (The tensile strength of Shanghai), https://read01.com/Rg45ma.html, accessed June 19, 2016.
114 Kuoshu, *Metro Movies*, 29–30.
115 Liu Sheng, "Left Behind."
116 Because the financial status of these individuals was in general much higher than that of average business owners in commerce (mostly retail businesses).
117 *Time*, June 8, 1987, p. 42.
118 *Time*, February 5, 2007.
119 Nien Cheng, *Life and Death in Shanghai*, 224.
120 Even after she was released from prison in 1973 in the midst of the Cultural Revolution, she was allocated a house in an elegant subdivision on Taiyuan Road (Route Delastre), where her neighbors were old Republican-era elites such as the son of President Li Yuanhong (1864–1928) and the daughter of CCP founder Chen Duxiu (1879–1942). Zhao Zhiming, "Zheng Nian yu yige shidai de 'Shanghai shengsi jie.'"
121 Ibid., 3.
122 Nien Cheng, *Life and Death in Shanghai*, 4.
123 Shell's head office was at No. 1 the Bund, the McBain Building; see Hibbard, *The Bund Shanghai*, 88. The company had a depot in Yangshupu in northeast Shanghai.
124 Shell Companies in China, *Looking to the Long Term*, 18–19.
125 Nien Cheng, *Life and Death in Shanghai*, 120.
126 Zhang Min interview with Nien Cheng broadcast on August 9, 1998. The transcript is in Zhang Min, *Chuanqiang de duanbo*, 255–64.
127 Nien Cheng, *Life and Death in Shanghai*, 8–9.
128 Ibid., 83.

129 Zhao Zhiming, "Zheng Nian yu yige shidai de 'Shanghai shengsi jie.'"
130 After most foreigners left Shanghai in the early 1950s, the former "foreign alley" remained an upscale neighborhood that housed the party's "united front personages." Among Cheng's neighbors were the daughter of the CCP founder Chen Duxiu (1879–1942); Qin Shou'ou (1908–1993), a prominent writer of the "Mandarin Duck and Butterfly" school; Shen Kefei (1898–1972), China's top neurosurgeon; and Gu Kaishi (1913–2005), China's top cardiac surgeon.
131 Zhu Dake, "Zheng Nian."
132 Saich, *The Origins of the First United Front in China*, 3.
133 Zhonggong zhongyang wenxian yanjiushi, *Liu Shaoqi lun gongren yundong*, 350–1.
134 Zhonggong zhongyang wenxian yanjiushi, *Liu Shaoqi nianpu*, 2:190–208.
135 Liu Shaoqi, *Liu Shaoqi xuanji*, 2:180–1.
136 Bo Yibo, *Ruogan zhongda jueci yu shijian de huigu*, 1:39.
137 See Mao's speech of October 29, 1955, *Mao Zedong wenji* (Collected works of Mao Zedong), 6:494–6, 181; *Liu Shaoqi xuanji*, 2:488.
138 The Common Program was adopted by the First Plenary Session of the CPPCC on September 29, 1949, in Beijing. See Zhongguo renmin zhengzhi xieshang huiyi, *Important Documents of the First Plenary Session of the Chinese People's Political Consultative Conference*, 10 (Article 26).
139 Mao, *Mao Zedong wenji*, 7:181.
140 Ibid., 7:180.
141 Tang Diyin, *The Pen and I*, 143.
142 Van Slyke, *Enemies and Friends*, 221.
143 A frequently quoted work of Lenin's in this regard is his *"Left-Wing" Communism, an Infantile Disorder*. A relevant paragraph reads: "The more powerful enemy can be vanquished only by exerting the utmost effort, and without fail, most thoroughly, carefully, attentively and skillfully using every, even the smallest, 'rift' among the enemies, of every antagonism of interest among the bourgeoisie of the various countries and among the various groups or types of bourgeoisie within the various countries, and also by taking advantage of every, even the smallest, opportunity of gaining a mass ally even though this ally be temporary, vacillating, unstable, unreliable and conditional. Those who fail to understand this, fail to understand even a particle of Marxism, or of scientific, modern Socialism in general." Lenin, *Selected Works*, vol. II, part 2: 67.
144 In Chinese, *zichan jieji faquan*; or, since 1979, translated as *zichan jieji quanli*.
145 Marx and Engels, *Selected Works in Three Volumes*, 3:13–30; Lenin, *Lenin Collected Works*, 25 (June–September 1917): 471–2.
146 See the CCP Central Bureau of Translation's official announcement regarding the translation, *Renmin ribao*, December 12, 1977. For information on the revisions of the translation, see Chen Zhongcheng and Shao Aihong, "'Faquan' haishi 'quanli' zhi zheng." For an insightful account of the politics of translation in this particular case, see Tomba, *Paradoxes of Labour Reform*, 47–50.

147 *Renmin ribao*, October 13, 1958. The article was first published in issue no. 6 (September 15, 1958) of the *Jiefang* (Liberation). See also Dittmer, *Liu Shao-ch'i and the Chinese Cultural Revolution*, 186.
148 According to Zhou Erfu (1914–2004), vice minister of the Ministry of Culture, Zhang's article was commissioned by Ke Qingshi (1902–1965), the then Shanghai party boss. On several occasions Ke listened in person to Mao's comments on "bourgeois right." In other words, Zhang's article was written according to Mao's ideas on the subject; see Zhou Erfu, *Wangshi huishou lu*, 2:225.
149 For a summary of the use of the term and its impact on various campaigns and the political vocabulary in Mao's China, see Wang Shaoguang, *Zhongguo zhengdao*, chap. 5.
150 Tomba, *Paradoxes of Labour Reform*, 49.
151 The expression famously appears in Mao's poem "The Capture of Nanking," written in April 1949; for an English translation, see Mao Zedong, *The Poems of Mao Zedong*, 75.
152 "Zhongguo Gongchandang dibajie Zhongyang Weiyuanhui dishici quanti huiyi gongbao" (Communiqué of the Ten Plenary Session of the Eighth Central Committee of the Chinese Communist Party), in *Renmin ribao*, September 29, 1962.
153 Malraux, *Anti-Memoirs*, 373.
154 *Renmin ribao*, February 9, 1975; Zhonggong zhongyang dangshi yanjiushi, *Zhongguo Gongchandang lishi*, 2, part 2.
155 *Renmin ribao*, June 18, 1966.
156 Mittler, *A Continuous Revolution*, 32. Matthew Johnson has also noted in a case study on Shanghai that the Chinese party-state was less effective in controlling cultural affairs at the grassroots level than people have generally thought. Johnson, "Beneath the Propaganda State."

2 The Stinking Number Nine

1 Mao's speech at the "Highest Meeting on State Affairs," October 13, 1957. Mao Zedong, *Mao Zedong sixiang wansui*, 131.
2 In a speech on September 10, 1956, Mao indicated that "we inherited a hundred thousand high-level intellectuals from old China. Our plan is to create one to one and a half million high-level intellectuals (including university and college graduates) in a period of three five-year plans." *Mao Zedong wenji*, 7:101–2.
3 U, *Creating the Intellectual*, 12.
4 College graduates after the early 1950s were not necessarily called "bourgeois intellectuals." However, in the mid-1960s, Mao proclaimed that the bourgeoisie dominated Chinese higher education, and hence it became unclear whether or not PRC-trained college graduates were "bourgeois intellectuals."
5 Mao Zedong, *Mao Zedong wenji*, 7:273; MacFarquhar, Cheek, and Wu, *The Secret Speeches of Chairman Mao*, 225–6.
6 Zhu Zheng, *Fan Youpai douzhen quanshi*, 2:342.

7 Deng Xiaoping, "Guanyu zhengfeng yundong de baogao" (A report on the rectification movement), *Renmin ribao*, October 19, 1957.
8 Two conferences on "intellectuals' issues," one held in Beijing in January 1956 and the other in Guangzhou in March 1962, signaled short periods of relaxation in the onslaught against intellectuals. At both conferences, Premier Zhou Enlai gave a speech claiming that the party regarded the great majority of intellectuals as part of the working people. Zhou's speech at the 1956 meeting was published in *People's Daily* (January 30, 1956) but his 1962 speech was only circulated internally, a result of a split among the party's top leadership on this issue. For Zhou's speeches, see Zhou Enlai, *Zhou Enlai xuanji*, 2:158–89, 353–69. On the "intellectuals' spring," see Shen Zhihua, *Sikao yu xuanze—cong zhishifenzi huiyi dao fanyou yundong*, 13–78; and Wu Xiaoni, "1956 nian zhishifenzi wenti huiyi yanjiu shuping"; Qian Bocheng, *Wensi ji*, 265–78.
9 For a discussion of the concept of the "old society," see Smith, *Thought Reform and China's Dangerous Classes*, 62–4.
10 Kraus, *Pianos and Politics in China*, 76.
11 On the democratic party system, see the State Council of the People's Republic of China, *Zhongguo zhengdang zhidu* (The Chinese political party system), published November 15, 2007, Beijing, http://cpc.people.com.cn/GB/64107/65708/66065/66076/7210918.html.
12 The term was derived from the lineup of political outcasts of the time: landlords, rich peasants, counterrevolutionaries, bad elements (moral degenerates), rightists, renegades, enemy agents, capitalist roaders, and intellectuals. It is believed that this list was a mutation of the Yuan dynasty ranking of ten categories of people in society under Mongol rule: officeholders, government employees, monks, Taoists, doctors, workers, hunters, common folk, intellectuals, and beggars. Note that intellectuals ranked number nine, one notch above beggars. Kwok-sing Li, *A Glossary of Political Terms of the People's Republic of China*, 27–8; MacFarquhar and Fairbank, *The Cambridge History of China*, 15 (part 2):79.
13 See Fu Lei, *Fu Lei yiwen ji*.
14 For Chinese who grew up in the 1960s and 1970s, Fu Lei's translations were often what got them interested in French literature. His translations were used as texts to study French. Shi Kangqiang, *Zishuo zihua*, 79.
15 Mingyuan Hu, *Fou Lei*, 7.
16 Lou Shiyi, "Fu Lei de xingge."
17 Ye Yonglie, *Jiedu Fu Lei yijia*, 84–5.
18 The college was renamed China Foreign Affairs University in 2005; it remains a major school for training Chinese diplomats.
19 These articles are reprinted in Fu Lei, *Fu Lei yinyue jiangtang*, 204–25.
20 The meeting was held in Beijing, March 6–13.
21 Fu Lei, *Fu Lei wenji shuxin juan*, 200.
22 Ibid., 201.
23 Zhou Erfu, *Wangshi huishou lu*, 2:234. Professionally, Zhou Yang was a literary theorist and a Russian literature specialist. His translation of Leo Tolstoy's *Anna Karenina* remains a classic in China.

278 Notes to pages 60–67

24 On March 15, 1957, Mao wrote an article, "Things Are Beginning to Change," for circulation among party cadres in which he declared that up to 10 percent of intellectuals outside the party were rightists. Mao Zedong, *Selected Works of Mao Zedong*, 5:441. See also MacFarquhar and Fairbank, *The Cambridge History of China*, 14:257.
25 The house, at 284 Jiangzu Road, Number Five, is still there. Jin Shenghua, *Fu Lei he ta de shijie*, 309.
26 The rent is recorded in the 1966 penal court file sixty of Changning District, Shanghai; see Ye Yonglie, *Tiegu Fu Lei*, 198. Fu Lei's will lists it as 55.29 yuan.
27 Mingyuan Hu, *Fou Lei*, 208.
28 Shanghai youdian zhi bianzuan weiyuanhui, *Shanghai youdian zhi*, 393, 405–6. The number of household phone lines in Shanghai decreased steadily after Liberation, making telephone service even more precious for the very privileged few.
29 Fu Lei, *Fu Lei quanji*, 20:227.
30 Kraus, *Pianos and Politics in China*, 72.
31 Fu Min's letter to Ye Yonglie, September 9, 2004; Ye Yonglie, *Tiegu Fu Lei*, 100.
32 Fu Lei, *Fu Lei wenji shuxin juan*, 624. The book was published in 1978, twelve years after his death.
33 *Wenhui bao* (Wenhui Daily), October 1, 1959, and September 2, 1987; Ye Yonglie, *Tiegu Fu Lei*, 155–7.
34 Chen Jianhua, "Yi jiu liu ling niandai de wenxue zhuiyi."
35 Su Yuanyuan, "Yijie shixue zhuanzhu zhi zhuanjia – Xie Defeng."
36 Chen Lai, *Buxi ji*, 74–5. In 2002, Yale University Press published Zhang Dainian's *Key Concepts in Chinese Philosophy*, translated by Edmund Ryden.
37 Letter to Fu Cong, April 20, 1961, in Fu Lei, *Fu Lei wenji shuxin juan*, 277–8.
38 Based on Mrs. Fu's Letter to Fu Cong, November 26, 1965, in ibid., 446.
39 Letter to Fu Cong, April 20, 1961, in ibid., 278.
40 Letter to Fu Cong, April 24, 1964, in ibid., 411.
41 Ye Yonglie's interview of Ding Ji'nan, July 15, 1987, Shanghai, *Tiegu Fu Lei*, 193.
42 Based on the 1966 penal court file 60 of Changning District; see Ye Yonglie, *Tiegu Fu Lei*, 198–9.
43 Kraus, *Pianos and Politics in China*, 70.
44 Jiang's letter to Yu Kaiwei, January 23, 1998, in Yu Kaiwei, "Jiangnan qi'nü jin youzai." See also Ye Yonglie, *Ta, yige ruo nüzi*, 1–14.
45 Shen Jianzhong, *Shi Zhecun xiansheng biannian shilu*, 1:694.
46 Shi Zhecun, "Jinian Fu Lei." See also, Shi Zhecun, *Shashang de jiaoyin*, 141–4.
47 The expression *tuo mian zi gan* is attributed to Lou Shide (630–699), a Tang dynasty government minister. Chen Rong and Ye Xin, comps., *Zhongguo chengyu diangu kaoshi*, 944–5.
48 According to Yale University Professor Sun Kangyi (1944–), who kept in touch with Shi in his late years. Shen Jianzhong, *Shi Zhecun xiansheng biannian shilu*, 1:2.

49 Lee, *Shanghai Modern*, 153–89.
50 Wang Junxi, "Wo de lilong zhengchanzu wangshi."
51 Ibid.; Ke Linjuan and Du Yaping, *Jianshuo liangzhi de fanyijia*, 67–71.
52 Cao Ying, "Wo benlai bing buxiang zuo wenxue"; Cao Ying, *Wo yu Eluosi wenxue*, 190–1.
53 CCTV interview, aired June 8, 2009, script published online June 9, 2009, http://news.xinhuanet.com/video/2006-06/09/content_4667772.htm, accessed July 24, 2014.
54 Wang Junxi, "Wo de lilong zhengchanzu wangshi."
55 Ke Linjuan and Du Yaping, *Jianshuo liangzhi de fanyijia*, 90–4.
56 *Qianjiang wanbao* (Qianjiang Evening News), Hangzhou, October 27, 2015.
57 Wang Zhiliang, *Wangshi yu huainian*, 14–19.
58 Li Hui, *Hu Feng jituan yuan'an shimo*, 54–7.
59 He Qifang, *Yige pingchang de gushi*, 142. For a discussion of He as one of the most talented modern Chinese poets, see David Der-wei Wang, *The Lyrical in Epic Time*, 117–31.
60 Ye Kai, "Zuowei zishifenzi de Zhou Yang."
61 For a comprehensive examination of China's *hukou* (household registration) system, see, Fei-ling Wang, *Organizing through Division and Exclusion*; for a case study of rural-urban disparity related to hukou in the Mao era, see Brown, *City versus Countryside in Mao's China*, especially chap. 2.
62 Schoenhals, *Spying for the People*, especially chaps. 4–6.
63 Wang Zhiliang, *Wangshi yu huainian*, 71–8, 101–46.
64 Brown, *City Versus Countryside in Mao's China*, 137.
65 Chen Zhu, "Bei yiwang zai fanyi de shijie li."
66 The phrase refers to Old Customs, Old Culture, Old Habits, and Old Ideas. It first appeared in a *People's Daily* editorial titled "Sweeping Away All the Demons," published on June 1, 1966. See also Kwok-sing Li, *A Glossary of Political Terms of the People's Republic of China*, 427.
67 Mao, *Selected Works of Mao Tse-tung*, 3:22.
68 Wang Zhiliang, *Wanshi yu huainian*, 28–9. Wang's translation of *Eugene Onegin* was published in 1982, thirty-five years after he first started the translation. In 1999, the government of the Russian Federation awarded Wang a Pushkin Souvenir Medal for his contribution to introducing Russian literature to foreign readers. *Xin Jingbao* (Beijing News), September 26, 2013.
69 An example of an intellectual who was anxious about the future of intellectuals in China is the renowned writer Eileen Chang, who had just reached her thirties at the time of Communist takeover. After hesitating for three years, she eventually left Shanghai in July 1952. Chen Zishan, *Zhang Ailing congkao*, 2:262–71.
70 On the "yellow music" of Li Jinhui, see Jones, *Yellow Music*, 73–104; on May Fourth intellectuals, see Schwarcz, *The Chinese Enlightenment*.
71 On rental deposits in Shanghai, see Hanchao Lu, *Beyond the Neon Lights*, 160–7.
72 The alleyway house complex is still known as Siming Villa (*Siming bieshu*). The current street address of Li's home is 576 Yuyuan Road, Number Forty-Three.

73 Li Sui, *Mingguo fenghua*, 193.
74 Ibid., 196–7; Zhang Weiqun, *Shanghai longtang yuanqi*, 302–3; Zhang Weiqun, *Siming Bieshu duizhao ji*, 448.
75 Li Sui, *Mingguo fenghua*, 194; Zhang Weiqun, *Shanghai longtang yuanqi*, 301, 313.
76 Liu Shaoqi, *Liu Shaoqi xuanji*, 192.
77 Li Sui, *Mingguo fenghua*, 193–4.
78 Ibid., 203–4.
79 Zhang Weiqun, *Siming Bieshu duizhao ji*, 460.
80 *Jiefang ribao* (Liberation Daily), July 24, 1950.
81 Li Sui, *Minguo fenghua*, 189; Zhang Weiqun, *Shanghai longtang yuanqi*, 314. The Literature and Arts Conference was held at Shanghai's Liberation Theater (Jiefang Juchang) on July 24–29, 1950. This was the first conference of its kind after the Communist takeover. *Jiefang ribao* (Liberation Daily), July 24, 1950.
82 The maxim is from the Confucian classic *Book of Rites* (*Liji*), chap. 41.
83 Zhang Weiqun, *Shanghai longtang yuanqi*, 315.
84 Li Sui, *Minguo fenghua*, 204.
85 Ibid.; Li Jinhui, *Li Jinhui ertong gewuju*, 56. The film, released in 1959, was directed by Yu Zheguang (1906–1991).
86 Li Sui, *Minguo fenghua*, 194; Zhang Weiqun, *Shanghai longtang yuanqi*, 343; Zhang Weiqun, *Siming Bieshu duizhao ji*, 446, 458–9.
87 Li Sui, *Minguo fenghua*, 191, 206.
88 Ibid., 205.
89 The Li family had eight brothers whose accomplishments in their respective fields earned them the epithet "The Eight Talents of the Lis" (*Li shi ba jun*). For short biographies of the eight brothers, see Li Sui, *Mingguo fenghua*, 216–31.
90 Sun Ji'nan, *Li Jinhui yu Lipai yinyue*, 263–4.
91 Li Sui, *Mingguo fenghua*, 197; Zhang Weiqun, *Siming Bieshu duizhao ji*, 462.
92 Hahn, *China to Me*, 8–10. The story is candidly told in Emily Hahn's 1942 book, *Mr. Pan: A Memoir*. For a scholarly discussion of Hahn and Shao, see Cuthbertson, *Nobody Said Not to Go*, 140–7; and Leo Ou-fan Lee, *Shanghai Modern*, 241–4.
93 Jung Chang, *Big Sister, Little Sister, Red Sister*. The biography titled *The Soong Sisters* was published in 1942 (London: Robert Hale).
94 Hutt, "Monstre Sacré."
95 His grandfather Shao Youlian (1840–1901) served as the governor of Hunan and Taiwan and was also a leading diplomat. His maternal grandfather, Sheng Xuanhuai (1844–1916), was the Minister of Imperial Posts and Transportation late in the Qing Empire.
96 On Lu Xun's satirical criticisms (always published anonymously) of Shao, see Lu Xun, *Lu Xun quanji*, 5:264–5, 274–5, and 6:38–41.
97 For Shao Xunmei's life before 1949, see Grescoe, *Shanghai Grand*, Part III.
98 Zhang Changhua, *Cengjing fengya*, 160. For the rules and politics of ranking top academics at universities in the years 1950–1990, see Ge Jianxiong, "1949 nian yihou jiaoshou ruhe pingding dengji he gongzi."

99 Shao Shaohong, *Wo de baba Shao Xunmei*, 343.
100 Sheng Peiyu, *Shengshi jiazu*, 273 and 279.
101 *Liuyi* (Six Arts), February 15, 1936.
102 Such as the actresses Zhou Xuan (1920–1957) and Li Lihua (1924–2017). Emily Hahn, who encouraged Shao to move to the neighborhood, lived at Number Six on the same alley.
103 Xu Hongxin, "Jiari li guangguang Shanghai lao longtang."
104 Interview with Fang Ping, *Nanfang dushi bao* (Southern Metropolis Daily), Guangzhou, www.ruanyifeng.com/blog/2008/10/translator_fang_ping_passed_away.html.
105 On urban neighborhood organizations in China, see Chapter 4.
106 Sheng Peiyu, *Shengshi jiazu*, 270–96.
107 Shao asked his friend Ye Lingfeng (1905–1975), then a Hong Kong-based writer who had close ties with the party, to mail the letter in Hong Kong. Apparently, the letter was confiscated by customs.
108 According to the rehabilitation letter of the Shanghai Public Security Bureau issued in February 1985 (file 26811), Shao was jailed from October 1958 to April 1962 on the charge of being a "historical counterrevolutionary." Shao Xiaohong, *Wo de baba Shao Xunmei*, 361. Shao's wife, Sheng Peiyu, however, recalled that Shao was released in 1961. Sheng Peiyu, *Shengshi jiazu*, 299.
109 On Shao's life in prison, see Jia Zhifang, *Wo de rensheng dang'an*, 288–94. Jia was locked in the same cell with Shao in 1960–1961.
110 Sheng Peiyu, *Shengshi jiazu*, 300–4; Shao Xiaohong, *Wo de baba Shao Xunmei*, 352; Zhang Changhua, *Cengjing fengya*, 163; Yiming, "Minguo diyi haomen."
111 Newman, *Farewell, My Beijing*, 2.
112 An oil painting that she did as a homework assignment, for instance, was appreciated by a foreign visitor so much that he immediately paid the school 200 francs in order to take the painting back home. This unusual case made Lu well-known in the school. Lu Zonglin, "Huiyi gumu Lu Xiaoman," 129.
113 Chai Cao, *Lu Xiaoman zhuan*, 3–4.
114 Lu Zonglin, "Huiyi gumu Lu Xiaoman."
115 Chai Cao, *Lu Xiaoman zhuan*, 73.
116 Liu Haisu, "Wo suo renshi de Xu Zhimo he Lu Xiaoman."
117 Jane Zheng, *The Modernization of Chinese Art*, 296.
118 Xu's best-known poem is "Taking Leave of Cambridge Again." For an English translation of the poem by Guohua Chen, see Pagnamenta, *The University of Cambridge*, 29.
119 See Pang-Mei Chang, *Bound Feet & Western Dress*; and Tony S. Hsu, *Chasing the Modern*.
120 In 1928, Lu and Xu moved to Fuxi Road, Number Two (the present-day address is 913 Middle Yan'an Road). The Hardoon Garden, covering more than 28 acres, was the largest private garden in Shanghai. Silas Aaron Hardoon (1851–1931), a Jewish business tycoon of British nationality, built it as part of his residence in 1909.
121 Liu Haisu, "Wo suo renshi de Xu Zhimo he Lu Xiaoman."

Notes to pages 84–90

122 Xu took the trip to attend a talk by Lin Huiying, whom Xu continued to admire even after he married Lu Xiaoman.
123 Chen Jianhua, "Lu Xiaoman de 'fengjing' neiwai."
124 It is unclear if Lu and Weng were officially married. Lu, however, identified Weng as her husband in her personnel file at the Shanghai Academy of Chinese Painting.
125 Shanghai Zhongguo huayuan, *Shanghai Zhongguo huayuan 1956–2004*, 169.
126 *Shanghai meishu tongxun neikan* (Shanghai Art Information, Internal Edition), no. 8 (June 1960).
127 The Institute of Culture and History (*Wenshiguan*) was a nationwide organization with branches in most provinces and major cities.
128 The Chinese Peasants and Workers Democratic Party (*Zhongguo nonggong minzu dang*), founded in 1930, is one of the eight non-Communist parties officially recognized in the PRC and is represented in the CPPCC. The name of the party is somewhat misleading as most of its members (about 144,000 in 2015) are elite professionals working in the fields of public health, medicine, and environmental science.
129 Founded in February 1951 as a consulting group to the municipal government.
130 Shanghai funü zhi bianzuan weiyuanhui, *Shanghai funü zhi*, 618.
131 Based on the personnel files at the Shanghai Institute of Culture and History (SICH). The system usually designated one's work unit (*danwei*) as the main payer. It is unclear whether the stipend was paid by SICH or the Academy of Chinese Painting, which was Lu's primary work unit. My thanks to Shen Zuwei, Director of SICH, for access to the file. For slightly different figures, see also Ding Yanzhao, *Beiqing Lu Xiaoman*, 255.
132 Shanghai Academy of Chinese Painting, "Lu Xiaoman" personnel file. The exchange rate was 100 HKD = 42.70 yuan during much of the 1960s.
133 Shanghai Academy of Chinese Painting, "Lu Xiaoman" personnel file.
134 Lu Xiaoman's home address: 1157 Middle Yan'an Road, Number Thirty-Five, Jing'an District.
135 The phone number was 369163. Ding Yanzhao, *Beiqing Lu Xiaoman*, 253.
136 Ibid., 262.
137 Shanghao yancao zhi bianzuan weiyuanhui, *Shanghai yancao zhi*, 179; Tang Longbiao, "Huixiang 'Zhonghua' juanyan 50 duo nian fazhan shi."
138 In 1988 when the cigarette was finally available on the market, it sold for 72 yuan per carton (ten packs), equivalent to the monthly salary of a college graduate. Zhonghua xiangyan jianjie (A brief introduction to Zhonghua cigarettes), www.sina.com.cn, June 24, 2009; see also Xue Na, *Jingdian pinpai gushi quji*, 100–1.
139 Zhang Fanghui, "Gensui Lu Xiaoman xuehua."
140 The club is located at 306 Taixing Road, Jing'an District.
141 Wang Jingzhi, *Lengdong sanshi nian*, 136–7.
142 Shen Zhihua, *Sikao yu xuanze*, 644–6.
143 Zhang Fanghui, "Gensui Lu Xiaoman xuehua."
144 Zhang Re, "'Xiang dang jiaoxin' de qianyin houguo."

145 Wang Jingzhi, *Lengdong sanshi nian*, 61–2.
146 Zhang Fanghui, "Gensui Lu Xiaoman xuehua."
147 Shanghai Zhongguo Huayuan, *Shanghai Chinese Painting Academy 1956–2004*, 169.
148 The main building of the hospital was designed by László Hudec in 1923 and construction was completed in 1926. For recent research on the Shanghai Municipal Council and its role in the development of the city, see Jackson, *Shaping Modern Shanghai*.
149 *China Press*, June 9, 1926, supplement; Wakeman, *The Shanghai Badlands*, 102n52.
150 Lu Zonglin, "Huiyi gumu Lu Xiaoman." Mao's *On Contradiction* (*Maodun lun*), first published in 1937, consists of about 25,000 Chinese characters.
151 Chen Yi zhuan bianxie zu, *Chen Yi zhuan*, 25.
152 Liu Shufa, *Chen Yi nianpu*, 1:72–3.
153 Xu Zhimo, *Xu Zhimo quanji*, 2:352–9.
154 *Jingbao* (Beijing News), February 4, 1926.
155 Lu Zonglin, "Huiyi gumu Lu Xiaoman," 128–46; Zhao Jiabi, "Huiyi Xu Zhimo he 'Zhimo quanji.'"
156 Cai Cao, *Zhongshuo fenyun Lu Xiaoman*, 21, 219, 230.
157 For a critical biography of Hu, see Min-chih Chou, *Hu Shih and Intellectual Choice in Modern China*.
158 For Chinese translations of the letters, see Zibo, *Shijian yi wu Hu Shizhi*, 115–18.
159 See Xu Zhimo's letter to Xiaoman dated February 23, 1926, Yu Kunlin, *Kuse de lianqing*. One of the autographed photographs Lu sent to Hu Shi was displayed at the "Exhibition of Manuscripts and Precious Documents of Famous People in Modern China," held at the Shanglin Academy in Fuzhou, February 25–March 15, 2013.
160 Chen Julai, *Anchi renwen suoyi*, 67.
161 Geng Yunzhi, *Hu Shi yigao ji micang shuxin*, 34:535–6.
162 For Mao's comments on the possibility of Hu running for president, see Wang Xiangkun, *Jiang Jieshi yu Mao Zedong hezuo suiyue*, 284.
163 Zhang Fanghui, "Gensui Lu Xiaoman xuehua."
164 Mao Zedong, *Mao Zedong zaoqi wen'gao*, 494; Snow, *Red Star Over China*, 148; Hu Songping, *Hu Shizhi xiansheng nianpu changbian chugao*, 5:1895. See also Gong Yuzhi, *Dangshi zhaji er ji*, 34; Zhao Yinglin, "Mao Zedong yu Hu Shi."
165 Tang Tao, "Chuntian de huainian."
166 From October 1954 to August 1955, the CCP launched an intense campaign criticizing Hu. In 1955, Sanlian shudian (Joint Publishing) published a book of over two million words titled *Hu Shi sixiang pipan lunwen huibian* (Collection of essays criticizing Hu Shi's thought). A condensed version of the book was published in 1959.
167 Gong Yuzhi, *Dangshi zhaji er ji*, 43.
168 MacFarquhar, Cheek, and Wu, *The Secret Speeches of Chairman Mao*, 225–6.
169 Goldman, *China's Intellectuals and the State*, 3.

284 Notes to pages 99–101

3 The Power of Balzac

1. de Certeau, *The Practice of Everyday Life*, 18.
2. Halbwachs, *On Collective Memory*, 38–9.
3. Jiang Xiaoyuan, "Huixiang dangnian du jinshu." The author is a professor of the history of science at Shanghai Jiaotong University and the founding dean of the university's School of Humanities.
4. Liang Qichao, *Yinbinshi heji*, 1:67; Schwartz, *In Search of Wealth and Power*, 91–112; Huang Chunyu, "Hanyi mingzhu wangshi."
5. Liang Qichao, *Liang Qichao wenxuan*, 2:308.
6. Lu Xun, *Diary of a Madman and Other Stories*, 21–8.
7. Pollard, *Translation and Creation*, 9.
8. Ibid., 16. According to one account, Lu Xun translated more than 200 foreign works by close to 100 authors from fourteen countries. Half of his published works – in total over ten million Chinese words – are translations. Tao Hongling, "Lu Xun shouxian shi fanyijia."
9. Zhongguo banben tushuguan, *1949–1979 fanyi chuban waiguo wenxue zhuzuo mulu he tiyao*.
10. Literacy rates from the 1950s onward chart an upward climb, with most estimates indicating that on average four million people per year became literate. Bhola, "The Anti-illiteracy Campaigns in the People's Republic of China."
11. Chen Zhongyi, "Huigu yu fansi waiguo wenxue fanyi yu yanjiu liushi nian."
12. Russian literature began to be introduced to China around the 1910s, but in terms of the number of foreign literature translations, Russian occupied a distant third place after English and French prior to the 1950s. Gamsa, *The Reading of Russian Literature in China*, 3–4, 121–3.
13. Goldman, "The Rectification Campaign at Peking University."
14. Fang Huawen, *20 shiji Zhongguo fanyi shi*, 435–6.
15. *Beijing qingnian zhoukan* (Beijing Youth Weekly), August 13, 2009.
16. Shi Kangqiang, *Zishuo zihua*, 13–17.
17. As discussed in Chapter 2, Fu Lei gained fame primarily for his translations of the works of Balzac and Romain Rolland. Shanghai's first library open every day till midnight is named after Fu Lei. His birthplace (where he lived for the first four years of his life) and his childhood home (where he lived till he left Shanghai for Paris in 1927) are in the district of Pudong, and both have been designated as a commemorative museum. For her translations of French literature, Luo Yujun's residence in Shanghai's former French Concession (555 Yongjia Road) has been designated a "Cultural Relic Subject to Preservation." *Xinmin wanbao* (Xinmin Evening News), February 17, 2012.
18. See Mao's 1942 speech at the Yan'an Forum on Literature and Art, which served as the ultimate guideline for Chinese writers in his era. Mao Zedong, *Selected Works of Mao Tse-tung*, 3:69–97.
19. This rationale was widely known but considered a sham or a type of officialese. One reader commented: "My siblings and I all loved nineteenth-century European literature. Before the Cultural Revolution these world classics had a legitimate place in socialist China. Supposedly, they would enhance our knowledge of the evils of capitalist society. I suspect it was a

pretext invented by a huge body of intellectuals and translators who love Western literature or made a comfortable living from it." Zhong, Wang, and Bai, *Some of Us*, 45.
20 Mao's letter to Lu Dingyi, September 27, 1964. Zhonggong zhongyang wenxian yanjiusi, *Mao Zedong shuxin xuanji*, 558.
21 Marx and Engels were well acquainted with classical literature and admired Aeschylus, Shakespeare, Dickens, Fielding, Goethe, Schiller, Heine, Cervantes, Balzac, Dante, Chernyshevsky, and Dobrolyubov. They were also acquainted with the works of less prominent and even little-known writers both among their contemporaries and those who lived and worked in more distant times. They also displayed a love for popular art, for the epics of various nations and other types of folklore: Songs, tales, fables and proverbs. See Andy Blunden, "Preface" in Marx and Engels, *Marx, Engels on Literature and Art*, 15.
22 I-7, I-8, and I-9.
23 From 1966 to 1970, China printed 1.053 billion copies of *Quotations from Chairman Mao* and 2.409 billion of *Selected Readings of the Works of Mao Zedong*. Dangdai Zhongguo congshu bianjibu, *Dangdai Zhongguo de chuban shiye*, 1:77.
24 Zhou Yang, *Makesi Engesi Liening lun yishu*.
25 Zhou Yang, *Makesi zhuyi yu wenyi*.
26 *Jiefang ribao* (Liberation Daily), April 8, 1944.
27 Mao's letter to Zhou Yang, January 22, 1939. Mao Zedong, *Mao Zedong shuxin xuanji*, 228.
28 Feng Xianguang, "Liushi nian Makesi zhuyi wenxue lilun de yijie he yanjiu."
29 *New York Tribune*, August 1, 1854 (transcribed by Andy Blunden), in Marx and Engels, *Marx, Engels on Literature and Art*, 339–40.
30 Engels to Margaret Harkness in London, April 1(c.), 1888, in Marx and Engels, *Marx, Engels on Literature and Art*, 92.
31 Ibid., 91 (brackets in the original).
32 V. I. Lenin, "Leo Tolstoy as the Mirror of the Russian Revolution," in Vladimir Lenin, *Lenin Collected Works*, 15:202–9. Originally published in *Proletary*, no. 35, September 11 (24), 1908.
33 Marx and Engels, *Marx, Engels on Literature and Art*, 162.
34 Mao, *Selected Works of Mao Tse-tung*, 2:272.
35 Victor Hugo, "The Chinese Expedition: On the Sack of the Summer Palace," a letter to Captain Butler, November 25, 1861 (*UNESCO Courier*, November 1985).
36 Ibid.
37 Vladimir Ilyich Lenin, "Imperialism, the Highest Stage of Capitalism," Lenin, *Selected Works* (1963), 1:667–76.
38 On Romain Rolland's anti-imperialism, see Fisher, *Romain Rolland and the Politics of International Engagement*, 39–48, 156–7.
39 Dittmer, *Liu Shao-ch'i and the Chinese Cultural Revolution*, 268.
40 For a discussion on the rural–urban divide among party cadres, see Gao, *The Communist Takeover of Hangzhou*, 257–60.
41 Li Hui, "Yu Xia Yan tan Zhou Yang"; MacFarquhar and Fairbank, *The Cambridge History of China*, 14:434.
42 Yang Jianmin, "Xia Yan Muqin yiben de bozhe."

43 Hanchao Lu, *Beyond the Neon Lights*, 168.
44 For a literary study of Mao Dun's work, including *Midnight*, see Yu-Shih Chen, *Realism and Allegory in the Early Fiction of Mao Dun*.
45 Although Zhou translated only half of the book, he claimed credit for the entire translation. See Ye Deyu, *Wangshi tanwei*, 11.
46 Ma Maoru, "Wo suo jingli de 'Zhongxuanbu yanwangdian yuan'an ji pingfan"; *Renmin ribao* (People's Daily), January 16, 1979; MacFarquhar and Schoenhals, *Mao's Last Revolution*, 95.
47 Zhang Hua and Su Caiqing, *Huishou "wen'ge,"* 1:327–8.
48 *Renmin ribao* (People's Daily), December 22, 1968.
49 They were the Shanghai Library, Shanghai Municipal Library of Historical Documents, Shanghai Municipal Library of Periodicals, Shanghai Municipal Library of Science and Technology, and Shanghai Municipal Library for Children and Juveniles. Shanghai tushuguan shiye zhi bianzuan weiyuanhui, *Shanghai tushuguan shiye zhi*, Section 2.
50 Ibid.
51 Ibid., Section 4.
52 The following is the number of books in a few university library collections in Shanghai at the end of 1965: Fudan University, 1,215,535; Jiaotong University, more than 610,000; Tongji University, 477,171; East China Normal University, more than 125,000; East China College of Chemistry, 310,349; Shanghai College of Foreign Languages, more than 248,000. Ibid., Section 3.
53 For details about the changes in the early PRC publishing industry, see Culp, *The Power of Print in Modern China*, 185–213.
54 Zhonggong Shanghai dang zhi bianzuan weiyuanhui, *Zhonggong Shanghai dang zhi*, 446; Shanghai chuban zhi bianzuan weiyuanhui, *Shanghai chuban zhi*, 992.
55 *Renmin ribao*, October 30, 1954.
56 Shanghai chuban zhi bianzuan weiyuanhui, *Shanghai chuban zhi*, 898 and 904. Xinhua Bookstore was founded in Yan'an in April 1937 and its Shanghai branch was opened on September 1, 1949.
57 Chen Jianhua, "Yi jiu liu ling niandai de wenxue zhuiyi."
58 Zhou Zhenhe, "Shanghai shudian yijiu."
59 Dingyuwa, "Shanghai jiushudian" (Shanghai's used-book stores), http://blog.sina.com.cn/s/blog_69db613d0101ec9h.html, accessed December 2015.
60 Chen Jianhua, "Yi jiu liu ling niandai de wenxue zhuiyi"; for the works of the Saturday School and its popularity, see Link, *Mandarin Ducks and Butterflies*, 165–6, 253–4.
61 Zhou Zhenhe, "Shanghai de jiu yangshu." The line, "Endless awe-inspiring views atop the precipitous peaks," is from a poem Mao wrote in 1961 for a photograph of the Yellow Mountains (Huangshan) taken by his wife, Jiang Qing. The poem was circulated widely during the Cultural Revolution.
62 Xiao Gongqin, "Zai jingshen ziyou zhong fansi."
63 Zhou Zhenhe, "Shanghai jiushudian yijiu."
64 Dingyuwa, "Shanghai jiushudian."
65 I-10.

66 Kang Xuepei, *Zhiqing*, 79.
67 Xiaoping Fang, *Barefoot Doctors and Western Medicine in China*, 58–60.
68 Shanghai Zhongyi xueyuan, *Cejiao yisheng shouce*, 19–20. The handbook was reprinted numerous times across the country and in Hong Kong. For an English translation, see *A Barefoot Doctor's Manual: The American Translation of the Official Chinese Paramedical Manual* (Philadelphia, PA: Running Press, 1977).
69 Zhao Tielin, *Wo de laosanjie suiyue*, 114.
70 Canran, "Shouchaoben."
71 Link, "Hand-Copied Entertainment Fiction from the Cultural Revolution," 33.
72 Yang Dongxiao, "Shaonü zhi xin."
73 In 2004 when a press in Inner Mongolia planned to publish the manuscript, it had become a book of 140,000 Chinese characters. Although the galley proofs came out in January and were exhibited at a book fair in Beijing, in February the government called off the publication. Canran, "Shouchaoben."
74 It was not until Dr. Hu Yanyi's book *Xingzhishi mantan* (General discussions on sexual knowledge) was published in 1985 that sex-education books were openly sold in bookstores. Zhong Gang and Chen Xuelian, "'Huangse' shouchaoben *Shaonü zhi xin*."
75 Shanghai huaijing weisheng zhi, comp., *Shanghai huaijing weisheng zhi* 5:1:3, pp. 198–201. While these public toilets were provided to meet the needs of pedestrians and local residents, they were also an important source of nightsoil used to fertilize farms in Shanghai's suburbs and in the provinces of Jiangsu and Zhejiang. In the 1950s–1970s, human waste from Shanghai was such a "precious commodity" that it was rationed to these farms. Ibid., 3:3:1, pp. 160–3.
76 I-32, I-33, I-34. One of the informants commented that the song might also have been an oblique criticism of the severe shortage of meat and cooking oil at the time.
77 Honig, "Socialist Sex."
78 I-32, I-33, and I-34.
79 Y. Yvon Wang, *Reinventing Licentiousness*, 196.
80 Honig, "Socialist Sex."
81 Yang Shiyang, "Xunzhao geming zhixia de xue yu rou"; I-14, I-28.
82 Ibid.
83 Chen Jianhua, "Yi jiu liu ling niandai de wenxue zhuiyi."
84 In the first five years of the Cultural Revolution (1966–1970), China published an astonishing amount of material that fed the cult of Mao, including 4,206 million volumes of Mao Zedong's works, 4,155 million of Mao's portraits (photographs and paintings), and 2,072 million posters with Mao's quotations. Dangdai Zhangguo congshu bianjibu, *Dangdai Zhongguo de chuban shiye*, 1:77. *People's Daily* claimed that from 1958 to 1966, five million copies of the *Poems of Mao Zedong* were printed, while in 1967 alone, fifty-seven million copies were published. *Renmin ribao*, December 26, 1967.
85 Chen Jianhua, "Yi jiu liu ling niandai de wenxue zhuiyi."
86 Shanghai tushuguan shiye zhi bianzuan weiyuanhui, *Shanghai tushuguan shiye zhi*, Introduction (*zongshu*) section. See also Denise Ho, *Curating Revolution*, 175–7.

288   Notes to pages 114–119

87 For instance, in 1966, the library of Xuhui district had a collection of 120,000 books; like all libraries in the country, it closed in late 1966. When it reopened in 1973, only 37,000 books remained. More than 50,000 volumes had been destroyed (mainly, sent to recycling centers) and the rest were missing, that is, stolen during the chaos. Shanghai tushuguan shiye zhi bianzuan weiyuanhui, *Shanghai tushuguan shiye zhi*, section 2.
88 Mittler, *A Continuous Revolution*, 130.
89 Chen Jianhua, "Yi jiu liu ling niandai de wenxue zhuiyi."
90 Mittler, *A Continuous Revolution*, 135.
91 Brehm and Brehm, *Psychological Reactance*, 11–56.
92 Lin Yutang, *The Importance of Living*, 131–6, 383; John Ching-Yu Wang, *Chin Sheng t'an*, 27–8.
93 Zhu Dake, *Gudu de daduoshu*, 59.
94 Zhu Dake, *Jiyi de hongpishu*, 85. The influence of *Jean-Christophe* in China was long-lasting and affected generations of Chinese readers in the twentieth century. See, for example, Denton, *The Problematic of Self in Modern Chinese Literature*, 193–4, 239.
95 Chen Cun, *Chen Cun zuopin jingxuan*, 80–1.
96 Wang Weiming, *Shanghai qiqing liuyu*, 208.
97 de Certeau, *The Practice of Everyday Life*, 173.
98 Cheng Naishan, *Shanghai Fashion*, 72.
99 Wang Anyi and Zhang Xinying, *Tanhua lu*, 23.
100 Zhong, Wang, and Bai, *Some of Us*, 44.
101 Ibid., 45.
102 Yin Huifen, *Shanghai linli*, 149.
103 Zheng Jian, "Huayuan yangfang hao dushu."
104 The owner of the house, Zhou Zongliang, left Shanghai in 1948 and died in Hong Kong in 1957. Zhou's daughter Zhou Yunqin and her husband, Xu Xingye (1917–1990), lived in the house (Zhou Yunqin left China in 1957 for her father's funeral and never returned). Xu, who became an award-wining writer in the 1990s, was an editor and low-level cadre in the 1960s, which helped the house escaped the Red Guard's home-raid list.
105 Zheng Jian, "Huayuan yangfang hao dushu." The January Revolution, also known as the January Storm, was a major event in January 1967 in Shanghai where so-called proletarian revolutionaries, that is, Maoist "rebels" and Red Guards, took control of the Shanghai municipal government. This month-long "seizure of power" marked the beginning of a nationwide power transition from established party leaders to Maoist radicals during the Cultural Revolution.
106 Chen Sihe, *1966–1970*, 188.
107 Mittler, *A Continuous Revolution*, 130 (the brackets are in the original).
108 Zhu Dake, *Jiyi de hongpishu*, 85.
109 Yin Huifen, *Shanghai linli*, 120 and 149.
110 Mao's comments on Chinese higher education, known as the "721 Instruction" (because Mao made the comments on July 21 of 1968), were published in *Renmin ribao*, July 22, 1968; Theodore Chen, *Chinese Education since 1949*, 96.
111 Wang Jingzhi, *Lengdong sanshi nian*, 175.

112 Wang's translation of *The Greek Coffin Mystery* was published in 2008 (Beijing: Xinxing chubanshe).
113 For a few case studies on restricted books, see Shen Zhanyun, *Huipishu, huangpishu*.
114 In the PRC administrative twenty-four-grade ranking system established in mid-1950s, cadres ranked up to grade twelve were "high ranking"; those between thirteen and sixteen were "middle ranking"; those seventeen and above were "ordinary ranking." Yang Kuisong, "Guanyu jianguo yilai dangzheng ganbu de shouru." For a discussion of the establishment of the system, see Barnett and Vogel, *Cadres, Bureaucracy, and Political Power in Communist China*.
115 Zhongguo banben tushuguan, *1949–1986 quanguo neibu faxing tushu zongmu*.
116 Jiang Xiaoyuan, "Huixiang dangnian du jinshu."
117 Zhu Xueqin, "'Niangxipi' he 'shengjunji'—'wen'ge' dushu ji." In 1953, the school was renamed Jiguang Middle School, after China's Korean War hero Huang Jiguang (1931-1952).
118 See Chapter 4 for further discussion of recycling centers in China's cities.
119 Wei Guangqi and Ding Dong, "Meiyou kongbai—Wen'ge shiqi de dushu shenghuo" (No blankness: Reading time during the Cultural Revolution), www.edubridge.com/erxiantang/12/dushushenghuo.htm.
120 He Zixi, "Wen'ge zhong de yici ziwo jiushu." For a similar case, see Yu Xiaoping, "Wen'ge gaochao, shushan tanbao."
121 Yang Jian, *1966–1976 de dixia wenxue*, 116.
122 The list of works includes *Anna Karenina, Resurrection, Crime and Punishment, The Brothers Karamazov, Quiet Flows the Don*, "Fate of a Man", *Bel-Ami, Nana, Ninety-Three, Les Misérables, The Man Who Laughs, The Red and the Black, Carmen, Don Juan, Selected Lyric Poetry of Pushkin,* and *The Golden Rose*. Ge Yan, "Qishi niandai: jiyi zhong de Xi'an dixia dushu huodong."
123 Qing Qiuzi, *Zheteng shinian*, 8.
124 Ibid., 32, 58–9.
125 Dai Sijie, *Balzac and the Little Chinese Seamstress*, 110.
126 Ibid., 56.
127 Ibid., 57.
128 Buckley, "Chinese Village Where Xi Jinping Fled Is Now a Monument to His Power."
129 Edward Wong, "Myth of a Chinese Leader Is Traced Back to Its Roots."
130 *Renmin ribao*, October 14, 2016.
131 Ibid.
132 Ibid.
133 Ibid.
134 Buckley, "Xi Starts New Term in China, With Trusted Deputy to Deal with Trump." Chinese sources indicate that Wang took the book when Xi paid him a visit. *Huanqiu renwu* (Global Figures), no. 22 (November 2017): 16–18.
135 Today the address is Hongxing Road, Number Eighty, Hefei City, Anhui.
136 Li Keqiang, "Zhuiyi Li Cheng xiansheng."

137 The event was clearly an attempt by Xi to imitate the 1942 Yan'an Forum on Literature and Art at which Mao delivered important speeches dictating that all forms of literature and arts should serve proletarian politics.
138 The "great masters" (*dashi*) of literature on Xi's list are from four European nations and the United States. Russia: Pushkin, Gogol, Lermontov, Turgenev, Dostoyevsky, Nekrasov, Chernyshevsky, Tolstoy, Chekhov, Gorky, and Sholokhov; France: Rabelais, La Fontaine, Molière, Stendhal, Balzac, Hugo, Dumas, Dumas fils, Maupassant, and Romain Rolland; the United Kingdom: Chaucer, Milton, Byron, Shelley, Keats, Dickens, Hardy, and George Bernard Shaw; Germany: Lessing, Goethe, Schiller, and Heine; United States: Hawthorne, Longfellow, Stowe, Whitman, Mark Twain, Dreiser, Jack London, and Hemingway. *Renmin ribao*, October 15, 2015. Four days later, Xi's speech was published as a pamphlet and all major Chinese media reported the publication.
139 Zhang Guangzhao, "Wang Qishan weihe tuijian *Jiu zhidu yu da geming*?"
140 "One step further than comrades" was a common circumlocution, usually used by men, to propose a dating relationship.
141 Shuxin, "Feng Deying 'sanhua' lanman."
142 Ibid. For discussions of the novel's depiction of sexuality, see also Cai Xiang, *Revolution and Its Narratives*, 183; and Lu Tonglin, *Misogyny, Cultural Nihilism, and Oppositional Politics*, 55–7.
143 Yan Feng, "Yuedu 50 niandai" (Reading the 1950s), http://blog.sina.com.cn/s/blog_64909a7d0102vxyu.html?tj=1, accessed April 23, 2015. For an English translation of the book, see Chu Po, *Tracks in the Snowy Forest* (Beijing: Foreign Languages Press, 1978).
144 Li Zhencun, "Zuojia Qu Bo yishuang Liu Bo laoren jiangshu *Linhai xueyuan* gushi"; Yao Dan, "Chonghui linhai xueyuan."
145 Yang Li, "How Is Revolution 'Popularized?'" 69.
146 See Yang Mo, *The Song of Youth*.
147 Mo Yan, "Nanwang na daizhe kouzhao jiewen de ai." Mo himself was part of the generation that was hungry for reading – when he had no books to read, he read the *Xinhua Dictionary*. Zhu Shoutong, "Guanzhu Mo Yan, lijie Mo Yan."
148 On the influence of *Steel* in China from the late 1930s to the present, see Green, "The Cultural Indigenization of a Soviet 'Red Classic' Hero," and King, *Milestones on a Golden Road*, 101–5.
149 Ostrovsky, *How the Steel Was Tempered*, 2:105, translation modified. Ostrovsky was a Ukrainian; Jin Chongji, "Huiyi liushi nian qian de shi."
150 Gamsa, *The Reading of Russian Literature in China*, 115.
151 *Steel* was first translated into Chinese from a Japanese edition in June 1937, but Mei Yi's translation was most influential; reportedly, from October 1949 to December 1952, 2,070,000 copies were sold. Zou Zhenhuan, *Yingxiang Zhongguo jindai shehui de yibai zhong yizuo*, 409–10.
152 Tang Zhengmang, "Xinzhi shudian yu Gangtie shi zenyang lancheng de Zhongwen yiben."
153 By 1995, it had been printed fifty-seven times over forty-four years, with a total of 2.5 million copies sold. *Guangming ribao*, February 26, 2000.

154 Ostrovsky, *How the Steel Was Tempered*, 1:59.
155 Wang Xinli, *Yuegui nianling*, 30.
156 Gamsa, *The Reading of Russian Literature in China*, 12.
157 Liu Xiaofeng, "Jilian Dongniya."
158 Wang Gang, "Ye jilian Dongniya" (Also in love with Tonya), www.xys.org/xys/ebooks/literature/prose/Dongniya_too.txt, posted April 24, 2001.
159 Krebs and Lu, *China in Family Photographs*, 68. The scene is described in Ostrovsky, *How the Steel Was Tempered*, 2:86–90.
160 Han Qiulin, "Dongniya 'qingjie.'"
161 Ostrovsky, *How the Steel Was Tempered*, 1:80.
162 Mo Yan, *Lingting yuzhou de gechang*, 149–50. For the part of the novel that Mo Yan refers to, see *Steel*, 1:215–16.
163 Jing Fang, *Wo shi 60 huo*, 219–20.
164 Mao Yuyuan, *Zaijian Dongniya*, 35–118.
165 ChinaSunTV interview with Mao Yuyuan, published on January 10, 2011, www.youtube.com/watch?v=2fTASw2iMnk.
166 Wang Gang, "Ye jilian Dongniya," www.xys.org/xys/ebooks/literature/prose/Dongniya_too.txt.
167 Ostrovsky, *How the Steel Was Tempered*, 2:90.
168 Kaufman and Libby, "Changing Beliefs and Behavior through Experience-Taking."
169 Gamsa, *The Reading of Russian Literature in China*, chap. 1.
170 Shanghai's Russian community erected the bust in 1937 to commemorate the hundredth anniversary of his death in a duel. It was located at the intersection of Fenyang Road (formerly, Route Pichon), Yueyang Road (Route Ghisi), and Taojiang Road (Route Henri Riviere).
171 *New York Times*, August 20, 1972.
172 I-11.
173 Zhang Da-Peng, *Life Under Mao Zedong's Rule*, 509–10.
174 Perry and Lu, "Narrating the Past to Interpret the Present"; Mah, *Falling Leaves*, 222.
175 Chen Danyan, *Shang de fenghua xueyue*, 83; Hanchao Lu, "Nostalgia for the Future."
176 As recently as 2009, Chinese media still used the expression; see, for example, *Qinghai ribao*, September 18, 2009.
177 Wu Liang, *Wo de Luotuosi*, 107.
178 "Gambara" was translated into Chinese by Gao Mingkai (1911–1965) and published by the Shanghai New Literature and Art Press in 1953.
179 The alleyway house compound is in Lane 833, Middle Huaihai Road.
180 Wu Liang, *Wo de Luotuosi*, 101.
181 Wu Liang, *Zhaoxia*, 132.
182 Wang Weiming, *Shanghai qiqing liuyu*, 43.
183 Ibid., 42–3.
184 Sun Peidong, "Jingshui shenliu."
185 Wang Anyi, *The Song of Everlasting Sorrow*. For a review of Wang Anyi's novel of nostalgia, see Howard Choy, *Remapping the Past*, 169–80.
186 Pan Ling, *In Search of Old Shanghai*, 130.

292   Notes to pages 137–140

187 Wang Anyi, *Xiaoshuojia de shisan tang ke*, 311.
188 Ibid., 1–2; Zhang Ying, "Daxue neng bu neng peiyang zuojia?"
189 Xudong Zhang, "Shanghai Nostalgia," 382.
190 Chen Danyan, *Shanghai sela*, 169.
191 Tencent, "Chen Danyan he ta bixia de Shanghai nüren men."

4 Alleyway Women's Detachments

1 Deng Yingchao, *Deng Yingchao wenji*, 126.
2 Richman, *Industrial Society in Communist China*, 304. This figure does not include women workers employed in neighborhood industry, discussed later.
3 Zuo Jiping, *Work and Family in Urban China*, 27.
4 Davin, *Woman-Work*, 165.
5 The term originally derived from a seventh-century women's insurgent army led by the third daughter of Li Yuan (566–635), the founding emperor of the Tang dynasty (618–907). It has often been used as a witty way of referring to an all-female cohort. *Niangzijun* became a household word after 1958 in the face of a barrage of reportage using that term. *Niangzijun* was the title and subject of a drama and then a movie in 1961 and a ballet in 1964. The last was in turn made into one of the so-called eight model plays engineered and promoted by Jiang Qing during the Cultural Revolution.
6 MacFarquhar, *The Origins of the Cultural Revolution 2*, 336; Teiwes, *China's Road to Disaster*, 5–6.
7 "Resolution on Certain Questions in the History of our Party since the Founding of the People's Republic of China, June 27, 1981," see the Wilson Center Digital Archive International History Declassified, https://digitalarchive.wilsoncenter.org/document/121344.pdf?v=d461ad5001da989b8f96cc1dfb3c8ce7.
8 Jiang Yongping, "50 nian Zhongguo chengshi nüxing jiuye de huigong yu fansi," 154–6; Zuo and Jiang, *Shehui zhuanxing zhong chengzhen funü de gongzuo he jiating*, 30–1. This reflected a clear consensus among my interviewees, including women and men as well as former APT workers and non-APT employees, on this point. Several of my informants claimed that this is something "everybody knows." I-13, I-14, I-15, and I-19.
9 Research Institute of All-China Women's Federation, *Statistics on Chinese Women*, 241, 245.
10 Shanghaishi tongzhi bianzuan weiyuanhui, *Shanghai tongzhi*, 11:2.1.
11 Shanghai funü zhi bianzuan weiyuanhui, *Shanghai funü zhi*, 5:2.1; SMA, C31-1-61; SMA, B182-1-1111-1.
12 Qiu Guosheng, "Ershi shiji wushi niandai Shanghai de funü jiefang yu canjia jiti shengchan"; Xu Gang, *Xiang xiang chengshi de fangfa*, 247–9; Zhang Niumei, "Lizhi yihuo kuangre."
13 Volgyes, "Blue-Collar Working Women and Poverty in Hungary."
14 Harsch, *Revenge of the Domestic*, 3.
15 Evans, *The Subject of Gender*, 105.

16 Here, "unskilled women workers" is a government category referring to housewives who had not worked outside the home before they were recruited into an APT. It should be noted that a gender bias is entangled in the term as it ignores the fact that homemaking and childrearing are skills.
17 Eyferth, *How China Works*, 3–4; Shaw, *Social Control in China*; Lü and Perry, *The Danwei*.
18 The People's Congress of the PRC passed a neighborhood organization statute on December 31, 1954. A revised statute was passed by the Congress on December 26, 1989, and remains in effect to this day.
19 Read, *Roots of the State*.
20 Schurmann, *Ideology and Organization in Communist China*, 374–80; Salaff, "Urban Residential Committees in the Wake of the Cultural Revolution"; Whyte and Parish, *Urban Life in Contemporary China*, 22–4.
21 "Shanghai shi jumin weiyuanhui zhengdun gongzuo qingkuang" (Rectification of the residents' committees in Shanghai municipality), *Jiefang ribao*, December 17, 1954.
22 For more on street factories set up as part of the urban people's commune movement in 1959 in five cities (Beijing, Tianjin, Guangzhou, Harbin, and Shanghai), see Ch'eng-chih Shih, *Urban Commune Experiments in Communist China*, 81–90.
23 Ma Wenrui, "Jin yi bu jiefang funü laodongli."
24 Jing'anqu difangzhi bianzuan weiyuanhui, *Jing'anqu zhi*, 101.
25 Shanghaishi tongzhi bianzuan weiyuanhui, *Shanghai tongzhi*, 18:2:1.
26 Among the workshops and service units were 4,334 APTs with 95,389 workers, and 6,839 service units with 44,241 workers. SMA, B182-1-1111-1.
27 SMA B127-1-157; Xiong Yuezhi, *Shanghai tongshi*, 13:227.
28 Shanghaishi tongjiju, *Xin Shanghai sishi nian*, 107; SMA, B29-2-899.
29 In rural areas, officially reported rates of women's participation in agricultural production were 60–70 percent in 1957 and 90 percent by 1958. Thereafter, reported rates dropped. See Hershatter, *Women in China's Long Twentieth Century*, 61. Cities followed a similar trajectory. See also Croll, *Women and Rural Development in China*, 23–8.
30 SMA, A20-2-24.
31 SMA, B123-5-327-11.
32 SMA, A20-2-24.
33 SMA, B158-2-9-66.
34 By January 1973 daily pay ranged from 0.70 to 0.90 yuan. Shanghaishi Xuhuiqu zhi bianzuan weiyuanhui, *Xuhuiqu zhi*, 20:3:5.
35 Shanghai laodong zhi bianzuan weiyuanhui, *Shanghai laodong zhi*, 339.
36 SMA, B158-2-9-66.
37 Ibid. Shanghaishi tongzhi bianzuan weiyuanhui, *Shanghai tongzhi*, 18:3:1.
38 SMA, C21-2-2895.
39 SMA, B246-2-423-1.
40 Bauer et al., "Gender Inequality in Urban China."
41 SMA, B158-2-9-66.
42 Hanchao Lu, "Arrested Development."
43 SMA, A20-2-17; I-16, I-17, and I-18.

294   Notes to pages 146–152

44 In 1960 alone, Shanghai's six industrial bureaus in charge of machinery, electronics, instrumentation, chemicals, textiles, and light industry outsourced eighty products with a total output value of 260 million yuan to neighborhood workshops. SMA, A20-2-6-23.
45 SMA, A20-2-15-15.
46 Goldstein, "The Remains of the Everyday."
47 Hu Weixing, "Laodizi feipin huishou ke jiejian."
48 SMA, B182-1-1111-1, "Guanyu zuzhi lilong shengchan fuwu xing shiye de yijian (taolungao)."
49 "Rang 'Shanghai jingnian' huo dao Shanghai – cong feipin huishou kan xunhuan jijing" (Let the "Shanghai experience" return to Shanghai: Examining the recycling economy from the perspective of waste reclamation), Shanghai municipal government website, January 11, 2005, www.shanghai.gov.cn/nw2/nw2314/nw2315/nw4411/u21aw98824.html.
50 Yang Lang, "Wo de jiesheng de waigong."
51 Wu Xiaoming, "Chengshi zhongchan."
52 United Nations, Department of Economic and Social Affairs, Population Division, *World Population Prospects: The 2010 Revision*, 188, 266.
53 "Longtang gongchang li de nüren men: zouchu jiamen tisheng diwei" (Women in the alleyway factories: Walking out the door to raise their status), *Wenhui dushu zhoubao*, May 12, 2011. Although free care did not last long, day-care centers continued to operate in Shanghai's neighborhoods well into the post-Mao era.
54 Fang Xiaoping, *Barefoot Doctors and Western Medicine in China*, 95. In the 1970s, four editions of training textbooks for barefoot doctors nationwide were published in Shanghai. Ibid., 58.
55 I-19 and I-25.
56 Li Rui, *Dayuejin qinli ji*, 170–1; Li Zhisui, *The Private Life of Chairman Mao*, 275–84.
57 Yang Yalun, "'Chengshi renmin gongshe hua' zai Shanghai."
58 Watson, "Feeding the Revolution."
59 The maxim "serve the people" is the title of one of Mao's best-known essays (written in 1944). "Serve the people," arguably became the most popular maxim in the PRC.
60 Watson, "Feeding the Revolution."
61 SMA, B246-2-423-1.
62 SMA, B252-2-58. This echoed the low rate of female membership in the Communist Party in general. As recently as 2017, only 26 percent of the members of the party were women.
63 Ibid.
64 SMA, B158-1-569-134. Of Shanghai's 137 work units that made toys, 101 were APTs. SMA, B158-1-459-42.
65 SMA, B252-2-58.
66 SMA, B246-2-423-1.
67 Heitlinger, "Marxism, Feminism, and Sex Equality."
68 Shanghaishi Xuhuiqu zhi bianzuan weiyuanhui, *Xuhuiqu zhi*, 20:3:5.
69 Shanghai funü zhi bianzuan weiyuanhui, *Shanghai funü zhi*, 2.

70 Hanchao Lu, *Beyond the Neon Lights*, chap. 4.
71 A government report gives the following numbers on the sources of neighborhood workshop facilities in Jing'an district in west Shanghai: 55.44 percent borrowed from residents, 22.48 percent borrowed from factories, 20 percent purchased, 2.05 percent others. SMA, A20-1-58. Another report provides the following data on Liyuan Street in Nanshi district: 70 percent borrowed from residents, 12.8 percent borrowed from factories, and 17.2 percent purchased. SMA, A20-1-30.
72 "Longtang gongchang li de nüren men" (see note 52 above).
73 Liu Ping, "Chachu weifa dajian de xiangguan falü wenti yanjiu."
74 A brief border war with the Soviet Union on the Ussuri River in March 1969 prompted a nationwide surge in China of preparations for war from 1969 to 1971; this notably included launching a mass campaign to construct air-raid shelters in cities. For the politics of the Ussuri River incident and its aftermath, see MacFarquhar and Schoenhals, *Mao's Last Revolution*, 308–23.
75 Shanghaishi tongzhi bianzuan weiyuanhui, *Shanghai tongzhi*, 18:3:2.
76 SMA, A20-1-58.
77 SMA, A20-2-15-15.
78 SMA, A20-1-52-97.
79 Ibid.
80 "Guanyu ganbu xiafang jinxing laodong duanlian he canjia jiceng gongzuo de wenti" (Issues about transferring cadres downward to take part in manual labor and participate in grassroots-level work), *Laodong* (Labor), 1958 (1), 8.
81 "Duanping" (Short comments), *Renmin ribao*, March 8, 1958.
82 "Jin yibu di jiefang funü laodongli" (Further liberating women's labor power), *Laodong*, 1958 (15), 4.
83 Heilmann and Perry, *Mao's Invisible Hand*. For a review of the recent literature on resilience and adaptation in the China field and a detailed analysis of the limits of this approach, see Howell, "Adaptation under Scrutiny."
84 SMA, A20-1-52-97. According to the report, unmarried women under the age of twenty-five were particularly unsettling.
85 Ibid., 3–5.
86 Ibid.
87 Andors, *The Unfinished Liberation of Chinese Women, 1949–1980*, 94.
88 The average monthly pay for sailors was 104 yuan in the early 1950s. After a salary adjustment in May 1954, this was reduced to 88 yuan and largely kept at that level throughout the Mao era. Shanghai Changjiang hangyun zhi bianzuan weiyuanhui, *Shanghai Changjiang hangyun zhi*, 9:2.
89 "Longtang gongchang li de nüren men," *Wenhui dushu zhoubao*, May 12, 2011.
90 I-22.
91 Ibid.
92 I-17 and I-22.
93 SMA, B246-2-423.
94 I-23.

95 On Shanghai's neighborhood stores, see Hanchao Lu, "Away from Nanking Road."
96 I-23.
97 I-24.
98 I-25 and I-26.
99 *Jiafang ribao*, April 4, 2015. The recorded interview was part of an oral history project started in 2008 and presided over by He Amao's grandson, Li Yaohua (1970–).
100 These words will not be found in Mao's formal writings. However, Chinese official media reported on this comment of Mao's on various occasions and used it for propaganda purposes. "Mao Zhuxi Liu Zhuxi changyou Shisanling shuiku" (Chairman Mao and Chairman Liu enjoyed swimming in the Shisanling reservoir), *Renmin ribao*, May 27, 1965, and "Funü neng ding banbiantian" (Women hold up half the sky), *Renmin ribao*, March 8, 1970; see also Zhong Xueping, "Women Can Hold Up Half the Sky."
101 On the sent-down movement of urban youth during the Cultural Revolution, see Bernstein, *Up to the Mountains and Down to the Villages*; Bonnin, *The Lost Generation*; Rene, *China's Sent-Down Generation*; and Honig and Zhao, *Across the Great Divide*, which has a focus on sent-down youth of Shanghai.
102 SMA, B127-2-133-58; SMA, B127-1-157.
103 Shanghaishi tongzhi bianzuan weiyuanhui, *Shanghai tongzhi*, 18:4: 1.
104 Goldman, *Women at the Gates*, 115.
105 Zaleski, *Planning for Economy Growth in the Soviet Union*, 58.
106 Goldman, *Women at the Gates*, 6–7.
107 In China's first five-year plan period (1953–1958), investment in heavy industry as a percentage of total industrial investment increased from 35.5 to 45; still, the rate was significantly lower than that in the Soviet Union's first five-year plan. Wang Haibo, *Xin Zhongguo gongye jingji shi*, 562–6. For a discussion of the Soviet industrialization as a model, see Kemp, *Industrialization in the Non-Western World*, 50–83; on the influence of the "Soviet model" on Chinese industry, see Kaple, *Dream of a Red Factory*, especially 5–18.
108 Gender identities at industrial workplaces in the two countries in the pre-revolutionary era (Russia before 1917, China before 1949) were not significantly different. For a comparison between St. Petersburg and Shanghai in this regard, see Smith, *Revolution and the People in Russia and China*, 131–44.
109 Zimmermann, "Gender Regime and Gender Struggle in Hungarian State Socialism."
110 Siemieńska, "Women, Work, and Gender Equality in Poland," 307.
111 Harsch, *Revenge of the Domestic*, 99–100.
112 Volgyes, "Blue-Collar Working Women and Poverty in Hungary."
113 For a study of "socialist state feminists" and the high politics of the CCP from the perspective of gender, see Wang Zheng, "'State Feminism'?" and *Finding Women in the State*.
114 In this regard Lenin explicitly stated that the real emancipation of women "will begin only where and when an all-out struggle begins (led by the proletariat wielding the state power) against this petty housekeeping." Lenin, *On the Emancipation of Women*, 64.

Notes to pages 163–170

115 Perry and Selden, *Chinese Society*, 11.
116 I-23 and I-27.
117 Croll, *Women and Rural Development in China*, 34–5.
118 Ibid., 35.
119 SMA, A20-2-15-15. On gender-based job segregation, see Yao and Xie, "The Economic Effects of Occupational Segregation."
120 Zheng Wang, "'State Feminism'?"
121 Sociological and anthropological studies have found that similar considerations contributed to women in Latin America considering "informal employment" as a relatively desirable alternative. See Maloney, "Informality Revisited."
122 Jiang Yongping, "50 nian Zhongguo chengshi nüxing jiuye de huigong yu fansi."
123 Howell and Pringle, "Shades of Authoritarianism and State–Labour Relations in China," 6.
124 Brown and Johnson, *Maoism at the Grassroots*, 6–7.
125 Zhang Weiguo, "Mao Zedong shidai de yundong yu zuiming." Tens of thousands of rural communes and their short-lived communal dining halls established during the GLF were also created under the banner of liberating women's labor power.
126 MacFarquhar, *The Origins of the Cultural Revolution 2*, 326.

5 Everyday Flora

1 Hanchao Lu, "Creating Urban Outcasts."
2 Zhonggong Shanghai shiwei dangshi yanjiushi, *Shanghai zhichi quanguo*.
3 Japanese scholar Sanetō Keishū (1896–1985) did remarkable research on the Japanese influence on modern Chinese vocabulary. On the term *lühua*, see Shitun Huixiu (Sanetō Keishū), *Zhongguoren liuxue Riben shi*, 282. See also Zhao Ji-jun, "'Lühua' gainian de chansheng yu yanbian."
4 The revolutionary Sun Yat-sen (1866–1925), for instance, was an advocate of greening as part of China's nation-building. For his contributions, the date of Sun's death, March 12, is designated as Arbor Day in China. See Sun Wen (Sun Yat-sen), *Jianguo fanglüe*, 135, 199.
5 Verdurization was part of the Soviet Union's urban planning model, which included such things as formalistic street patterns, huge public squares, and the predominance of master plans. Wing-Shing Tang, "Chinese Urban Planning at Fifty."
6 Zhao Ji-jun, "'Lühua' gainian de chansheng yu yanbian."
7 The Chinese expression *huayuan chengshi* (garden city) was used during the campaign, but there is little evidence that the term was inspired by Ebenezer Howard's notion of the "garden city." The latter is alternatively translated in Chinese as *tianyuan chengshi* (pastoral city). A Chinese translation of Howard's *Garden Cities of To-morrow* was first published in 2000 (translated by Jin Jingyuan; Beijing: Commercial Press).
8 Shanghai kancha sheji zhi bianzuan weiyuanhui, *Shanghai kancha sheji zhi*, 611.

298   Notes to pages 170–173

9 Shanghai renmin zhengfu zhi bianzuan weiyuanhui, *Shanghai renmin zhengfu zhi*, 751; Shanghai chengshi guihua zhi bianzuan weiyuanhui, *Shanghai chengshi guihua zhi*, 388.
10 Composed by Guo Shifu (1929–2007); *Zhongguo yinyue bao*, December 24, 2007.
11 China's largest beverage company, Wahaha, founded in 1987 in Hangzhou, is named after the song. The song's name recognition contributed significantly to the company's success in the food and beverage market, and also caused a major lawsuit in 2007 against the company over the right to use the name. See Luo Jianxing, *Zong Qinghou yu* Wahaha, 77–8; *South China Morning Post*, April 11, 2007, p. B3.
12 *Renmin ribao*, February 26, 1958.
13 Zhao Zukang, reporting on the preliminary plan for verdurization in Shanghai, *Renmin ribao*, February 26, 1958.
14 Shanghaishi Huangpuyu zhi bianzuan weiyuanhui, *Huangpuqu zhi*, 585.
15 Ibid., 590. By 1992, there were 11,900 street trees in the district, which was about 7–8 square miles (19 square kilometers).
16 The Resolution on a Few Issues Concerning the People's Communes was passed at the sixth meeting of the CCP's Eighth Central Committee held in Wuchang, November 28–December 10, 1958. The document was published in *Renmin ribao*, December 19, 1958.
17 Zhonggong zhongyang wenxian yanjiushi, *Mao Zedong lun linye*, 51.
18 From January to November 1958, Mao gave no less than fifteen speeches or written instructions on verdurization, advocating the so-called three-three system, with one-third of all farmland to be devoted to grain production, another third to trees, and the last third to be left fallow. Zhonggong zhongyang wenxian yanjiushi, *Mao Zedong lun linye*, 44–64.
19 Shanghai renmin zhengfu zhi bianzuan weiyuanhui, *Shanghai renmin zhengfu zhi*, 751.
20 In the city proper there were 119,500 street trees in 1962, an increase of only 3,400 from the number in 1957. Shanghai yuanlin zhi bianzuan weiyuanhui, *Shanghai yuanlin zhi*, 388.
21 Ibid., 430.
22 Galston, *Daily Life in People's China*, 130. Arthur Galston (1920–2008) was a professor of botany at Yale University and the first US scientist to have visited the PRC after 1949.
23 Shanghai kancha sheji zhi bianzuan weiyuanhui, *Shanghai kancha sheji zhi*, 611.
24 The weight of the tael varied considerably, but in most cases was equivalent to 1.3 ounces of silver.
25 Shanghai yuanlin zhi bianzuan weiyuanhui, *Shanghia yuanlin zhi*, 387.
26 Zhou Erfu, *Morning in Shanghai*, 1.
27 See, for example, the popular reading, Wang Anyi's *The Song of Everlasting Sorrow*, and the academic work, Hanchao Lu, "Nostalgia for the Future."
28 Nanjingshi difangzhi bianzuan weiyuanhui, *Nanjing yuanlin zhi*, 396.
29 Ru Zhijuan, *Gaogao de baiyangshu*. Using trees as symbols remains common. Yomi Braester has noted that Beijing had 141,796 trees in 1980; the locust tree stood out by being regarded as "the national locust tree" and in 1986

was chosen as Beijing's "city tree" for its perceived social and cultural value. Braester, *Painting the City Red*, 125–6.
30 Shanghai yuanlin zhi bianzuan weiyuanhui, *Shanghia yuanlin zhi*, 388.
31 The insects became quite a hazard. For instance, in summer 1973, in eight elementary schools along Zaojiabang Road where white poplars had been planted, 373 kilograms (746 *jin*) of bristle insect pupa were collected from the trees. Shanghai Municipal Archives, File B252-2-41-15.
32 Shanghai yuanlin zhi bianzuan weiyuanhui, *Shanghia yuanlin zhi*, 388, 591.
33 Da Qizhen, "Shanyin Lu de qianshi jinsheng." Starting from October 1971, the Shanghai municipal government undertook a number of park and promenade garden renovations in preparation for Nixon's visit in February 1972; see *Shanghai yuanlin zhi*, 35. For Shanghai on the day of Nixon's visit, see Qiu Xiaolong, *Years of Red Dust*, 59–70, and Jibisou, *Shanghai chuantangfeng*, 98–100.
34 Shanghai yuanlin zhi bianzuan weiyuanhui, *Shanghai yuanlin zhi*, 388; Shanghai kancha sheji zhi bianzuan weiyuanhui, *Shanghai kancha sheji zhi*, 611–12.
35 Shanghai renmin zhengfu zhi bianzuan weiyuanhui, *Shanghai renmin zhengfu*, 750.
36 These parks were all built in the former foreign concessions. For a detailed account of parks in pre-1949 Shanghai, see Xiong Yuezhi, "Jindai Shanghai gongyuan yu shehui shenghuo."
37 Shanghai tongzhi bianzuan weiyuanhui, *Shanghai tongzhi*, vol. 26, chap. 8; Shanghai yuanlin zhi bianzuan weiyuanhui, *Shanghai yuanlin zhi*, 5.
38 See Mao's opening address at the First Plenary Session of the Chinese People's Political Consultative Conference delivered on September 21, 1949. Mao Zedong, *Mao Zedong xuanji*, 5:15–18.
39 Nanjing Road refers to both Nanking Road (present-day East Nanjing Road) and Bubbling Well Road (present-day West Nanjing Road).
40 The enforcement of the ban varied over time but before June 1928, most Chinese, save for a few amahs and individuals with special permission, were barred from the park. For details of the ban and a revisionist view on the controversies over it, see Bickers and Wasserstrom, "Shanghai's 'Dogs and Chinese Not Admitted' Sign."
41 Shanghaishi difangzhi bangongshi and Shanghaishi lühua guanliju, *Shanghai mingyuan zhi*, 122. In 1996, the Shanghai municipal government designated the park as a "base for educating youth in patriotism."
42 At the time it was located at the corner of Nanking Road and Honan Road.
43 In September 1951, the southern part of the racecourse was made into People's Square, a 35-acre open, public space.
44 Shanghaishi difangzhi bangongshi and Shanghaishi lühua guanliju, *Shanghai mingyuan zhi*.
45 The construction budget was of 56,200 taels of silver. Henriot, "Shanghai zujie gongmu yanjiu, 1844–1949."
46 Henriot, *Scythe and the City*, 204, 188–9.
47 Shanghaishi difangzhi bangongshi and Shanghaishi lühua guanliju, *Shanghai mingyuan zhi*, 216–17.

48 The origins of Jing'an Temple can be traced back to the year 247, but much of its structure was destroyed during the Taiping Rebellion in 1860. It was rebuilt in 1880–1881 with donations from merchant Hu Xueyan (1823–1885) and others and survived into the PRC.
49 Shanghai kancha sheji zhi bianzuan weiyuanhui, *Shanghai kancha sheji zhi*, 599.
50 Jing'anqu renming zhengfu, *Shanghaishi Jing'anqu diming zhi*, 282.
51 By 2003, of the 133 parks in Shanghai, ninety were admission-free; *Renmin ribao*, April 18, 2003, p. 13.
52 The monthly pass was not valid for Xijiao Park, which was a zoo and charged 10 cents for single-entry admission.
53 Shanghai laodong zhi bianzuan weiyuanhui, *Shanghai laodong zhi*, 339.
54 Shanghai yuanlin zhi bianzuan weiyuanhui, *Shanghai yuanlin zhi*, 588.
55 Zhu Bangxing, Hu Lin'ge, and Xu Sheng, *Shanghai chanye yu Shanghai gongren*, 79–80.
56 Xiong Yuezhi, "Jindai Shanghai gongyuan yu shehui shenghuo."
57 Shanghai yuanlin zhi bianzuan weiyuanhui, comp., *Shanghai yuanlin zhi*, 588.
58 Cheng Naishan, "Xiari ougan."
59 Wang Tao, *Yinru zazhi*, 14–15; Zheng Yimei, "TongGuang nianjian de juhuahui."
60 *North China Herald*, May 29, 1875.
61 Shanghaishi shili yuanlinchang, *Zai ju shu*.
62 Shanghai yuanlin zhi bianzuan weiyuanhui, *Shanghai yuanlin zhi*, 361–2.
63 Xijiao Park was renamed Shanghai Zoo in 1980. Shanghaishi difangzhi bangongshi and Shanghaishi lühua guanliju, *Shanghai mingyuan zhi*, 112.
64 Shanghai yuanlin zhi bianzuan weiyuanhui, *Shanghai yuanlin zhi*, 361.
65 Ibid.
66 Nixon's visit in 1972 and Deng Xiaoping's return to power from 1973 to 1975 contributed to a relatively relaxed atmosphere in Chinese society; flower shows were part of that general trend.
67 See Shanghai tongzhi bianzuan weiyuanhui, *Shanghai tongzhi*, vol. 3, chap. 1.
68 Hanchao Lu, *Beyond the Neon Lights*, chap. 4.
69 Wang Shaozhou and Chen Zhimin, *Lilong jianzhu*, 161–72.
70 Balzac, *The Works of Honoré de Balzac*, 86. Also, Balzac, *Comédie Humaine*, 22:301.
71 The saying is generally attributed to Taoist poet Wang Kangju, who lived during the Eastern Jin dynasty (317–420). Zhong Laiyin, *Zhonggu xian dao shi jinghua*, 278.
72 See Lao-Tzu, *Tao Te Ching*, 41.
73 Xia Renhu, *Zhi chao si shu/Jiu Jing suo ji*, 83.
74 Ibid.
75 Hanchao Lu, *Beyond the Neon Lights*, 154.
76 Fan Qian, "Shanghai longtang."
77 Ye Shengtao, "Tianjing li de zhongzhi."
78 *Renmin ribao*, March 1, 1958, p. 2.

79 Ibid.
80 Scott, *Seeing Like a State*, 82.
81 *Ziliao xuanbian* (Selected materials), dated February 1967, housed in the library of the Institute of Modern History, Chinese Academy of Social Sciences, Beijing; see also the Red Guard publication titled *Mao Zedong sixiang wansui* (Long live Mao Zedong Thought) (n.p.: 1967), 2:332.
82 In 1988, twelve years after Zhou's death, his wife wrote an essay, "The Crabapple at the West Hall of Flowers Bloomed Again," about the affection of her husband of fifty years. Zhang Zuoliang, *Zhou Enlai de zuihou shinian*.
83 Lin Yutang, *The Importance of Living*, 304. The other three "gentlemen" are the calyx canthus (wintersweet), bamboo, and chrysanthemum. Zhang Xingcheng, "Yimin qingjie yu wenren lanhua shihua zhuantong de hua."
84 Zheng Jingzhong, "Wo zai Zhongnanhai jian dao de Zhu laozhong."
85 Yang Jisheng. *Tiandi fanfu*, 54.
86 Beijing Forestry Institute and the Shanghai Park Office Red Guard Newspaper, undated, http://blog.people.com.cn/article/1319690443872.html.
87 You-Sheng Li, *A New Interpretation of Chinese Taoist Philosophy*, 213.
88 Jung Chang, *Wild Swans*, 10.
89 Li Chengpeng, *Quan shijie renmin dou zhidao*, 4–5.
90 *Renmin ribao*, overseas edition, October 12, 2009, p. 7.
91 Shanghai yuanlin zhi bianzuan weiyuanhui, *Shanghai yuanlin zhi*, 516–19.
92 Da Qizhen, "Shanyin Lu de qianshi jinsheng."
93 Zheng Jian, *Shanghai chuantangfeng*, 22–3.
94 There was widespread prejudice toward people of Subei (northern Jiangsu province) origin in Shanghai. See Honig, *Creating Chinese Ethnicity*.
95 Hanyan, *Wuchang zhi mei*, 139–55.
96 The "backyard furnaces" refer to the efforts to make iron and steel through a mass movement in 1958–1959. For an eyewitness account of the campaign, see Li Zhisui, *The Private Life of Chairman Mao*, 272–4, 277.
97 Zhang Da-Peng, *Life Under Mao Zedong's Rule*, 221, 239.
98 Wang, *The Song of Everlasting Sorrow*, 5, 17, 237, 429.
99 Ibid., 253.
100 Jian Fan, *Canghai*, 3:225–8.
101 Ibid.; Zhang Da-peng, *Life Under Mao Zedong's Rule*, 384–6.
102 Tan Yingzhou, "Shiliu huakai, qianban ganhuai."
103 Tan Yingzhou, "Hongse de niaoluo" (The red cypress vine), *Xinmin wanbao*, July 27, 2013; Tan Yingzhou, *Renjian huashi*.
104 Da Qizhen, "Shanyin Lu gushi."
105 Li Chengpeng, *Quan shijie renmin dou zhidao*, 4–5.
106 *Xiamen ribao*, August 3, 2014.
107 Ma Jun, "Lao Shanghai Bailemen wuting de chuangban yu xingshuai."
108 Yuyuan (literally, "pleasant garden") was a new-style alleyway-house subdivision on Avenue Joffre; its current address is Lane 1350, Huaihai Zhonglu.
109 Li Man, "Shanghai Bailemen chuangshiren Sheng qi xiaojie."
110 Nie Chongbin, "Wo de guju wo de muxiao."

111 Zhonggong Shanghai dang zhi bianzuan weiyuanhui, *Zhonggong Shanghai dang zhi*, 5:3:1.
112 Tang Baolin, *Jujue nuxing*, 266–73.
113 For a discussion of cultural gaps between southbound cadres and urban bourgeois, see James Gao, *The Communist Takeover of Hangzhou*, 257–60.
114 Huang Shi, *Zui mei de Shanghai*, 72.
115 In 1992, the resident of the house on Panyu Road moved to an apartment high-rise and, writing under the pen name Yunjian Shanjiao (Cloudy Mountains Woodman), waxed nostalgic about the joy of gardening and the "authentic organic food" that came from the garden, and lamented that "the pastoral pleasure is gone forever." Yunjian Shanjiao, "Shiqu de doushi huayuan caidi."
116 Zhou Haiying, *Lu Xun yu wo qishi nian*, 33–7. Mrs. Uchiyama's husband, Uchiyama Kanzō (1885–1959), was a close friend of Lu Xun's during Lu Xun's last ten years in Shanghai.
117 I-28.
118 Shanghai Municipal Archive website, www.archives.sh.cn/shjy/shzg/201303/t20130319_38144.html.
119 Zhou Peihong, *Shanghai siren ditu*, 8.
120 Da Qizhen, "Shanyin Lu gushi"; I–29.
121 Shanghai sichou zhi bianzuan weiyuanhui, *Shanghai sichou zhi*, 6:3:2.
122 Shanghai nongye zhi bianzuan weiyuanhui, *Shanghai nongye zhi*, 5:4:1.
123 Yuan Nianqi, "Can baobao."
124 Chen Jianxing, "Yangcan qushi."
125 Zhu Dake, *Jiyi de hongpishu*, 91.
126 Chen Jianxing, "Yangcan qushi."
127 Dongfang Television Station, script: http://bbs.tianya.cn/post-books-74913-1.shtml, March 15, 2006.
128 *Zhongguo lüse shibao*, April 29, 2014. According to Lei, one reason for the near disappearance of the mulberry trees from Shanghai is that they were regarded as too Chinese and rustic and the authorities favored planting exotic foreign spices such Canary Island date palms.
129 Zhang Da-Peng, *Life Under Mao Zedong's Rule*, 473–4. Present-day Shanghai is greener than it was in the late twentieth century, but bees have become rare. According to a 2014 report of the Shanghai Insect Institute, "in recent years, the numbers of bees, butterflies, frogs, and even earthworms have plunged." Professor Wu Zhixing of the Shanghai Landscape Garden Association pointed out that "in spring wisteria is the flower that attracts bees the most, but now although wisteria is booming, bees are absent." Air pollution and excessive use of pesticides were generally blamed. *Xinwen chengbao*, April 15, 2014.
130 Karl Gerth's recent study of consumerism in Mao's China provides many pieces of evidence for this argument. See Gerth, *Unending Capitalism*.
131 Zhonggong zhongyang wenxian yanjiushi, *Mao Zedong lun linye*, 51.
132 Ibid., 74.
133 See Scott, *Seeing Like a State*, especially chap. 1, for an analysis of scientific and state-sponsored forestry. For case studies of China's failed state programs that caused ecological disasters, see Smil, *China's Environmental Crisis*, and Shapiro, *Mao's War against Nature*.

Notes to pages 199–208

134 Dong Jianhong, *Zhongguo chengshi jianshe shi*, 386–98.
135 See Table 5.1; Shanghai chengshi guihua zhi bianzuan weiyuanhui, *Shanghai chengshi guihua zhi*, 386–8. See also *Lüye* (*Green Leaf*, a monthly magazine published in Beijing), no. 9 (September 2009): 85.
136 Li Zhisui, *The Private Life of Chairman Mao*, 504.

6 In the Eyes of Foreign Onlookers

1 de Certeau, *The Practice of Everyday Life*, 115.
2 Shanghaishi gong'an ju, *Shanghai gong'an zhi*, 284–5; He Yaping, *Shanghai guoji hua renkou yanjiu*, 76–7.
3 He Yaping, *Shanghai guoji hua renkou yanjiu*.
4 Shanghaishi gong'an ju, *Shanghai gong'an zhi*, 288; He Yaping, *Shanghai guoji hua renkou yanjiu*, 77–8.
5 *Boston Globe*, October 16, 1955, p. 32.
6 Cameron, *Mandarin Red*, 193.
7 Chipp, "Shanghai Retains 'Vitality' under Reds."
8 Gerth, *Unending Capitalism*, 191.
9 Chipp, "Shanghai Retains 'Vitality' under Reds."
10 Ibid.
11 Bisch, "This Is the China I Saw," 618.
12 Rossi, *The Communist Conquest of Shanghai*, 106.
13 Guillain, "Shanghai Living Subtle New Life."
14 Kin-ming Liu, *My First Trip to China*, 86.
15 Wilson, *Anatomy of China*, 46. In addition to writing numerous works on China, Wilson was also the editor of the influential journal *China Quarterly* from 1975 to 1980.
16 Karol, *China*, 208.
17 Koningsberger, *Love and Hate in China*, 50.
18 Ibid., 51.
19 Hunter, *Shanghai Journal*, 89.
20 *New York Times*, November 29, 1970, p. 10; also, *Washington Post*, December 28, 1970, p. A16.
21 John Roderick and the staff writers and photographers of the Associated Press, *What You Should Know about the People's Republic of China*, 3.
22 *Los Angeles Times*, April 25, 1971, p. 12.
23 Ibid.
24 MacMillan, *Nixon and Mao*, 313.
25 Kraft, *The Chinese Difference*, 37 (italics in the original).
26 Qiu Xiaolong, *Years of Red Dust*, 62; Zhang Hanzhi, *Kuaguo houhou de da hongmen*, 256–57; Jibisou, *Shanghai chuantangfu*, 98–100.
27 Peddlers, whose typical sale of green onions and ginger root was one or two cents, were allowed to sell their goods at the entrance of every food market. All the peddlers were old women.
28 I-4 and I-33.
29 Zhang Hanzhi, *Kuaguo houhou de da hangmen*, 257.
30 *Washington Post*, September 3, 1972, p. F1.

304   Notes to pages 208–218

31 Ibid.
32 Snow, *The Other Side of the River*, 531.
33 Ibid., 531–3.
34 Karol, *China*, 207–8. Dick Wilson had a similar experience at the Great World amusement center in 1964; see Wilson, *Anatomy of China*, 47.
35 McCullough, "Shanghai: Decorum Replaces Bars and Dance Halls."
36 Shanghai qiaowu zhi bianzuan weiyuanhui, comp., *Shanghai qiaowu zhi*, 165.
37 For instance, in the early 1960, a Shanghai municipal government project to mobilize residents who had overseas connections was able to obtain enough overseas remittances to import 11,000 tons of chemical fertilizer for farms in suburban Shanghai. Ibid., 164.
38 Shanghai riyong gongye pin shangye zhi bianzuan weiyuanhui, comp., *Shanghai riyong gongye pin shangye zhi*, 10:3:3, 353–5.
39 Shanghai qiaowu zhi bianzuan weiyuanhui, *Shanghai qiaowu zhi*, 164.
40 *Shanghai qiaobao* (Shanghai Overseas Chinese News), February 2, 2009.
41 I-34.
42 *Washington Post*, September 3, 1972.
43 For example, *The Diary of Lei Feng* (*Lei Feng riji*), one of most widely circulated propaganda pamphlets in China, has an entry that reads in part: "Today, our territory Taiwan is still occupied by the American imperialists and Chiang Kai-shek. Two-thirds of the people in the world have not been liberated. They don't have food to eat and clothing to wear, they are suppressed and exploited. I will never let them be bullied and humiliated, and I will carry out the revolution to the end to liberate all the people who are suffering" (March 10, 1960).
44 Huang Hu, "Zhongguo dalu yi yue you."
45 Wilson, *Anatomy of China*, 48.
46 For details about these neighborhoods (known as *lilong* or, more colloquially, *longtang*), see Hanchao Lu, *Beyond the Neon Lights*, chaps. 5–6.

7 The Essential Does Not Change

1 Sheringham, *Everyday Life*, 332.
2 Ibid., 180.
3 Barber, *The Fall of Shanghai*, 187.
4 The Zhongshan suit was based on a Japanese military uniform that was brought by Sun Yat-sen (best known in China as Sun Zhongshan) to Shanghai around 1920. It was promoted by the Nationalist government in the late 1920s as a sort of standard men's suit. Hanchao Lu, *Beyond the Neon Lights*, 253–4.
5 Ke Ling, "Yaoji Zhang Ailing."
6 The novel was first published in *I Bao* (*Yibao*), a Shanghai-based tabloid from April 25, 1950, to February 11, 1951 (a stand-alone reprint was published by the same newspaper in November 1951). A slightly revised edition was published in Taiwan in 1969 as *Bansheng yuan* by Crown Publishing. An English translation, *Half a Lifelong Romance*, was published in Great Britain by Penguin Books in 2014.

7 Chang's essay, "Chinese Life and Fashions," was published by a Shanghai-based English journal, *20th Century* (January 1943 issue, 54–61); a revised Chinese version, "Gengyi ji" (A chronicle of changing clothes), was almost simultaneously published in the Chinese journal *Gujin* (Past and Present), 36 (1943): 25–9. Both essays are important in the study of fashion and psychoanalysis in modern China. For a "triangulated translation into English of Chang's translation [of "Gengyi ji"]" into Chinese, see Zhang and Jones, "Chronicle of Changing Clothes."
8 Zhang Zijing, *Wo de jiejie Zhang Ailing*, 184 and 190.
9 For real life stories of people from Shanghai fleeing overseas on the 1949 Communist takeover, see Helen Zia, *Last Boat Out of Shanghai*.
10 *Qingnan bao* (Youth News), May 17, 1955.
11 Finnane, *Changing Clothes in China*, 210–11; see also Gerth, *Unending Capitalism*, 84–87.
12 Zhang Chunqiao, *Longhua ji*, 158.
13 I-35.
14 Finnane, *Changing Clothes in China*, 247–55.
15 *Renmin ribao*, August 19, 1966.
16 The restriction on the rise of trousers was less strictly enforced than the width of the trouser legs; compromises were allowed to accommodate individual physiques.
17 I-25 and I-36; Wang Anyi, *Xunzhao Shanghai*, 33–4, 44, 52.
18 Boehler, "North Korea Remembers a Jacket."
19 Ji Zong, "Shinian xishi manlu."
20 Huang Shansong, "Mantan Wen'ge shiqi Shanghai jumin de yi shi zhu xing."
21 Qing Qiuzi, *Zheteng shinian*, 44.
22 "Chou, 73, and 'Team Hippie' Hit It Off," *New York Times*, April 15, 1971. See also the April 26, 1971, issue of *Time* magazine.
23 Wang Weiming, *Shanghai qiqing liuyu*, 17.
24 *Waitan huabao* (Bund Pictorial), no. 513 (November 1, 2012).
25 *Zhongguo qingnian bao* (Chinese Youth News), October 22, 2012.
26 Cheng Naishan, *Shanghai nüren*, 107–8.
27 Chen Junyi, *Wenrou de xiehou*, 207. Also, I-14 and I-37.
28 *Zhongguo qingnian bao*, October 22, 2012.
29 *Washington Post*, December 7, 1969.
30 Jin Dalu, "Chong 'wu' de shenmei ji qi tuibian."
31 He Bingdi et al., *LiuMei Huayi xuezhe chongfang Zhongguo guangan ji*, 46.
32 *Renmin ribao*, April 4, 1972, p. 2.
33 Lin Biao (1907–1971), one of the ten marshals of the PRC, was officially designated as Mao's successor in the late 1960s. He died in an air crash while allegedly fleeing to the Soviet Union after a failed attempt to murder Mao.
34 The popularity of do-it-yourself tailoring is also reflected in books on tailoring. During the Republican era ten tailoring books and eleven knitting books were published in Shanghai. From 1950 to 1964, 167 tailoring and knitting books were published. Shanghai chuban zhi bianzuan weiyuanhui, *Shanghai chuban zhi*, 410.
35 I-38. For a discussion of "capitalist tails," see *Renmin ribao*, April 10, 1972.

36 Zhong Fulan, *Shanghai jietou longkou*, 4.
37 Shanghai fangzhi gongye zhi bianzuan weiyuanhui, *Shanghai fangzhi gongye zhi*, 1:10:1.
38 On the Singer company founded by Isaac Merritt Singer (1811–1875), see Brandon, *A Capitalist Romance*; on the spread of sewing machines in China, see Krebs and Lu, eds., *China in Family Photographs*, 22–6.
39 Shanghai tongzhi bianzuan weiyuanhui, *Shanghai tongzhi*, 17(1):5:7. This number does not distinguish between household and industrial sewing machines. Based on early data, household sewing machines were always the majority – around 80 percent of the sewing machines produced annually. See also Buck, *Constructing China's Capitalism*, 42–45.
40 Shanghai fangzhi gongye zhi bianzuan weiyuanhui, *Shanghai fangzhi gongye zhi*, 1:10:1.
41 Wang You, "Fengrenji pinpai Hudie shangwei xiaoshi."
42 Shanghai fangzhi gongye zhi bianzuan weiyuanhui, *Shanghai fangzhi gongye zhi*, 1:10:1.
43 Zhong Fulan, *Shanghai jietou longkou*, 4.
44 Shanghaishi Jing'anqu zhi bianzuan weiyuanhui, *Shanghaishi Jing'anqu zhi*, 164–5.
45 Cheng Naishan, *Shanghai Fashion*, 80.
46 In Chinese, *jia lingzi*; more commonly in the Shanghai dialect, *jia lingtou*.
47 In a scene in the 1937 movie *Street Angel* (*Malu tianshi*) one of the protagonists takes a false collar from his wardrobe and puts it on before donning his Western-style outfit, suggesting that it was already common in Shanghai at the time. The scene appears about twenty minutes after the beginning of the movie.
48 There were two different standard widths of cotton fabric: 2.4 *chi* (2.6 feet) and 2.7 *chi* (2.95 feet). During the famine, the ration was based on the narrow type. The standard width for fabric for bed sheets was 3.3 *chi* (3.6 feet). I-39; Shanghai Municipal Archives website, *Jihua jingji shiqi de piaozheng* (Coupons and vouchers at the time of the planning economy), www.archives.sh.cn/dabl/zjjm/201203/t20120313_8502.html.
49 Shen Jialu, *Shanghai ren huofa*, 5.
50 *Guangzhou ribao*, September 15, 2009; Cen Rong, "Jialing shi Shanghai ren de faming ma?"
51 Chen Peizong, "Na ge niandai na xie shi."
52 Shen Jialu, *Shanghai ren huofa*, 5–6.
53 Xu Xiaodi, *Diandao suiyue*, 219–20.
54 *Nanfang ribao*, June 23, 2009, p. B5.
55 Peng Zuji, *Xiri Shanghai fengqing*, 44–5.
56 I-40.
57 Bray, *Technology and Gender*, 239, 252–60.
58 Wu Jimin, "Shen Laizhou yu rongxian dawang Hengyuanxiang." Xingsheng Jie is today Yongsheng Lu.
59 Pan Zhen, *Suiyue fengjing*, 204–5.
60 Zhong Fulan, *Shanghai jietou longkou*, 12.
61 Cheng Naishang, *Shanghai nüren*, 107.

Notes to pages 232–241   307

62 Zhongyang wenxian yanjiusi, *Jianguo yilai Mao Zedong wen'gao*, 7:53; *Renmin ribao*, editorial, March 27, 1958.
63 Wang Jingzhi, *Lengdong sanshi nian*, 215.
64 I-27 and I-41; Ernie, "Wen'ge zhong de Shanghai shangpin gongying xishi."
65 The typical amount of wool yarn (in catties) needed for smaller items: A pair of gloves, 0.2; a hat, 0.25; a high collar, 0.15; a scarf, 0.25 to 0.3. I-39.
66 I-36 and I-39; Zhong Fulan, *Shanghai jietou longkou*, 12.
67 Xu Longhua, *Shanghai fuzhuang wenhua shi*, 300.
68 Zhu Dake, *Jiyi de hongpi shu*, 123–4.
69 Jin Dalu, *Feichang yu zhengchang*, 1:214. The five streets were East Nanjing Road, West Nanjing Road, Huahai Road, North Sichuan Road, and Tibet Road.
70 Link, *An Anatomy of Chinese*, 27, 61.
71 Lin Jian, *Shanghai shishang*, 73–74; Jin Dalu, *Feichang yu zhengchang*, 1:214.
72 Jin Dalu, *Feichang yu zhengchang*, 1:210–11.
73 Chen Danyan, *Shanghai Princess*, 195–6.
74 Jia Zhifang, *Wo de rensheng dang'an*, 40.
75 I-45.
76 Chen Danyan, *Shanghai Princess*, 196.
77 Gunde, *Culture and Customs of China*, 116.
78 Hanchao Lu, *Beyond the Neon Lights*, 199, 260–3.
79 Shanghai yinshi fuwu ye zhi bianzuan weiyuanhui, *Shanghai yinshi fuwu ye zhi*, 49, 52.
80 In Chinese, *fuqi laopo dian*, equivalent to "mom-and-pop shop" in US English.
81 Dong Qian, *Gaizhao richang*, 199.
82 Shen Jialu, *Shanghai laoweidao*, 263. This was Shen's first job, at the age of eighteen. He later became a leader of Shanghai's restaurant employees' union.
83 Terrill, *800,000,000*, 41–2.
84 Ibid.
85 The retail prices (per 50 kilogram/yuan) of the staple foods were: Japonica rice (round-grained rice), 16.40; long-grained rice, 14.30; wheat flour, 17.00. I-44.
86 Hanchao Lu, *Beyond the Neon Lights*, 275.
87 Pan Ling, *In Search of Old Shanghai*, 100; Hanchao Lu, *Beyond the Neon Lights*, 194.
88 Shanghai liangshi zhi bianzuan weiyuanhui, *Shanghai liangshi zhi*, 2:2:2 and 2:3:1.
89 Shanghai fushipin shangye zhi bianzuan weiyuanhui, *Shanghai fushipin shangye zhi*, 1:1:3.
90 Shanghai sucai shangye zhi bianzuan weiyuanhui, *Shanghai sucai shangye zhi*, chap. 7.
91 The average retail price for vegetables was calculated based on the prices of the following twenty-seven vegetables: Bok choy, feather-shaped greens, cabbage, spinach, celery, Chinese cabbage, shepherd's purse, savoy cabbage,

three-colored amaranth, daikon radish (round), daikon radish (long), celtuce (stem lettuce), wax gourd (winter gourd), pumpkin, green cucumber, potato, taro, soybean, cowpea, green bean, tomato, eggplant, pepper, chive, cauliflower, water bamboo, and arrowhead (*cigu*). Shanghai jiage zhi bianzuan weiyuanhui, *Shanghai jiage zhi*, 1:9.
92 In Chinese, *cailanzi gongcheng*. The term *cailanzi* literally means "vegetable basket," which, prior to the widespread use of plastic containers in the 1980s, referred to bamboo baskets only.
93 Shanghai sucai shangye zhi bianzuan weiyuanhui, *Shanghai sucai shangye zhi*, 7:3.
94 Ibid.
95 Hanchao Lu, "Away from Nanking Road."
96 Shanghai fushipin shangye zhi bianzuan weiyuanhui, *Shanghai fushipin shangye zhi*, 1:1:3.
97 James Z. Gao, "Eating, Cooking, and Shanghai's 'Less-Than Manly Men'"; Long Yingtai, "Ah, Shanghai nanren."
98 I-19, I-28, I-F36, and I-43. See also Dong Qian, *Gaizhao richang*, 215–22.
99 Rations in Shanghai were much more generous than in most other places in the country. The writer Zhang Xianliang (1936–2014) recalled that in the Ningxia farm where he worked from 1957 to 1979, every two months each person was allocated only 1.1 ounces (one sixteenth of a *jin*) of cooking oil. Zhang satirically described how he coped with the meager ration: "What kind of container would you use for an amount of cooking oil that is less than a mouthful of saliva? And how could you manage to have the oil evenly used in your daily cooking for sixty days? I'll bet this is beyond your imagination. But I, a person with great wisdom, quickly found a solution: An eyedrop bottle! This way, I could squeeze a drop of cooking oil not only every day but even for every meal. The invention spread quickly to the whole farm – the only pity was that at that time no one had such a concept as intellectual property." See Hanchao Lu, "The Significance of the Insignificant," 155–6.
100 Shanghai fushipin shangye zhi bianzuan weiyuanhui, *Shanghai fushipin shangye zhi*, 1:1:3; Jin Dalu, "Guanyu 'piaozheng shidai' de jiti jiyi."
101 Hanchao Lu, "The Tastes of Chairman Mao."
102 Ristaino, *Port of Last Resort*, 5.
103 Gerth, *Unending Capitalism*, 148.
104 I-47. This father–daughter conversation occurred in the 1980s when the political atmosphere had become much more relaxed.
105 The idea behind the value accorded to rumors was that if news circulated in the marketplace, it must be widely known, even though it was not yet official. A number of informants recalled that they learned about the Lin Biao incident of 1971 from fellow shoppers while waiting in line in the markets; I-35 and I-45. Even in the early twentieth-first century, when there were many more channels for people to get information, roadside food markets remained a common place for neighbors to get information via chatting. See Zhu Jiangang, *Guo yu jia zhi jian*, 41–2, 47.
106 Yiqiao, *Tanshi ji*, 280.
107 Hanchao Lu, *Beyond the Neon Lights*, 98.

Conclusion

1. Babiarz et al., "An Exploration of China's Mortality Decline under Mao."
2. Peterson, *The Power of Words*, 3.
3. Ross, "China Country Study."
4. The exact death toll of the Great Famine is unknown – estimated numbers range between eighteen million and forty-five million. Several scholarly monographs on the famine have been published in English since 1984. See, for example, Yang Jisheng, *Tombstone: The Great Chinese Famine, 1958–1962*, and Frank Dikötter, *Mao's Great Famine: The History of China's Most Devastating Catastrophe, 1958–62*.
5. For a recent study of China's sent-down youth based on their own memories, see Xu, *Chairman Mao's Children*. For general history of the movement, see Bonnin, *The Lost Generation*, and Bernstein, *Up to the Mountains and Down to the Villages*.
6. Weber, *Weber's Rationalism and Modern Society*, chap. 7.
7. Leese, *Mao Cult*, 59.
8. It is of course ironic that the Weberian concept of traditional authority also includes monarchical rule, to which Mao's rule bore some resemblance.
9. Two *People's Daily* editorials set the tone for the discourse: "Linhun shenchu nao geming" (Have a revolution deep in one's soul), published October 22, 1966, and "'Dousi pixiu' shi wuchan jieji wenhua da geming de genben fangzhen" ("Fight selfishness, repudiate revisionism" is the guiding principle of the Great Proletarian Cultural Revolution), published October 6, 1967.
10. Hong Yung Lee, *From Revolutionary Cadres to Party Technocrats in Socialist China*, 2–3.
11. Smith, *Thought Reform and China's Dangerous Classes*, 53.
12. Goffman, "The Interaction Order," 9.
13. Whyte, *Street Corner Society*, xix.
14. Hegel, *Hegel's Preface to the Phenomenology of Spirit*, 88.
15. Perry, *Anyuan*, 4.
16. Misztal, *Informality*, 41.
17. Ibid., 44.
18. Mack, *Invisible Resistance to Tyranny*.
19. Terrill, *Flowers on an Iron Tree*, 43.
20. Machonin, "The Social Structure of Soviet-Type Societies"; Dikötter, "The Second Society."
21. Mao, *Mao Zedong wenji*, 7:321; Zhonggong zhongyang wenxian yanjiusishi, *Mao Zedong nianpu*, 3:237. Mao was in the habit of quoting Chinese classics in his speeches and writings. The line is from the famous eighteenth-century novel *Dream of the Red Chamber* (*Honglou meng*), Chapter 82.
22. Dutton, *Policing Chinese Politics*, 197.
23. Watson, *Class and Social Stratification in Post-Revolution China*, 15.
24. Brown and Johnson, *Maoism at the Grassroots*, 12.
25. Zhang Chunhua, *Hucheng suishi quge*, 23.
26. See, for example, Forbes, *Five Years in China*, 13–14.
27. Wang Tao, *Yingru zazhi*, 8; Hanchao Lu, "Arrested Development."
28. Shanghai Bowuguan, *Shanghai beike zilao xuanji*, 38–9.

29 Hanchao Lu, *Beyond the Neon Lights*, 308–15; Yang Dongping, *Chengshi jifeng*.
30 Zou Yiren, *Jiu Shanghai renkou bianqian de yanjiu*, chap. 4. According to a collection of biographies of Shanghai's so-called celebrities published in 1930, only 10 percent of them – that is, the most prominent persons who played a leading role in various fields in Shanghai – were born in Shanghai. See Haishang mingren zhuan bianjibu, *Haishang mingren zhuan*.
31 *China Weekly Review*, December 4, 1926, p. 15; Murphey, *Shanghai*, 85.
32 Bergère, *Shanghai*, 5.
33 Hanchao Lu, "Nostalgia for the Future."
34 The southern tour refers to Deng Xiaoping's inspection trip to southern China, including visits to Shenzhen, Zhuhai, Guangzhou, and Shanghai, from January 18 to February 21, 1992. Deng's talks and remarks during the tour became guidelines for China to reinforce the "Reform and Opening-up" policy that had been in limbo after the 1989 Tiananmen Incident.
35 Deng Xiaoping, *Deng Xiaoping wenxuan*, 3:376.
36 When the "reform and opening up" policy was launched, making Shanghai an SEZ would have fitted uncomfortably with the image of Shanghai's colonial past, especially the city's well-known foreign concessions, which were seen as manifestations of China's "national humiliation." There were debates among the leadership on this issue, and both *People's Daily* and Shanghai's *Liberation Daily* carried articles about the history of the *zujie* (foreign concessions) to imply that the SEZs might put Shanghai back on the old road to ruin. By the mid-1980s, more liberal voices seemed to win out, suggesting that even the foreign concessions imposed on China from 1845 to 1943 had a positive impact on China. See Xiong Yuezhi, "Lüelun Shanghai zujie de shuangchong yingxiang."
37 Deng was more candid in private conversations about the value of the West. Li Shenzhi (1923–2003), a senior leader who accompanied Deng on his visit to the United States in 1979, recalled that on the plane he asked Deng why China should open and open primarily to the West. Deng replied to the effect that looking back over the past few decades, all countries and regions with good relations with the United States had become rich. Li Pu, *Huainian Li Shenzhi*, 2:293; Zhao Kejin, "Meiguo mei qita lieqiang huai shi shishi."
38 Wen-hsin Yeh, *Shanghai Splendor*, 205, 215.

References

Archives

Chinese University of Hong Kong database.
Minjian lishi (Folk History) http://mjlsh.usc.cuhk.edu.hk/

Shanghai Municipal Archives (SMA)

(File titles are provided whenever they are available in the original)
SMA, A20-1-30.
SMA, A20-1-52-97. *CCP Changbai Street Committee neighborhood industry investigation report*, August 20, 1961.
SMA, A20-1-58. CCP Committee of Yangpu District, Shanghai, "Lilong funü canjia shehui laodong hou chuxian de xin maodun" (New contradictions arising from neighborhood women participating in the social workforce), July 1961.
SMA, A20-2-6-23. Industrial bureau report, May 10, 1960.
SMA, A20-2-7.
SMA, A20-2-15-15. Zhabei district report, "Jiedao lilong shengchan de qingkuang he zhuyao wenti" (The conditions of neighborhood production and key issues), August 4, 1961.
SMA, A20-2-17. *CCP Shanghai municipal branch internal bulletin*, March 16, 1961.
SMA, A20-2-24.
SMA, A33-6-13:33.
SMA, A33-6-13:42.
SMA, B29-2-899. "Guanyu fazhan jiedao gongye shengchan zhong jige wenti de yijian" (Comments and recommendations on issues concerning the development of street industry), June 7, 1960.
SMA, B123-5-327-11.
SMA, B127-1-157. "Guanyu jinyibu jianshao chengzhen renkou he tuoshan anzhi shehui xiansan laodongli de huibao" (Report on further reducing the urban population and appropriately placing the social idle labor force).
SMA, B127-2-133-58 "Benshi xiansan laodongli de qingkuang he anzhi yijian huibao ziliao" (Reporting materials on the conditions of idle laborers in this city and views concerning their placement).
SMA, B127-2-410.

SMA, B158-1-459-42.
SMA, B158-1-569-134.
SMA, B158-2-9-66. CCP Shanghai Municipal Bureau of Handicraft Industry Committee Report, September 6, 1965.
SMA, B182-1-1111-1. "Guanyu zuzhi lilong shengchan fuwu xing shiye de yijian (taolungao)" (Points of view concerning organizing alleyway production and service enterprises [draft for discussion]).
SMA, B246-2-423.
SMA, B246-2-423-1. Shanghai Handicraft Bureau investigation team report on APTs, March 4, 1969.
SMA, B252-2-41-15.
SMA, B252-2-58. Shanghai Municipal Revolutionary Committee statistics report, 1973.
SMA, C21-2-2895. Shanghai Municipal Bureau of Labor meeting minutes, July 25, 1966.
SMA, C31-1-61. Shanghai Municipal Women's Federation report, "Shanghaishi funü zuzhi qingkuang (1952)" (Organizational circumstances of Shanghai's women, 1952).
SMA, C48-2-2471-54.
SMA, Q194/1/285/2-12.
SMA, Q196-1-468.

Others

All About Shanghai and Environs: A Standard Guide Book. Shanghai: Shanghai University Press, 1935. Reprinted, Taipei: Ch'eng Wen, 1973.
Allison, Graham. *Destined for War: Can America and China Escape Thucydides's Trap?* New York: Mariner Books, 2017.
Altehenger, Jennifer. *Legal Lessons: Popularizing Laws in the People's Republic of China, 1949–1989.* Cambridge, MA: Harvard University Asia Center, 2018.
Andors, Phyllis. *The Unfinished Liberation of Chinese Women, 1949–1980.* Bloomington: Indiana University Press, 1983.
Apter, David E., and Tony Saich. *Revolutionary Discourse in Mao's Republic.* Cambridge, MA: Harvard University Press, 1994.
Babiarz, Kimberly Singer, Karen Eggleston, Grant Miller, and Qiong Zhang. "An Exploration of China's Mortality Decline under Mao: A Provincial Analysis, 1950–80." *Population Studies: A Journal of Demography* 69, no. 1 (March 2015): 39–56.
Bai Hua. *Rumeng suiyue* (The surreal time). Shanghai: Xuelin chubanshe, 2002.
Ball, Alan M. *Russia's Last Capitalists: The Nepmen, 1921–1929.* Berkeley: University of California Press, 1987.
Balzac, Honoré de. *Comédie Humaine.* Philadelphia: Gebbie Publishing Co., 1898.
Balzac, Honoré de. *The Works of Honoré de Balzac.* Philadelphia: Avil Publishing Co., 1901.
Barber, Noel. *The Fall of Shanghai.* New York: Coward, McCann & Geoghegan, 1979.
Barnett Doak A., and Ezra F. Vogel. *Cadres, Bureaucracy, and Political Power in Communist China.* New York: Columbia University Press, 1967.

Bauer, John, Wang Feng, Nancy E. Riley, and Xiaohua Zhao. "Gender Inequality in Urban China: Education and Employment." *Modern China* 18, no. 3 (July 1992): 333–70.

Bergère, Marie-Claire. *Shanghai: China's Gateway to Modernity*. Stanford, CA: Stanford University Press, 2009.

Bernstein, Thomas P. *Up to the Mountains and Down to the Villages: The Transfer of Youth from Urban to Rural China*. New Haven: Yale University Press, 1977.

Bhola, H. S. "The Anti-illiteracy Campaigns in the People's Republic of China: From the 1950s to the 1980s." In H. S. Bhola, *Campaigning for Literacy: Eight National Experiences of the Twentieth Century with a Memorandum to Decision-Makers*, 73–90. Paris: UNESCO, 1984.

Bickers, Robert A., and Jeffrey N. Wasserstrom. "Shanghai's 'Dogs and Chinese Not Admitted' Sign: Legend, History and Contemporary Symbol." *China Quarterly* 142 (1995): 444–66.

Bisch, Jørgen. "This Is the China I Saw." *National Geographic* 126, no. 5 (November 1964): 591–640.

Bo Yibo. *Ruogan zhongda juece yu shijian de huigu* (Recollections of several important decisions and events). 2 vols. Beijing: Zhonggong dangshi chubanshe, 2008.

Boecking, Felix. *No Great Wall: Trade, Tariffs, and Nationalism in Republican China, 1927–1945*. Cambridge, MA: Harvard University Asia Center, 2017.

Boehler, Patrick. "North Korea Remembers a Jacket." *Time*, December 3, 2012.

Bonnin, Michel. *The Lost Generation: The Rustication of China's Educated Youth (1968–1980)*. Hong Kong: Chinese University of Hong Kong, 2013.

Braester, Yomi. "'A Big Dying Vat': The Vilifying of Shanghai during the Good Eighth Company Campaign." *Modern China* 31, no. 4 (October 2005): 411–47.

Braester, Yomi. *Painting the City Red: Chinese Cinema and the Urban Contract*. Durham, NC: Duke University Press, 2010.

Brandon, Ruth. *A Capitalist Romance: Singer and the Sewing Machine*. Philadelphia: J.B. Lippincott, 1977.

Bray, Francesca. *Technology and Gender: Fabrics of Power in Late Imperial China*. Berkeley: University of California Press, 1997.

Brehm, Sharon S., and Jack W. Brehm. *Psychological Reactance: A Theory of Freedom and Control*. New York: Academic Press, 1981.

Brown, Jeremy. *City Versus Countryside in Mao's China: Negotiating the Divide*. Cambridge, NY: Cambridge University Press, 2012.

Brown, Jeremy, and Matthew D. Johnson, eds. *Maoism at the Grassroots: Everyday Life in China's Era of High Socialism*. Cambridge, MA: Harvard University Press, 2015.

Brown, Jeremy, and Paul Pickowicz, eds. *Dilemmas of Victory: The Early Years of the People's Republic of China*. Cambridge, MA: Harvard University Press, 2007.

Buck, Daniel. *Constructing China's Capitalism: Shanghai and the Nexus of Urban-Rural Industries*. New York: Palgrave Macmillan, 2012.

Buckley, Chris. "Chinese Village Where Xi Jinping Fled Is Now a Monument to His Power." *New York Times*, October 8, 2017.
"Xi Starts New Term in China, with Trusted Deputy to Deal with Trump." *New York Times*, March 16, 2018.
Cai Xiang. *Revolution and Its Narratives: China's Socialist Literary and Cultural Imaginaries, 1949–1966*. Edited and translated by Rebecca E. Karl and Xueping Zhong. Durham, NC: Duke University Press, 2016.
Cameron, James. *Mandarin Red: A Journey Behind the Bamboo Curtain*. London: Michael Joseph, 1955.
Canran. "Shouchaoben: xiangjian buru huainian" (Hand-copied manuscripts: It is better to cherish them than to read them). *Xinwen zhoukan* (News Weekly), March 9, 2004.
Cao Cheng. *Yi huan bei chang ji* (A record of the sufferings from a barbarian invasion). Shanghai: Shanghai guji chubanshe, 1989 [1876].
Cao Juren. *Shanghai Chunqiu* (Shanghai spring and autumn). Shanghai: Shanghai renmin chubanshe, 1996.
Cao Ying. "Wo benlai bing buxiang zuo wenxue" (Originally, I did not want to work on literature). Chinese University of Hong Kong database, *Minjian lishi* (Folk History).
Cao Ying. *Wo yu Eluosi wenxue – fanyi shengya liushi nian* (Russian literature and me: A sixty-year career in translation). Shanghai: Wenhui chubanshe, 2003.
Cen Rong. "Jialing shi Shanghai ren de faming ma?" (Is the false collar an invention of the Shanghainese?). *Shenzhen shangbao* (Shenzhen Business Daily), December 12, 2013.
Chai Cao. *Lu Xiaoman zhuan* (Biography of Lu Xiaoman). Tianjin: Baihua wenyi chubanshe, 2002.
Chang, Jung. *Big Sister, Little Sister, Red Sister: Three Women at the Heart of Twentieth-Century China*. New York: Knopf, 2019.
Chang, Jung. *Wild Swans: Three Daughters of China*. New York: Simon & Schuster, 2003.
Chang Pang-Mei. *Bound Feet & Western Dress*. New York: Doubleday, 1996.
Chao, Kang. "Industrialization and Urban Housing in Communist China." *Journal of Asian Studies* 25, no. 3 (May 1966): 381–96.
Cheek, Timothy. *The Intellectual in Modern Chinese History*. Cambridge, UK: Cambridge University Press, 2015.
Chen Cun. *Chen Cun zuopin jingxuan* (A collection of carefully selected works of Chen Cun). Beijing: Huaxia chubanshe, 2008.
Chen Danqing. *Duoyu de sucai* (Superfluous materials). Guilin: Guangxi Normal University Press, 2007.
Chen Danyan. *Shanghai de fenghua xueyue* (title in English: *Shanghai Memorabilia*). Beijing: Zuojia chubanshe, 1998.
Chen Danyan. *Shanghai Princess: Her Survival with Pride & Dignity*. New York: Better Link Press, 2010.
Chen Danyan. *Shanghai sela* (Shanghai salad). Beijing: Zuojia chubanshe, 2001.
Chen Haiwen, comp. *Peace and Prosperity: Classic Buildings of Jing'an District, Shanghai*. Shanghai: Shanghai wenhua chubanshe, 2004.
Chen Jianhua. "Lu Xiaoman de 'fengjing' neiwai" (Lu Xiaoman's "scenery" and beyond). Chinese University of Hong Kong database, *Minjian lishi* (Folk History).

References 315

Chen Jianhua. "Yi jiu liu ling niandai de wenxue zhuiyi" (Recollecting the literature in the 1960s). *Shucheng* (Book Town), no. 40 (September 2009).
Chen Jianxing. "Yangcan qushi" (The fun of raising silkworms). *Xinmin wanbao* (Xinmin Evening News), March 18, 2018.
Chen Julai. *Anchi renwen suoyi* (Miscellaneous recollections of the people I knew). Shanghai: Shanghai shuhua chubanshe, 2011.
Chen Junyi. *Wenrou de xiehou* (English title: *An Enchanting Encounter*). Keller, TX: Fellows Press of America, 2010.
Chen Kun. "Wo de bofu Luo Ji'nan" (My uncle Lu Ji'nan). *Lao zhaopian* (Old Photos) 24 (August 2002): 1–13.
Chen Lai, ed. *Buxi ji: huiyi Zhang Dainian xiansheng* (Working without a break: Reflections on Mr. Zhang Dainian). Beijing: Peking University Press, 2005.
Chen Mingyuan, ed. *Jiaru Lu Xun huozhe* (If Lu Xun were alive). Shanghai: Wenhui chubanshe, 2003.
Chen Peizong. "Na ge niandai na xie shi" (Those things in that era). Chinese University of Hong Kong database, *Minjian lishi* (Folk History).
Chen Rong and Ye Xin, comps. *Zhongguo chengyu diangu kaoshi* (Philological studies of Chinese proverbs and literary allusions). Taiyuan: Shanxi jingji chubanshe, 1997.
Chen Sihe. *1966–1970: Andan suiyue* (1966–1970: A gloomy time). Shanghai: Shanghai shudian chubanshe, 2013.
Chen, Theodore Hsi-en. *Chinese Education since 1949: Academic and Revolutionary Models*. New York: Pergamon, 1981.
Chen Yi zhuan bianxie zu, comp. *Chen Yi zhuan* (Biography of Chen Yi). Beijing: Dangdai Zhongguo chubanshe, 1991.
Chen, Yu-Shih. *Realism and Allegory in the Early Fiction of Mao Dun*. Bloomington: Indiana University Press, 1986.
Chen Zhongcheng and Shao Aihong. "'Faquan' haishi 'quanli' zhi zheng" (The debate on using "legal rights" or "right"). *Faxue (Law)* 6 (1999): 2–3.
Chen Zhongyi. "Huigu yu fansi waiguo wenxue fanyi yu yanjiu liushi nian" (Review and reflection on sixty years of foreign literature translation and research). Keynote speech at the Sixth National Conference of the Chinese Association for Translation, Beijing, November 12–13, 2009.
Chen Zhu. "Bei yiwang zai fanyi de shijie li" (Being forgotten in the world of translation). *Zhongguo qingnian bao* (China Youth News), May 9, 2012.
Chen Zishan. *Zhang Ailing congkao* (Studies on Eileen Chang). Beijing: Haitun chubanshe, 2015.
Cheng Naishan. "Nanjing Xi Lu Huayuan Gongyu: wo de Haipai wenhua de qimeng keben" (Garden Villas on West Nanjing Road: My enlightenment textbook of Shanghai culture). *Shanghai wenxue* (Shanghai Literature), February 2013: 58–67.
Cheng Naishan. *Shanghai Fashion*. Shanghai: Shanghai wenyi chubanshe, 2005.
Cheng Naishan. *Shanghai luomanshi* (Shanghai romance). Shanghai: Shanghai cishu chubanshe, 2006.
Cheng Naishan. *Shanghai nüren* (Shanghai women). Hangzhou: Zhejiang sheying chubanshe, 2003.
Cheng Naishan. *Shanghaijie qinghua* (Sweet nothings in Shanghai's streets). Shanghai: Xuelin chubanshe, 2007.

Cheng Naishan. "Xiari ougan" (Random thoughts on a summer day). Posted August 10, 2013. http://blog.sina.com.cn/s/blog_4aba2161010178ag.html.
Cheng, Nien. *Life and Death in Shanghai*. New York: Penguin, 1988.
Chipp, David. "Shanghai Retains 'Vitality' under Reds." *Washington Post and Times Herald*, September 8, 1957.
Chou, Min-chih. *Hu Shih and Intellectual Choice in Modern China*. Ann Arbor: University of Michigan Press, 1984.
Choy, Howard Y. F. *Remapping the Past: Fictions of History in Deng's China, 1979–1997*. Leiden: Brill, 2008.
Cochran, Sherman, ed. *The Capitalist Dilemma in China's Communist Revolution*. Ithaca, NY: Cornell East Asia Program, 2014.
Cochran, Sherman, and Andrew Hsieh. *The Lius of Shanghai*. Cambridge, MA: Harvard University Press, 2013.
Croll, Elisabeth J. *Women and Rural Development in China: Production and Reproduction*. Geneva: International Labour Office, 1985.
Culp, Robert. *The Power of Print in Modern China: Intellectuals and Industrial Publishing from the End of Empire to Maoist State Socialism*. New York: Columbia University Press, 2019.
Cuthbertson, Ken. *Nobody Said Not to Go: The Life, Loves and Adventures of Emily Hahn*. New York: Faber & Faber, 1998.
Da Qizhen. "Shanyin Lu de qianshi jinsheng" (The past and present of Shanyin Road). Chinese University of Hong Kong database, *Minjian lishi* (Folk History).
Da Qizhen. "Shanyin Lu gushi: yi Dashen Xiaoqing xiongmei" (The story of Shanyin Road: Reminiscences of brother and sister Dashen and Xiaoqing). Chinese University of Hong Kong database, *Minjian lishi* (Folk History).
Dai Sijie. *Balzac and the Little Chinese Seamstress*. New York: Anchor, 2002.
Dangdai Zhongguo congshu bianjibu, ed. *Dangdai Zhongguo de chuban shiye* (Publishing enterprises in contemporary China). Beijing: Dangdai Zhongguo chubanshe, 1993.
Davin, Delia. *Woman-Work: Women and the Party in Revolutionary China*. Glasgow: Oxford University Press, 1976.
de Certeau, Michel. *The Practice of Everyday Life*. Translated by Steven F. Rendall. Berkeley: University of California Press, 1984.
Deng Xiaoping. *Deng Xiaoping wenxuan* (Selected works of Deng Xiaoping). Beijing: Renmin chubanshe, 1993.
Deng, Yingchao. *Deng Yunchao wenji* (Collected works of Deng Yunchao). Beijing: Renmin chubanshe, 1994.
Denton, Kirk A. *The Problematic of Self in Modern Chinese Literature: Hu Feng and Lu Ling*. Stanford, CA: Stanford University Press, 1998.
Dikötter, Frank. *The Cultural Revolution: A People's History, 1962–1976*. London: Bloomsbury, 2019.
Dikötter, Frank. *Mao's Great Famine: The History of China's Most Devastating Catastrophe, 1958–62*. London: Bloomsbury, 2017.
Dikötter, Frank. "The Second Society." In *Popular Memories of the Mao Era: From Critical Debate to Reassessing History*, edited by Sebastian Veg, 183–98. Hong Kong: Hong Kong University Press, 2019.

References

Dikötter, Frank. *The Tragedy of Liberation: A History of the Chinese Revolution 1945–1957*. London, UK: Bloomsbury, 2017.

Ding Yanzhao. *Beiqing Lu Xiaoman* (Sorrowful Lu Xiaoman). Shanghai: Shanghai renmin chubanshe, 2008.

Dittmer, Lowell. *Liu Shao-ch'i and the Chinese Cultural Revolution: The Politics of Mass Criticism*. Berkeley: University of California Press, 1974.

Dong Jianhong. *Zhongguo chengshi jianshe shi* (A history of Chinese urban construction). Beijing: Zhongguo jianzhu gongye chubanshe, 2004.

Dong Qian. *Gaizhao richang: Xinmin wanbao yu shehui zhuyi Shanghai shenhuo kongjian zhi jianguo (1949–1966)* (Reforming the quotidian: *Xinmin Evening News* and the reconstruction of life space in socialist Shanghai [1949–1966]). Shanghai: Shanghai shiji chuban jituan, 2016.

Dong Zhujun. *Wode yige shiji* (My hundred years). Beijing: Sanlian shudian, 1997.

Dutton, Michael. *Policing Chinese Politics: A History*. Durham, NC: Duke University Press, 2005.

Ernie. "Wen'ge zhong de Shanghai shangpin gongying xishi" (Small details on merchandise supplies in Shanghai during the Cultural Revolution). Chinese University of Hong Kong database, *Minjian lishi* (Folk History).

Evans, Harriet. *The Subject of Gender: Daughters and Mothers in Urban China*. Lanham, MD: Rowman & Littlefield, 2008.

Eyferth, Jacob. *How China Works: Perspectives on the Twentieth-Century Industrial Workplace*. New York: Routledge, 2006.

Fan Qian. "Shanghai longtang" (Shanghai's alleyways). *Shijie ribao fukan (World Journal Supplement)*, February 6, 2009.

Fang Huawen. *20 shiji Zhongguo fanyi shi* (A history of translation in twentieth-century China). Xi'an: Xibei daxue chubanshe, 2008.

Fang Xiaoping. *Barefoot Doctors and Western Medicine in China*. Rochester, NY: University of Rochester Press, 2012.

Farrer, James, and Andrew David Field. *Shanghai Nightscapes: A Nocturnal Biography of a Global City*. Chicago: University of Chicago Press, 2015.

Feng Xianguang. "Liushi nian Makesi zhuyi wenxue lilun de yijie he yanjiu" (Sixty years of translation of and research on Marxist theories on literature). *Shehui kexue zhanxian* (Social Science Front) 10 (October 2009): 1–7.

Finnane, Antonia. *Changing Clothes in China: Fashion, History, Nation*. New York: Columbia University Press, 2008.

Fisher, David James. *Romain Rolland and the Politics of International Engagement*. Berkeley: University of California Press, 1988.

Forbes, F. E. *Five Years in China*. London: Richard Bentley, 1848.

Fu Lei. *Fu Lei quanji* (Complete works of Fu Lei). Shenyang: Liaoning jiaoyu chubanshe, 2002.

Fu Lei. *Fu Lei wenji shuxin juan* (A collection of the works of Fu Lei, volume of letters). Beijing: Dangdai shijie chubanshe, 2006.

Fu Lei. *Fu Lei yinyue jiangtang* (English title in original: *Fu Lei's Talks on Music*). Taipei: Sanyanshe, 2003.

Fu, Lei. *Fu Lei yiwen ji* (Collected works of translation of Fu Lei). Hefei: Anhui wenyi chubanshe, 1998–2010.
Galston, Arthur W., with Jean S. Savage. *Daily Life in People's China*. New York: Thomas Y. Crowell, 1973.
Gamsa, Mark. *The Reading of Russian Literature in China: A Moral Example and Manual of Practice*. New York: Palgrave Macmillan, 2010.
Gao, James Z. *The Communist Takeover of Hangzhou: The Transformation of City and Cadre, 1949–1954*. Honolulu: University of Hawai'i Press, 2004.
Gao, James Z. "Eating, Cooking, and Shanghai's 'Less-Than Manly Men': The Social Consequences of Food Rationing and Economic Reforms." *Frontiers of History in China* 8, no. 2 (2013): 259–93.
Gardner, John. "The Wu-fan Campaign in Shanghai: A Study in the Consolidation of Urban Control." In *Chinese Communist Politics in Action*, edited by A. Doak Barnett, 477–539. Seattle: University of Washington Press, 1969.
Gaulon, Richard. "Political Mobilization in Shanghai, 1949–1951." In *Shanghai: Revolution and Development in an Asian Metropolis*, edited by Christopher Howe, 35–65. Cambridge, UK: Cambridge University Press, 1981.
Ge Jianxiong. "1949 nian yihou jiaoshou ruhe pingding dengji he gongzi" (How professors were ranked and their salaries after 1949). www.thepaper.cn/newsDetail_forward_1345800
Ge Yan. "Qishi niandai: jiyi zhong de Xi'an dixia dushu huodong" (The 1970s: Recollection of underground readings in Xi'an). Chinese University of Hong Kong database, *Minjian lishi* (Folk History).
Geertz, Clifford. *Interpretation of Cultures*. New York: Basic Books, 1973/2000.
Geng Yunzhi, ed. *Hu Shi yigao ji micang shuxin* (Hu Shi's posthumous manuscripts and private correspondence). Hefei: Huangshan shushe, 1994.
Gerth, Karl. *Unending Capitalism: How Consumerism Negated China's Communist Revolution*. Cambridge, UK: Cambridge University Press, 2020.
Gerth, Karl. "Wu Yunchu and the Fate of the Bourgeoisie and Bourgeois Lifestyles under Communism." In *The Capitalist Dilemma in China's Communist Revolution*, edited by Sherman Cochran, 175–201. Ithaca, NY: Cornell University East Asia Program, 2014.
Goffman, Erving. "The Interaction Order." *American Sociological Review* 48, no. 1 (February 1983): 1–17.
Goldman, Merle. "The Political Use of Lu Xun." *China Quarterly* 91 (September 1982): 446–61.
Goldman, Merle, with Timothy Cheek and Carol Lee. *China's Intellectuals and the State: In Search of a New Relationship*. Cambridge, MA: Harvard University Asia Center, 1987.
Goldman, René. "The Rectification Campaign at Peking University: May–June 1957." *China Quarterly* 12 (October–December 1962): 138–53.
Goldman, Wendy Z. *Women at the Gates: Gender and Industry in Stalin's Russia*. Cambridge, UK: Cambridge University Press, 2002.

References

Goldstein, Joshua. "The Remains of the Everyday: One Hundred Years of Recycling in Beijing." In *Everyday Modernity in China*, edited by Madeleine Yue Dong and Joshua Goldstein, 206–302. Seattle: University of Washington Press, 2006.

Gong Yuzhi. *Dangshi zhaji er ji* (Various notes on party history, second collection). Hangzhou: Zhejiang renmin chubanshe, 2004.

Green, Frederik H. Green. "The Cultural Indigenization of a Soviet 'Red Classic' Hero: Pavel Korchagin's Journey through Time and Space." In *The Making and Remaking of China's "Red Classics,"* edited by Rosemary Roberts and Li Li, 136–55. Hong Kong: Hong Kong University Press, 2017.

Grescoe, Taras. *Shanghai Grand: Forbidden Love and International Intrigue in a Doomed World.* New York: St. Martin's Press, 2016.

Gu Meizhong. "Wo de pengyou Zhou Yi" (My friend Zhou Yi). *Shanghai tan* (January 2006): 22–3.

Gu Zhenyang. "Baiquelin de gushi" (The Pehchaolin story). Chinese University of Hong Kong database, *Minjian lishi* (Folk History).

Guangming ribao (Guangming Daily). Beijing.

Guillain, Robert. "Shanghai Living Subtle New Life." *Los Angeles Times*, October 22, 1964.

Gunde, Richard. *Culture and Customs of China*. Westport, CT: Greenwood Press, 2002.

Hahn, Emily. *China to Me: A Partial Autobiography*. Philadelphia: Blakiston, 1944.

Hahn, Emily. *Mr. Pan: A Memoir*. New York: Doubleday, 1942.

Haishang mingren zhuan bianjibu, comp. *Haishang mingren zhuan* (Biographies of Shanghai's celebrities). Shanghai: Wenmin shuju, 1930.

Halbwachs, Maurice. *On Collective Memory*. Edited, translated, and with Introduction by Lewis A. Coser. Chicago: University of Chicago Press, 1992.

Han Qiulin. "Dongniya 'qingjie'" (The Tonya "complex"). *Zhonghua dushu bao* (China Reading News), August 23, 2006.

Hanyan. *Wuchang zhi mei* (Variable beauty). Shanghai: Wenhui chubanshe, 2018.

Harsch, Donna. *Revenge of the Domestic: Women, the Family, and Communism in the German Democratic Republic*. Princeton, NJ: Princeton University Press, 2008.

He Bingdi (Ping-ti Ho) et al. *LiuMei Huayi xuezhe chongfang Zhongguo guangan ji* (A collection of essays by Chinese American scholars on revisiting China). Hong Kong: Qishi niandai zazhi chubanshe, 1974.

He Qifang. *Yige pingchang de gushi* (An ordinary tale). Tianjin: Baihua wenyi chubanshe, 1982.

He Yaping. *Shanghai guoji hua renkou yanjiu* (English title in original: *A Study on the Internationalized Population of Shanghai*). Shanghai: East China Normal University Press, 2012.

He Zixi. "Wen'ge zhong de yici ziwo jiushu—feipin shouguozhan xunbao ji" (A self-redemption in thought during the Cultural Revolution: A record of hunting for treasures in a recycling center). *Jiyi* (Remembrance) 143 (November 15, 2015): 60–4.

Hegel, Georg Wilhelm Friedrich. *Hegel's Preface to the Phenomenology of Spirit.* Translation and running commentary by Yirmiyahu Yovel. Princeton, NJ: Princeton University Press, 2005.

Heilmann, Sebastian, and Elizabeth J. Perry, eds. *Mao's Invisible Hand: The Political Foundations of Adaptive Governance in China.* Cambridge, MA: Harvard University Press, 2011.

Heitlinger, Alena. "Marxism, Feminism, and Sex Equality." In *Women in Eastern Europe and the Soviet Union*, edited by Tova Yedlin, 9–20. New York: Praeger, 1980.

Henriot, Christian. *Scythe and the City: A Social History of Death in Shanghai.* Stanford, CA: Stanford University Press, 2016.

Henriot, Christian. "Shanghai zujie gongmu yanjiu, 1844–1949" (The colonial space of death in Shanghai). www.virtualshanghai.net/Texts/Articles?ID=81.

Hershatter, Gail. *Women in China's Long Twentieth Century.* Berkeley: University of California Press, 2007.

Hibbard, Peter. *The Bund Shanghai: China Faces West.* Hong Kong: Odyssey Books and Guides, 2007.

Ho, Denise Y. *Curating Revolution: Politics on Display in Mao's China.* Cambridge, UK: Cambridge University Press, 2017.

Honig, Emily. *Creating Chinese Ethnicity: Subei People in Shanghai, 1850–1980.* New Haven, CT: Yale University Press, 1992.

Honig, Emily. "Socialist Sex: The Cultural Revolution Revisited." *Modern China* 29, no. 2 (April 2003): 143–75.

Honig, Emily, and Xiaojian Zhao. *Across the Great Divide: The Sent-Down Youth Movement in Mao's China, 1968–1980.* New York: Cambridge University Press, 2019.

Howe, Christopher. "The Level and Structure of Employment and the Sources of Labor Supply in Shanghai, 1949–57." In *The City in Communist China*, edited by John Wilson Lewis, 215–34. Stanford, CA: Stanford University Press, 1971.

Howell, Jude. "Adaptation under Scrutiny: Peering through the Lens of Community Governance in China." *Journal of Social Policy* 45, no. 3 (July 2016): 487–506.

Howell, Jude, and Tim Pringle. "Shades of Authoritarianism and State-Labour Relations in China." *British Journal of Industrial Relations*, 2018.

Hsu, Tony S. *Chasing the Modern: The Twentieth-Century Life of Poet Xu Zhimo.* Cambridge, UK: Cambridge Rivers Press, 2017.

Hu, Mingyuan. *Fou Lei: An Insistence on Truth.* Leiden: Brill, 2017.

Hu Songping, comp. *Hu Shizhi xiansheng nianpu changbian chugao* (The first draft of the long chronicle of Mr. Hu Shizhi). Taipei: Lianjing, 1984.

Hu Weixing. "Laodizi feipin huishou ke jiejian" (The practice of waste reclamation in the past can inform future practice). *Xinmin wanbao* (Xinmin Evening News), November 20, 2013.

Hu Yanyi. *Xingzhishi mantan* (General discussions on sexual knowledge). Nanchang: Jiangxi Science and Technology Press, 1985.

Huang Chunyu. "Hanyi mingzhu wangshi" (Past events in Chinese translations of famous works). *Wenhui bao* (Wenhui Daily), March 4, 2016.

Huang Hu. "Zhongguo dalu yi yue you" (A month of travel in mainland China). *Xin wanbao* (Hong Kong), March 3–15, 1974; *Cankao xiaoxi* (Reference News) (Beijing), October 13, 1974.

Huang Shansong. "Mantan wen'ge shiqi Shanghai jumin de yi shi zhu xing" (A random talk on Shanghai residents' clothing, food, housing, and transportation during the Cultural Revolution). www.16lo.com/article/376056.

Huang Shi, comp. *Zui mei de Shanghai* (The most beautiful Shanghai). Changsha: Hunan renmin chubanshe, 2013.

Huang Zongying. "Wo qinling Mao Zedong Lu Ji'nan duihua" (I listened in person to the conversation between Mao Zedong and Lu Ji'nan). *Nanfang zhoumo* (Southern Weekly), October 21, 2003.

Hunter, Neale. *Shanghai Journal: An Eyewitness Account of the Cultural Revolution.* New York: Frederick A. Praeger, 1969.

Huntington, Samuel P. *The Clash of Civilizations and the Remaking of World Order.* New York: Touchstone, 1997.

Hutt, Jonathan. "Monstre Sacré: The Decadent World of Sinmay Zau." *China Heritage Quarterly*, Australian National University, 22 (June 2010).

Jackson, Isabella. *Shaping Modern Shanghai: Colonialism in China's Global City.* Cambridge, UK: University of Cambridge Press, 2017.

Ji Zong. "Shinian xishi manlu: wen'ge shiqi de Shanghai shangpin gongying" (Random records on a decade of trivial matters: Commodity supplies in Shanghai during the Cultural Revolution). www.edubridge.com/erxiantang/l2/shanghai_wujia.htm.

Jia Zhangke. *Haishang chuanqi* (Shanghai legends). Ji'nan: Shandong huabaoshe, 2010.

Jia Zhifang. *Wo de rensheng dang'an* (An archive of my life). Nanjing: Jiangsu wenyi chubanshe, 2009.

Jian Fan. *Canghai* (The ocean). Beijing: Renmin wenxue chubanshe, 2000.

Jiang Weimin. *Shimao waipo: zhuixun lao Shanghai de shishang shenghuo* (Original English title: *Vogue Grandma: In Search of the Fashionable Life of the Old Shanghai*). Shanghai: Sanlian shudian, 2003.

Jiang Xiaoyuan. "Huixiang dangnian du jinshu" (Recollection of reading banned books in those years). *Minzhu yu kexue* (Democracy and Science), no. 3 (1998).

Jiang Yongping. "50 nian Zhongguo chengshi nüxing jiuye de huigong yu fansi" (Reflections on fifty years of female employment in urban China). In *Ban'ge shiji de funü fazhan* (Half a century of women's development), edited by Li Qiufang, 152–62. Beijing: Dangdai Zhongguo chubanshe, 2001.

Jibisou. *Shanghai chuantangfeng* (Shanghai, the breeze that blew through the hallway). Shanghai: Shanghai wenhua chubanshe, 2015.

Jiefang ribao (Liberation Daily). Shanghai.

Jin Chongji. "Huiyi liushi nian qian de shi" (Recalling things of sixty years ago). *Dushu* (Reading) 9 (September 2012): 3–8.

Jin Dalu. "Chong 'wu' de shenmei ji qi tuibian" (Aesthetical appreciation for "material strength" and its transformation). *Shehui guancha* (Social Observation), May 2006.

Jin Dalu. *Feichang yu zhengchang: Shanghai "Wen'ge" shiqi de shehui shenghuo* (Abnormality and normality: Society and life in Shanghai during the Cultural Revolution). Shanghai: Shanghai cishu chubanshe, 2011.

Jin Dalu. "Guanyu 'piaozheng shidai' de jiti jiyi" (On collective memories of the "age of the ration coupons"). *Shehui kexue* (Social Sciences), 8 August 2009.

Jin Shenghua, ed. *Fu Lei he ta de shijie* (Fu Lei and his world). Beijing: Sanlian chubanshe, 1997.

Jing Fang. *Wo shi 60 huo, 1968–1978* (I am of the post-1960 generation, 1968–1978). Beijing: Xinxing chubanshe, 2010.

Jing'anqu difangzhi bianzuan weiyuanhui, comp. *Jing'anqu zhi* (Gazetteer of Jing'an district). Shanghai: Shanghai Academy of Social Sciences Press, 1996.

Jing'anqu renming zhengfu, comp. *Shanghaishi Jing'anqu diming zhi* (Gazetteer of toponyms in the Jing'an district of Shanghai). Shanghai: Shanghai Academy of Social Sciences Press, 1988.

Johnson, Matthew D. "Beneath the Propaganda State: Official and Unofficial Cultural Landscapes in Shanghai, 1949–1965." In *Maoism at the Grassroots*, edited by Jeremy Brown and Matthew D. Johnson, 199–229.

Jones, Andrew F. *Yellow Music: Media Culture and Colonial Modernity in the Chinese Jazz Age*. Durham, NC: Duke University Press, 2001.

Kang Xuepei, ed. *Zhiqing: Stories from China's Special Generation*. Huntsville: Texas Review Press, 2014.

Kaple, Deborah A. *Dream of a Red Factory: The Legacy of High Stalinism in China*. New York: Oxford University Press, 1994.

Karol, K. S. *China: The Other Communism*. New York: Hill and Wang, 1967.

Kaufman, Geoff F., and Lisa K. Libby. "Changing Beliefs and Behavior through Experience-Taking." *Journal of Personality and Social Psychology* 103, no. 1 (July 2012): 1–19.

Ke Ling. "Yaoji Zhang Ailing" (To Eileen Chang from afar). *Dushu* (Reading) 2 (April 1985).

Ke Linjuan and Du Yaping. *Jianshuo liangzhi de fanyijia: Cao Ying zhuan* (The translator who follows his conscience: A biography of Cao Ying). Nanjing: Jiangsu renmin chubanshe, 2010.

Kemp, Tom. *Industrialization in the Non-Western World*. London: Longman, 1989.

King, Richard. *Milestones on a Golden Road: Writing for Chinese Socialism, 1945–80*. Vancouver: UBC Press, 2013.

Kirby, William. "Continuity and Change in Modern China: Economic Planning on the Mainland and on Taiwan, 1943–1958." *Australian Journal of Chinese Affairs* 24 (1990): 121–41.

Kirkby, Richard J. R. *Urbanization in China: Town and Country in a Developing Economy, 1949–2000 AD*. New York: Columbia University Press, 1985.

Koningsberger, Hans. *Love and Hate in China*. New York: McGraw-Hill, 1966.

Kraft, Joseph. *The Chinese Difference*. New York: Saturday Review, 1972.

Kraus, Richard Curt. *Pianos and Politics in China: Middle-Class Ambitions and the Struggle over Western Music*. New York: Oxford University Press, 1989.

Kraus, Willy. *Private Business in China: Revival between Ideology and Pragmatism*. Honolulu: University of Hawaii Press, 1991.

Krebs, Ed, and Hanchao Lu, eds. and trans. *China in Family Photographs: A People's History of Revolution and Everyday Life*. Encino, CA: Bridge 21 Publications, 2018.

Kuoshu, Harry H. *Metro Movies: Cinematic Urbanism in Post-Mao China*. Carbondale: Southern Illinois University Press, 2011.
Laodong (Labor). Beijing.
Lao-Tzu. *Tao Te Ching*. Indianapolis: Hackett Publishing, 1993.
Lee, Hong Yung. *From Revolutionary Cadres to Party Technocrats in Socialist China*. Berkeley: University of California Press, 1991.
Lee, Leo Ou-fan. *Shanghai Modern: The Flowering of New Urban Culture in China, 1930–1945*. Cambridge, MA: Harvard University Press, 1999.
Leese, Daniel. *Mao Cult: Rhetoric and Ritual in China's Cultural Revolution*. New York: Cambridge University Press, 2011.
Leighton, Christopher Russell. "Capitalists, Cadres, and Culture in 1950s China." PhD diss., Harvard University, 2010.
Lenin, Vladimir. *Lenin Collected Works*. Moscow: Progress Publishers, 1973.
Lenin, Vladimir Ilyich. *On the Emancipation of Women*. Moscow: Progress Publishers, 1965.
Lenin, Vladimir Ilyich. *Lenin Collected Works*. Moscow: Progress Publishers, 1977.
Lenin, Vladimir Ilyich. *Selected Works*. Moscow: Foreign Languages Publishing House, 1952.
Lenin, Vladimir Ilyich. *Selected Works*. Moscow: Progress Publishers, 1963.
Li Chengpeng. *Quan shijie renmin dou zhidao* (The whole world knows). Beijing: Xinxing chubanshe, 2013.
Li Hui. *Hu Feng jituan yuan'an shimo* (The unjust case concerning the Hu Feng clique). Wuhan: Hubei renmin chubanshe, 2003.
Li Hui. "Yu Xia Yan tan Zhou Yang" (Conversations with Xia Yan about Zhou Yang). *Suibi* (Random Essays) 6 (June 1995): 46–7.
Li, Jie. *Shanghai Home: Palimpsests of Private Life*. New York: Columbia University Press, 2015.
Li Jinhui. *Li Jinhui ertong gewuju* (Li Jinhui's musical theater). Beijing: Renmin jiaoyu chubanshe, 2012.
Li Keqiang. "Zhuiyi Li Cheng xiansheng" (Reminiscing about Mr. Li Cheng). *Anhui ribao* (Anhui Daily), May 15, 1997.
Li, Kwok-sing. *A Glossary of Political Terms of the People's Republic of China*. Translated by Mary Lok. Hong Kong: Chinese University Press, 1995.
Li Man. "Shanghai Bailemen chuangshiren Sheng qi xiaojie" (The founder of the Shanghai Paramount Miss Sheng Number Seven). https://kknews.cc/history/zp44jzg.html.
Li Pu, ed. *Huainian Li Shenzhi* (In commemoration of Li Shenzhi). Two vols. Xianggang: Shidai chaoliu chubanshe, 2003.
Li Rui. *Dayuejin qinli ji* (Personal experiences of the Great Leap Forward). Haikou: Nanfang chubanshe, 1999.
Li Sui. *Mingguo fenghua: wo de fuqin Li Jinhui* (Talent in the Republic: My father Li Jinhui). Beijing: Tuanji chubanshe, 2011.
Li Weiyi. *Zhongguo gongzhi zhidu* (China's wage system). Beijing: Zhongguo laodong chubanshe, 1991.
Li, Yang. "How Is Revolution 'Popularized'? Rereading *Tracks in the Snowy Forest*." In *The Making and Remaking of China's "Red Classics,"* edited by Rosemary Roberts and Li Li, 59–73. Hong Kong: Hong Kong University Press, 2017.

Li, You-Sheng. *A New Interpretation of Chinese Taoist Philosophy: An Anthropological/Psychological View*. London: Taoist Recovery Centre, 2005.

Li Zhencun. "Zuojia Qu Bo yishuang Liu Bo laoren jiangshu *Linhai xueyuan* gushi" (The writer Qu Bo's widow, Liu Bo, tells the story about *Tracks in the Snowy Forest*). *Liaosheng wanbao* (Liaosheng Evening News), January 25, 2005.

Li Zhisui. *The Private Life of Chairman Mao*. New York: Random House, 1994.

Liang Qichao. *Liang Qichao wenxuan* (Selected works of Liang Qichao). Beijing: Zhongguo guangbo dianshi chubanshe, 1992.

Liang Qichao. *Yinbinshi heji* (Collected writings from the Ice Drinker's Studio). Beijing: Zhonghua shuju, 1989 [1936].

Lin, Jennifer. *Shanghai Faithful: Betrayal and Forgiveness in a Chinese Christian Family*. Lanham, MD: Rowman & Littlefield, 2017.

Lin Jian, ed. *Shanghai shishang: 160 nian Haipai shenghuo* (Shanghai vogue: 160 years of Shanghai lifestyles). Shanghai: Shanghai wenhua chubanshe, 2005.

Lin Yutang. *The Importance of Living*. New York: John Day, 1937.

Link, Perry. *An Anatomy of Chinese: Rhythm, Metaphor, Politics*. Cambridge, MA: Harvard University Press, 2013.

Link, Perry. "Hand-Copied Entertainment Fiction from the Cultural Revolution." In *Unofficial China: Popular Culture and Thought in the People's Republic*, edited by Perry Link, Richard Madsen, and Paul Pickowicz, 17–36. Boulder, CO: Westview, 1989.

Link, Perry. *Mandarin Ducks and Butterflies: Popular Fiction in Early Twentieth-Century Chinese Cities*. Berkeley, Los Angeles, and London: University of California Press, 1981.

Liu, Haisu. "Wo suo renshi de Xu Zhimo he Lu Xiaoman" (Xu Zhimo and Lu Xiaoman as I knew them). *Renwu* (English title: *Portrait*), no. 5 (May 1989).

Liu, Kin-ming. *My First Trip to China: Scholars, Diplomats and Journalists Reflect on their First Encounters with China*. Hong Kong: East Slope Publishing Limited, 2012.

Liu Ping. 2007. "Chachu weifa dajian de xiangguan falü wenti yanjiu" (Research on legal issues regarding unauthorized building constructions.). Shanghai Institute of Administrative Law, *Zhengfu fazhi yanjiu*. http://cpfd.cnki.com.cn/Article/CPFDTOTAL-SXZF200700001013.htm.

Liu Shaoqi. *Liu Shaoqi xuanji* (Selected works of Liu Shaoqi). Beijing: Renmin chubanshe, 1985.

Liu Sheng. "Left Behind." *Global Times*, August 19, 2010.

Liu Shufa, ed. *Chen Yi nianpu* (A chronicle of Chen Yi). Beijing: Renmin chubanshe, 1995.

Liu Xiaofeng. "Jilian Dongniya" (Record on falling in love with Tonya). In *Zhe yidai ren de pa he ai* (Fear and love of this generation), 40–52. Beijing: Huaxia chubanshe, 2007.

Loh, Robert. *Escape from Red China*. New York: Coward-McCann, 1962.

Long Jianyu. *Mao Zedong jiaju* (The home life of Mao Zedong). Beijing: Zhonggong dangshi chubanshe, 2013.

Long Yingtai (Lung Ying-tai). "Ah, Shanghai nanren!" (Oh, Shanhgai men!). *Wenhui bao* (Wenhui Daily), January 7, 1997.

Lou Shiyi. "Fu Lei de xingge" (Fu Lei's character). In *Fu Lei yu ta de shijie* (Fu Lei and his world), edited by Jin Shenghua, 15–17. Beijing: Sanlian shudian, 1997.
Lu, Hanchao. "Arrested Development: Cotton and Cotton Markets in Shanghai, 1350–1843." *Modern China* 18, no. 4 (October 1992): 468–99.
Lu, Hanchao. "Away from Nanking Road: Small Stores and Neighbourhood Life in Modern Shanghai." *Journal of Asian Studies* 54, no. 1 (February 1995): 92–123.
Lu, Hanchao. *Beyond the Neon Lights: Everyday Shanghai in the Early Twentieth Century*. Berkeley: University of California Press, 1999.
Lu, Hanchao. "Creating Urban Outcasts: Shantytowns in Shanghai, 1920–1950." *Journal of Urban History* 21, no. 5 (July 1995): 563–96.
Lu, Hanchao. "Nostalgia for the Future: The Resurgence of an Alienated Culture in China." *Pacific Affairs* 75, no. 2 (Summer 2002): 169–86.
Lu, Hanchao. "The Significance of the Insignificant: Reconstructing the Daily Lives of the Common People of China." *China Journal* 1, no. 1 (March 2003): 144–58.
Lu, Hanchao. "The Tastes of Chairman Mao: The Quotidian as Statecraft in the Great Leap Forward and Its Aftermath." *Modern China* 41, no. 5 (October 2015): 539–72.
Lu, Tonglin. *Misogyny, Cultural Nihilism, and Oppositional Politics: Contemporary Chinese Experimental Fiction*. Stanford, CA: Stanford University Press, 1995.
Lü, Xiaobo, and Elizabeth J. Perry. *The Danwei: Changing Chinese Workplace in Historical and Comparative Perspective*. New York: M.E. Sharpe, 1997.
Lu Xun. *Diary of a Madman and Other Stories*. Translated by William A. Lyell. Honolulu: University of Hawaii Press, 1990.
Lu Xun. *Lu Xun quanji* (Completed works of Lu Xun). Beijing: Renmin wenxue chubanshe, 1991.
Lu Zonglin. "Huiyi gumu Lu Xiaoman" (Recollections about my aunt Lu Xiaoman). In *Zhongshuo fenyun Lu Xiaoman* (A wide diversity of opinions on Lu Xiaoman), edited by Chai Cao, 209–31. Taiyuan: Shanxi renmin chubanshe, 2006.
Luo Jianxing. *Zong Qinghou yu Wahaha: yige Zhongguo zhuming qiye de shendu yanjiu* (Zong Qinghou and Wahaha: An in-depth study of a famous Chinese enterprise). Beijing: Jixie gongye chubanshe, 2008.
Ma Jun. "Lao Shanghai Bailemen wuting de chuangban yu xingshuai" (The rise and fall of the Paramount Dance Hall in old Shanghai.) *Dongfang zaobao* (Oriental Morning Post), October 29, 2013.
Ma Maoru. "Wo suo jingli de 'Zhongxuanbu yanwangdian yuan'an ji pingfan" (My experiences with the unjust case of accusing the CCP propaganda department of being the headquarters of an underworld kingdom and its rehabilitation). *Bainianchao* (A Century of Tides) 8 (August 2013): 37–41.
Ma Wenrui. "Jin yi bu jiefang funü laodongli" (Further liberating women's labor power). *Laodong* (Labor) 15 (1958): 5–7.
MacFarquhar, Roderick. *The Origins of the Cultural Revolution 2: The Great Leap Forward 1958–1960*. York: Columbia University Press, 1983.

MacFarquhar, Roderick, and John K. Fairbank, eds. *The Cambridge History of China, Volumes 14–15.* Cambridge, UK: Cambridge University Press, 1987 and 1991.

MacFarquhar, Roderick, and Michael Schoenhals. *Mao's Last Revolution.* Cambridge, MA: Harvard University Press, 2008.

MacFarquhar, Roderick, Timothy Cheek, and Eugene Wu, eds. *The Secret Speeches of Chairman Mao from the Hundred Flowers to the Great Leap Forward.* Cambridge, MA: Council on East Asian Studies, Harvard University, 1989.

Machonin, Pavel. "The Social Structure of Soviet-Type Societies, Its Collapse and Legacy." *Czech Sociological Review* 1, no. 2 (Fall 1993): 231–49.

Mack, Jefferson. *Invisible Resistance to Tyranny: How to Lead a Secret Life of Insurgency in an Increasingly Unfree World.* Boulder, CO: Paladin, 2002.

MacMillan, Margaret. *Nixon and Mao: The Week That Changed the World.* New York: Random House, 2008.

Mah, Adeline Yen. *Falling Leaves: The True Story of an Unwanted Chinese Daughter.* New York: John Wiley & Sons, 1997.

Maloney, William F. "Informality Revisited." *World Development* 32, no. 7 (2004): 1159–78.

Malraux, André. *Anti-Memoirs.* New York: Holt, Rinehart and Winston, 1968.

Mao Yuyuan. *Zaijian Dongniya* (Farewell Tonya). Beijing: China CITIC Publishing Group, 2014.

Mao Zedong. *Mao Zedong sixiang wansui* (Long live Mao Zedong thought). Hong Kong: Bowen shuju, restricted publication, 1967 and 1969.

Mao Zedong. *Mao Zedong wenji* (Collected works of Mao Zedong). Beijing: Renmin chubanshe, 1999.

Mao Zedong. *Mao Zedong xuanji* (Selected works of Mao Zedong). Beijing: Renmin chubanshe, 1977.

Mao Zedong. *Mao Zedong zaoqi wen'gao 1912.6–1920.11* (Manuscripts of Mao Zedong in his early years, June 1912 to November 1920). Changsha: Hunan renmin chubanshe, 1990.

Mao Zedong. *The Poems of Mao Zedong.* Translated by Willis Barnstone. Berkeley: University of California Press, 2008.

Mao Zedong. *Selected Works of Mao Tse-tung.* Peking: Foreign Languages Press, 1965.

Marx, Karl, and Frederick Engels. *Karl Marx and Frederick Engels: Selected Works in Three Volumes.* Moscow: Progress Publishers, 1970.

Marx, Karl, and Frederick Engels. *Marx, Engels on Literature and Art.* Moscow: Progress Publishers, 1976.

McCullough, Colin. "Shanghai: Decorum Replaces Bars and Dance Halls." *Washington Post*, December 7, 1969.

Meng Shaoyi and Li Zhaidao, eds. *Zhongguo fanyi wenxue shi* (A history of translated literature in China). Beijing: Peking University Press, 2005.

Miller, William J. *The CCP's United Front Tactics in the U.S., 1972–1988.* Bakersfield, CA: Charles Schlacks Jr., 1988.

Misztal, Barbara A. *Informality: Social Theory and Contemporary Practice.* London: Routledge, 1999.

Mittler, Barbara. *A Continuous Revolution: Making Sense of Cultural Revolution Culture*. Cambridge, MA: Harvard University Asia Center, 2012.

Mo Yan. *Lingting yuzhou de gechang* (Listen to the singing of the universe). Beijing: Zhongguo wenshi chubanshe, 2012.

Mo Yan. "Nanwang na daizhe kouzhao jiewen de ai" (Unforgettable love by kissing through a facemask). www.kanunu8.com/book3/8253/182347.html, archived May 30, 2020.

Murphey, Rhoads. *Shanghai: Key to Modern China*. Cambridge, MA: Harvard University Press, 1953.

Nanjingshi difangzhi bianzuan weiyuanhui. *Nanjing yuanlin zhi* (Gazetteers of gardening in Nanjing). Beijing: Fangzhi chubanshe, 1997.

Newman, Chi. *Farewell, My Beijing: The Long Journey from China to Tucson*. Tucson, AZ: Wheatmark, 2008.

Nie Chongbin. "Wo de guju wo de muxiao" (My former residence and my alma mater). http://blog.sina.com.cn/s/blog_6796d0b80100w4rj.html, accessed April 3, 2014.

Ostrovsky, Nikolai. *How the Steel Was Tempered*. Moscow: Foreign Languages Publishing House, 1952.

Pagnamenta, Peter, ed. *The University of Cambridge: An 800th Anniversary Portrait*. London: Third Millennium Publishing, 2008.

Pan, Ling. *In Search of Old Shanghai*. Hong Kong: Joint Publishing, 1982.

Pan, Zhen. *Suiyue fengjing* (Time and scenery). Shanghai: Fudan University Press.

Pantsov, Alexander, with Steven I. Levine. *Mao: The Real Story*. New York: Simon & Schuster, 2012.

Peng Zuji. *Xiri Shanghai fengqing* (Culture and customs of old Shanghai). Shanghai: Shanghai renmin chubanshe, 2011.

Perry, Elizabeth J. *Anyuan: Mining China's Revolutionary Tradition*. Berkeley: University of California Press, 2012.

Perry, Elizabeth J. "Trends in the Study of Chinese Politics: State-Society Relations." *China Quarterly* 139 (September 1994): 704–13.

Perry, Elizabeth J., and Hanchao Lu. "Narrating the Past to Interpret the Present: A Conversation with Elizabeth J. Perry." *Chinese Historical Review* 22, no. 2 (November 2015): 1–14.

Perry, Elizabeth J., and Mark Selden, eds. *Chinese Society: Change, Conflict and Resistance*. London: Routledge, 2010.

Peterson, Glen. *The Power of Words: Literacy and Revolution in South China, 1949–95*. Vancouver: University of British Columbia Press, 1997.

Pollard, David, ed. *Translation and Creation: Readings of Western Literature in Early Modern China, 1840–1918*. Amsterdam: John Benjamins, 1998.

Poncellini, Luca. "Laszlo Hudec in Shanghai (1919–1947): The Brilliant Trajectory of a Hungarian Architect in the Process of Modernization of the Greatest City of the East." Unpublished manuscript, Turin, Italy, (September) 2007.

Qian Bocheng. *Wensi ji* (A collection of inquiries and deliberations). Shanghai: Zhongxi shuju, 2011.

Qin Feng lao zhaoxiang guan, comp. *Shanghai zhizhao, 1950–1960 niandai* (Shanghai-made: The 1950s to 1960s). Guilin: Guangxi Normal University Press, 2010.

Qing Qiuzi. *Zheteng shinian: wo de qingcong suiyue* (Tossing about for ten years: My green years). Hefei: Anhui wenyi chubanshe, 2006.

Qishi niandai zazhishe, ed. *LiuMei Huayi xuezhe chongfang Zhongguo guangan ji* (A collection of the impressions of China from Chinese American scholars who revisited China). Hong Kong: Qishi niandai zazhishe, 1974.

Qiu Guosheng. "Ershi shiji wushi niandai Shanghai de funü jiefang yu canjia jiti shengchan" (Women's liberation and participation in collective production in 1950s Shanghai). *Dangdai Zhongguo shi yanjiu* (Studies of the History of Contemporary China) 16, no. 1 (2009): 70–7.

Qiu Xiaolong. *Years of Red Dust: Stories of Shanghai*. New York: St. Martin's, 2010.

Read, Benjamin L. *Roots of the State: Neighborhood Organization and Social Networks in Beijing and Taipei*. Stanford, CA: Stanford University Press, 2012.

Rene, Helena K. *China's Sent-Down Generation: Public Administration and the Legacies of Mao's Rustication Program*. Washington, DC: Georgetown University Press, 2013.

Renmin chubanshe, comp. *Sanfan Wufan yundong wenjian huibian* (A collection of documents on the Three-Anti and Five-Anti campaigns). Beijing: Renmin chubanshe, 1953.

Renmin ribao (People's Daily). Beijing.

Research Institute of the All-China Women's Federation. *Statistics on Chinese Women (1949–1989)*. Beijing: China Statistical Publishing House, 1991.

Richman, Barry M. "Capitalists and Managers in Communist China." *Harvard Business Review* 45 (January–February 1967): 57–78.

Richman, Barry M. *Industrial Society in Communist China: A Firsthand Study of Chinese Economic Development and Management, With Significant Comparisons with Industry in India, the U.S.S.R., Japan, and the United States*. New York: Random House, 1969.

Ristaino, Marcia Reynders. *Port of Last Resort: The Diaspora Communities of Shanghai*. Stanford, CA: Stanford University Press, 2001.

Roberts, Rosemary, and Li Li, eds. *The Making and Remaking of China's "Red Classics": Politics, Aesthetics, and Mass Culture*. Hong Kong: Hong Kong University Press, 2017.

Roderick, John, and the staff writers and photographers of the Associated Press. *What You Should Know about the People's Republic of China*. New York: Associated Press, 1972.

Ross, Heidi. "China Country Study." UNESDOC program and meeting document. Paris: UNESCO, 2005.

Rossi, Paolo. *The Communist Conquest of Shanghai*. Arkington, VA: Crestwood Books, 1970.

Ru Zhijuan. *Gaogao de baiyangshu* (The tall white poplars). Shanghai: Shanghai wenyi chubanshe, 1959.

Saich, Tony. *The Origins of the First United Front in China: The Role of Sneevliet (Alias Maring)*. Leiden: E. J. Brill, 1991.

Salaff, Janet Weitzner. "Urban Residential Committees in the Wake of the Cultural Revolution." In *The City in Communist China*, edited by John Wilson Lewis, 289–323. Stanford, CA: Stanford University Press, 1971.

References

Schoenhals, Michael. *Spying for the People: Mao's Secret Agents, 1949–1967*. New York: Cambridge University Press, 2013.
Schurmann, Franz. *Ideology and Organization in Communist China*. Berkeley: University of California Press, 1968.
Schwartz, Benjamin I. *In Search of Wealth and Power: Yen Fu and the West*. Cambridge, MA: Harvard University Press, 1964.
Scott, James C. *Seeing Like a State: How Certain Schemes to Improve the Human Condition Have Failed*. New Haven, CT: Yale University Press, 1998.
Scott, James C. *Weapons of the Weak: Everyday Forms of Peasant Resistance*. New Haven, CT: Yale University Press, 1987.
Shanghai Bowuguan, comp. *Shanghai beike zilao xuanji* (Selections of stelae materials of Shanghai). Shanghai: Shanghai renmin chubanshe, 1980.
Shanghai Changjiang hangyun zhi bianzuan weiyuanhui. *Shanghai Changjiang hangyun zhi* (Gazetteer of Shanghai's Yangtze River shipping and navigation). Shanghai: Shanghai shehui kexueyuan chubanshe, 1997.
Shanghai chengshi guihua zhi bianzuan weiyuanhui, comp. *Shanghai chengshi guihua zhi* (Gazetteer of urban planning in Shanghai). Shanghai: Shanghai Academy of Social Sciences Press, 1999.
Shanghai chuban zhi bianzuan weiyuanhui, comp. *Shanghai chuban zhi* (Gazetteer of publishing in Shanghai). Shanghai: Shanghai Academy of Social Sciences Press, 2000.
Shanghai fangzhi gongye zhi bianzuan weiyuanhui, comp. *Shanghai fangzhi gongye zhi* (Gazetteer of the textile industry in Shanghai). Shanghai: Shanghai Academy of Social Sciences Press, 1998.
Shanghai funü zhi bianzuan weiyuanhui, comp. *Shanghai funüzhi* (Gazetteer of Shanghai women). Shanghai: Shanghai Academy of Social Sciences Press, 2000.
Shanghai fushipin shangye zhi bianzuan weiyuanhui, comp. *Shanghai fushipin shangye zhi* (Gazetteer of non-staple foods in Shanghai). Shanghai: Shanghai Academy of Social Sciences Press, 1998.
Shanghai gongshang shetuan zhi bianzuan weiyuanhui, comp. *Shanghai gongshang shetuan zhi* (Gazetteer of Shanghai mass organizations in industry and commerce). Shanghai: Shanghai Academy of Social Sciences Press, 2001.
Shanghai hongwei zhanbao (Shanghai Red Guard battlefield report), May 15, 1968.
Shanghai huaijing weisheng zhi, comp. *Shanghai huaijing weisheng zhi* (Gazetteer of environmental hygiene in Shanghai). Shanghai: Shanghai Academy of Social Sciences Press, 1996.
Shanghai jiage zhi bianzuan weiyuanhui, comp. *Shanghai jiage zhi* (Gazetteer of prices in Shanghai). Shanghai: Shanghai Academy of Social Sciences Press, 1998.
Shanghai kancha sheji zhi bianzuan weiyuanhui, comp. *Shanghai kancha sheji zhi* (Gazetteer of prospective designs of Shanghai). Shanghai: Shanghai Academy of Social Sciences Press, 1998.
Shanghai laodong zhi bianzuan weiyuanhui, comp. *Shanghai laodong zhi* (Gazetteer of labor in Shanghai). Shanghai: Shanghai shehui kexueyuan chubanshe, 1998.

Shanghai liangshi zhi bianzuan weiyuanhui, comp. *Shanghai liangshi zhi* (Gazetteer of staple food grains in Shanghai). Shanghai: Shanghai Academy of Social Sciences Press, 1995.
Shanghai nongye zhi bianzuan weiyuanhui, comp. *Shanghai nongye zhi* (Gazetteer of the agriculture of Shanghai). Shanghai: Shanghai Academy of Social Sciences Press, 1996.
Shanghai qiaowu zhi bianzuan weiyuanhui, comp. *Shanghai qiaowu zhi* (Gazetteer of Shanghai's overseas Chinese affairs). Shanghai: Shanghai Academy of Social Sciences Press, 2001.
Shanghai renmin zhengfu zhi bianzuan weiyuanhui, comp. *Shanghai renmin zhengfu zhi* (Gazetteer of the People's Government of Shanghai). Shanghai: Shanghai Academy of Social Sciences Press, 2004.
Shanghai riyong gongye pin shangye zhi bianzuan weiyuanhui, comp. *Shanghai riyong gongye pin shangye zhi* (Gazetteer of daily commercial products in Shanghai). Shanghai: Shanghai Academy of Social Sciences Press, 1999.
Shanghai sichou zhi bianzuan weiyuanhui, comp. *Shanghai sichou zhi* (Gazetteer of silk in Shanghai). Shanghai: Shanghai Academy of Social Sciences Press, 1998.
Shanghai sucai shangye zhi bianzuan weiyuanhui. *Shanghai sucai shangye zhi* (Gazetteer of the vegetable business in Shanghai). Shanghai: Shanghai Academy of Social Sciences Press, 1996.
Shanghai tongzhi bianzuan weiyuanhui, comp. *Shanghai tongzhi* (Comprehensive gazetteer of Shanghai). Ten vols. Shanghai: Shanghai renmin chubanshe, 2005.
Shanghai tushuguan shiye zhi bianzuan weiyuanhui, comp. *Shanghai tushuguan shiye zhi* (Gazetteer of Shanghai's library enterprises). Shanghai: Shanghai Academy of Social Sciences Press, 1996.
Shanghai yancao zhi bianzuan weiyuanhui, comp. *Shanghai yancao zhi* (Gazetteer of the tobacco industry in Shanghai). Shanghai: Shanghai Academy of Social Sciences Press, 1998.
Shanghai yinshi fuwuye zhi bianzuan weiyuanhui, comp. *Shanghai yinshi fuwuye zhi* (Gazetteer of the restaurant and service businesses in Shanghai). Shanghai: Shanghai Academy of Social Sciences Press, 2006.
Shanghai youdian zhi bianzuan weiyuanhui, comp. *Shanghai youdian zhi* (Gazetteer of postal and telecommunication service in Shanghai). Shanghai: Shanghai Academy of Social Sciences Press, 1999.
Shanghai yuanlin zhi bianzuan weiyuanhui, comp. *Shanghai yuanlin zhi* (Gazetteer of Shanghai's gardens). Shanghai: Shanghai Academy of Social Sciences Press, 2000.
Shanghai Zhongguo huayuan, comp. *Shanghai Zhongguo huayuan 1956–2004* (Shanghai Academy of Chinese Painting, 1956–2004). Shanghai: Shanghai renmin meishu chubanshe, 2004.
Shanghai Zhongyi xueyuan, comp. *Cejiao yisheng shouce* (Barefoot doctor's manual). Shanghai: Shanghaishi chuban geming zu, 1970.
Shanghai zhuzhai jianshe zhi bianzuan weiyuanhui, comp. *Shanghai zhuzhai jianshe zhi* (Gazetteer of Shanghai residential housing development). Shanghai: Shanghai Academy of Social Sciences Press, 1998.
Shanghaishi difangzhi bangongshi, comp. *Shanghai ming jianzhu zhi* (Gazetteer of famous architecture in Shanghai). Shanghai: Shanghai Academy of Social Sciences Press, 2005.

Shanghaishi difangzhi bangongshi and Shanghaishi lühua guanliju, comps. *Shanghai mingyuan zhi* (Gazetteer of famous gardens in Shanghai). Shanghai: Shanghai huabao chubanshe, 2007.

Shanghaishi gong'an ju gong'an shizhi bianzuan weiyuanhui, comp. *Shanghai gong'an zhi* (Gazetteer of Shanghai public security). Shanghai: Shanghai Academy of Social Sciences Press, 1997.

Shanghaishi Huangpuqu shangyezhi bianzuan weiyuanhui, comp. *Shanghaishi Huangpuqu shangyezhi* (Gazetteer of commerce in Huangpu district, Shanghai). Shanghai: Shanghai kexue jishu, 1995.

Shanghaishi Huangpuqu zhi bianzuan weiyuanhui, comp. *Huangpuqu zhi* (Gazetteer of Huangpu district). Shanghai: Shanghai Academy of Social Sciences Press, 1996.

Shanghaishi Jing'anqu zhi bianzuan weiyuanhui, comp. *Shanghaishi Jing'anqu zhi* (Gazetteer of Jing'an district). Shanghai: Shanghai Academy of Social Sciences Press, 1996.

Shanghaishi shili yuanlinchang, comp. *Zai ju shu: Shanghaishi di san jie juhua zhanlanhui dashiji* (The art of chrysanthemum planting: Memorabilia of the Third Chrysanthemum Exhibition of Shanghai). Shanghai: Shanghaishi shili yuanlinchang, 1933.

Shanghaishi tongjiju. *Xin Shanghai sishi nian* (Forty years of new Shanghai). Beijing: China Statistics Press, 1989.

Shanghaishi Xuhuiqu zhi bianzuan weiyuanhui. *Xuhuiqu zhi* (Gazetteer of Xuhui district). Shanghai: Shanghai Academy of Social Sciences Press, 1997.

Shao, Qin, and Frank Dikötter. "History as Humanity's CV: A Conversation with Frank Dikötter." *Chinese Historical Review* 24, no. 2 (November 2017): 166–82.

Shao Shaohong. *Wo de baba Shao Xunmei* (English title in original: *My Father Sinmay Zau*). Shanghai: Shanghai shudian, 2005.

Shaoshan Mao Zedong tongzhi jinianguan, comp. *Mao Zedong yiwu shidian* (A catalog of things left behind by Mao Zedong). Beijing: Hongqi chubanshe, 1996.

Shapiro, Judith. *Mao's War against Nature: Politics and the Environment in Revolutionary China.* New York: Cambridge University Press, 2001.

Shaw, Victor N. *Social Control in China: A Study of Chinese Work Units.* Westport, CT: Praeger, 1996.

Sheehan, Brett. *Industrial Eden: A Chinese Capitalist Vision.* Cambridge, MA: Harvard University Press, 2015.

Shell Companies in China. *Looking to the Long Term: The Story of Shell in China.* Beijing: Shell China Beijing Office, 2004.

Shen Jialu. *Shanghai laoweidao* (The old tastes of Shanghai). Shanghai: Shanghai wenhua chubanshe, 2007.

Shen Jialu. *Shanghai ren huofa* (How the Shanghainese live). Shanghai: Shanghai wenhua chubanshe, 2008.

Shen, Jianzhong, comp. *Shi Zhecun xiansheng biannian shilu* (A biographical annual of Mr. Shi Zhecun). Shanghai: Shanghai guji chubanshe, 2013.

Shen Zhanyun. *Huipishu, huangpishu* (Gray-covered books and yellow-covered books). Guangzhou: Huacheng chubanshe, 2007.

Shen Zhihua. *Sikao yu xuanze—cong zhishifenzi huiyi dao fanyou yundong* (Deliberation and selection: From the Conference on Intellectuals to the Anti-Rightist movement). Hong Kong: University of Hong Kong Contemporary Chinese Cultural Center, 2008.

Shen Zhihua. *Sulian zhuanjia zai Zhongguo (1948–1960)* (Soviet experts in China, 1948–1960). Beijing: Shehui kexue wenxian chubanshe, 2015.
Sheng Peiyu. *Shengshi jiazu: Shao Xunmei yu wo* (The Sheng lineage: Shao Xunmei and I). Beijing: Renmin wenxue chubanshe, 2004.
Sheringham, Michael. *Everyday Life: Theories and Practices from Surrealism to the Present*. Oxford: Oxford University Press, 2006.
Shi Kangqiang. *Zishuo zihua* (Talking to oneself). Wuhan: Hubei jiaoyu chubanshe, 2002.
Shi Zhecun. "Jinian Fu Lei" (In memory of Fu Lei). *Xinmin wanbao* (Xinmin Evening News), September 3, 1986.
Shi Zhecun. *Shashang de jiaoyin* (Footprints in the sand). Shenyang: Liaoning jiaoyu chubanshe, 1995.
Shih, Ch'eng-chih. *Urban Commune Experiments in Communist China*. Westport, CT: Greenwood, 1974.
Shitun Huixiu (Sanetō Keishū). *Zhongguoren liuxue Riben shi* (A history of Chinese studying in Japan). Beijing: Peking University Press, 2012.
Shuxin. "Feng Deying 'sanhua' lanman" (Feng Deying's bright-colored "three flowers"). *Guangming ribao*, April 9, 2015.
Siemieńska, Renata. "Women, Work, and Gender Equality in Poland: Reality and Its Social Perception." In *Women, State, and Party in Eastern Europe*, edited by Sharon L. Wolchik and Alfred G. Meyer, 305–22. Durham, NC: Duke University Press, 1985.
Smil, Vaclav. *China's Environmental Crisis: An Inquiry into the Limits of National Development*. Armonk, NY: M.E. Sharpe, 1993.
Smith, Aminda M. *Thought Reform and China's Dangerous Classes: Reeducation, Resistance, and the People*. Lanham, MD: Rowman & Littlefield, 2013.
Smith, Stephen A. *Revolution and the People in Russia and China: A Comparative History*. Cambridge, UK: Cambridge University Press, 2008.
Snow, Edgar. *Red China Today: Revised and updated edition of The Other Side of the River*. New York: Vintage Books, 1970.
Snow, Edgar. *Red Star Over China*. New York: Grove, 1994.
Snow, Edgar. *The Other Side of the River*. New York: Random House, 1961.
So, Bennis Wai-yip. "The Policy-Making and Political Economy of the Abolition of Private Ownership in the Early 1950s: Findings from New Material." *China Quarterly* 171 (September 2002): 682–703.
Su Yuanyuan. "Yijie shixue zhuanzhu zhi zhuanjia—Xie Defeng" (Xie Defeng: An expert in translating and introducing historical monographs). *Jiannan wenxue* (Jiannan Literature) 10 (May 2013): 254–55.
Sun Ji'nan. *Li Jinhui yu Lipai yinyue* (Li Jinhui and the Li syle of music). Shanghai: Shanghai Conservatory of Music Press, 2007.
Sun Peidong. "Jingshui shenliu: wen'ge shiqi Jing Hu zhiqing de jiecheng hua geren yuedu" (A deep and silent undercurrent: Stratified individual reading among educated youth in Beijing and Shanghai during the Cultural Revolution). *Ershi yi shiji* (Twenty-first Century), Hong Kong 156 (August 2016): 78–98.
Sun Shufen. *Sheng si jie* (A tale of life and death). Hong Kong: Tiandi tushu, 1994.

Sun Wen (Sun Yat-sen). *Jianguo fanglüe* (Plans and strategies of nation-building). Shanghai: Minzhi shuju, 1925.
Sun, Yaodong and Cheng Naishan. "Hushang diyi meishijia Shen Jingsi" (Shen Jingsi: The number one gastronome of Shanghai). *Shipin yu shenghuo* (Food and Life) 12 (2005).
Swislocki, Mark. *Culinary Nostalgia: Regional Food Culture and the Urban Experience in Shanghai*. Stanford, CA: Stanford University Press, 2009.
Tan Yingzhou. "Hongse de niaoluo" (The red cypress vine). *Xinmin wanbao* (Xinmin Evening News), July 27, 2013.
Tan Yingzhou. *Renjian huashi* (Flowers in the human world). Guilin: Lijiang chubanshe, 2018.
Tan Yingzhou. "Shiliu huakai, qianban ganhuai" (Reminiscing when pomegranates are in bloom). *Shanghai wenxue* (Shanghai Literature) 4 (April 2012): 83–5.
Tang Baolin. *Jujue nuxing – Zhonggong mimi Nanjing shiwei shuji Chen Xiuliang zhuan* (Refusing servility: A biography of Chen Xiuliang, CCP's underground party secretary of Nanjing municipality). Hong Kong: Zhonghe chuban youxian gongsi, 2012.
Tang Diyin. *The Pen and I: The Autobiography of a Shanghai Businesswoman*. Beijing: New World Press, 1985.
Tang Longbiao. "Huixiang 'Zhonghua' juanyan 50 duo nian fazhan shi" (Recollections of over fifty years of the history of the development of Zhonghua cigarettes). *Shanghai yanye bao* (Shanghai Tobacco Business News), January 22, 2008.
Tang Tao. "Chuntian de huainian" (Cherishing the memory of spring). In *Fengyu tongzhou sishi nian 1949–1989* (Traveling over forty years on the same boat in winds and rain, 1949–1989), edited by Jin Ruiying. Beijing: Zhongguo wenshi chubanshe, 1990.
Tang Wing-Shing. "Chinese Urban Planning at Fifty: An Assessment of the Planning Theory Literature." *Journal of Planning Literature* 14, no. 3 (February 2000): 347–66.
Tang Yanming and Tang Yaming. *Mao Zhuxi yulu de dansheng ji qita: Tang Pingzhu wen'ge shilu* (The birth of the *Quotations of Chairman Mao* and others: Tang Pingzhu's Cultural Revolution memoir). Hong Kong: Chinese University of Hong Kong Press, 2019.
Tang Zhengmang. "Xinzhi shudian yu Gangtie shi zenyang lancheng de Zhongwen yiben" (Xinzhi bookstore and the Chinese translation of *How the Steel Was Tempered*). *Dangshi tiandi* (Party History Forum) 11 (April 2000).
Tao Hongling. "Lu Xun shouxian shi fanyijia" (Lu Xun was first of all a translator). *Nanfang ribao* (Southern Daily), November 30, 2006.
Tata, Sam. *Shanghai 1949: End of an Era*. Introduction by Ian McLachlan. New York: New Amsterdam Books, 1989.
Teiwes, Frederick C., with Warren Sun. *China's Road to Disaster*. Armonk, NY: M.E. Sharpe, 1999.
Tencent. "Chen Danyan he ta bixia de Shanghai nüren men" (Chen Danyan and the Shanghai women she writes about). http://archive.fo/E4tXh, posted April 8, 2008.

Terrill, Ross. *800,000,000: The Real China*. Boston: Little, Brown, 1972.
Terrill, Ross. *Flowers on an Iron Tree: Five Cities of China*. Boston: Little, Brown, 1975.
Tomba, Luigi. *Paradoxes of Labour Reform: Chinese Labour Theory and Practice from Socialism to Market*. Honolulu: University of Hawai'i Press, 2002.
Trumbull, Robert, ed. *This Is Communist China*. By the staff of Yomiuri Shimbun. Tokyo, New York: David McKay Company, Inc., 1968.
U, Eddy. *Creating the Intellectual: Chinese Communism and the Rise of a Classification*. Berkeley: University of California Press, 2019.
U, Eddy. "Dangerous Privilege: The United Front and the Rectification Campaign of the Early Mao Years." *China Journal* 68 (July 2012): 32–57.
United Nations, Department of Economic and Social Affairs, Population Division. *World Population Prospects: The 2010 Revision*. New York: United Nations, 2011.
Van Slyke, Lyman P. *Enemies and Friends: The United Front in Chinese Communist History*. Stanford, CA: Stanford University Press, 1967.
Veg, Sebastian, ed. *Popular Memories of the Mao Era: From Critical Debate to Reassessing History*. Hong Kong: Hong Kong University Press, 2019.
Volgyes, Ivan. "Blue-Collar Working Women and Poverty in Hungary." In *Women, State, and Party in East Europe*, edited by Sharon L. Wolchik and Alfred G. Meyer, 221–33. Durham, NC: Duke University Press, 1985.
Wakeman, Frederic E. Jr. *Red Star over Shanghai: The Communist Transformation of the Municipal Police, 1942–1952 / Hongxing zhaoyao Shanghai cheng: Gongchandang dui shizheng jingcha de gaizao*. Translated into Chinese by Liang He. Beijing: Renmin chubanshe, 2011.
Wakeman, Frederic E. Jr. (Weifeide). *The Shanghai Badlands: Wartime Terrorism and Urban Crime, 1937–1941*. Cambridge, UK: Cambridge University Press, 2002.
Walder, Andrew G. *China under Mao: A Revolution Derailed*. Cambridge, MA: Harvard University Press, 2015.
Wang Anyi. *The Song of Everlasting Sorrow: A Novel of Shanghai*. Translated by Michael Berry and Susan Chan Egan. New York: Columbia University Press, 2008.
Wang Anyi. *Xiaoshuojia de shisan tang ke* (A novelist's thirteen lectures). Shanghai: Shanghai wenyi chubanshe, 2005.
Wang Anyi. *Xunzhao Shanghai* (Searching for Shanghai). Shanghai: Xuelin chubanshe, 2001.
Wang Anyi and Zhang Xinying. *Tanhua lu* (Records of conversations). Beijing: Renmin wenxue chubanshe, 2011.
Wang, David Der-wei. *The Lyrical in Epic Time: Modern Chinese Intellectuals and Artists through the 1949 Crisis*. New York: Columbia University Press, 2015.
Wang, Fei-ling. *Organizing through Division and Exclusion: China's Hukou System*. Stanford, CA: Stanford University Press, 2005.
Wang Gang. "Ye jilian Dongniya" (Also a record of falling in love with Tonya). www.xys.org/xys/ebooks/literature/prose/Dongniya_too.txt.
Wang, George, and Betty Barr. *Between Two Worlds: Lessons in Shanghai*. Hong Kong: Old China Hand Press, 2004.

Wang, George, and Betty Barr. *Shanghai Boy, Shanghai Girl: Lives in Parallel*. Hong Kong: Old China Hand Press, 2002.
Wang Haibo. *Xin Zhongguo gongye jingji shi, 1949.10–1957* (A history of the industrialization of new China, October 1949 to 1957). Beijing: Jingji guanli chubanshe, 1994.
Wang Jingzhi. *Lengdong sanshi nian* (Frozen for thirty years). Hong Kong: Mingbao chubanshe, 1996.
Wang, John Ching-Yu. *Chin Sheng t'an*. New York: Twayne, 1972.
Wang Ju. *Jindai Shanghai mianfangye de zuihou huihuang (1945–1949)* (The last boom of modern Shanghai's textile industry, 1945–1949). Shanghai: Shanghai Academy of Social Science Press, 2004.
Wang Junxi. "Wo de lilong shengchanzu wangshi" (My recollections of the neighborhood workshop). *Xinmin wanbao* (Xinmin Evening News), November 1, 2011.
Wang Laidi. "Mao Zedong de zhishifenzi zhengce" (Mao Zedong's intellectual policy). *Modern China Studies* 3 (2003). www.modernchinastudies.org/us/issues/past-issues/82-mcs-2003-issue-3/1300-2012-01-06-09-16-39.html.
Wang Li. *Wang Li fansilu* (Wang Li's reflections). Hong Kong: Beixing chubanshe, 2001.
Wang Shaoguang. *Zhongguo zhengdao* (China: The political path). Beijing: Chinese People's University Press, 2014.
Wang Shaozhou and Chen Zhimin, comps. *Lilong jianzhu* (Architecture of alleyway houses). Shanghai: Shanghai kexue jishu wenxian chubanshe, 1987.
Wang Tao. *Yinru zazhi* (Seashore miscellanea). Shanghai: Shanghai guji chubanshe, 1989 [1875].
Wang Weiming. *Shanghai qiqing liuyu* (English title in original: *Shanghai's Fleeting Fashions*). Shanghai: Shanghai wenyi chubanshe, 2005.
Wang Xiangkun. *Jiang Jieshi yu Mao Zedong hezuo suiyue* (The time when Chiang Kai-shek and Mao Zedong cooperated). Beijing: Zhonggong dangshi chubanshe, 2013.
Wang Xinli. *Yuegui nianling* (Rebellious ages). Nanjing: Fenghuang chubanshe, 2009.
Wang, Y. Yvon. *Reinventing Licentiousness: Pornography and Modern China*. Ithaca, NY: Cornell University Press, 2021.
Wang You. "Fengrenji pinpai Hudie shangwei xiaoshi" (Butterfly brand sewing machines have not vanished). *Diyi caijing ribao* (First Financial Daily), August 8, 2009.
Wang, Zheng. *Finding Women in the State: A Socialist Feminist Revolution in the People's Republic of China, 1949–1964*. Berkeley: University of California Press, 2016.
Wang, Zheng. "'State Feminism'? Gender and Socialist State Formation in Maoist China." *Feminist Studies* 31, no. 3 (Fall 2005): 519–51.
Wang Zhiliang. *Wangshi yu huainian* (Past events and reminiscences). Nanning: Guangxi shifan daxue chubanshe, 2013.
Watson, James L., ed. *Class and Social Stratification in Post-Revolution China*. Cambridge, UK: Cambridge University Press, 1984.

Watson, James L., ed. "Feeding the Revolution: Public Mess Halls and Coercive Commensality in Maoist China." In *Handbook of Food and Anthropology*, edited by Jakob A. Klein and James L. Watson, 308–20. London: Bloomsbury, 2016.

Weber, Max. *Weber's Rationalism and Modern Society*. Translated and edited by Tony Waters and Dagmar Waters. New York: Palgrave Macmillan, 2015.

Wei Guangqi and Ding Dong. "Meiyou kongbai—Wen'ge shiqi de dushu shenghuo" (No gaps: Reading life during the Cultural Revolution). https://news.boxun.com/news/gb/z_special/2005/05/200505090516.shtml.

Wemheuer, Felix. *A Social History of Maoist China: Conflict and Change, 1949–1978*. Cambridge, UK: Cambridge University Press, 2019.

Wenhui bao (Wenhui Daily). Shanghai.

Wenhui dushu zhoubao (Wenhui Reader's Weekly). Shanghai.

Whyte, Martin King, and William L. Parish. *Urban Life in Contemporary China*. Chicago: University of Chicago Press, 1984.

Whyte, William Foote. *Street Corner Society: The Social Structure of an Italian Slum*. Chicago: University of Chicago Press, 1993.

Wickeri, Philip L. *Seeking the Common Ground: Protestant Christianity, the Three-Self Movement, and China's United Front*. Eugene, OR: Wipf and Stock, 2011.

Wilson, Dick. *Anatomy of China: An Introduction to One Quarter of Mankind*. New York: Weybright and Palley, 1968.

Wong, Edward. "Myth of a Chinese Leader Is Traced Back to Its Roots." *New York Times*, February 17, 2011, Section A: 8.

Wu Jimin. "Shen Laizhou yu rongxian dawang Hengyuanxiang" (Shen Laizhou and Hengyuanxiang, the King of the Worsted). In *Dangnian naxie ren* (People in those years), edited by Dang'an Chunqiu zazhi she, 246–57. Beijing: Wenhua chubanshe, 2009.

Wu Liang. *Wo de Luotuosi: Shanghai qishi niandai* (My own Rhodes: Shanghai in the seventies). Beijing: Renmin wenxue chubanshe, 2011.

Wu Liang. *Zhaoxia* (Sunglow). Beijing: Renmin wenxue chubanshe, 2016.

Wu Xiaobo. *Lidai jingji bian'ge deshi* (Success and failure of economic reforms in history). Hangzhou: Zhejiang University Press, 2013.

Wu Xiaoming. "Chengshi zhongchan: weihe jiaolü? ruhe xiaofei?" (The urban middle class: Why feel anxious? How should one consume?). *Shanghai Observer*, November 16, 2015. www.shobserver.com/news/detail?id=7610.

Wu Xiaoni. "1956 nian zhishifenzi wenti huiyi yanjiu shuping" (A commentary on the research on the 1956 conference on the intellectual issues). *Dangshi yanjiu yu jiaoxue* (Research and Teaching on Party History) 1 (2013): 67–70.

Xia Renhu. *Zhi chao si shu / Jiu Jing suo ji* (My four accounts / Miscellanea of old Beijing). Shenyang: Liaoning jiaoyu chubanshe, 1998 [1943].

Xiao Gongqin. "Zai jingshen ziyou zhong fansi" (Reflections in spiritual freedom). In *Wang jin tianya lu—dangdai xueren zishu* (A long journey to go: Accounts in their own words by contemporary scholars), edited by Ge Jianxiong, Ding Dong, and Xiang Jidong, 174–88. Nanchang, Jiangxi: Ershi yi shiji chubanshe, 2013.

Xibo. *Shanghai wangshi* (Things past in Shanghai). Shanghai: Wenhua chubanshe, 2008.

Xinmin wanbao (Xinmin Evening News). Shanghai.

Xiong Yuezhi. "Jindai Shanghai gongyuan yu shehui shenghuo" (Parks and social life in modern Shanghai). *Shehui kexue* (Social Sciences) (Shanghai) 5 (May 2013): 129–39.

Xiong Yuezhi. "Lishi shang de Shanghai xingxiang sanlun" (On the historical images of Shanghai). *Shilin* (Historical Review) 43 (1996): 139–53.

Xiong Yuezhi. "Lüelun Shanghai zujie de shuangchong yingxiang" (On the dual influence of Shanghai's foreign concessions). *Wenhui bao* (Wenhui Daily), November 11, 1986.

Xiong Yuezhi, ed. *Shanghai tongshi* (A general history of Shanghai). 15 vols. Shanghai: Shanghai renmin chubanshe, 1999.

Xu, Bin. *Chairman Mao's Children: Generation and the Politics of Memory in China.* Cambridge, UK: Cambridge University Press, 2021.

Xu Gang. *Xiang xiang chengshi de fangfa* (The way the city was perceived). Taipei: Xinrui wenchuang, 2013.

Xu Hongxin. "Jiari li guangguang Shanghai lao longtang" (Touring Shanghai's old alleyways during the holidays). *Jiefang ribao* (Liberation Daily), January 1, 2010.

Xu Jilin and Luo Gang, eds. *Chengshi jiyi: Shanghai wenhua de duoyuan lishi chuantong* (Urban memories: Multi-historical traditions in the culture of Shanghai). Shanghai: Shanghai shudian chubanshe, 2011.

Xu Longhua. *Shanghai fuzhuang wenhua shi* (A cultural history of clothing in Shanghai). Shanghai: Dongfang wenhua zhongxing, 2010.

Xu Xiaodi. *Diandao suiyue* (Deranged times). Beijing: Sanlian shudian, 2012.

Xu Zhimo. *Xu Zhimo quanji* (Complete works of Xu Zhimo). Tianjin: Tianjin renmin chubanshe, 2005.

Xu Zhongni. "Fangwen Shanghai zibenjia Rong Yiren" (Visiting Shanghai capitalist Rong Yiren). *Xinhua yuekan* (New China Monthly) 4 (April 1956): 76–77.

Xue Na, ed. *Jingdian pinpai gushi quji* (A complete collection of tales on classic brands). Beijing: Jincheng chubanshe, 2006.

Yan Ming. *Yimen xueke yu yige shidai* (One principle and one era). Beijing: Tsinghua University Press, 2004.

Yang Dongping. *Chengshi jifeng* (City monsoon). Beijing: Dongfang, 1994.

Yang Dongxiao. "Shaonü zhi xin: nage niandai de xing yu zui" (A Maiden's Heart: Sex and crime in that age). *Kan lishi* (English title in original: *History*). (Chengdu) 11 (2010).

Yang Jian. *1966–1976 de dixia wenxue* (Underground literature from 1949 to 1976). Beijing: Zhonggong dangshi chubanshe, 2013.

Yang Jianmin. "Xia Yan Muqin yiben de bozhe" (The twists and turns of Xia Yan's translation of *Mother*). *Zhonghua dushubao* (China Reading Weekly), March 19, 2014.

Yang Jisheng. *Tiandi fanfu: Zhongguo wenhua dageming shi* (The world turned upside down: A history of the Chinese Cultural Revolution). Hong Kong: Tiandi tushu, 2018.

Yang Jisheng. *Tombstone: The Great Chinese Famine, 1958–1962*. New York: Farrar, Straus and Giroux, 2012.

Yang Kuisong. "Guanyu jianguo yilai dangzheng ganbu de shouru" (On the income of party and government cadres since the establishment of the PRC). *Nanfang zhoubao* (Southern Weekly), August 29, 2007.

Yang Lang. "Wo de jiesheng de waigong: wei ban'ge shiji qian de shimin shenghuo jianying" (My thrifty grandpa: Sketches of the lives of city residents half a century ago). *Wenhui bao* (Wenhui Daily), April 5, 2016.

Yang Mo. *The Song of Youth*. Translated by Nan Ying. Beijing: Foreign Languages Press, 1958.

Yang Shiyang. "Xunzhao geming zhixia de xue yu rou" (Searching for flesh and blood under the revolution). *Zhongguo xinwen zhoukan* (Chinese News Weekly), August 16, 2011.

Yang Shuming. "1978–1979: luoshi dang dui minzu zichan jieji zhengce" (1978–1979: Fulfilling the party's policies on national capitalists). Interview script, in *Zhonggong dangshi yanjiu* (Research on the History of the Chinese Communist Party) 11 (2011): 87–94.

Yang Yalun. "'Chengshi renmin gongshe hua' zai Shanghai" (The urban people's commune program in Shanghai). In *Jiannan tansuo suo 1956–1965* (Arduous explorations, 1956–1965), vol. 1, edited by Xu Jiangang, 59–71. Shanghai: Shanghai shudian chubanshe, 2001.

Yao Dan, "Chonghui linhai xueyuan – Qu Bo fangtan lu" (Returning to tracks in the snowy forest – an interview with Qu Bo). *Xin wenxue shiliao* (Historical Materials of the New Literature) 1 (January 2012): 86–97.

Yao Xianguo and Xie Sisheng. "The Economic Effects of Occupational Segregation: An Analysis on Occupational Discrimination against Chinese Urban Female Labor." *Journal of Zhejiang University (Humanities and Social Sciences)* 36, no. 2 (March 2006): 73–9.

Ye Deyu. *Wangshi tanwei: Zhongguo wenhua shawang Zhou Yang* (Exploring the past: China's cultural tsar Zhou Yang). Taipei: Xiuwei, 2013.

Ye Kai. "Zuowei zishi fenzi de Zhou Yang" (Zhou Yang as an intellectual). *Dushu* (Reading) 4 (2001): 40–5.

Ye Shengtao. "Tianjing li de zhongzhi" (Planting on a patio). *Zhongxuesheng* (Middle School Students) 52 (February 1, 1935).

Ye Yonglie. *Jiedu Fu Lei yijia* (Unscrambling Fu Lei's family). Beijing: Jincheng chubanshe, 2010.

Ye Yonglie. *Sirenbang xingwang* (The rise and fall of the Gang of Four). Beijing: Renmin ribao chubanshe, 2009.

Ye Yonglie. *Ta, yige ruo nüzi* (She, a vulnerable woman). Changsha: Hunan renmin chubanshe, 2011.

Ye Yonglie. *Tiegu Fu Lei* (The unyielding character of Fu Lei). Shanghai: Wenhui chubanshe, 2010.

Yeh, Wen-hsin. *Shanghai Splendor: A Cultural History, 1843–1949*. Berkeley: University of California Press, 2007.

Yiming. "Minguo diyi haomen" (The number one rich and powerful family of the Republic). Chinese University of Hong Kong database, *Minjian lishi* (Folk History).

Yin Huifen. *Shanghai linli* (Shanghai neighbors). Shanghai: Shanghai wenhua chubanshe, 2009.

Yiqiao. *Tanshi ji* (Records of voracity). Beijing: Sanlian shudian, 2012.
Yu Guangren and Ji Yibing. "Zhishifenzi jieji shuxing rending de jiannan lichen" (The arduous course to defining intellectuals' class attributes). *Yanhuang chunqiu* (China Through the Ages) 1 (2002).
Yu Kaiwei. "Jiangnan qi'nü jin youzai" (Jiangnan still has outstanding women). *Shuwu* (Book House) 5 (1998).
Yu Kunlin, comp. *Kuse de lianqing* (Painful love). Taiyuan: Shanxi renmin chubanshe, 2006.
Yu Xiaoping. "Wen'ge gaochao, shushan tanbao" (Hunting for treasures in a mountain of books at the height of the Cultural Revolution). *Jiyi* (Remembrance) 143 (November 2015): 55–7.
Yuan Nianqi. "Can baobao" (Silkworm babies). *Jiefang ribao* (Liberation Daily), April 7, 2014.
Yuan Rong. "Fengrenji yu Minguo shiqi Shanghai siying junzhuang gongye" (Sewing machines and the private military uniform industry in Shanghai during the Republican period). *Junshi lishu yanjiu* (Military History Research) 4 (2008): 97–105.
Yunjian Shanjiao. "Shiqu de doushi huayuan caidi" (Urban gardens and vegetable plots that are no more). Blog entry, March 20, 2009. http://blog.sina.com.cn/s/blog_49c8b90c0100cyuc.html.
Zaleski, Eugene. *Planning for Economy Growth in the Soviet Union, 1918–1932*. Chapel Hill: University of North Carolina Press, 1971.
Zhang, Ailing, and Andrew F. Jones. "A Chronicle of Changing Clothes." *Positions: East Asia Cultures Critique* 11, no. 2 (Fall 2003): 427–41.
Zhang Changhua. *Cengjing fengya: wenhua mingren beiying* (Elegant once upon a time: Profiles of cultural celebrities). Guilin: Guangxi Normal University Press, 2012.
Zhang Chunhua. *Hucheng suishi quge* (Seasonal folk songs of Shanghai). Shanghai: Shanghai guji chubanshe, 1989 [1839].
Zhang Chunqiao. *Longhua ji* (Essays of Longhua). Shanghai: Shanghai wenyi chubanshe, 1960.
Zhang, Da-Peng. *Life Under Mao Zedong's Rule*. Translated and annotated by George A. Fowler. North Charleston, SC: CreateSpace, 2013.
Zhang, Dainian. *Key Concepts in Chinese Philosophy*. Translated by Edmund Ryden. New Haven, CT: Yale University Press, 2002.
Zhang Fanghui. "Gensui Lu Xiaoman xuehua" (Studying painting with Lu Xiaoman). *Wengu* (Reviewing the Past) 15 (March 2009): 95–101.
Zhang Guangzhao. "Wang Qishan weihe tuijian *Jiu zhidu yu da geming*?" (Why did Wang Qishan recommend *The Old Regime and the Revolution*?). *Renmin ribao* (People's Daily), overseas edition, January 18, 2013.
Zhang Hanzhi. *Kuaguo houhou de da hongmen* (Crossing the thick red door). Shanghai: Wenhui chubanshe, 2002.
Zhang Hongming and Pang Yuan. *Zhongguo fangdichan guanli yuanli, fangfa, he shijian* (The principles, methodologies, and practices of Chinese real estate management). Shanghai: Shanghai Academy of Social Sciences Press, 2006.
Zhang Hua and Su Caiqing, eds. *Huishou "wen'ge": Zhongguo shinian "wen'ge" de fenxi yu fansi* (Looking back on the Cultural Revolution: Analyses

and reflections on the decade of China's Cultural Revolution). Beijing: Zhongyang dangshi chubanshe, 2000.

Zhang Jishun. *Yuanqu de duoshi: 1950 niandai de Shanghai* (English title in original: *A City Displayed: Shanghai in the 1950s*). Beijing: Social Sciences Academic Press, 2015.

Zhang Min, ed. *Chuanqiang de duanbo* (The short waves that can penetrate walls). Suyan shushe, 2012.

Zhang Niumei. "Lizhi yihuo kuangre: Shanghai jiating funü canyu gongye shengchan yanjiu" (English title in original: "Reason or Fanaticism? Study on the Shanghai Housewives' Participation in Industrial Production from 1958 to 1962"). *Journal of East China Normal University (Philosophy and Social Sciences)* 1 (January 2014): 78–84.

Zhang Re. "'Xiang dang jiaoxin' de qianyin houguo" (The cause and effects of the campaign of "Submitting your hearts and minds to the party"). *Yanhuang chunqiu* (Yan-Huang Historical Review) 12 (December 2010): 58–62.

Zhang Weiguo. "Mao Zedong shidai de yundong yu zuiming" (Political campaigns and accusations in Mao's era). *NewCenturyNet,* September 9, 2016. http://2newcenturynet.blogspot.de/2016/09/blog-post_50.html.

Zhang Weiqun. *Shanghai longtang yuanqi: genju yiqian ling yi jian dangce yu wenshu fuxian de Siming Bieshu lishi* (The vitality of a Shanghai alleyway: A history of Siming Villa based on 1,001 archival and other documents). Shanghai: Shanghai renmin chubanshe, 2007.

Zhang Weiqun. *Siming Bieshu duizhao ji—yi tiao Shanghai longtang zhushi* (Siming Villa in comparison: Various histories of a Shanghai alleyway). Beijing: Zhongyang bianyi chubanshe, 2013.

Zhang Xingcheng. "Yimin qingjie yu wenren lanhua shihua zhuantong de hua" (English title in original: "An Analysis of the Image-Literary Intertextuality between the Remnant Complex and Literati's Orchid Poetry and Painting Tradition"). *Journal of Southwest University (Social Science Edition)* 44, no. 5 (May 2018): 117–26.

Zhang, Xudong. "Shanghai Nostalgia: Postrevolutionary Allegories in Wang Anyi's Literary Production in the 1990s." *Positions: East Asia Cultures Critique* 8, no. 2 (Fall 2000): 349–87.

Zhang Yihe. *Wangshi bingbu ruyan* (Past events have not faded like a puff of smoke). Beijing: Renmin wenxue chubanshe, 2004.

Zhang Ying. "Daxue neng bu neng peiyang zuojia?" (Can universities train writers?). *Nanfang zhoumo* (Southern Weekend), April 4, 2014.

Zhang Zijing, with Ji Ji. *Wo de jiejie Zhang Ailing* (My sister Zhang Ailing). Shanghai: Wenhui chubanshe, 2003.

Zhang Zugan. "Qing xi Huxiang" (Emotional connections to Huxiang). Chinese University of Hong Kong database, *Minjian lishi* (Folk History).

Zhang Zuoliang. *Zhou Enlai de zuihou shinian* (Zhou Enlai's last ten years). Shanghai: Shanghai renmin chubanshe, 1998.

Zhao Ji-jun. "'Lühua' gainian de chansheng yu yanbian" (English title in original: "The Origin and Development of the Concept of '*Lühua*' [Greening]"). *Zhongguo yuanlin* (English title in original: *Journal of Chinese Landscape Architecture*) 2 (February 2013): 57–59.

Zhao Jiabi. "Huiyi Xu Zhimo he 'Zhimo quanji'" (Looking back on Xu Zhimo and the *Complete Works of Zhimo*). *Xinwenxue shiliao* (Historical materials on the New Literature) 4 (1981): 93–107.

Zhao Kejin. "Meiguo mei qita lieqiang huai shi shishi" (It is a fact that the United States is not as bad as other world powers). *Huanqiu shibao* (Global Times), January 17, 2012.

Zhao Tielin. *Wo de laosanjie suiyue* (My life as a student of the old three classes). Beijing: Renmin wenxue chubanshe, 2010.

Zhao Yinglin. "Mao Zedong yu Hu Shi" (Mao Zedong and Hu Shih). *Wengu* (Reviewing the Past) 9 (September 2007): 70–80.

Zhao Zhiming. "Zheng Nian yu yige shidai de 'Shanghai shengsi jie'" (Nien Cheng and an era's "Life and Death in Shanghai"). Chinese University of Hong Kong database, *Minjian lishi* (Folk History).

Zheng, Jane. *The Modernization of Chinese Art: The Shanghai Art College, 1913–1937.* Leuven, Belgium: Leuven University Press, 2016.

Zheng Jian. "Huayuan yangfang hao dushu" (A garden house good for reading). *Shanghai wenxue* (Shanghai Literature) 3 (March 2015).

Zheng Jian. *Shanghai chuantangfeng* (Shanghai, the wind passing through the hallway). Shanghai: Wenhua chubanshe, 2015.

Zheng Jingzhong. "Wo zai Zhongnanhai jian dao de Zhu laozong" (The Commander Zhu I saw in Zhongnanhai). *Tongzhou gongjin* (Together in the Same Boat) 1, 2015.

Zheng Yimei. "TongGuang nianjian de juhuahui" (Chrysanthemum shows during the Tongzhi and Guangxu periods). *Xinmin wanbao* (Xinmin Evening News), October 8, 1956.

Zhong Fulan. *Shanghai jietou longkou* (English title in original: *Shanghai Folklore*). Shanghai: Shanghai cishu chubanshe, 2006.

Zhong Gang and Chen Xuelian. "'Huangse' shouchaoben *Shaonü zhi xin*: yidairen de yueduji" ("Yellow" hand-copied manuscript of *A Maiden's Heart*: Record of a generation's reading). www.zgnfys.com/a/nfrw-10077_3.shtml.

Zhong Laiyin. *Zhonggu xian dao shi jinghua* (The best Taoist poems of medieval times). Nanjing: Jiangsu wenyi chubanshe, 1994.

Zhong Xueping. "Women Can Hold Up Half the Sky." In *Words and Their Stories: Essays on the Language of the Chinese Revolution*, edited by Wang Ban, 227–48. Leiden: Brill, 2010.

Zhong Xueping, Wang Zheng, and Bai Di, eds. *Some of Us: Chinese Women Growing up in the Mao Era*. New Brunswick, NJ: Rutgers University Press, 2001.

Zhonggong Shanghai dang zhi bianzuan weiyuanhui. *Zhonggong Shanghai dang zhi* (Gazetteer of the Shanghai branch of the Chinese Communist Party). Shanghai: Shanghai Academy of Social Sciences Press, 2001.

Zhonggong Shanghai shiwei dangshi yanjiushi, ed. *Shanghai shehui zhuyi jianshe wushi nian* (Fifty years of socialist construction in Shanghai). Shanghai: Shanghai renmin chubanshe, 1999.

Zhonggong Shanghai shiwei dangshi yanjiushi, ed. *Shanghai zhichi quanguo 1949–1976* (Shanghai supports the whole nation, 1949–1976). 2 vols. Shanghai: Shanghai shudian chubanshe, 2011.

Zhonggong Shanghai shiwei tongzhanbu, Zhonggong Shanghai shiwei dangshi yanjiushi, Shanghaishi dang'anguan, comps. *Zhongguo ziben zhuyi gongshangye de shehui zhuyi gaizhao: Shanghai juan* (The socialist reform of China's capitalist industry and commerce: Shanghai volume). Beijing: Zhonggong dangshi chubanshe, 1993.

Zhonggong zhongyang dangshi yanjiushi. *Zhongguo Gongchandang lishi* (A history of the Chinese Communist Party). Beijing: Zhonggong dangshi chubanshe, 2011.

Zhonggong zhongyang wenxian yanjiushi, comp. *Chen Yun nianpu* (A chronicle of Chen Yun's life). Beijing: Zhonggong zhongyang wenxian chubanshe, 2000.

Zhonggong zhongyang wenxian yanjiushi, comp. *Liu Shaoqi lun gongren yundong* (Liu Shaoqi on the labor movement). Beijing: Zhongyang wenxian chubanshe, 1988.

Zhonggong zhongyang wenxian yanjiushi, comp. *Liu Shaoqi nianpu, 1898–1969* (A chronicle of Liu Shaoqi's life, 1898–1969). Beijing: Zhongyang wenxian chubanshe, 1996.

Zhonggong zhongyang wenxian yanjiushi, comp. *Mao Zedong lun linye* (Mao Zedong on forestry). Beijing: Zhongyang wenxian chubanshe, 2003.

Zhonggong zhongyang wenxian yanjiushi, comp. *Mao Zedong nianpu* (A chronicle of Mao Zedong's life). Beijing: Zhongyang wenxian chubanshe, 2013.

Zhonggong zhongyang wenxian yanjiushi, comp. *Mao Zedong shuxin xuanji* (Selected correspondence of Mao Zedong). Beijing: Renmin chubanshe, 2003.

Zhonggong zhongyang zuzhi bu and Zhonggong zhongyang wenxian yanjiushi, comps. *Zhishifenzi wenti wenxian xuanbian* (Selected documents on the issues regarding intellectuals). Beijing: Renmin chubanshe, 1983.

Zhongguo banben tushuguan, comp. *1949–1979 fanyi chuban waiguo wenxue zhuzuo mulu he tiyao* (Catalogs and synopses of translated foreign literature published from 1949 to 1979). Nanjing: Jiangsu renmin chubanshe, 1986.

Zhongguo banben tushuguan, comp. *1949–1986 quanguo neibu faxing tushu zongmu* (A complete catalog of internal circulation books published from 1949 to 1986). Beijing: Zhonghua shuju, 1988.

Zhongguo fanyijia cidian bianxiezu, comp. *Zhangguo fanyijia cidian* (Dictionary of Chinese translators). Beijing: Zhongguo duiwai fanyi chuban gongsi, 1988.

Zhongguo renmin zhengzhi xieshang huiyi, comp. *The Important Documents of the First Plenary Session of the Chinese People's Political Consultative Conference*. Peking: Foreign Languages Press, 1949.

Zhongguo yinyue bao (Chinese Music News). Beijing.

Zhongyang wenxian yanjiusi, comp. *Jianguo yilai Mao Zedong wen'gao* (Mao Zedong's manuscripts after 1949). Beijing: Zhongyang wenxian chubanshe, 1992.

Zhou Enlai. *Zhou Enlai xuanji* (Selected works of Zhou Enlai). 2 vols. Beijing: Renmin chubanshe, 1997.

Zhou Erfu. *Morning in Shanghai*. Translated by A. C. Barnes. Beijing: Foreign Languages Press, 1962.

Zhou Erfu. *Wangshi huishou lu* (Records of things in the past). Beijing: Zhongguo gongren chubanshe, 2004.

Zhou Haiying. *Lu Xun yu wo qishi nian* (Seventy years of Lu Xun and I). Haikou: Nanhai chubanshe, 2001.
Zhou Peihong. *Shanghai siren ditu* (A private map of Shanghai). Beijing: Zhongyang guangbo dianshi daxue chubanshe, 2013.
Zhou Yang, comp. *Makesi, Engesi, Liening lun yishu* (Marx, Engels, and Lenin on the arts). Yan'an: Yan'an Lu Xun yishu wenxueyuan, 1940.
Zhou Yang, comp. *Makesi zhuyi yu wenyi* (Marxism and literature and art). Yan'an: Jiefangshe, 1944.
Zhou Zhenhe. "Shanghai de jiu yangshu" (Old foreign books in Shanghai). *Xinwen wanbao* (Evening News), January 4, 2013.
Zhou Zhenhe. "Shanghai jiushudian yijiu" (Recollections of Shanghai's used-book stores). *Xinmin wanbao* (Xinmin Evening News), September 24, 2014.
Zhu Bangxing, Hu Lin'ge, and Xu Sheng. *Shanghai chanye yu Shanghai gongren* (Industries and workers in Shanghai). Shanghai: Shanghai renmin chubanshe, 1984 [1939].
Zhu Dake. *Gudu de daduoshu* (The lonely majority). Beijing: Zhongguo shuji chubanshe, 2012.
Zhu Dake. *Jiyi de hongpishu* (English title in original: *The Memory of a Red-Covered Book*). Guangzhou: Huacheng chubanshe, 2008.
Zhu Dake. "Zheng Nian: Bi guci geng mei geng ying de linghun" (Zheng Nian: A soul harder and more beautiful than curio china). *Yazhou zhoukan* (Asia Weekly), March 31, 2011.
Zhu Jiangang. *Guo yu jia zhi jian: Shanghai lingli de shimin tuanti yu shequ yongdong de minzhu zhi* (English title in original: *Between the Family and the State: An Ethnography of the Civil Associations and Community Movement in a Shanghai Lilong Neighborhood*). Beijing: Social Sciences Academic Press, 2010.
Zhu Shoutong. "Guanzhu Mo Yan, lijie Mo Yan" (Pay attention to Mo Yan and understand Mo Yan). *Aomen ribao* (Macau Daily), December 3, 2014.
Zhu Xueqin. "'Niangxipi' he 'shengjunji'—'wen'ge' dushu ji" ("Damn it" and "the provincial and military-command ranks": A record of reading during the Cultural Revolution). Chinese University of Hong Kong database, *Minjian lishi* (Folk History).
Zhu Zheng. *Fan Youpai douzhen quanshi* (A complete history of the Anti-Rightist campaign). Taipei: Xiuwei zixun keji, 2013.
Zhuang Qidong, Yuan Lunqu, and Li Jianli. *Xin Zhongguo gongzhi shigao* (A draft history of wages in new China). Beijing: Zhongguo caizheng jingji chubanshe, 1986.
Zia, Helen. *Last Boat Out of Shanghai: The Epic Story of the Chinese Who Fled Mao's Revolution*. New York: Ballantine Books, 2019.
Zibo. *Shijian yi wu Hu Shizhi* (The world lost Hu Shih). Beijing: New World Press, 2016.
Zimmermann, Susan. "Gender Regime and Gender Struggle in Hungarian State Socialism." *Aspasia* 4 (2010): 1–24.
Zou Yiren. *Jiu Shanghai renkou bianqian de yanjiu* (Research on population change in old Shanghai). Shanghai: Shanghai renmin chubanshe, 1980.

Zou Zhenhuan. *Yingxiang Zhongguo jindai shehui de yibai zhong yizuo* (A hundred translated works that influenced modern Chinese society). Beijing: Zhongguo duiwai fanyi chuban gongsi, 1996.

Zuo, Jiping. *Work and Family in Urban China: Women's Changing Experience since Mao*. New York: Palgrave Macmillan, 2016.

Zuo Jiping and Jiang Yongping. *Shehui zhuanxing zhong chengzhen funü de gongzuo he jiating* (Urban women's work and the family in social transition). Beijing: Contemporary China Publishing House, 2009.

Index

Adaptive governance, 155
Adventures of Tom Sawyer, The, 79
Agriculture and Forestry, Department of, 187
Ai Qing, 64
All-China Federation of Industry and Commerce, 42, 51
alleyway houses, 10, 74, 80, 87, 132
alleyway production teams (APTs), 140, 141, 145, 146
alleyway women's detachments, 139–41
An Ideal Husband, 81
Anda Cotton Mill, 31
Anding Fang, 60
Anna Karenina, 105
Anti-Rightist Campaign, 13, 58, 60, 90, 249
Anti-Rightist movement, 89
Art moderne structure, 41
As Time Goes By (from *Casablanca*), 31
Associated Press, The, 206
Avenue Foch in the French Concession, 86
Avenue Joffre, 34, 35, 43, 79, 108

Bai Hua, 38
Bai Juyi (772–846), 68
Backyard furnaces, 190
Balzac and the Little Chinese Seamstress, 122
Balzac, Honoré de (1799–1850), 63, 99, 100, 103
bamboo basket, 243–5
Bankers, 2
Baoqing Road, 43
Barber of Seville, The, 33
Barefoot doctor, 109, 149
Beckett, Samuel (1906–1989), 216
Beethoven, 4, 33
  and *Fate Symphony*, 33
  and Ninth, 4
  and *Pastoral Symphony*, 33

Bei Dao (1949–), 201
Bei Runsheng, 41
Beijing News Supplement (Jingbao fukan), 92
Beijing Road West, 89
Beijing style, 184, 254
Being Frozen for Thirty Years, 30
Beiyang era (1916–1927), 86
Bergère, Marie-Claire, 28
Big-character poster, 66, 69, 112, 113, 206
Birth rate, 149
Bisch, Jørgen, 203
Bitter Flower (Kucai hua), 121
Bizarre dress and outlandish clothing (*qizhuang yifu*), 221
Black-light dance parties, 44
Blanket endorsement, 28
Bloodworth, Dennis (1919–2005), 202
blue ants, 204, 222
bookstores
  in Fuzhou Road, 107
  specialized, 107
  used-book stores, 109
  Xinhua Bookstore, 35, 106, 214
Boston Globe, 202
bourgeoisie, 22, 24, 50, 52, 92, 219, 270
  and bourgeois ideology, 21
  and bourgeois right, 52–4
  in comfortable lifestyle, 12, 31, 39, 45, 52, 54, 59, 62, 78, 86, *See also* Bourgeois comforts
  dance parties, 43–4
  in dissolute lifestyle, 111
  and fixed interest, 22, 24, 27, 30, 37, 51
  habit, 38
  and high pay, 71
  and home parties, 46
  and intellectuals, 54
  life, 25
  and national capitalists, 24, 26, 51
  toys, 34
  upscale restaurants, 37, 38
  works, 125

345

Bourgeois books/literature
  fengzixiu, 99
  and gray-covered books, 119
  for internal circulation only, 119
  and "negative materials that serve as a lesson" (*fanmian jiaocai*), 119
  and shalong ("*salon*"), 121
  Tonya complex, 130
  and yellow-covered books, 119
Bourgeois comforts, 28, 30, 31, 33–40
  and "As Time Goes By" (from *Casablanca*), 31
  and Beethoven, 4
  coffee, 35, 38, 39, 42, 46
  and Garden Villas, 33
  and Green House, 41, 43
  Jinjiang Hotel, 37
  Mozart, 33
  Mr. Three R's, 40
  My Fair Lady, 33
  "One Day When We Were Young" (from *The Great Waltz*), 33
  Peace Hotel (Cathay Hotel), 206, 208, 210, 273
  piano, 31, 33, 34, 51, 82, 277, 278
  Shanghai Culinary School in 1963, 36
  Siming Villa, 34
  training programs and cooking competitions, 36
  Yan Qingxiang, 36, 37
  Ye Xingshan, 38
  Zhang Da-Peng (1941–), 35, 44, 189, 190, 191, 198, 272, 274, 291
  Zhou Yi (1931–), 34
bourgeois intellectuals, 13, 14, 19, 55, 56
Bright Moon Music Society, 75
Bubbling Well Cemetery, 176
Bubbling Well Road, 5, 31, 108, 175, 299n39
Buddha Bathing Festival, 205
buke ("makeup class"), 60
bulaji, 218
Bund, the, 5, 71, 170, 172
  and Garden, 174
Bureaucratic capitalists, 40
Butterfly brand, The, 227
Butterfly Lovers (Liang Zhu), 74
Byron, 101, 103

Cameron, James (1911–1985), 202
Campaign for the Socialist Transformation of *China Weekly Review*, 3, 209
Capitalist Industry and Commerce. *See* Socialist Nationalization Campaign

Cao Ying (1923–2015), 67, 68, 73
capitalism, 17, 19, 24, 50, 53
capitalist agents, 47–50
capitalist restoration, 54
capitalist roaders, 53
capitalist tail, 227
casual military uniform, 223
Cathay Hotel, 208, 210
CCP. *See* Chinese Communist Party (CCP)
César Birotteau, 64
Changchun (city), 121
charismatic mobilization, 250
Chen Cun (1954–), 115
Chen Danqing, 33, 40, 198
Chen Danyan (1958–), 136, 137, 292
Chen Hanbo (1914–1988), 64
Chen Jianhua (1947–), 113, 114, 278, 282, 286–8
Chen Julai (1904–1984), 90
Chen Junyi, 305
Chen Sihe (1954–), 118
Chen Yi (1901–1972, Shanghai mayor), 25, 37, 86, 91–3, 96
  and *Beijing News Supplement* (*Jingbao fukan*), 92
  and Li Shuhua, 91
  Lu Xiaoman, 82–6, 89
  and *Morning News Supplement* (*Chenbao fukan*), 92
  (visiting) Shanghai Institute of Culture and History, 93
  Voltaire College of ZhongFa University, 91
  Xu Zhimo, 82, 83, 91, 92
Chen Yun, 37
Chen Zhongyi, 284
Cheng Muhao, 30
Cheng Naishan (1946–2013), 31, 42, 288, 305
Chengdu (city), 187
Chernyshevsky, Nikolay, 123
Chiang Kai-shek, 6, 84, 95
  old regime of quislings, 26
China Press, 283
China to Me, 78
China's urban-based private businesses, 27
Chinese capitalist acquaintance, 31
Chinese Communist Party (CCP), 139
  and capitalist restoration, 53
  cultural affairs of, 64
  and hierarchy of, 50
  member of the CCP politburo, 92
  national capitalists, 24, 26, 27
  for nationalization, 31

party's policies, 78
political campaigns of, 24
sense of conscience and mortal integrity, 68
Shanghai Cultural Bureau, 75
the united front policy of, 42
Chinese Communist system, 26
Chinese education system, 118
Chinese Institute of Music, 75
Chinese liberalism, 83
Chinese literature, 67
Chinese National Silk Company, 197
Chinese opera, 84
Chinese Peasants and Workers Democratic Party, 87
Chinese People's Political Consultative Conference (CPPCC), 11, 32, 42, 75
Chinese poetry movement, 83
China-Soviet Union Friendship Hall, The, 169
Chinese tradition, 66
Chinese Writer's Association, 58
Chipp, David (1927–2008), 203
Chrysanthemums, 60 show, 179
cimaochong ("bristle insects"), 173
class and class struggle, 10, 11, 18, 53, 130
climbing plants, 185
Clothing: amateur tailor, 226, 227, 231
bizarre dress and outlandish clothing (*qizhuang yifu*), 221
"blue ants", 222
bulaji, 218
Butterfly brand, The, 227
casual military uniform, 223
Clothing, 1957–1958 (manual), 218
Common Knowledge of Worsted Knitting, 232
false collar, 230, 231
flowery dresses (*huayifu*), 218, 219
"Imelda style", 23
nühong (women's needlework), 232
qipao, 218
and Shanghai Clothing Company, 218
Shanghai Knitting Crafts Factory, 233
Siberian Fur Store, 229
vast ocean of gray, 222
worsted business, 232
youth jackets, student jackets, dual-purpose jackets, 222
Zhongshan suit, 217
Clothing, 1957–1958 (manual), 218
for Kang's (party), 46
Coffee, 35, 38, 39, 42, 46. *See also* bourgeois comforts

Cold War, 9, 26
collections of feudalism, capitalism and revisionism, 114
Columbia University, 83
Comintern, 50
Commercial Press, 64
Common Knowledge of Worsted Knitting, 232
Communal canteens, 149
Communism, 29, 38, 46
achieving Communism before the Soviet Union, 268n47
Chinese translation of, 51
coping with 251
lived under, 57, 192, 204
struggle for 252
sympathy to, 55
a yardstick of, 169
Communist
cadres of, 70
and class system, 24
egalitarianism and asceticism, 24
ideology of, 25, 36
and nation-building, 56
orthodoxy, 203
revolution of, 24
rule, 24
system, 26
terminology, 54
victory, 42
Communist model of gender equality, 152
Communist Party. *See* Chinese Communist Party (CCP)
Communist revolution, 48, 54
Communist Youth League, 44, 49, 58
Communists' policy of scrutinizing people's lives, 46
compradors, 2
bourgeoisie, 40
bureaucratic capitalists, 26
Zhou Zongliang, 43
comrades in revolution, 125
continuous revolution, 54
coolies, 2, 248
Count of Monte Cristo, The, 116, 136
Country Hospital (Hong'en Hospital), 91
Cowan, Glenn L (1952–2004), 224
Crescent Moon literary society, 78, 83
Critical realism, 101
Critique of the Gotha Program, 52
Cuckoo Waltz, The, 33
cultural demon, 77, 78
Cultural Revolution, 24, 34, 37, 39–41, 45, 48, 50, 54, 66, 73, 81, 105, 111
victims of, 57

"Cutting off Poisonous Roots, Completely Destroy Yellow Music", 75

Da Qizhen (1952–), 188, 301
Dai Sijie (1954–), 122
Dalong Machine Plant, 36
danwei (work unit), 141, 157
Das Leben Jesu, 103
day-care centers, 148, 149
de Certeau, Michel, 18, 99
Deirdre, 206
Democratic party (eight), 56, 87
Democratic personage, 91
Deng Xiaoping, 55, 92
Deng Yingchao (1904–1992), 108
Deng Yunchao, 292
denouncing meetings, 7, 76
deviation, 10, 45, 70
Dialectical materialism and historical materialism, 80. *See also* Marist theory
Diao Deren, 34
dictatorship of the proletariat, 21, 24
Ding Ji'nan, 65, 278
District's bureau of handicraft industries, the, 151
domestic servants/maid, 40
Don Quixote, 101
Dream of Red Chamber, The, 119
Drzewiecki, Zbigniew (1890–1971), 58
dushuren, 71
Dutton, Michael, 252

East China Normal University, 68
East Europe, 140
École du Sacré-Coeur, 82
egalitarian society, 53
Eight model works, The, 118
Eight [Taoist] Immortals, 153
Eileen Chang (Zhang Ailing, 1920–1995), 40, 137, 217
Engels, 15, 52, 72, 97
Episcopal Church of the United States, 34
Eugene Onegin, 68, 69
Experience-taking, 131

Fairbank, John. King, 119
false collar, 230, 231, 306n47
Fang Ping, 80
fashion, 219
"Fate of a Man", 67
Fate Symphony, 33
Faust, 123
Fei Dinghan (1944–), 108
feipin (scrap or waste material), 146
Feng Qiuping (1911–2001), 232

Fengzixiu (feudalism, capitalism, revisionism), 99
Fenyang Road, 38
feudal bureaucratic class, 78
Five-Anti Campaign, 21, 24, 28, 35
   of 1952, 21
fixed interests (*dingxi*), 24, 27, 31, 35, 36, 51
flora, 169, 170
flower planting, 184–7
flower shows, 181
flowering garden, 170–4
Flowery dresses (*huayifu*), 218, 219
folk songs, 33, 111
food
   bamboo basket projects, 243
   in cheap restaurants, 239
   eat this bowl of rice, 238
   European cuisines, 238
   everyday dishes, 37
   fan (the staple food) and *cai* (mainly, meat and vegetables), 238
   gastronomists, 36
   home-cooked dishes (*jiachang cai*), 246
   noodles (boiled or fried), 240
   official Shanghai Municipal Public Food and Drink Company, 36
   pickled fresh (*yanduxian*), 247
   public canteen, 81
   puluo restaurants, 238
   Russian soup, 247
   Shanghai Culinary School in 1963, 36
   Shen Jingshi (1898–1992), 36
   sunny spring noodles, 238, 239
   xiaochi (little food, street food), 239
foreign alley, 49
foreigners, 2, 31, 50, 83, 105, 178, 202
Forty Golden Years, The, 30
four o'clock flower, 192
Four Olds, 72
French Concession, 35, 45, 50, 173
   and International Settlement, 48
French parasol-tree-lined streets, 167
French Park, 181
Friendship Store, the, 211, 214 fig. 6.4
Fu Cong (Fou Ts'ong, 1934–2020), 57–61, 65
Fu Lei (1908–1966), 57–62, 64–6, 73
Fu Min (1937–), 59, 60
Fudan University, 79
Fuzhou Road, 107

Galston, Arthur W. (1920–2008), 172
Gang of Four, 6, 181
gangsters, 2, 38

Index

Gansu (province), 71
garages
  of the houses, 40
  as home for old rich, 25, 37, 50
  of private homes or apartment buildings, 153
Garden landscapes campaign, 169
Gardening
  Da Qizhen (1952–), 188, 301
  landscaping, 171, 185
  Liu Haisu (1896–1994), 83
  within marketplace (*shi*), 182
  Marks Terrace, 189
  Nie Chongbin (1957–), 193, 301
  orchid, 186
  Tan Yingzhou (1966–), 191, 301
  West Hall of Flowers (Xihuating), 186
  Xia Yiqiao (1918–2012), 191
  Ye Shengtao (1894–1988), 184
  Zhang Da-Peng (1941–), 35, 44, 189, 190, 191, 198, 272, 274, 291
Garden Villas, 31, 33
Ge Yan (1957–), 121
Geertz, Clifford, 10
gender equality and women's role in society, 161
George Kwok Bew (1868–1932), 236
George Wang (1927–), 3
Gerth, Karl, 247
Gone with the Wind, 108
Good Number Eight Company of Nanjing Road (*Nanjing lu shang hao ba lian*), 219
Gordon Road (Jiangning Road), 5
Gorky, Maxim (1868–1936), 101
Gorky Prize in 1987, 68
Grand Theater, 41
Great Famine of the early 1960s, 37
Great Leap Famine, 37, 62
Great Leap Forward (GLP) of 1958–1960, 15, 120, 139, 171, 190, 199, 203
  and backyard furnaces, 190
Great Proletarian Cultural Revolution, 43, 49
Great Wall, 82
Great Wall Cinema, The, 108
Green House, 41, 43
Gu Zhimin (1903–1956), 30
Guangming Daily, 74
Guillain, Robert (1908–1998), 31, 204

Hahn, Emily, 78
Haiying (1929–2011), 196
Halbwachs, Maurice, 99
Han Qiulin (1962–), 129
Hardoon Garden, 29 fig. 1.4, 84, 169, 178, 281n120

Hartling, Poul, 53
He Amao (1922–), 160
He Qifang (1912–1977), 69, 70
Hebei, 71
Hegel, Georg, 251
high-level intellectuals, 57
High socialism, 10, 25, 164, 266n28
Historia Romana, 64
History of the Peloponnesian War, 64
Home-cooked dishes (*jiachang cai*), 246
home a site of inquiry, 26
The Home and the World, Two Sisters, and Four Chapters, 79
home gardening, 170, 181, 182, 184, 200
Hong Kong, 42, 43, 87, 95
Hope, Bob (1903–2003), 46
housewives, 141, 154, 157
How the Steel Was Tempered, 126, 291
Hu Dongxiu, 93
Hu Feng (1902–1985), 70
Hu Shih (1891–1962), 83, 84, 93–5
Hu Sidu, 95
Hu Yaobang (1915–1989), 58
Hua Du'an, 31
Huadong Hospital, 65, 91
Huaihai Road, 34, 35, 79
Huaihai Road Number 2 Residential Committee, 80
Huang Shi, 302
Huang Zongying (1925–), 13, 14
Huangpu Park, 174
Huashan Road, 33, 35
Hudec, Ladislav, 41
Hugo, Victor (1802–1885), 104
Hundred Flowers Campaign, 13, 75, 100, 267. *See also* Anti-Rightist Campaign
Hundred Flowers exhibition, 179
Hunter, Neale, 206

Ian McLanchlan, 4
Imelda Marcos (1929–), 233
independent production, 145
indoor food market, 244
Institute of Literature of the Chinese Academy of Social Sciences in Beijing, 69
intellectuals
  bourgeois. *See* bourgeois intellectuals
  high-level intellectuals, 56, 57
(1955) International Chopin Piano Competition, 58
International Settlement, 3
  and French Concession, 33
Itō Hirobumi (1841–1909), 82
Ivan Kovalev (1901–1993), 3

Jean-Christophe, 62, 115, 122
Jenner, W.J.F. (1940–), 204
Jia Zhifang (1916–2008), 237
Jian Fan, 301
Jiang Qing (Mao's wife), 219
Jiang Xiaoyan (1939–), 65
Jiang Xiaoyuan (1955–), 119
Jiangsu, 2, 3, 5
Jin Shengtan (1608–1661), 115
Jing'an district, 295
Jing'an Park, 176–8
Jing'an Temple, 39, 87–8, 176, 196, 204
Jiangsu Road/Edinburgh Road, 115
Jing Fang, 291
Jingpai (Beijingstyle), 254
Jinjiang Hotel, 37
Joffre, Marshal Joseph, 82
"joint state–private ownership" (*gongsi heyin*), 22–4, 31, 52, 244
Jung Chang (1952–), 187

Kang Tongbi, 45
Kang Youwei, 45
Karol, K. S. (1924–2014), 204, 209, 266, 303, 304
Ke Ling, 304
Ke Qingshi (1902–1965), 60, 276
Kim Jong-il (1941–2011), 222
knitting, 231–6, 305
Konigsberger, Hans (1921–2007), 204, 303
Koo, Wellington (1888–1985), 82
Korchagin, Pavel, 126
Korean War (1950–1953), 21
Kovalev, Ivan (1901–1993), 3
Kraus, Richard Curt, 56
Kun opera, 84
Kwok, Daisy, 28, 277, 279

Lake Tai, 38
Laodong (magazine), 295
laokele, 47, 236
law-abiding, 21
law-breaking capitalists, 28
Le Bon Marché, 84
Le Monde, 5, 265n15
Leese, Daniel, 309
Lefebvre, Henri, 216
Leigh, Vivien(1913–1967), 46
Lenin, 72, 275, 285, 296
and Communism, 92
Lennon, John, 168
Les Contemporains (Xiandai zazhi), 66
Les Misérables, 137
Li Cheng (1906–1977), 124
Li Chengpeng (1968–), 187, 192, 301

Li Jinhui, 74–6, 78
Li Keqiang (1955–), 124, 289
Li Shuhua, 91
Liang Huifang (1917–2008), 75
Liang Qichao (1873–1929), 100, 284
Liangjiahe (village), 122, 123
Liberating women's labor power, 139, 141, 151, 161, 164, 166
Liberation, 53, 140, 149, 152–4, 156, 179, 217, 265–7, 276, 278, 280
Liberation Daily, 14, 102, 232, 280, 285, 310
Library, 106, 114, 120, 122, 129
 of Fudan University, 106
 of high school, 129
 municipal libraries, 106
 public library, 106
 Shanghai Library, 114
 Shanghai Library Tower, 175
 rent-only bookshops, 106
 roadside portable picture-book libraries, 106
Life and Death in Shanghai, 47, 274, 283
Light Cavalry Overture, 33
lilong (alleyway house), 304
Lin Biao incident, 305, 308
Lin Huiyin (1904–1955), 80, 83
Literature, bourgeois/translated/foreign literature (CCP's policies and figures of)
 as critical realism, 101
 by Fu Lei (1908–1966), 57–62, 64–6, 73
 and Hundred Flowers Campaign in 1957, The, 13, 75, 100, 267
 Jiang Qing (1914–1991), 105
 and Lou Shiyi (1905–2001), 105
 Mao Dun (1896–1981), 105
 Mei Yi (1913–2003), 127
 "reading is useless", 105, 118
 Xia Yan, 104
 Zhou Erfu (1914–2004)
 Zhou Yang, 102
Literature and Arts Conference (1950), 76
literature youth, 269, 272, 277, 279, 280, 284, 285, 288, 290, 291, 295
Liu Haisu (1896–1994), 83
Liu Hexiang, 35
Liu Hongsheng (1888–1956), 28, 270
Liu Shaoqi (1898–1969), 50, 269, 275, 280
Liu Tsing-kew (1902–1997), 31, 32 fig. 1.5
Liu Xiaofeng, 291
London School of Economics, 48
Lou Shiyi (1905–2001), 105. *See also* literature

Index

Love of Marriage, The (Jiehun de ai), 108
Lu Ding, 82
Lu Jiansan, 83
Lu Xiaoman (1903–1965), 82–6, 89
  in Anti-Rightist Campaign, 13, 58, 60, 90, 249
  and Chen Julai (1904–1984), 90
  with Chen Yi, 86, 91–3, 96
  using École du Sacré-Coeur, 82
  with Hu Shih (1891–1962), 83
  and Koo, Wellington (1888–1985), 82
  Le Bon Marché, 84
  Marshal Joseph Joffre [1852–1931], 82
  and Wang Geng (colonel, 1895–1942), 83
  Weng Duanwu (1899–1960), 84
  and Xu Zhimo (1895–1931), 82, 83, 91, 92
  and Zhonghua (cigarette), 88, 89
Lu Xun (1981–1936), 13, 66, 78, 100, 267, 271, 280, 284, 302
Lü Nengzhong (1932–), 123
Lühua (verdurization), 297. *See also* gardening, and park
Luo Ji'nan (1898–1971), 14, 267
Luo Shiyi (1905–2001), 58, 277
Luo Yujun (1907–1988), 101

Ma Jun, 301
Ma Wenrui (1912–2004), 141
Macao regions, 211
MacArthur, Douglas, 256
Mahathir Mohamad, 18
mahjong, 36
Maiden's Heart (*Shaonü zhi xin*), A, 109
Mak Lai-heung, 4
Malraux, André (1901–1976), 53, 276
manifestation of the human need, 310
Mao Dun (1896–1981), 173, 266–6, 299
Mao suit. *See* Zhongshan suit
Mao Wenrui (1912–2004), 141
Mao Xiaolu, 80
Mao Yuyuan (1956–), 130, 291
Mao Zedong, 50–5
  and Cultural Revolution, 187, 188, 191–5, 200
  On Contradiction, 91
  on garden landscaping, 171, 185
  on Hu Shih, 93
  on Rong Yiren, on Chinese intellectuals, 28, 29, 271
  politicization of flower planting, 184–7
  potted flowers, 185, 187
  Quotations of Chairman Mao, 46
  "reading is useless", 105, 118
  salary, 27

Selected Works of Mao Zedong, 46
Mao's political campaigns, 76
Mao's revolution, 203
Mao's tyranny, 66
Maoism
  on class analysis, 239, 270
  and class struggle, 130, 184, 205, 232
  Four Olds, 72
  and garden landscaping, 171, 185
  Good Number Eight Company of Nanjing Road (*Nanjing lu shang hao ba lian*), 219
  notion of continuous revolution, 9, 19
  Patriotic capitalists, 26
  Patriotic hygiene movement, 81
  patriotic personages, 19, 65
  petty bourgeois, 12, 26, 27
  proletarian dictatorship, 20, 54, 111, 288, 290, 309
  on redemption policy, 52
  Reform Our Study, 72
  Selected Works of Mao Zedong, 72
  "up to the mountains and down to the countryside", 161
  on "women hold up half the sky", 161
Maoist Politics, 50–4, 70, 82
Maoming Road, 34
Marching toward science, 56
Mario Paci (1878–1946), 58
Marketplace (*shi*), 182
Marks Terrace, 189
Márquez, Gabriel García (1927–2014), 137
Marriage Law of 1950, 8, 97
marvel-of-Peru (flower), 192, 196
Marx, 72, 97, 267, 275, 285
Marxism and Literature and Arts (by Zhou Yang in 1944), 102
Marxist theory, 50–4
  on "bourgeois right", 52
  of class warfare, 19
  Critique of the Gotha Program, 52
  dialectical materialism and historical materialism, 80
  means of production/livelihood, 52
Marxist world outlook, 95
May Fourth movement, 83
  Hu Shih, (1891–1962), 83, 84, 93–5
  Lu Xun (1981–1936), 13, 66, 78, 100, 267, 271, 280, 284, 302
McCullough, Colin, 209, 304
McLachlan, Ian, 4
Medhurst College, 119
Medhurst Road, 86
Mengchang, Lord, 79

Menu, at canteen, 150
  at cheap restaurants, 237–9
  of common households, 246
Middle Yan'an Road, 87
Mittler, Barbara, 114
Mo Yan (1954–), 125, 126, 130, 268, 274, 282, 284–6, 290, 291
morning glories (flower), 189, 193, 298
Morning in Shanghai, 173
Morning News Supplement (Chenbao fukan), 92
Mount East (Dongshan), 38
Mozart, 33
Mr. Three R's (American Ray-Ban sunglasses, British Raleigh bicycles, and German Rolleiflex camera), 35
"museum of global architecture", 40
Music
  "As Time Goes By" (from *Casablanca*), 31
  Fate Symphony, 33
  Lennon, John, 168
  Mozart, 33
  My Fair Lady, 33
  "One Day When We Were Young" (from *The Great Waltz*), 33
  Pastoral Symphony, 33
  piano, 31, 33, 34, 51, 82, 277, 278
  Schubert, 33
  Schumann, 38
  Serenade for Strings, 33
  Wagner, Richard, 116
My Fair Lady, 33

Nanjing Road, 23, 170
Nanking Road, 5
national capitalists, 24, 26, 27, 266, 267, 270, 271, 298, 310
  with fixed interests (*dingxi*), 24, 27, 31, 35, 36, 51
  Gu Zhimin (1903–1956), 30
  Kwok, Daisy, 28, 277, 279
  Liu Hongsheng (1888–1956), 28, 270
  Liu Tsing-kew (1902–1997), 31
  national total of fixed-interest recipients, 27
  "objects of the united front" (*tongzhan duixiang*), 25
  private businesses, 26
  retention pay, 27, 270
  Rong Yiren (1916–2005), 28, 29, 32, 51, 271
  wartime supply system, 27
  Xu Meifeng (1902–1996), 28
  Xu Yuanzhang (1946–2015), 43, 46
National Day, 36, 112, 179, 268, 281, 284, 290, 293, 294, 297, 299, 302, 308
National Music Week (in Beijing), 75
Nationalist, 3, 270, 304
neighborhood committee, 111, 155, 190, 275, 281, 292, 294, 296, 304
neighborhood organizations, 71, 140–2, 144, 145, 148, 149, 281, 293
Neighborhood workshops
  alleyway production teams (APTs), 140, 141, 145, 146
  alleyway women's detachments, 139–41
  barefoot doctor, 149
  big/small collectives, 142
  communal canteens, 149, 150
  dichotomy between the exploitation and empowerment, 141
  district's bureau of handicraft industries, 151
  feipin (scrap or waste material), 146
  He Amao (1922–), 160
  Mao Wenrui (1912–2004), (four categories of APTs) independent producers, members of a neighborhood industry, 139, 140
  neighborhood organization-sponsored work units, 144
  and piece-rate wage system, 159
  production chain, service, waste reclamation, 145
  as reservoir of labor, 155
  self-governing mass organization, 141
  sent-down youth in, 39, 120, 122, 123, 161, 226, 230
  service stations, 148
  Shanghai Waste Reclamation Company, The, 147
  street factories, 142
  street office, the, 150–1
  unskilled laborers, 162
  volunteerism, 152–4
  waste recycling centers, 147
  "women hold up half the sky", 161
  Zhangjiazhai, 131
  zichanzixiao, 145
New Chronicle of London, 203
Nie Chongbin (1957–), 193, 301
Nien Cheng (1915–2009), 47–50
Nietzsche, 116
Nixon, Richard, 174
Nixon's visit, delegation, press, 299, 300
Nonparty democratic patriots, 56
non-staple foods in Shanghai, 242
North Sichuan Road, 108
nostalgia/nostalgy, 46, 133, 173, 273, 291, 292, 298, 310
nühong (women's needlework), 232

Index

Objects of the united front (*tongzhan duixiang*), 25
On Contradiction, 91, *See also* Mao Zedong
"One Day When We Were Young" (from *The Great Waltz*), 33
Opium War, The, 2, 253–4.
Orchids planting, 186, 187
Ordinary people, 9, 170, 200, 251
Ostrovsky, Nikolai (1904–1936), 126
An Outline of Chinese Philosophy, 64
Overseas Chinese Store, 211, 212, 304, 305
Overseas connections, 208, 209, 211, 213, 215
Overseas remittances, 210, 211, 213

Pacific War
  in December 1941, 3, 86
Pan Ling, 291
Paramount (nightclub), 88, 193
park building, 174–6, 178, 179
  chrysanthemum show, 179, 181
  with entrance fee, 178
  Hundred Flowers exhibition, 179
  Nanyang Park, 178
  Public Garden (Huangpu Park, Bund Park), the, 174
  the rule excluding "Chinese and dogs", 175
  seasonal flower shows, 179
  Xijiao Park, 179, 181, 300
  Xikang Park, 178
Park Hotel, 37, 41
party-imposed social norms in clothing, 236
Pastoral Symphony, 33
Patriotic capitalists, 26
Patriotic hygiene movement, 81
patriotic personages, 19, 65
Peace Hotel (Cathay Hotel), 206, 208, 210, 273
Peking University, 83
Peng Zuji (1940–), 231
People's Congress or of the Chinese People's Political Consultative Committee, 27
People's Daily, 17, 53, 123, 155, 187, 226, 232, 266–72, 275–7, 279, 282–4, 286, 287, 292–4, 296, 298, 299, 301, 303–5, 308–10
People's Liberation Army (PLA), 2, 137, 195, 219, 223, 265, 292
People's Literature Press, 58, 62, 79, 102, 278, 287, 290, 291, 297, 303
People's Park, 169, 175, 176, 179, 180, 253
People's Square, 175
Perry, Elizabeth J., 251, 266, 291, 293, 295, 297, 309
  and adaptive governance, 155

petty bourgeois, 12, 26, 27
petty urbanites, 10, 137
piano, 31, 33, 34, 51, 82, 277, 278. *See also* bourgeois comforts
Pickled fresh (*yanduxian*), 247
piece-rate wage system, 159
pigeon lofts, 41
Pingliang Road, 8
Ping-pong diplomacy of 1971, 224
Planned economy, 8
Poems of Dai Wangshu, 64
policy of redemption, 22
political anathema, 25
political and financial pressure, 23
A Political Biography, 119
political campaigns and propaganda, 133
Political Consultative Conference, 89
political convictions, 74
political liability, 24
politics of downsizing, 154–6
Polland, David E, 100
Potemkin metropolis, 207
potted flowers, 185, 187, 266, 301
pre-Liberation life, 42
private real estate, 41
professed volunteerism, 152, 153
proletarian dictatorship, 20, 54, 111, 288, 290, 309
proletarian masses, 101
Prometheus Unbound, 79
prostitutes, 2
Psychological reactance, 115
public green space per capita, 170
Public Security Bureau, 71, 282, 287, 297, 299

Qing Qiuzi (1952–), 121–223, 289, 305
Qu Bo (Chu Po, 1923–2002), 125
Quiet Flows the Don, 67
Quotations from Chairman Mao, 102, 285, 287

ration coupons, 211, 306, 308
Reading
  Bitter Flowers, 125
  centers, 120, 146–8, 289
  How the Steel Was Tempered, 126
  recyclable paper, 146
  recycling, 146, 160
  Red and the Black, The, 101, 136, 289
  The Song of Youth, 126
  Tracks in the Snowy Forest, 125
Red Flag (CCP's monthly journal), 28, 97, 113
Red Guards, 38, 41, 42, 48, 49, 57, 72, 97, 105, 113, 114, 117, 128, 132, 187, 221, 235, 236, 288

Red Rose and the White Rose, The, 40
Redemption policy, 52
reductionism, 82
Reform Our Study, 72
Renmin ribao. See People's Daily
Republican China, 77 fig. 2.2, 82, 229
Republican era, 81, 107, 134, 217, 274, 305
Republican Revolution of 1911, 2
residence permit (*hukou*), 70, 281, 284
Restaurant
   government-run, 89, 239
   high-end restaurants, 36, 37
   high-priced dishes, 37
   Jinjiang Hotel, 37
   restaurants price, 87, 150
   Peace Hotel (Cathay Hotel), 206, 208, 210, 273
   public canteen, 81
   puluo restaurants, 238
   Shen Jingshi (1898–1992), 36
Revolutionization (*geminghua*), 226
Riboud, Marc, 209
Richman, Barry, 30
rickshaw pullers, 167
rightist, 30, 45, 60, 62, 64, 69–71, 267, 277, 278
Robert Guillain (1908–1998), 5, 31, 204
Roderick, John (1914–2008), 206, 266, 303
Rolland, Romain (1866–1944), 104
Romance of the Three Kingdoms, 119
Rong Yiren (1916–2005), 28, 29, 32, 51, 271
roses, 60, 189, 190
Rossi, Paolo Alberto (1887–1969), 204, 266, 303
Ruijin Hospital, 65
Russian revolutionaries, 67

Saich, Tony, 50
Sassoon, Victor (1881–1961), 208
Schubert, 33
Schumann, 38
Scott, James, 18, 185
Selected Works of Mao Zedong, 72
Self-denunciation, 75
Self-governing mass organization, 141
semi-law-abiding, 21
sent-down youth, 39, 120, 122, 123, 161, 226, 230
Serenade for Strings, 33

The Service Industry Should Be Better at Serving the Workers, Peasants, and Soldiers, 226
Service stations, 148
sewing machines, 227, 229
sewing workshops, 153
sexual frustration, 111
   and public lavatory graffiti, 111
   random male-female relationships, 112
   and sex-related topics, 108, 111
   and sexual misconduct, 111
shalong ("salons"), 121
shangfang baojian, 101
Shanghai, 71
   Cemetery of Revolutionary Martyrs, 66
   China's "real city," 208
   Clothing Company, 218
   during Cultural Revolution, 206–8
   First Literature and Arts Conference, 75
   Flower and Bird Store, 188
   foreign concessions, 86
   French Concession, 48, 118
   Fuxing Road, 108
   Fuzhou Road, 107
   Hongkou, 33
   international experiences, 208
   International Settlement, 86
   keenness about the West, 213
   middle class, 215
   North Sichuan Road, 108
   street factories, 144
   streets, 4
Shanghai Academy of Chinese Painting, 87
Shanghai Administration Institute, 34
Shanghai alleyway house for decades, 82
Shanghai Animated Films Studio, 7
Shanghai-based "bourgeois intellectuals"
   as democratic personage, 90, 91
   family financial situation of, 87
   socialist educational programs, 58
   tobacco availabilty, 88
   upscale neighborhoods, 96
Shanghai-based British soft drink company Aquarius, 31
Shanghai capitalists, 41
Shanghai Clothing Company, 218
Shanghai College of Chinese Medicine, 109
Shanghai Communiqué, 207
Shanghai Conservatory, 33
Shanghai Culinary School in 1963, 36
Shanghai Cultural Bureau, 75
Shanghai Exhibition Center, The, 169
Shanghai Film Studio, 74

Index

Shanghai First Literature and Arts Conference, 75
Shanghai Flowers and Plants Company, 188
Shanghai Foreign Language Institute, 206
Shanghai Foreign Trade Company, The, 195
Shanghai Institute of Culture and History, 93
Shanghai in the Morning (1950s), 105
Shanghai Knitting Crafts Factory, 233
Shanghai Library, 114, 175
Shanghai Lifetime Achievement for Literature and Arts Award in 2014, 68
Shanghai Mansions (Broadway Mansions), 206
Shanghai Municipal Bureau of Statistics, 142
Shanghai Municipal CCP Committee, 80
Shanghai Municipal Communist Youth League Committee, 235
Shanghai Municipal Council, 91
Shanghai Municipal Government, 36
  payroll records, 27
Shanghai Municipal Public Food and Drink Company, 36
Shanghai Municipal Revolutionary Committee, 114
Shanghai nostalgia, 137
Shanghai Number Two Medical College, 45
Shanghai School of Fine Arts, 57
Shanghai Science and Technology Information Institute, 71
Shanghai Textile Industry Bureau, 227
Shanghai Waste Reclamation Company, 147
Shanghai Xuhui District Committee, 87
Shanghai's Parks, 181
Shanghai's Private Telephone Lines, in Mao Era, 62
Shanghai's restaurants in the Mao era, 37. *See also* restaurant
Shanghainese, 7, 64, 106, 108, 132, 152, 182, 204
Shanyin Road, 174, 188, 196
Shao Xunmei, 74, 78, 79, 81, 82
Shell Oil's stay in China, 49
Shelley, Percy Bysshe, 79, 101, 103
Shen Jialu (1956–), 239
Shen Jingshi (1898–1992), 36. *See also* food and restaurant
Sheng Aiyi (1900–1983), 192
Sheng Peiyu (1905–1989), 80, 281
Sheng Xuanhuai [1844–1916], 80, 280
Shi Kangqiang, 284

Shi Ximin (1912–1987), 80
Shi Zhecun, 80
Shimu, 86
Sholokhov, Mikhail (1905–1984), 67
Shopping, 208, 212
  at food markets, 243, 244
  at indoor food market, 244
  Jing'an Temple shopping area, 39, 87, 88
  by maid (middle-aged housewives hired to shop), 245
  waiting in line, 247
  Wujiaochang (Pentagonal Square), 237
Siberian Fur Store, 229
Sihanouk, Monique (1936–), 224, 225
Sihanouk, Norodom (1922–2012), 224
silkworm babies (*can baobao*), 197
Siming Villa, 34
Sino-Japanese War, 79
Sino-Soviet Friendship Hall, 29, 169
Slyke, Lyman Van, 52
Smith, Steve A., 250, 277
Snow, Edgar (1905–1972), 2, 208
social butterfly, 82–4, 86. *See also* Lu Xiaoman
social gatherings, 43
socialist, 73
Socialist Nationalization Campaigns, 22, 24, 26, 27, 29, 41, 106, 111, 153, 188, 227, 229, 239
socialist nationalization of private businesses, 29
socialist society, 73
Socialist state feminism, 162, 164
  liberating women's labor power, 139, 141, 151, 151, 161, 164, 166
  "woman's army" (*niangzijun*)., 139
  "women hold up half the sky", 161
socialist system, 38
Song of Everlasting Sorrow, The, 137, 190
Song Zi'an, 84
Soong, T.V. (1894–1971), 34, 84, 193
Soviet Communist Party, 30
Soviet model of industrial development, 162
Soviet social imperialists, 153
Soviet Union, 161, 162, 169, 218, 221
Spare-time university (*yeyu daxue*), 80
Special Economic Zone (SEZ), 255, 310
St. John's University, 34, 42
Stalin, 30, 72, 77, 99, 105, 161, 226, 269n8
Stalinist, 162
State and Revolution, 52
State Council meeting, 95
Stendhal, 101

Stephens, Robert Henry, 119
Stinking Number Nine, 55–7
Street office, the, 150–1
Sun Dayu, 80
Sun Hengfu, 76
Sun Xiang (1957–), 136
Sunglow, 135
supply network points, 243
Suzhou creek, 3, 174
Swislocki, Mark, 37

Tagore, Rabindranath, 79
tai-chi, 18, 253
Taiping Rebellion, 172
Tale of the White Serpent (Baishe zhuan), 74
Tall White Poplars, The (Gaogao de baiyangshu), 173
Tan Yingzhou (1966–), 191, 301
Tang Zhengmang, 290
Taoist
  hermit, 182
  orchids, 186
  poem, 300
Taylor, Robert (1911–1969), 46
telephone booths, 148
Terrill, Ross (1938–), 240, 252, 266
Textile Industry Bureau, in 1949, 227
thick description, 10
Three Butterflies, 76
Tiananmen crisis of 1989, 155
Tiananmen Square, 22, 76, 221
tianfandifu, 53
Tianjin, 51, 219, 293
Tibet Road, 16
Tilanqiao (prison), 81
"As Time Goes By" (from *Casablanca*), 31
tobacco, Dunhill's Royal Yacht pipe, 62
Tolstoy, Leo (1828–1910), 101, 103, 118
Tongren Road, 41
Tonya complex, 125–7, 129–32
Tracks in the Snowy Frost, 125
transliterated European names, 135
Trumpeter of revisionism, 67
Twain, Mark, 79
Two Hundred Foreign Folk Songs, 33
tyranny of informality, 252

Under the Eaves of Shanghai (1937) (by Xia Yan), 104
unified purchase and sale, 241
united front, 11, 12, 267, 270, 275, 290, 294, 310
united front personages, 11, 275, 89
United Nations, 208, 272, 285, 290, 294

United States Military Academy (West Point), 83
University of Cambridge, 83
University of Michigan, 116
Unskilled laborers, 162
Up to the mountains and down to the countryside, 161
urban culture, 82, 266, 279, 281, 285, 293, 296, 297, 302
urban farming, 194–200
urban greening. *See also* gardening and verdurization (*lühua*)
  China as a gigantic garden, 170
  flower stores, 188
  French parasol tree, 173
  home gardening, 170, 181, 182, 184, 200
  London plane trees or platanus, 172, 174
  street trees, 133, 170–2
  white poplars, 173
Urban idle labor force, 71, 161, 190
Urban people's commune campaign in 1958, 81
urban youth generation, 115

Van Slyke, Lyman, 11
vast ocean of gray, 222
Verdurization (*lühua*), 81, 169, 199, 297
  chrysanthemum show, 179
  and *cimaochong* ("bristle insects"), 172
  "Eulogizing the White Poplar" (*Baiyang lizan*), 172
  French parasol tree, 172
  French parasol-tree-lined streets, 167, 172
  garden landscaping, 171, 185
  Hundred Flowers exhibition, 179
  London plane trees, 174
  Mao Dun (1896–1981), 173
  "marketplace" (*shi*), 182
  Richard Nixon's visit in February 1972, 174
  seasonal flower shows, 179
  as "socialist paradise on earth", 171
  "turn the earth into a garden", 171
Victorian/Edwardian terraced houses, 152
Voltaire College of ZhongFa University, 91
volunteerism, 152–4

wages, 64, 144, 159
Wagner, Richard, 116
Walder, Andrew, 22

Index

Wang Anyi (1954–), 39, 116, 136, 137, 148, 190, 273, 288, 291, 305
Wang Dongxing (1916–2015), 185
Wang Gang, 291
Wang Geng, 83
Wang Hongwen (1935–1992), 27
Wang Jingzhi, 30, 89–90, 119, 232, 271n39
Wang Qianguo (1930–), 228
Wang Qishan (1948–), 124
Wang Weiming, 288
Wang Xinli, 291
Wang Zheng (1952–), 116
Wang Zhiliang (1928–), 69, 73, 279
    Anti-Rightist Campaign to the Cultural Revolution, 69
    cultural affairs, 70
    labor reform, 69
    medical treatment, 70
    notion of humanity, 72
    party's anti-intellectualism, 71
    party's policies, 71
    political outcast, 70
    resignation and urge, 70
    urban idle labor force, 71
War and Peace, 137
Warsaw Conservatory, 58
Wartime supply system, 27
Washington Post, 208
waste reclamation, 145–7, 294
Waste recycling centers, 147
Water Margin, 119
Watson, James L., 253, 309
Weberian tripartite classification of political authority, 249
Wei Guangqi (1950–), 120
Wen Jiabao (1942–), 68
Weng Duanwu, 84
Weng Xiangguang, 87
Wenhui Daily, 59
West Hall of Flowers (Xihuating), 186
West Nanjing Road, 5, 31, 108, 112, 175
Western classics, 34
Western influences in Shanghai, 45
Western literature, 35
White Russians, 30, 247
Whyte, Martin King, 3
Wilde, Oscar, 81
William Tell Overture, 33
Wilson, Dick (1928–2011), 204, 213, 266, 303
Wing-On, department store, 206
"woman's army" (*niangzijun*), 139
women
    labor power, 139, 155, 161–5

liberating women's labor power, 141, 155, 164
participation in paid labor, 163
wear lipstick, 207
Women hold up half the sky, 161
Women's liberation, 162–4
workers, 139, 140, 154, 162, 163, 232, 292, 293
Wu Liang (1955–), 134, 135, 291
Wu Tongwen, 41
Wukang Road, 31
Wuyuan Road, 193, 196

xenophobia, 211
Xi Jinping (1953–), 97, 122
Xi Zhongxun (1913–2002), 123
Xia Yan, 75, 79, 96
Xia Yiqiao (1918–2012), 191
Xiamen (city), 192
Xiao Gongqin (1946–), 108
Xiaocun, 43
Xiaokai ("little open"), 35
xiaoyao pai (clique of the free and unfettered), 114
XieDefeng (1906–1980), 64
Xijiao Park, 179, 181, 300
Xindaxiang Silk and Fabric Store, 23
Xinghuo Food Store, 16
Xinhua Bookstore, 35, 106, 112, 214
Xinhua Cinema, 112
Xinzha Road, 16
Xu Chi, 80
Xu Meifeng (1902–1996), 28
Xu Yuanzhang (1946–2015), 43, 46
Xu Zhimo, 82, 83, 91, 92
Xuhui district, 81, 288
Xujiahui, 2

Yan Fu (1854–1921), 100
Yan Qingxiang, 36, 37
Yan'an period (1935–1948), 102
Yang Diaofang, 34
Yang Li, 290
Yang Shiyang, 287
Yang Zhenning, 33
Yangren ("ocean people"), 209
Yangzi delta region, 157, 184, 197, 201, 247
Ye, Wen-hsin, 255
Ye Shengtao (1894–1988), 184
Ye Xingshan, 38
Ye Yonglie, 271, 277, 278
yellow croaker car, 156, 157
Yellow music, 74
Yin Huifen (1949–), 116, 288

Yishi (clothing and food), 216
YMCA, 206
Yong'an Cemetery, 65
Youth News, 218, 305
Yu Dafu (1896–1945), 83
Yuanmingyuan (looting), 104
Yuyuan Road, 77

zashu (miscellaneous books), 105
Zhabei, 185
Zhaibei railway station, 204
Zhang Bojun, 45
Zhang Chunqiao (1917–2005), 14, 53, 219
Zhang Dainian (1909–2004), 64
Zhang Da-Peng (1941–), 35, 44, 189, 190, 191, 198, 272, 274, 291
Zhang Fanghui, 90
Zhang Guangzhao, 290
Zhang Hanzhi (1935–2008), 208, 303
Zhangjiazhai, 141
Zhang Leping (1911–1992), 196
Zhang Weiguo, 297
Zhang Weiqun (1949–2015), 34, 280
Zhang Xinying, 288
Zhang Yihe (1942–), 45
Zhang Youyi (1898–1989), 83
Zhang Zugan (1947–), 33

Zhejiang, 2
Zhejiang Road, 244
Zheng Jian (1952–), 117, 189, 288
Zheng Wang, 297
Zhong Fulan, 227, 306
Zhonghua cigarettes, 88, 89
Zhongnanhai, 185–6
Zhongshan Park, 186, 198
Zhongshan suit, 217
Zhou Enlai (1898–1976), 22, 27, 49, 65, 75, 92, 96, 108, 185, 224, 268, 270, 277
Zhou Erfu, 105
Zhou Peihongh (1951–), 196
Zhou Xiliang, 80
Zhou Xinfang, 34
Zhou Yang (1908–1989), 60, 81, 102, 104, 285
Zhou Yi (1931–), 34
Zhou Zhenhe (1941–), 108
Zhou Zongliang, 43
Zhu Dake (1957–), 115, 118, 275, 288, 307
Zhu De (1886–1976), 185
Zhu Meifu (1913–1966), 60
Zhu Xueqin (1952–), 119
zichan zixiao, 145
Zimmermann, Susan, 162